Phenomenology of Youth Cultures and Globalization

This edited collection brings together scholars who draw on phenomenological approaches to understand the experiences of young people growing up under contemporary conditions of globalization. Phenomenology is both a philosophical and pragmatic approach to social sciences research, which takes as central the meaning-making experiences of research participants. One of the central contentions of this book is that phenomenology has long informed critical empirical approaches to youth cultures, yet until recently its role has not been thusly named. This volume aims to resuscitate and recuperate phenomenology as a robust empirical, theoretical and methodological approach to youth cultures. Chapters explore the lifeworlds of young people from countries around the world, revealing the tensions, risks and opportunities that organize youth experiences.

Stuart R. Poyntz is an Associate Professor in the School of Communication at Simon Fraser University.

Jacqueline Kennelly is an Associate Professor in the Department of Sociology and Anthropology at Carleton University.

Routledge Studies in Social and Political Thought

For a full list of titles in this series, please visit www.routledge.com

66 **Liberalism, Neoliberalism, Social Democracy**
Thin Communitarian Perspectives on Political Philosophy and Education
Mark Olssen

67 **Oppositional Discourses and Democracies**
Edited by Michael Huspek

68 **The Contemporary Goffman**
Edited by Michael Hviid Jacobsen

69 **Hemingway on Politics and Rebellion**
Edited by Lauretta Conklin Frederking

70 **Social Theory in Contemporary Asia**
Ann Brooks

71 **Governmentality**
Current Issues and Future Challenges
Edited by Ulrich Bröckling, Susanne Krasmann and Thomas Lemke

72 **Gender, Emotions and Labour Markets—Asian and Western Perspectives**
Ann Brooks and Theresa Devasahayam

73 **Alienation and the Carnivalization of Society**
Edited by Jerome Braun and Lauren Langman

74 **The Post-Colonial State in the Era of Capitalist Globalization**
Historical, Political and Theoretical Approaches to State Formation
Tariq Amin-Khan

75 **The Psychology and Politics of the Collective**
Groups, Crowds and Mass Identifications
Edited by Ruth Parkin-Gounelas

76 **Environmental Solidarity**
How Religions Can Sustain Sustainability
Pablo Martínez de Anguita

77 **Comedy and the Public Sphere**
The Rebirth of Theatre as Comedy and the Genealogy of the Modern Public Arena
Arpad Szakolczai

78 **Culture, Class, and Critical Theory**
Between Bourdieu and the Frankfurt School
David Gartman

79 Environmental Apocalypse in Science and Art
Designing Nightmares
Sergio Fava

80 Conspicuous and Inconspicuous Discriminations in Everyday Life
Victor N. Shaw

81 Understanding the Tacit
Stephen P. Turner

82 The Politics of Expertise
Stephen P. Turner

83 Globalized Knowledge Flows and Chinese Social Theory
Xiaoying Qi

84 Reconstructing Social Justice
Lauretta Conklin Frederking

85 The Dialectics of Inquiry Across the Historical Social Sciences
David Baronov

86 How Groups Matter
Challenges of Toleration in Pluralistic Societies
Edited by Gideon Calder, Magali Bessone and Federico Zuolo

87 The Politics of Rationality
Reason through Occidental History
Charles P. Webel

88 Gramsci, Materialism, and Philosophy
Esteve Morera

89 Emotions and Social Change
Historical and Sociological Perspectives
Edited by David Lemmings and Ann Brooks

90 John Rawls and the History of Political Thought
The Rousseauvian and Hegelian Heritage of Justice as Fairness
Jeffrey Bercuson

91 What Holism Can Do for Social Theory
Barbara Hanson

92 The Sociology of Knowledge in a Time of Crisis
Challenging the Phantom of Liberty
Onofrio Romano

93 Cosmopolitanism and the Legacies of Dissent
Tamara Caraus and Camil-Alexandru Parvu

94 The Metaphysics of Technology
David Skrbina

95 The Political Thought of Hume and His Contemporaries: Enlightenment Projects Vol 1
Frederick G. Whelan

96 The Political Thought of Hume and His Contemporaries: Enlightenment Projects Vol 2
Frederick G. Whelan

97 Rosa Luxemburg In Action: For Revolution and Democracy
Rosemary H. T. O'Kane

98 Innovation Contested: The Idea of Innovation Over the Centuries
Benoît Godin

99 Phenomenology of Youth Cultures and Globalization
Lifeworlds and Surplus Meaning in Changing Times
Edited by Stuart R. Poyntz and Jacqueline Kennelly

Phenomenology of Youth Cultures and Globalization

Lifeworlds and Surplus Meaning in Changing Times

Edited by Stuart R. Poyntz and Jacqueline Kennelly

Routledge
Taylor & Francis Group
NEW YORK AND LONDON

First published 2015
by Routledge
711 Third Avenue, New York, NY 10017

and by Routledge
2 Park Square, Milton Park, Abingdon, Oxon OX14 4RN

Routledge is an imprint of the Taylor & Francis Group, an informa business

Library of Congress Cataloging-in-Publication Data
Phenomenology of youth cultures and globalization : lifeworlds and surplus meaning in changing times / edited by Stuart R. Poyntz and Jacqueline Kennelly.
pages cm. — (Routledge studies in social and political thought ; 99)
Includes bibliographical references and index.
1. Youth—Social conditions—21st century. 2. Youth—Cross-cultural studies. 3. Globalization—Social aspects. 4. Phenomenological sociology. I. Poyntz, Stuart R. II. Kennelly, Jacqueline.
HQ796.P4694 2015
305.235009′05—dc23
2014035772

ISBN: 978-0-415-72070-0 (hbk)
ISBN: 978-1-315-86678-9 (ebk)

Typeset in Sabon
by Apex CoVantage, LLC

For Pennie and Hamish
—Stuart R. Poyntz

For KaiLin and Desmond
—Jacqueline Kennelly

Contents

Acknowledgments

Stuart and Jacqueline would like to thank all of the contributors for their fabulous work, and a special acknowledgement of Paul Ugor, who was part of the original triumvirate that hatched this project. Thanks also to the generous peer reviewers who gave of their expertise in ways that helped improve each chapter in this volume, and to Jo-Anne Dillabough, for her constant support of this project and her efforts on our behalf. We look forward to working with her further as this volume goes out into the world. Finally, we extend our gratitude to Max Novick, Jennifer Morrow and the rest of the staff at Routledge for their prompt and supportive efforts in bringing this project to a conclusion.

Individually, Jacqueline would like to acknowledge the research assistance of Christopher Enman, Ryan Boyd, Amelia Curran and Jessica Azevedo. She is also grateful to her co-editor, Stuart Poyntz, for his cheerful solidarity and extraordinary organizational skills. Special thanks and a toast to my phenomenology reading group at Carleton University: Danielle DiNovelli-Lang, Peter Gose, Bernhard Leistle and Frances Slaney. And to my life partner, Alex Campbell: Words are not sufficient.

Stuart would like to acknowledge the timely research assistance of Graham Mackenzie and Sophie Dempsey. He is also grateful to Chery Meszaros, someone who is no longer with us, but who played a formative role in organizing a remarkable reading group in Vancouver that nurtured Stuart's interest in phenomenology and youth studies. Finally, a special thanks to my co-editor, Jacqueline, who has proven to be a generous, brilliant and energetic scholar and friend throughout two major projects we have now completed together.

1 Introduction

Phenomenology of Youth Cultures and Globalization: Lifeworlds and Surplus Meaning in Changing Times

Jacqueline Kennelly and Stuart R. Poyntz[1]

INTRODUCTION

Globalization is one of the central philosophemes of our era, a focal objectification of lived experience in space and time, and a concept that continues to help explain the fundamental dynamics of human experience today. Globalization references the ever-accelerating interconnections of diverse human lives at the political, economic, social and cultural levels. If at times the very ubiquity of the term can appear to leave the concept barren of meaning, we contend that it remains a fundamental resource for orienting ourselves in contemporary life. It is with this in mind that we have turned to phenomenology, a philosophical tradition with roots in early twentieth-century European thought, currently being reinvigorated across diverse disciplines as a crucial approach for tackling complex questions regarding lived experience, meaning-making processes and subjectivity. Phenomenology is concerned with the ways subjects orient to worlds through an array of symbolic articulations. In this edited collection we have sought to draw from phenomenology in order to specify how globalization is unfolding amongst young people living in various regions and under diverse conditions around the world. In so doing, we contend that phenomenology and phenomenologically imbued modes of analysis can help us to better diagnose the present and future by 'thickening up' our understanding of the sense-making practices deployed by young people in the current period of asymmetrical globalization.

In turning to phenomenology to understand how young people are living out their contemporary lives, we intend to keep central the body of evidence which makes clear that globalization has unfolded within social networks, among communities and within the complexities of the new global metropolis through novel and profound forms of inequity. We contend, however, that all of us—young and old, those from the global North and South—are also already agents in and of globalization. Consequently, young people in particular would appear to have existential evidence "at ontic and mundane levels" of what it means to live, survive and even flourish under the constraints of a new global order (Mendieta, 2007, 40). In saying this, we do not wish to privilege youth voice as a medium of truth. Rather, we contend that because the particular, subjective accounts of young people are always symbolically enacted in a specific space and time, they contain what Paul Ricoeur (1976) would call a "surplus of meaning," an excess through which it becomes possible to chart the social imaginaries of youth cultures unfolding in the new and oftentimes perilous circumstances of global futurity. Richard Kearney (2004, 86) explains that social imaginaries refer to what Ricoeur understood as:

> That body of collective stories, histories and ideologies which inform our modes of socio-political action. Social imagination . . . is constitutive of our lived reality. . . . [But this means t]he social imagination serves both an ideological role of identification and a utopian role of disruption. The former preserves and conserves; the latter projects alternatives.

Where globalization is a worldview or philosopheme, it is also a system through which individual lifeworlds are structured in particular ways: Most profoundly today, this has included a de-structuring of older lifeworlds, the result of which is the development of "processes that have given rise to new horizons of experience and expectation" (Mendieta, 2007, 20).

The task of this book, then, is to draw on phenomenologically informed inquiries to describe youth experience as it is lived in the context of globalization, to understand the patterns of meaning that emerge in the midst of the totality of human being-in-the-world (Heidegger, [1927] 1962). To do this, a key objective is to identify young people's "symbolic worlds as a detour through [which] other spatial, structural, moral and temporal narratives and registers" might be addressed (Dillabough and Kennelly, 2010, 51). Thereby, the 'boundedness' of young people in the context of global life, including that which is preserved and conserved, and those social, political and cultural possibilities that are emergent among contemporary youth, might be revealed.

INTERSUBJECTIVITY, EMBODIMENT, TEMPORALITY AND MEANING-MAKING

Amongst its many contributions, phenomenology offers a means by which to attend to the directly lived experiences of young people within globalizing times without succumbing to the temptation of positing their experiences as ahistorical or fragmented. As has often been the case in youth research that relies on postmodernist or 'voice-centered' interpretations of young people's experiences, a focus on identity, transitions, and individualization can render young people's lives as separated from the structures and histories that shape them. Phenomenology, on the other hand, permits the focus of meaning-making to rest with the experiences of the youth themselves, but does not end there, for "the problem of meaning is a time problem" (Schutz, [1932] 1967, 12). That is, rather than taking the experiences of youth under globalization as an exemplar case of detraditionalization (Beck, 2009; Beck, Giddens and Lash, 1994), phenomenology permits an analysis that focuses on contemporary meaning-making processes within the context of a much larger historical frame. It thus posits such experiences as emerging from a past, while lived in the present. At the same time, the centrality of globalization as an organizing structure helps to reveal what has been recalibrated, shifted, and/or dissolved under social relations that must account for the intensification of global flows of information, finance, and (in some cases) bodies (Appadurai, 1996, 2013).

At the core of a phenomenological approach to young people's lives is the recognition of the centrality of *intersubjectivity* within human experience, what Arendt (1958) calls the "web of relations" that bind together a plurality of people across a shared horizon of social life. Intersubjectivity draws attention to the specific way consciousness and intentionality are taken up in phenomenology. Neither term should be interpreted in an idealist sense, in relation to the subject as 'universal thinker,' as "the positing power who subjects the manifold to the law of the understanding, in so far as [she] is to be able to put together a world" (Merleau-Ponty, 2004, 74). In phenomenology, subject and world dwell in each other. Husserl's early supposition (e.g., see *The Cartesian Meditations* or *Ideas*) that the contingency of meaning might be escaped by a reduction to "the pure immanence of a transcendental subjectivity" is thus not of interest here (Kearney, 2004, 15). We begin rather from Ricoeur's assumption (shared by Heidegger, Merleau-Ponty and the later Husserl) that consciousness is always finite. It is born in the wash of a language horizon "whose meanings precede our own subjective creations" (ibid., 16). This move aligns our work with various analyses of young people's social being today. What phenomenology brings to the analysis of subject and world is, however, a focus on meaning. But in phenomenology meaning-making processes are always understood to be oriented toward or around something, which is another way of saying "consciousness is always directed toward objects and hence is always worldly, situated and embodied" (Ahmed, 2006, 544). Intersubjectivity thus refers to a necessary intimacy between subject and world. And because young people's symbolic articulations are necessarily of the world, "phenomenology is the attempt to articulate the 'operative intentionality' that is antecedent to conscious thought" (Merleau-Ponty, 2004, 63). The task before us is not just to describe youth lives, then, but to interpret what they simultaneously conceal about the machinations of global life.

The consequence of this is that phenomenology requires of us, as researchers and as fellow human beings, to approach our interpretation of the other via what Schutz ([1932] 1967) refers to as *durée*—life as experienced across time and space, belonging to each one of us as individuals but also residing within a shared social world. Under phenomenology, the concepts we are working with begin to change; common sociological and cultural themes are taken up differently.

For instance, we can talk about the public (as Arendt does), but 'publicness' in a phenomenological sense is understood to be a creatively co-constituted space of interconnections, activities, stories and effects through which our appearances together constitute threads of human possibility. Pubic life is not strictly about rational communication oriented toward a Habermasian consensus, in other words, nor is it about something 'out there,' a space to be designed by careful urban planning or prudent politicians (Bridge and Watson, 2011). Public life is about speech and action that counteract thoughtlessness and produce spaces of communicative plurality that reveal the contingencies and materialities that affect people's ability to act with others (Poyntz, 2012; Gallagher, this volume; Asthana, this volume). Roger Silverstone (2002, 766) captures this well when he writes: "The possibility of public life depends on the mutuality of seeing and hearing [others] and seeing and hearing depends on the recognition of both difference and identity amongst those involved in the interaction."

Phenomenology also addresses measures of time and temporality, but here again, such measures are understood within the everyday, as each is experienced through the body, language and human relationships (Rasmussen, this volume; Taylor, this volume). Within youth cultures these temporal aspects might manifest as tattoo designs or the lingering resilience of certain subcultural taunts, changing yet constant, not emerging from nowhere yet also constantly interpellated through the subjective experiences of those creating meaning in that particular moment.

How else then, except through phenomenology, can we account for the manner in which the past lives through us in the present, embodied through everyday meaning practices that rely on interlocking webs of relationships? And how better to account for both the flux and sedimentation of globalization's effects on young people, where global flows meet futurity and the stubborn resilience of social structures that reproduce persistent inequalities that plague our globalized world? Certainly the social sciences have grappled with the monumental changes happening at an unprecedented pace under high modernity (of which globalization is one aspect). Ulrich Beck's (2009; see also Beck, Giddens and Lash, 1994) detraditionalization thesis is but one (albeit highly influential) theoretical approach that has attempted to account for the rapidity of global change and its meaning for social systems. Under the detraditionalization thesis, the ties that bind societies have loosened, emphasizing risk and contingency but also possibilities and the chance to re-make one's own biography. A phenomenological approach to globalized social contexts, on the other hand, questions the 'newness' of 'new times' (Hall, 1996a), re-attaching them to the reins of history, the body and an interlocking web of human relationships. "Knowing that there has always been flow, exchange, and mixture across social boundaries in human history," (Appadurai, 2013, 65), we take seriously the need for the *longue durée*. Not succumbing to the temptation to account for complex social lives through a singular or linear trajectory, phenomenological approaches to youth cultures permit a complex accounting of the constellations of contemporary youth experiences. Such constellations contain the residues of a deep past, but of course there is little doubt that the speed of cultural exchange has accelerated in the new millennium, as "global cultural flows have lost [their] selective and cumbersome qualities," which for so long mitigated their transit across the arc of human history (ibid., 63). In contrast, today global flows—whether political, cultural, social or economic—are a constant factor in young lives, and as the chapters in this collection indicate, they give shape and form to the production of local subjectivities and conditions under which youthful lives unfold.

SITUATING PHENOMENOLOGY WITHIN YOUTH CULTURAL THEORY

One of the central contentions of this collection is that phenomenology has long informed critical empirical approaches to youth cultures, yet until recently its role has not been thusly named. Part of our project, then, is to resuscitate and recuperate phenomenology as a robust empirical, theoretical and methodological approach to youth cultures. Some of the seminal influences on youth cultural theory have come from theorists who themselves disavow or understate their links to phenomenology, and yet whose work lends itself directly to phenomenological approaches. Pierre Bourdieu is the most prominent of these. Right up until the year of his death, he declared that his work was not phenomenological (see Bourdieu's response to Throop and Murphy, 2002), and yet subsequent theorists throughout the social sciences have linked Bourdieu's highly complex and influential corpus to that of various phenomenologists (e.g., Charlesworth, 2000; Throop and Murphy, 2002). In developing her study of queer bodily orientations, for instance, Ahmed (2006, 552) notes that "[p]henomenology helps us explore how bodies are shaped by histories, which they perform in their comportment, their posture, and their gestures." She ties her concerns to that of Husserl and Merleau-Ponty, who argue that bodily orientations are forms of "sedimented histories," *and* to Bourdieu, who describes such orientations as part of the *habitus*, the " 'system of durable, transposable, dispositions,' which integrate past experiences through the very 'matrix of perceptions, appreciations and actions' that are necessary to accomplish 'infinitely diversified tasks' " (ibid., 552–553; Bourdieu, quoted in text).

In a different way, we also note connections between Paulo Friere and phenomenology. Long a formative influence in the fields of youth studies, critical pedagogy and media education (cf. Giroux, McLaren, Soep and Chávez, etc.), the central Frierean notion of dialogic pedagogy is more often than not interpreted in relation to a Hegelian dialectic of *conscientizacion*. In this way Friere is attached to a tradition of immanent critique that runs through Kant to Hegel to Marx to the Frankfurt School, and so on. Here, critical consciousness emerges in the interchange between students and teachers as part of a problem-posing process wherein both parties experience forms of liberation through their connection with others. Duarte (2000) argues, however, that Friere's unique category of critical consciousness rests on a deeper form of inter-relatedness between dialogic subjects, one where student and teacher are understood to engage in a process of joining their expressions and thinking. Rather than a dialectic of self and other, here "the dialogic and communicative basis of problem-posing yields an experience of co-intentionality that is akin to a plurality of subjects thinking together as *One*" (Duarte, 2000, 186; emphasis in original). The upshot of this for youth research is that a Frierean-inspired pedagogy may have less to do with the production of a dialectic of immanent truth, and more to do with the way worldliness and a rich and full sense of the real are enabled through critical pedagogy and media education (c.f. Asthana, this volume; Hoechsmann and Poyntz, 2012; Silverstone, 2007; and Curtis, 1999).

Another highly influential theorist of contemporary culture is Raymond Williams, considered one of the 'founding fathers' of British Cultural Studies, from which youth cultural studies sprung. His seminal concept of "structures of feeling" (Williams, 1977) is easily co-locatable with phenomenological approaches, referencing as it does the process by which agents individually embody broader social structures. And Paul Willis's (1977) *Learning to Labour*, one of the most widely read and cited works of youth cultural theory, seeks to explain the everyday experiences of young men in 1970s Britain through an account of their everyday meaning-making practices, linking them to histories and structures highly reminiscent of phenomenological concerns (and, not coincidentally, using the work of Pierre Bourdieu to do so).

As the second director of the highly influential Birmingham Centre for Contemporary Cultural Studies in the UK, Stuart Hall has also played a formative role in shaping cultural studies more broadly, and youth cultural studies specifically. In his (2007) most extensive discussion of how phenomenology and cultural studies converge, Hall focuses on the phenomenological work of Schutz and the development of the sociology of knowledge in the American academy. He counters this development with the emergence of ideology critique in the Marxist tradition, and finds phenomenology lacking, particularly where the latter is conceived as the study of "the contents and structures of consciousness," rather than the social relations and conditions that make the history which subjects act in and through (Hall, 2007, 135). But Hall also notes that Schutz moves phenomenology away from the reduction of reality to what people think (i.e., to consciousness), to a concern for the way "thoughts [gain] an objective facticity in the world" and thereby shape human actions and the construction of reality (Hall, 2007, 138). Ricoeur ultimately moves this argument further along through his engagement with the so-called masters of suspicion—i.e., Marx, Nietzsche and Freud—whose respective critiques of false consciousness, the will-to-power and unconscious desire make evident the gaps and fissures that are part of meaning-making processes in the first instance. The effect of this is to reposition phenomenology as a hermeneutic exercise engaged in the examination of "the various inevitable detours which interpretation undergoes through language, myth, ideology, the unconscious and so on—*before* it arrives at the ultimate limit of Being" (Kearney, 2004, 22; emphasis in the original). In attending to the myriad forms of historical symbolization that knit to and are a consequence of Being, Ricoeur's phenomenology—including his concern for ideology and utopia—thus ultimately converges with Hall's work in cultural studies.

Meenakshi Gigi Durham (2011) agrees and notes that Hall's move away from Althusser's structuralist influence in cultural studies marks an important shift that brings cultural studies and phenomenological concerns into conversation. Hall never entirely abandoned Althusser's structuralist (and anti-phenomenological) concern for the way subjects are formed through processes of subjection that produce a speaking subject. Nonetheless, Hall did reconfigure Althusser's notion of subjectivation by making clear that subject positions are never fully fixed by some originary act of interpellation. Rather, subjectivities always "remain open to be positioned and 'subjected' in different ways, at different moments throughout our existence" (Hall, 1996b, 26). This shift plays a significant role in Hall's (1996c) theorizing of cultural identity, and it also marks a point at which Hall's thinking moves closer to phenomenology, to the extent that identities and bodies are now conceptualized as diachronic rather than synchronic forms. For Hall, identities are a consequence of our entanglement with rhetorics of power, but this does not mean the self is powerless. Self and world exist in a compact of social being, where subjectivities are a consequence of "[t]hat body of collective stories, histories and ideologies" that enable a self to be, and a source of potential disruption that forecasts a future (and possibly utopian) horizon yet to be realized (Kearney, 2004, 86).

Another important link between phenomenology and youth cultural theory is evident in feminist scholarship (see Fisher and Embree, 2000). Unlike the theorists noted above, feminism and phenomenology have long engaged in a rich and explicit exchange. Sara Heinämaa (2009) traces this back to Husserl's later work in *The Crisis of European Sciences and Transcendental Phenomenology*, where he notes "the problem of the sexes" among the genetic transcendental problems facing phenomenology. Simone de Beauvoir's *The Second Sex* ([1949] 1972) represents a more fully articulated encounter between feminism and phenomenology, in no small part because her famous observation that "one is not born, but, rather becomes, a woman" (295) remains a strikingly phenomenological account of gendered subjectivity. In her seminal essay, Judith Butler (2007) argues that the appeal of phenomenology among feminists has to do with the theory of 'acts' common to the tradition. Phenomenology draws attention to "the mundane ways social agents constitute social reality through language, gesture, and all manner of social symbolic sign" (ibid., 187). A major strain of phenomenology—one which we foreground in this collection—also suggests a more radical critique of how action is made possible in the first instance. Ricoeur alludes to this when he calls for a hermeneutics of the text: to understand that which writes us. In a similar way, Butler contends: "The social agent [is best understood] as an *object* rather than the subject of constitutive acts" (ibid.). Subjectivity is thereby rendered as a site of performance where social norms and taboos both enable and restrict social action. The reified gendered identities that result are always subject to forms of destabilization and transformation, but feminism's encounter with phenomenology has afforded researchers with a complex theory of action and subject formation that falls prey neither to naturalist conceptions of gender, nor highly individualized accounts of social change.

Heinämaa (2009) suggests that where sexual difference is concerned, phenomenology has thus contributed conceptual and methodological innovation as a philosophically grounded alternative to naturalism and constructivism. At the same time, feminism has reconfigured the place of the sexually neutral subject in phenomenology, thereby contributing to the project of reconceptualizing the role of a single transcendental subject in phenomenology. In youth research, the effect of feminism's encounter with phenomenology has been felt across a range of research, including: Dillabough and Kennelly's (2010) work on marginalized youth and global cities; Kennelly (2011) on youth citizenship and activism; Springgay (2007, 2008) on the pedagogies of touch and youth visual culture; Carrington (2002, 2009) on youth media and the family; Johnson (2000) on children's gender beliefs; Gallagher (2007) and Gallagher and Neelands (2013) on youth theatre and urban contexts; Crowley and Rasmussen (2010) on queer phenomenologies; and MacLeod (2012, 2013) on gendered history and learning. In the current collection, the intersection of feminism and phenomenology threads through a number of chapters (see for instance, Gallagher; Esfahani and Carrington; Rasmussen; and Taylor). Likewise, the ideas and concerns of other key youth cultural theorists noted above mark the accounts that follow, revealing important directions in the ways phenomenology is informing the future of youth research.

CREATING MEANINGFUL SOCIAL SCIENTIFIC RESEARCH

Phenomenology, as a field of inquiry, is notoriously broad and diverse; this might be one explanation for the reluctance of some theorists to align their work with the field. When invoking 'phenomenology,' one question that comes to mind for anyone even glancingly familiar with the field is 'which phenomenology?' Are we referring to Merleau-Ponty's embodied social perceptions? Husserl's pseudo-scientific call to return "back to the things themselves"? Heidegger's *Dasein*? Schutz's *schemas* and *durée*? Etc. Likewise, phenomenology has been most commonly associated with philosophy, and often elaborated as a philosophical approach to understanding human relations. This collection, by contrast, is focused on the *empirical applications* of phenomenological thinking; we gather together a range of youth theorists and researchers from across the global North and the global South who have used some aspects of phenomenology to better elaborate their understandings of young people's lives. We are not alone in seeing the potential of phenomenology for application to empirical studies; other disciplines that have made substantial use of phenomenological inquiry include nursing (Taylor, 1993), medicine (Carel, 2011) and psychology (Daanen, 2009; Langdridge, 2008). Our own collection draws from education, media studies, cultural studies, anthropology and sociology, reflecting both the diversity of youth cultural studies as well as the diversity of phenomenology itself.

Whereas it is true that a number of theorists from across a range of disciplines, geographic locations, and academic traditions have developed their own distinct forms of phenomenological inquiry, what ties them together is a certain style of thought and a focus on *meaning-making*, emerging from the individual but also tied to the social world around her. In this collection, we have focused on three key emergent themes that are common to the majority of phenomenological work: temporality and historicity (developed with the most attention by Paul Ricoeur), embodiment (often drawn from the work of Merleau-Ponty), and inter-relationality, or the connection between oneself and another.[2]

One of the qualities that makes phenomenology an interesting way to work with the social sciences is how it demands that we respond to the data; using a phenomenological lens, data cannot be viewed simply as truth claims elicited from unbounded rational subjects without a history of their own. Instead, phenomenological approaches to the social sciences demand a working-through of the meaning-making resources subjects use to orient and constitute their worlds. To work though such resources demands attentiveness to the "surface profusion of the world" (Curtis, 1999, 30), to the ways meaning-making contains a dense excess, a history of felt-ness and import that is revealed in tracing the social life of things and practices.

One of the driving questions that this project raises, then, is the purpose of the social sciences, and the ways we understand the meaningfulness of those projects and actions addressed in the chapters that follow. In particular, phenomenology requires us to question whether research is delivering the fullness of meaning suggested by the hermeneutic process of understanding. One problem that continues to pervade the social sciences, perhaps thanks to the positivist strains that bear down on so much academic research, is that we social scientists often remain content with achieving *explanation*—that something has happened, and how it has happened—but not *understanding*. But the latter objective tells us what it means to live something out as a meaningful relationship with the world.

Paul Ricoeur's concept of the long detour exemplifies a phenomenological approach that helps disrupt this tendency within the social sciences: For Ricoeur, the me that speaks is only conceivable after one makes sense of the world where the me is already speaking. Thus, in order to understand oneself, one has to go out into the world in order to return to oneself (Ricoeur, 1996). When one encounters the world, however, the self that one returns to is not a newly rendered transparent being, the so-called rational self, reminiscent of Descartes's dreams. Rather, what is unique about Ricoeur's phenomenological treatment is that there is no final accomplishment of the transparently evident self. Nor, we might add, can the social sciences ever produce a transparent picture of the world, including those worlds inhabited by young people today. Instead, what one gains from phenomenological investigations are richer sets of conditions and concerns for understanding self and world. This is what it means when we say, to explain more is to understand more. To understand more means nurturing a hermeneutics of truth, which is not the same as making claims to represent the truth. It is rather to see the social sciences as a broad field of research in which the fullness and substantiality of meaning-making is brought into view. This is what phenomenology calls on us as social scientists to do.

OVERVIEW OF CHAPTERS

In bringing phenomenology to the study of young people's lives in the context of globalization, the contributors to this collection demonstrate the depth and diversity of phenomenological concerns and their utility in responding to the question of *understanding* young people's lives. Intersubjectivity, embodiment, meaning-making, temporality and experience all make their appearance in the chapters that follow, and, as we have noted, each of these themes are central concepts within a phenomenological approach. Yet the authors here also raise questions and dilemmas that cut across epistemological positions, addressing them with the help of phenomenology but also recognizing that there are no easy answers to be found: questions surrounding the ethics of the research process itself, the capacity for agency under conditions of severe constraint, the potential for positive social change wrought by research participants and researchers alike. While seeking to expand understanding and reveal the interstices of young lives under globalization, the contributors to this volume also seek to trouble the very categories that shape the research process, such as 'researcher,' 'youth,' 'globalization,' even 'phenomenology.' In keeping the categories open, our hope is that this volume will begin a conversation about the ways in which phenomenology might help us think differently about young people under globalization, without dictating a singular or monolithic approach that forecloses other possibilities.

As noted above, one of the central themes that emerges when drawing on a phenomenological lens is *intersubjectivity*. Whether understood through Arendt's metaphor of a shared table or Merleau-Ponty's famous imagery of one hand touching the other, phenomenology takes at its core the understanding that we *interact* with one another, and in doing so, we *affect* one another. This raises important questions about efficacy and agency, themes that Sanjay Asthana and Kathleen Gallagher each explore in their respective chapters. In "Translocality, Imagination, and the Political: A Hermeneutic Exploration of Youth Media Initiatives from India and Palestine," Asthana explores the multifaceted media practices of two groups of young people in two very different parts of the world: New Delhi, India, and a Palestinian refugee camp in Bethlehem. His chapter uses Paul Ricoeur's phenomenological hermeneutics to theorize the political practices of agency embedded within the youths' engagement with multiple forms of media. With a particular focus on affect and embodiment, Asthana posits the potential for translocal media practices to extend 'spaces for dialogue' that contribute to an agonistic and relational public sphere. Resisting the common tendency to represent and perceive marginalized youth as somehow lacking in agency, Asthana also complicates the possibilities for political agency that can effect change. In doing so, he neither romanticizes nor dismisses the capacity for young marginalized people living in difficult circumstances to contribute to public life in meaningful, yet circumscribed, ways.

Kathleen Gallagher's chapter also asks us to consider questions of agency and the potential for change wrought through a shared public space. In "Performing Patriarchy: Indian Girls (En)gender a Social Imaginary," Gallagher phenomenologically explores questions of empathy and action in relation to the drama practices of the girls themselves. Based on her fieldwork at an innovative girls' school in Uttar Pradesh, India, Gallagher demonstrates the humour and enthusiasm with which these low-caste girls portray their everyday challenges in a rigidly sexist society. In witnessing their struggles, theatrically re-enacted, Gallagher asks us to consider not only how dramatic methods can contribute to a deeper understanding of young people's everyday lives, but also how audience members (researchers included) might be interpellated not as mere observers but instead as 'visitors,' following Hannah Arendt. Through 'visiting' the experiences of others, as accessed in this case via dramatic methods, Gallagher argues that we might be able to respond empathically and *politically* without erasing the differences of power that lie between us, permitting the possibility for action and change—however small such change might be in the constraints of the moment. As she notes, "The performance always exceeds in the abstract that which it symbolizes in the concrete" (p. 70, this volume); in other words, the dramatic methods used in Gallagher's research project produce surplus meanings (to borrow Ricoeur's turn of phrase) that make it possible to move both performers and audience to something *more*. As Arendt might argue, the 'more' can never be predicted at its genesis, but its potential is part of our human capacity for action that allows egregious social injustices to be fought and, eventually, to be changed.

Gallagher's concern with action and, centrally, the role of the researcher in contributing to positive social change, is echoed and reinforced by Clovis Bergère and Lauren Silver in their chapter, "Relational Phenomenology and the Politics of Global Urban Youth Research." Drawing on their own research with marginalized urban young people in Camden, NJ, USA, and Labé and Conakry in Guinea, West Africa, Bergère and Silver mobilize phenomenology to ask, "How can we do—a little more—justice to those lived experiences we claim to describe?" (p. 78, this volume). They see phenomenology as allowing researchers to shift their thinking incrementally towards a deeper understanding of our roles in relation to our research participants. Researchers, they suggest, when viewed phenomenologically, are not solely 'experts' engaged in the field to change it from without, but neither are they simply vessels through which to uncritically 'give voice' to young people. Instead, researchers are engaged inter-relationally with both the field and the participants within it, and are thus positioned to both comment on the social realities that shape young people's lives, and also to participate in changing unjust social conditions.

Also central to each of the chapters is a focus on youth experiences and their processes of meaning-making, themes that lie at the very core of phenomenological investigations. The means by which a subject makes sense of his or her own encounters with the world is one of the dilemmas that drove the development of phenomenology, as a result of dissatisfaction with the reigning Cartesian division between body and mind, emotion and reason. The power of phenomenological approaches for troubling these simple binaries is amply demonstrated in Ana Padawer's chapter, entitled "'When the Soil Is Just Right—It Has to Feel Like This': Peasant Youth of Northeastern Argentina: Experiences and Understanding." Drawing on five years of ethnographic research with Argentinian peasant youth, Padawer utilizes Paul Ricoeur's linguistic and temporal phenomenology to examine what she terms the 'enskilled translations' the youth engage with in their agricultural work. She sees Ricoeur's contribution on the relationship between language and interpretation as key to permitting her to theorize how the Argentinian youth experience *knowing* through *doing*. She uses Ricoeur's phenomenology to describe how knowledge becomes a part of predispositional understandings, while also based on socially and historically mediated practices. Similar to Bourdieu's *habitus* and Marx's *class consciousness*, Padawer sees Ricoeur's contribution through his notion of the distance (or distantiation) between experience and language as essential to the concept of enskilled translations. Following two young peasant men, Simon (age 19) and Damien (age 16), as they cultivate the land alongside their families, Padawer applies her insights to account for the interpretive work that is done by these young men, as they navigate between technical agricultural knowledge, their own different learning worlds, and their 'feel' for the land and its requirements.

On the other side of the world in an Australian urban centre, Naghmeh Nouri Esfahani and Victoria Carrington explore the meaning-making processes of young people interacting with a different aspect of cultural life—namely, young girls and their Barbie™ dolls. In "(Re)scripting Barbie: Postphenomenology and Everyday Artefacts," Esfahani and Carrington seek to apply and extend a postphenomenological approach to understanding young people's interactions with their everyday artefacts. As they note, the Barbie™ doll has been extensively analyzed by feminist theorists and through a cultural studies approach; by bringing postphenomenology to their examination, they seek to do something different. Following the work of Peter Paul Verbeek, they define postphenomenology as inspired by Heidegger's concern with the centrality of interactions to everyday life, but attempting to transcend Heidegger's suspicion of technology as inherently alienating. As such, postphenomenology "pays attention to the mediating role of technology in the construction and experience of everyday realities" (Esfahani and Carrington, p. 117, this volume). Applying this theoretical frame to the experiences of Nava, an eight-year-old girl living in suburban Australia, they demonstrate how Nava is both 'scripted' by Barbie™ and her design (e.g., through playing with her hair, as the designers intended for little girls), but also how Nava 'rescripts' Barbie™ to suit her own experiential needs and desires (e.g., through changing Barbie's™ hair and body, and enacting specific scenarios from her own life). Esfahani and Carrington conclude that Nava, and perhaps young girls more broadly, are not "passive recipient[s] of dolls' scripts." Instead, young girls may "actively and constantly look for connectivity, trying to discover or recall the links between" (p. 128, this volume) themselves and their dolls.

Paul Ugor's chapter, "Armed Insurgency, Young Women and the Feminization of Resistance in the Niger Delta," is also centrally concerned with experience, specifically the lived experiences of young women involved in the armed insurgency of the Niger Delta region between 2006 and 2009. Focusing on a group of youth whose voices have rarely been represented in either academic or media accounts of this conflict, Ugor's methodological choice is to present the young women's accounts of themselves without overt interference from himself as the researcher and author. In doing so, he is working to correct an institutional bias towards privileging men's stories of the insurgency and making women's participation invisible. He justifies this choice phenomenologically, asking us as readers to view the women's experiences through their own eyes, as much as might be possible within the distantiation already created by language. He points to the tensions inherent in bringing a European tradition to bear in order to account for postcolonial experiences of oppression and dispossession, noting that he has been challenged to answer the question of "the appropriateness of the so-called European theories for making sense of 'uniquely' African socio-cultural and political processes" (p. 137, this volume). Ugor's response is to suggest that phenomenology has something to offer that transcends the limits of its own origins, and might thus be fruitfully applied in diverse contexts. In the case of this chapter, he highlights the manner in which phenomenology focuses on "'the lived-world, the world of ordinary, immediate experience' (Stewart and Mickunas, 1974, 12), especially as felt and perceived by the thinking subject" (p. 137, this volume).

Leslie Robinson, Carolina Cambre, Andrew Jackson Obol and Cathy Mashakalugo likewise reflect on the relevance of phenomenology for exploring postcolonial experiences in "Phenomenological Passports: Youth and Experiences of Place, Mobility and Globalization." They turn to Frantz Fanon and W.E.B. DuBois, who they locate as belonging to a tradition of "Africana phenomenology" (p. 159, this volume), sharing in their "ethical commitment to those whose existence is subordinated and systemically excluded from traditional academic discourse in general" (p. 160, this volume). In this vigorous and experimental piece of collaborative writing, Robinson, Cambre, Obol and Mashakalugo explore their respective experiences of visiting the 'global' and globalized 'city of love.' Beginning with a vignette that illustrates their differing responses to the iconic image of the Eiffel Tower, the four authors offer phenomenological insights into the context of asymmetrical globalization through their differing perceptions of their time in Paris. Co-authored by two Ugandans, one Canadian and one Argentine immigrant to Canada, they work towards building collaborative meaning-making that is anti-colonial in its intent. All four authors belong to the broader category of 'youth,' whose dimensions have extended as the globalized lifecourse has shifted its parameters. In their reflections, we catch glimpses of the collisions between globalized knowledges, some shared, others patently in opposition. They offer not only their own experiences, but reflections on each other's, gathered through journal entries, poetry, drawings and oral recordings. As they note, "The process involved continuous reworking of reflections and stories with an emphasis on encouraging deep reflection and wondering and sitting with the stories" (p. 161, this volume); the result is a thoughtful and insightful contribution to ethical and personal questions about young people's lives and commitments within the context of post-colonial globalized relationships and their movement between cultural worlds. The chapter also illustrates the potential for inter-relationality as a means to produce knowledge, taking the phenomenological emphasis on the connection between 'I' and 'other' as their central methodological approach.

Embodiment is another central theme of phenomenological investigations, and is likewise a key theme in this volume. Mary Lou Rasmussen's chapter, "Sex education, Bodily Orientations and the Northern Territory 'Intervention,' " focuses squarely on embodiment when she asks us to consider what it might mean for Indigenous bodies to be oriented in specific ways via the cultural and educational work done by the Australian Northern Territory and Emergency Response (NTER). The NTER, known colloquially as 'the intervention,' is a policy initiative ostensibly designed to address allegations of child abuse within remote Indigenous communities. Rasmussen argues that this controversial initiative must be understood as much more than a straightforward government policy. Rather, she sees it as a social and political object that attempts to locate Indigenous people who live in remote areas "as specific sorts of sexual subjects inhabiting spaces that are depicted as culturally backward, sexually dangerous and particularly problematic for children and young people" (p. 183, this volume). Exploring the issue of the large blue signs that have been posted outside of remote Indigenous communities, prohibiting pornography and alcohol, and drawing on an ethnography of teenage girls' sexuality prior to 'the intervention,' Rasmussen uses Ahmed's and Povinelli's phenomenological approaches to ask, "What might it mean for bodies to be oriented in this way?" (p. 183, this volume). She concludes by suggesting that Indigenous people living in remote communities in Australia experience sexuality with and against 'the intervention.' The result is that "young people's experiences of sexuality and sexuality education are always betwixt and between Indigenous lifeworlds and liberal politics of recognition" (p. 207, this volume).

Yvette Taylor blends two core phenomenological themes—embodiment and temporality—when she asks us to consider which are the 'bodies that stay' and which are the 'bodies that travel'? Drawing on ethnographic research with young women living in the post-industrial North Eastern UK city of Newcastle, Taylor brings feminist phenomenology into conversation with cultural geography in her chapter entitled "Past, Present, Future Encounters: Bodies That Travel, Bodies That Stay." Caught between older histories of working-class industrial pride, stigma and struggles, and more recent efforts to rebrand Newcastle as a desirable urban destination for the middle classes, the young women of Taylor's study express their sense of belonging or displacement through reference to both the spatial and cultural resources that are associated with the city. Taylor explores how these experiences—of a body that stays, or a body that travels—are implicated by histories and geographies as well as the corporeal and inter-relational aspects of human experience. Through innovative focus group discussions and detailed interview excerpts, Taylor illuminates the weight of historicity and the geographies of class, race and gender that become embodied in the lived experiences of younger Newcastle women. In doing so, Taylor challenges her readers "to carve out a claim for plural futures." As she notes, "Not everyone can flexibly cast themselves through trajectories of regenerative potential, 'properly' orientating towards residential-consumer space—and not everyone wants to" (p. 230, this volume).

Aaron Klassen explores issues of embodiment at a different cultural moment and location in his chapter, "The Phenomenology of Authenticity Work: Merleau-Ponty and the 'Dissonant Sound' of The Clash." Revisiting an influential period in Western music history and the history of Western youth cultures—specifically, the emergence of 'punk' and the role that The Clash played in its formation—Klassen asks us to consider how we might see this moment differently if viewed through a phenomenological lens. He draws in particular on Merleau-Ponty's embodied phenomenology and the concept of 'authenticating work,' developed by R. A. Peterson, to explore the "way punk music both signifies *and* impresses itself upon the body, a process which in turn reconstitutes punk itself" (p. 236, this volume). Still attending to the political, cultural, and structural aspects of subcultures that were so thoroughly developed through the Birmingham school's approach to youth cultures, Klassen asks that we additionally consider the role of embodied experience, not only of the band but also of audience members and fans, who are part and parcel of the political, cultural, and social configuration of this thing we call 'punk.' One essential aspect of this experience is that of 'authenticity'—the claim to meaningfulness that punk performers and fans alike attribute to this particular cultural practice. Klassen suggests that 'authenticity' is itself a moving target, and the question is not whether or not punk performances and bands are *actually* authentic—a question that phenomenologists would refuse to answer—but whether the band and its fans successfully perform the 'authenticating work' necessary to ensure the band's association with this desirable trait.

In "Against All Odds: Making Underground Music in Iran," Daniel Ahadi also tackles a concept drawn from youth subcultural studies, in this case grounded in post-subcultural work that emerged after the Birmingham Centre for Contemporary Cultural Studies had substantially shaped the field. Looking to Will Straw's use of 'scene' to account for youth cultures that are perhaps not as coherent as the Birmingham tradition suggested, Ahadi approaches this concept phenomenologically in order to apply it to a context that has not been hitherto explored in great depth: that of the Iranian underground music scene. Literally located 'underground,' in the basements of those who dare to produce this banned form of culture in the Islamic Republic of Iran, the young people who make up the Iranian underground music scene must contend not only with the restrictions imposed by the regime, but also with the importation of Iranian diasporic music from Los Angeles. Characterized by the youth in Ahadi's study as "cheesy" music that offers little in terms of artistic merit to Iranian young people, the imported music from LA also marks the symbolic struggle being waged between Iranian youth culture producers and globalized cultural forms.

CONCLUSION

Globalization remains a central conceptual episteme of our time. Now thirty years since it came into popular use, the essays in this collection help us to understand how the inequities, speed and power of global forces are marking the social imaginaries of young lives. In taking up phenomenology as a uniquely helpful resource for understanding the shape and imprint of global conditions today, our collection also unwittingly draws attention to a new feature of globalization. Arjun Appadurai (2013, 3) has described this as the general "broadening of risk-taking and risk-bearing as properties of human life that link distant societies, cross national and market boundaries, and connect both the institutions of power and the agencies of ordinary human beings worldwide." To reference globalization in these terms is to acknowledge the influence that risk-based analyses have achieved over the past two decades (cf. Beck, 1992, 2000, 2009). It is also to draw attention to the way violence, uncertainty and, in some instances, possibility, have become markers of young lives, as the forces of markets, technological change, innovation and democratization have shaped our current situation. Risk and precarity have long been associated with what it means to be young. As the notion of youth culture emerged in the West in the early to mid-twentieth century, for instance, to be young seemed tied to experiences of transition and flux, which in turn gave shape to the identities, sexualities, bodies and dreams of youthful subjects. But when Appadurai speaks of the broadening of experiences of risk-taking and risk-bearing today, he points to a feature of the chapters included herein that was not our focus when the project began. As we have assembled the following stories and analyses of young people from across a range of geographies, classes, genders and histories, however, it has become evident that risk-based orientations have become a constant and persistent feature of youth experience. Such orientations mark the dangers and threats that haunt all our lives, revealing the intersubjective terms on which young people are charting their own uncertain futures. In the small stories, hopes and possibilities alluded to throughout the following chapters, however, there is also evidence of something more: the hint of a future horizon not yet fully visible or even conceivable, but one where we might yet foresee the possibilities for something other than the inequitable, asymmetrical world of globalization that is now before us. This is our hope at any rate, and one that we believe phenomenology helps us to anticipate.

NOTES

1. A note about author sequence: To reflect the collaborative nature of our process in developing this text, we have decided to list Poyntz as the first editor of the volume and Kennelly as first author of the Introduction. Both contributed equally, however, to the production of the text.
2. We are again indebted to Ricoeur for this turn of phrase, though inter-relationality has also been thoroughly investigated by Arendt, Schutz and Merleau-Ponty, amongst others.

REFERENCES

Ahmed, S. "Orientations: Toward a Queer Phenomenology." *GLQ: A Journal of Lesbian and Gay Studies* 12, no. 4, 2006. 543–574.

Appadurai, A. *Modernity at Large: Cultural Dimensions of Globalization*. Minneapolis: University of Minnesota Press, 1996.

———. *The Future as Cultural Fact: Essays on the Global Condition*. London: Verso, 2013.
Arendt, H. *The Human Condition*. 2nd ed. Chicago: University of Chicago Press, 1958.
Beck, U. *Risk Society: Towards a New Modernity*. London: Sage Publications, 1992.
———. *What Is Globalization?* London: Blackwell, 2000.
———. *World at Risk*. Translated by C. Cronin. Cambridge: Polity Press, 2009.
Beck. U., A. Giddens and S. Lash. *Reflexive Modernization: Politics, Tradition and Aesthetics in the Modern Social Order*. Stanford: Stanford University Press, 1994.
Bridge, G., and S. Watson. "Reflections on Publics and Cultures," in *The New Blackwell Companion to the City*. Edited by G. Bridge and S. Watson, 379–389. Malden: Wiley-Blackwell, 2011.
Butler, J. "Performative Acts and Gender Constitution: An Essay in Phenomenology and Feminist Theory," in *The Performance Studies Reader*. 2nd ed. Edited by H. Bial, 187–199. New York: Routledge, 2007.
Carel, H. "Phenomenology and Its Application in Medicine." *Theoretical Medicine and Bioethics* 32 no. 1, 2011. 33–46.
Carrington, V. *New Times: New Families*. Dordrecht: Springer, 2002.
———. " 'I Write, Therefore I Am': Texts in the City." *Journal of Visual Communication* 8, no. 4, 2009. 409–425.
Charlesworth, S.J. *A Phenomenology of Working Class Experience*. Cambridge: Cambridge University Press, 2000.
Crowley, V., and M.L. Rasmussen. "After Dark in the Antipodes: Pedagogy, Place, and Queer Phenomenology." *International Journal of Qualitative Studies in Education* 23, no. 1, 2010. 15–32.
Curtis, K. *Our Sense of the Real: Aesthetic Experience and Arendtian Politics*. Ithaca: Cornell University Press, 1999.
Daanen, P. "Conscious and Non-Conscious Representation in Social Representations Theory: Social Representations from the Phenomenological Point of View." *Culture & Psychology* 15, no. 3, 2009. 372–385.
de Beauvoir, S. *The Second Sex*. Translated and edited by H.M. Parshley. New York: Hammondsworth, (1949) 1972.
Dillabough, J., and J. Kennelly. *Lost Youth in the Global City: Class, Culture and the Urban Imaginary*. New York: Routledge, 2010.
Duarte, E.M. "Thinking Together as One: Friere's Rewriting of Husserl." *Philosophy of Education*, 2000. 180–188.
Durham, M.G. "Body Matters." *Feminist Media Studies* 11, no. 1, 2011. 53–60.
Fisher, L., and L. Embree (Eds.). *Feminist Phenomenology*. Dordrecht: Springer Publishing, 2000.
Gallagher, K. *The Theatre of the Urban: Youth and Schooling in Dangerous Times*. Toronto: University of Toronto Press, 2007.
Gallagher, K., and J. Neelands (Eds.). *Drama and Theatre in Urban Contexts*. London: Routledge, 2013.
Hall, S. "The Meaning of New Times," in *Stuart Hall: Critical Dialogues in Cultural Studies*. Edited by D. Morley and K. Chen, 223–237. New York: Routledge, 1996a.
———. "Signification, Representation, Ideology: Althusser and the Post-Structuralist Debates," in *Cultural Studies and Communications*. Edited by J. Curran, D. Morley and V. Walkerdine, 11–34. London: Arnold, 1996b.
———. "Who Needs Identity?" in *Questions of Cultural Identity*. Edited by S. Hall and P. de Gay, 1–17. Thousands Oaks: Sage Publishing, 1996c.
———. "The Hinterland of Science: Ideology and the 'Sociology of Knowledge,'" in *CCCS Selected Working Papers*. Edited by A. Gray and J. Campbell, 127–147. New York: Routledge, 2007.

Heidegger, M. *Being and Time*. Translated by J. Macquarrie and E. Robinson. New York: Harper, (1927) 1962.
Heinämaa, S. "Feminism," in *A Companion to Phenomenology and Existentialism*. Edited by H. Dreyfus and M. A. Wrathall, 502–515. Malden: Wiley-Blackwell, 2009.
Hoechsmann, M., and S.R. Poyntz. *Media Literacies: A Critical Introduction*. Malden: Wiley-Blackwell Publishing, 2012.
Johnson, A. "Understanding Children's Gender Beliefs," in *Feminist Phenomenology*. Edited by L. Fisher and L. Embree, 133–152. Dordrecht: Springer Publishing, 2000.
Kearney, R. *On Paul Ricoeur: The Owl of Minerva*. Aldershot: Ashgate Publishing, 2004.
Kennelly, J. *Citizen Youth: Culture, Activism, Agency in a Neoliberal Era*. New York: Palgrave Macmillan, 2011.
Langdridge, D. "Phenomenology and Critical Social Psychology: Directions and Debates in Theory and Research," *Social and Personality Psychology Compass* 2, no. 3, 2008. 1126–1142.
MacLeod, J. "Educating for 'World-Mindedness': Cosmopolitanism, Localism, and Schooling the Adolescent Citizen in Interwar Australia." *Journal of Educational Administration and History* 44, no. 4, 2012. 339–359.
———. " 'Touching Histories': Discipline, Gender and (Unwanted) Desire." *International Journal for the Historiography of Education* no. 1, 2013. 109–112.
Mendieta, E. *Global Fragments: Latinamericanisms, Globalizations, and Critical Theory*. Albany: State University of New York Press, 2007.
Merleau-Ponty, M. *Maurice Merleau-Ponty: Basic Writings*. Edited by T. Baldwin. New York: Routledge, 2004.
Poyntz, S.R. "Hannah Arendt: Pubic Action, Sociality, and Permanence in the World," in *Philosophical Profiles in the Theory of Communication*. Edited by J. Hannan, 9–33. New York: Peter Lang Publishers, 2012.
Ricoeur, P. *Interpretation Theory: Discourse and the Surplus of Meaning*. Fort Worth: Texas Christian University, 1976.
———. *Oneself as Another*. Translated by Kathleen Blamey. Chicago: University of Chicago Press, 1996.
Schutz, A. *The Phenomenology of the Social World*. Evanston: Northwestern University Press, (1932) 1967.
Silverstone, R. "Complicity and Collusion in the Mediation of Everyday Life." *New Literary History* 33, no. 4, 2002. 761–780.
———. *Media and Morality: On the Rise of the Mediapolis*. London: Polity Press, 2007.
Springgay, S. "An Intimate Distance: Youth Interrogations of Intercorporeal Cartography as Visual Narrative Text." *Visual Arts Research* 33, no. 2, 2007. 38–48.
———. *Body Knowledge and Curriculum: Pedagogies of Touch in Youth and Visual Culture*. New York: Peter Lang Publishing, 2008.
Taylor, B. "Phenomenology: One Way to Understand Nursing Practice." *International Journal of Nursing Studies* 30, no. 2, 1993. 171–179.
Throop, C.J., and K.M. Murphy. "Bourdieu and Phenomenology: A Critical Assessment." *Anthropological Theory* 2, no. 2, 2002. 185–207.
Williams, R. *Marxism and Literature*. Oxford: Oxford University Press, 1977.
Willis, P. *Learning to Labour: How Working Class Kids Get Working Class Jobs*. New York: Columbia University Press, 1977.

Section 1

Intersubjectivity

Oneself and Another

2 Translocality, Imagination and the Political

A Hermeneutic Exploration of Youth Media Initiatives from India and Palestine[1]

Sanjay Asthana

In recent years, a body of work grouped as nonrepresentational theories has emerged that takes into account the embodied nature of human experience while foregrounding the flow of practice in everyday life. Paulina Kirsi Kallio (2007), drawing upon the work of the feminist scholar Judith Butler, indicates that human agency is expressed not through language alone; rather, subjects make sense of their personal and social identities through specific "performances" via daily behaviors, habits and social norms. Kallio's line of inquiry has important implications for studying young people's understanding of politics, constitution of identity and experience. Contextualized in terms of embodiment and performativity, the subjective and sensory aspects of youth agency offer substantive analytic insights into the particular ways in which young people engage with, and produce, various media forms.[2] To understand children and young people's media engagements and their conception of the 'political,' it is important to examine the subjective and sensory aspects of their experiences through which they produce various media forms. To this end, I study two youth media initiatives from Palestine and India to understand how young people appropriate and reconfigure old and new media in the process of creating personal and social narratives.

The youth initiatives from Palestine and India bring to light difficult geopolitical challenges wrought by neoliberal globalization in New Delhi, and effects of the continuing Palestinian-Israeli conflict in Bethlehem.[3] While the Palestinian youth live in a constant 'state of emergency' in refugee camps surrounded by Israeli military barricades and borders, young people from poor neighborhoods of Delhi struggle against socio-economic and other forms of exploitation. In contrast to ICT and development policy frameworks that construct the poor as objects of their discourses, I consider poor youth as subjects engaging the world by appropriating ICTs and digital media forms. Indeed, the categories *poor* and *youth* are historical constructions grafted into public policies and social scientific research. I unpack the teleological assumptions about poor youth to examine how they create and develop a wide variety of media forms. Consequently, a primary task is to focus on youth identities and experiences that are multiple and variable across different geographical sites. However, their imagination is shaped not by despair, but to borrow Raymond Williams's (1989) felicitous phrase, by "resources of hope." In the face of looming violence and suffering, young people develop media forms and narratives that deal with their everyday life in the refugee camps, recuperation of individual and collective memories, identity and belonging. Although the youth-produced media forms take up the question of the political, two important elements are visible in the media narratives that this chapter will explore in specific detail: the role of affect and embodiment, and the issues of translocality that point toward potential 'spaces for dialogue.'

To grasp the full range and power dynamics of these performative acts that are not expressed in textual and linguistic registers, we need to draw upon concepts such as affect and embodied practices to analyze how human subjectivity is constituted. Without going into the extensive literature on affect, I will address the question of sensory experience by selectively drawing upon the writings of Paul Ricoeur that offer a substantive account into the embodied nature of human subjectivity while at the same time being alert to the quotidian aspects of everyday life. 'Affect' is understood in terms of a set of embodied practices and is largely defined as an unreflective and unstructured feeling and experience that cannot be realized in language. According to Jen Skattebol (2010, 78), "Affect theories dispute separations between mind and body; and between the individual, their communities and political contexts. Affect is a tangible, embodied force that operates between people and as such it adds complexity to the way we think about relationships in learning." Drawing upon phenomenological approaches and Ricoeur's hermeneutics, Vivian Sobchack (2004, 15) situates the notion of "embodiment" as a "radically material condition of human being that necessarily entails both the body and consciousness, objectivity and subjectivity, in an *irreducible ensemble*," where the meaning of experience is lived in context. To this end, I develop a theoretical framework to study the *ideological* and *affective* dimensions of youth media practices through the philosophical hermeneutics of Paul Ricoeur and feminist perspectives.

RICOEUR'S HERMENEUTIC APPROACH

Several interpretive frameworks consider youth as a relational category, but they do not account for the hermeneutic dimension of young people's experience. Ricoeur offers an understanding of the creative potential of agency and resistance that enables me to extend Cindy Katz's (2005) three overlapping categories of resilience, reworking and resistance, through which agency is exercised. Ricoeur's work, largely ignored in cultural and media studies, offers productive avenues for examining multiple temporalities in youth media practices in terms of the stories, the plots, and the intersubjective webs of relationships between and among the characters and their lifeworlds—visible in media produced by youth and in the lives of young people.[4] In recent years, however, few scholars have applied Ricoeur's hermeneutic framework to study children and young people. Sandy Farquhar (2010) studied early childhood education in New Zealand via Ricoeur's concept of narrative identity, and Jo-Anne Dillabough and Jacqueline Kennelly (2010) and Kennelly (2009) incorporated Ricoeur's phenomenological approach to examine marginalized urban youth in Canada. Arguing against the recent postmodern claims regarding the death of narrative due to the rise of the Internet and digital technologies, Caroline Bassett (2007) turned to Ricoeur's hermeneutic method to examine new media forms as complex narratives. Bassett's approach is refreshing, and provides a powerful counter to the various anti-narrative epistemologies. Mario Valdes (1991, 27), in his introductory overview, points out that Ricoeur's philosophical approach posits four dimensions—the formal, the historical, the phenomenological and the hermeneutic—forming a comprehensive framework for examining a variety of literary and cultural texts, including an "almost infinite variety of narrative expressions (oral, written, graphic, gestural) and the narrative classes (myths, folklores, legends, novels, epics, tragedies, drama, films, comic strips, etc.)."

Pursuing the key questions underlying his philosophical anthropology (What is the meaning of being human? And how does a 'subject' come to interpret itself?), Paul Ricoeur argues that the meaning of 'subject' is mediated through the process of interpretations—cultural, religious, political, historical and scientific. Paul Rabinow (1977) indicated that for Ricoeur, *hermeneutics,* in addition to concerning itself with the interpretation of literary works and cultural artifacts, *is about human action itself;* therefore, the task of hermeneutics becomes "the comprehension of the self by the detour of the comprehension of the other" (Rabinow, 1977, 5). More importantly, it presents an understanding of the human subject in terms of an embodied subjectivity that takes us beyond singular conceptions of identity, whether in terms of the abstract Cartesian subject or various other discourse-centered theorizations of subject. Indeed, Rabinow (1977, 5–6), who extended Ricoeur's hermeneutic method in his anthropological study in Morocco, noted that Ricoeur's notion of the self is not the Cartesian or psychoanalytic self, but a public self that is culturally mediated and historically situated in a continuously changing world. In an important way, Ricoeur's perspective has evolved into what has been characterized as 'poststructuralist' hermeneutics.[5]

Ricoeur (1996, 101) has argued that a person's narrative identity can be approached via two interconnected and overlapping notions of identity: *idem* (sameness) and *ipse* (selfhood). Whereas *idem*-identity refers to "sameness of body and character, our stability illustrated by genetic code," *ipse*-identity pertains to our "selfhood, the adjustable part of our identity," and furthermore, the two kinds of identities—of sameness and difference—offer coherence to the self and the possibility for change and reflexivity.

Indeed, the notion of ipse-identity emerges in narrative. Ricoeur's formulation of narrative might seem to suggest an ontological basis, but it does not impute a fixed self but rather a social self embedded in the everyday world.[6] According to Ricoeur (1996, 140, emphasis added), "Hermeneutic philosophy has attempted to demonstrate the existence of an opaque subjectivity which expresses itself through the detour of countless mediations—signs, symbols, texts and human *praxis* itself. The hermeneutic idea of subjectivity as a dialectic between the self and mediated social meanings has deep moral and political implications."

Feminist scholars have noted that in contrast to the various theories of identity and subjectivity, Ricoeur's work presents a persuasive account of the relational nature of identity through which one can grasp both the structural-ideological as well as the embodied and affective dimensions of selfhood. Indeed, as Lois McNay (1999, 316–317) noted, Ricoeur's temporalized notion of narrative identity as dialectic between idem–ipse (constancy and change) points to a dynamic unity of self, unlike various poststructuralist accounts of identity, where the self is fragmented and dispersed, which range from

> Baudrillard's celebration of the schizoid as the paradigm of subjectivity, through Lacan's stress on the lack that perpetually disrupts the illusion of symbolic unity, to Foucault's idea that identity is a socially specific phenomenon constructed through the interplay of technologies of domination and practices of the self.

Whereas Ricoeur's narrative model of identity opens up a more creative appropriation of agency, the poststructuralist model of identity deprives emancipatory theory of any concept of subjectivity through which the experiences of marginalized groups can be recovered and politicized.[7] The active dimensions of agency visible in the narrative construction of identity—as idem and ipse—acknowledge the inherent creativity in social action.[8] Although a subject or a self mediates his/her world within the constraints imposed by the social order, he/she is also able to produce forms of practices that question and resist domination and power. For Ricoeur, social action is to be understood as a dialectic of sedimentation and innovation; that is, action is neither purely creative nor authentic but constituted by a subject's ability to interpret and 'work through' a range of pre-reflexive behaviors and norms. Whereas Ricoeur emphasizes the centrality of language, action involves both the linguistic and nonlinguistic realms, because the subject is a corporeal and embodied self with desires and emotions. The notion of narrative identity as dialectic between idem–ipse and the idea of embodied subjectivity developed by Ricoeur offer analytic insights in the study of youth media practices, particularly because young people are involved in constructing personal and social narratives through creative and critical imaginaries. The ipse-identity of marginalized working-class and lower middle-class youth, among other things, is configured around questions of socio-economic inequities and the clash of religious and secular ontologies. Young people's narrative identity unfolds along multiple trajectories, simultaneous and nonsynchronous. Ricoeur's work, therefore, accords a more substantive understanding of youth subjectivity, one that offers productive avenues for examining youth media practices in terms of the stories, plots and intersubjective webs of relationships between and among young people and their lifeworlds. To this end, I propose that young people produce meanings through a phenomenological appropriation of the media forms: that is, the youth, drawing upon their subjective and quotidian experience, develop narratives as material artifacts where language and writing are woven into the auditory, sensory and visual.

OVERVIEW OF YOUTH MEDIA PROJECTS

The two youth media projects from Palestine and India considered as case studies span various media—print-based, radio, photography, video, television and the new media, particularly the multiple uses of the Internet. Young people gain access to tools of media production in a variety of ways: from training and imparting basic to advanced technical skills, using production facilities and equipment, and learning about script writing, storyboarding, lighting, set design, page design, layout, digital graphics and computers. In engaging with the media, youth explore and learn about themselves and the world around them. The criteria and rationale for selecting the case studies are based on several factors: the translocal nature of media production, engagement with a variety of media forms, collaboration with a range of institutions and dialogues between youth and their peers/mentors, and more importantly, the creative and critical ways through which young people relate to the dominant notions of participation, citizenship and politics through their media narratives (Soep and Chavez, 2010).

The Lajee Center (henceforth Lajee; in Arabic, *Lajee* means 'refugee'), located near the Aida camp in Bethlehem, was established in 2000.[9] The Palestinian youth initiative Lajee accords a central role to media that ranges from disseminating information about their activities to training young participants as future journalists. In fact, a significant amount of media work relates to developing creative and critical media narratives in printed, audio, video and digital formats. The young participants learn media-making and production activities from local and international volunteers and mentors. Youth members of Lajee have been involved in producing a magazine, radio broadcasts and a series of children's storybooks and photographic projects with mentoring and the help of the British creative artist and photographer Rich Wiles. The photographic narratives offer powerful accounts of daily life in refugee camps, the aspirations and hopes of children and young people for a better life, and observations of nature and landscape in and around their camps and villages. The photo exhibits and storybooks, *The Boy and the Wall, Dreams of Home, Our Eyes* and *Flying Home* were on display in several locations around the world. The highly acclaimed children's storybook *The Boy and the Wall* won several international awards. In addition, the film workshop "Dreaming in Palestine" resulted in several short films produced and directed by young participants at Lajee.

Cybermohalla (in Hindi-Urdu, 'cyber neighborhood') is an experimental project to enable democratic access to information and communication technologies among poor young women and men in Delhi, India. The initiative began in 2001 through an experimental collaborative project between the Sarai project of the Centre for the Study of Developing Societies (CSDS) and Ankur, a nongovernmental organization involving young people living in slum settlements and working-class neighborhoods in Delhi. The main aim is to provide a forum where young people not only explore their creativity but also comment on the social and moral topics that impact their lives. The three media labs of Cybermohalla are located in different parts of Delhi—four informal working-class settlements, LNJP, Dakshinpuri, Nangla Maanchi and Ghevra—and provide opportunities to young people to work individually and collectively. The idea of a *mohalla* as a locality and neighborhood exceeds the semantic connotations implied by the English term. As a social space, *mohalla,* with its sense of alleys and corners, can be conceived as 'dense nodes' where marginalized young people carry out their everyday activities. Formal schooling is out of reach or unaffordable for the youth. They visit the lab out of curiosity but soon get absorbed in the creative possibilities offered by computers and other media. These young participants, mostly school dropouts aged fifteen to twenty, visit the *compughar* (in Hindi, an abode of computers), a media lab with several low-cost desktop computers and free software, dictaphones (portable audio recorders), and digital and bromide print cameras, to freely express their ideas and imaginations from the mundane to the serious. Working at the media lab, participants write, draw and sketch a range of interesting verbal and visual narratives and texts published as books, diaries, magazines and wallpaper that become available in print as well as digitized formats.

LAJEE

Over the years, numerous photo workshops have been conducted by the British photographer and volunteer Rich Wiles, who is also actively involved as an editorial member of Lajee's magazine. Several of the photo-essays have been published and also are available on Lajee's website. The photo-essays are evocative accounts of young people's daily lives, reflections on their dreams, hopes, and nightmares, and conversations with grandparents about their ancestral villages. Young people also produce short digital stories that are composed of series of still images with audio—either commentary or music, or sometimes both. More recently, Lajee initiated the radio podcast projects set up by an Australian volunteer, Daz Chandler. Young people use inexpensive software and low-end ICTs to produce a weekly podcast that can be accessed on the Lajee website. The eight-week radio podcast workshops have generated great enthusiasm among the youth from Aida camp. Apart from the ability to operate and use low-end ICTs and digital media, youth gain exposure and learn about the arts and skills and journalistic practices that underpin media-making processes. Young people receive extended education and training in a wide variety of subjects and are involved in producing Lajee's quarterly magazine, *Our Voice*. Every year, sixty youth participants, male and female, selected from Aida and other refugee camps in Bethlehem, participate in lectures/workshops over several months. The youth participants follow a structured syllabus based on the following subjects: children's rights, human rights, democracy and peace-building strategies for conflict resolution, gender equality, journalism and photography. The lectures and workshops are led by academics and media professionals from Al Quds University and Birzeit University in Palestine and by other volunteers from outside Palestine. Some of the former youth members of Lajee lead the discussions on several topics. At the end of each session, the participants divide themselves into groups and begin developing ideas for features and stories for the magazine, collaborating on layout, graphics, photography, etc.

The photographic projects and digital stories incorporate hundreds of still images either taken by the young people themselves or assembled from newspapers. The photo-narratives provide evocative glimpses into the disruptions in the everyday lives of young people, their families and community. Yet, the young people do not seek the viewer's sympathy; rather, they demonstrate steadfastness *(sumud)* and resilience in the face of atrocities.

Children and youth participants at Lajee pursued a series of media and photographic workshops over an extended period of time. After receiving training and mentoring from Rich Wiles, the young people undertook several photographic projects to document life in the refugee camps where they lived; interviewed their own grandparents about the villages they were forced to flee during the *Al-Nakba* in 1948; later traveled to these depopulated villages to take pictures of the empty places, rocks, streams, cacti and olive trees, and the landscape; and talked about their dreams and nightmares. With this method, Wiles pointed out, it is not just the act of photography but also the entire process of collaborative thinking and creating media together that constituted learning and education. Children began to write and sketch out their deep-seated feelings, hopes and anxieties and gradually began talking to other participants and peers about their feelings and emotions. According to Wiles (2006, 1), initial workshops discussed the ideas of the project and what it was that participants wanted to say with their work. Basic notions of composition and light were discussed along with creative ideas about visual storytelling and photographic documentary work. Participants then worked daily, shooting images around Aida refugee camp and also the neighboring Al Azzeh camp.

The photography project created by young people at Lajee, *A Window to Our World*, a series of still images with short captions, was exhibited at several centers around the world. The photographic exhibits were also used in British schools to familiarize school children about the lives of Palestinian children. Developed and published in a photo-essay format, the images depict life inside a Palestinian refugee camp, showing cramped lanes and cluttered houses with adults and children working and playing. For instance, Nimer Al Azzeh's photo of a girl standing in front of her home and Miras Al Azza's photo of two girls playing in a narrow street of Aida camp were placed next to each other with commentary in English and Arabic.

In English it reads: "I want to take photographs again. I want to take pictures of a park with people playing in it. I would also like to photograph a beautiful city with wide streets that isn't crowded with narrow streets like the camp." Although the images render the palpable misery and suffering of people, the gestures, sighs and bodily dispositions of people in those images evoke steadfastness and fortitude that resemble what many have characterized as *sumud*, a Palestinian approach to life. The photo project, *A Child's Rights in Palestine*, explored the idea of human rights among the Lajee participants. The children, eight boys and twelve girls, all students from the United Nations Refugee Welfare Association schools, participated in several sessions on children's rights. Later, the young participants took pictures that

Figure 2.1 Girls playing in a narrow alley, Aida refugee camp. Lajee/Rich Wiles.

Figure 2.2 Girl in front of a refugee home. Lajee/Rich Wiles.

portrayed different aspects of children's rights. Describing the irony of the situation and the accompanying pain and anguish, Wiles (2006, 50) stated, "A couple of hours after the exhibition had opened in Aida Camp a 13-year-old child was shot in the head with a rubber coated steel bullet by the Israeli army less than 100 meters from the gallery in which children had proudly showed their work discussing human rights protection for children, a child's rights in Palestine."

Another project, *Dreams of Home,* is based on children's interviews with their grandparents who lived through the *Al-Nakba* events of 1948.[10] Following the interviews, the children visited the eight villages around Jerusalem, Bethlehem and Hebron to take pictures of the now depopulated villages. Thus, each child explored his/her grandparents' village and compared its present state with the grandparents' recollections. The project was published in the form of a photo-book. Ahmad Ibrahim Al-Aaraj, a fifteen-year-old visiting his ancestral village Al Walaja, in North Jerusalem, writes:

> The visit revived my tired feelings, and empowered my hope and belief that we will return. I drank from Ein Al Hanieh, one day my grandparents drank from this spring. I ate from the big fig tree that was planted by my great grandfathers. I will never forget this. I filled a bottle of water and gave it to my grandfather, Abu Fahmi, he was very excited. I felt proud and said to myself: how could he bear all this pain being a refugee in a camp that is located only 5 kilometers from Al Walaja.[11]

The grandparents' vignettes as bits of memories and experiences in the villages, and the children's images along with their brief comments, provide a powerful commentary on the hermeneutics of everyday life then and now. The social imaginaries of the first-generation *Al-Nakba* survivors and the acute awareness of the young fourth generation portrayed in the photobook, through the written and visual modalities, convey Thrift's (2007, 187) notion that the "space of embodiment [is] expanded by a fleeting but crucial moment set up by body practices which have complex and explicitly political genealogies." In Ricoeur's (1996) formulation of narrative identity as embodied subjectivity, the photographic projects of Lajee participants can be understood as a narrative modality of dialogue that does not seek consensus or impasse, but the act of distancing and appropriation of texts brings diverse perspectives in a state of tension—or as Ricoeur (1984) would indicate, a "concordant discordance."

The popular performance of *dabke* is an exemplification of what Thrift had indicated as "the flow of practice"—the spaces of affect and embodiment—through which children's aspirations and desires are expressed. Combining Palestinian *dabke* and the dance performances by young people from the refugee camp, along with interviews of the children about their daily life in the camps, the documentary mixes a variety of symbolic, musical and literary styles. Within the spaces of affect and embodiment, children's and women's bodies become a focus of meaning-making, and as the feminist scholars Saba Mahmood (2001, 210) and Paulina Kallio (2007, 132) point out, the body can articulate specific forms of agency and resistance to dominant discourses. Furthermore, Mahmood argues that agency should be considered "more in terms of capacities and skills required to undertake particular kinds of acts," and Kallio notes that "agencies and actions appear as statures, sighs, gazes, and movements" that transcend language, hence the recourse to nonrepresentational theories. I provide one last example of how the digital stories offer creative possibilities for the articulation of youth identity and political agency that is attentive to collective memory and dialogue with the other.

Examining Lajee's digital stories via affect and embodied subjectivity offers crucial insights into youth identity, agency and hermeneutic experience. The four digital stories by Abeer Malash, Miras Al-Azzah, Saddam Sadouk and Kholoud Ajarma, and the slideshow of still photographs with background voice-over narration, retrospectively deal with specific vital conjunctures in young people's lives (e.g., injuries caused by Israeli bullets fired on their homes, difficulties in moving within and beyond the city due to checkpoints). By narrating those events as they unfolded, young people offer powerful glimpses into the somatic and visceral experience of violence and unending conflict. The still photographs render palpable and actualize a repertoire of feelings—anguish, pain, suffering and sadness—not as emotions but as feelings that are grounded in the precognitive and nonlinguistic, per nonrepresentational theories. Such affective feelings are produced at the intra- and intersubjective levels, organizing young people's personal and social biographies. For instance, in "A Day Like Any Other Day," Abeer Malash, a fifteen-year-old, reflects on what it was like growing up as a refugee kid in the Aida camp. As he begins speaking in Arabic, several still photos of the refugee camp, his home, family, school and the pastoral land set up the visual context for the viewer. He says that he learned from his father that he and his family were refugees from the Ras Abu Amar village, not far from the Aida camp, and that Israelis have occupied their land.

Miras Al-Azzah in "The Day of Injury" and Saddam Sadouk in "Ruining Our Play" talk about their love of soccer and their inability to play the game with friends in their neighborhoods due to the restrictions imposed by Israeli military. Miras and Saddam also recount events from their childhood when they were injured by Israeli bullets. Both their digital stories open with their voice-over narration in Arabic along with several still photographs showing them with their friends playing at home, with their parents and depicting their injuries. Although the digital stories are about suffering and pain, they do not invoke pity in the viewer; instead, they open up a space for political engagement. Below are brief excerpts from the digital stories that map the contours of affect and embodiment:

Miras: One sunny Friday, my cousins and I were playing games on our balcony. We heard the sound of shooting—they were shooting at the balcony we were playing on. We got inside the room and we saw bullets flying through the window into the room. We rushed to the first floor and my sister started yelling, "Miras, you have a lot of blood all over." I put my hand on my stomach where the blood was. After that I knew I was injured.

Saddam: We used to play soccer in the Church field next to the camp. But the Israelis prevented us from playing there. The Israeli army confiscated that land to build the Wall. They destroyed the soccer field where we spent our time. My friends and I built a soccer field under the trees and began playing there. An army patrol came by and started shooting at us. As we ran away, my friend and I got shot. The guys carried me to Bet Jala hospital. I had a three-hour operation. When I woke up, my parents told me that my friend had died.

Abeer: One day in school. During second period, we heard shooting in all directions. I heard screams of fear. I was in 5th grade and was terrified. For the first time, I felt in danger and close to death. The principal and teachers directed us to hide in the lab. 400 of us gathered in this small room. Some girls held each other close. We were stuck there for an hour. Then, UN officials came and evacuated the school. On my way home I saw the soldiers for real and not just on TV. I

> was too afraid to go back to school, even though it was so close to home. Now that I am 16, I am embarrassed to say I was scared that day. I love to laugh and have fun. Sometimes when I see soldiers or shooting on TV, I get scared again. What I love most is being with my friends at Lajee Centre in the camp, sharing stories and laughing together. I want to eliminate fear of my childhood so that as I grow up, hope will grow in me.

For Miras and Saddam, the experiences recounted above signify the tragic moments of injury and death of a friend. Whereas the English translations on these pages offer partial access to affective dimensions of their identities, the series of photographs in their digital stories reveal a deeper understanding of how affect and embodiment frame their narratives. For instance, their accounts in Arabic of the specific events from childhood, particularly the moments of injury, uncertainty and fear, exceed the linguistic register, producing "felt thinking," where speech, voice and the series of still photographs that depict the moments shape their embodied subjectivities.[12] Consequently, their identity is revealed as ipseity, as dialectic between self and the other, creating new possibilities for both speaking and listening (Couldry, 2010). What is interesting in such digital stories is that as a youth cultural practice they offer a space for the exploration of the personal and quotidian elements of life, mixing the autobiographical with the historical. It is within the domain of the quotidian and the everyday that young people articulate the political. For Miras, Saddam and Abeer, the political structures their subjective experience of life in the refugee camps and the constant threat of Israeli violence.

In Palestine, the refugee camps as enclosed geographic areas operate as ghettos of another kind, where their lives are enclosed within the security wall, under constant surveillance by the Israeli security apparatus. Despite the politics of enclosure and isolation, Palestinians have developed extraordinary means of coping with the injustices. Even without the status of citizenship and as stateless persons, young Palestinians have been able to develop 'acts of citizenship' through which they construct the political. In her perceptive study of ordinary life in two Palestinian refugee camps in Jerusalem, Bulle (2009, 28) notes:

> The enclosed "citizen" who is in fact without citizenship uses her or his capacities to distinguish his or her intimate, individual and private world from "hostile" or "external" domination. Using the term "enclosed citizens" assumes, not only the trapped fatalism of the "ghetto" situation, but even more, the implementation of ordinary or everyday practices and policies of life that take advantage of the hope of resistance or patriotism and open new perspectives on individual liberalism and the theory of justice.

The digital stories are powerful examples of how young people produce narratives of hope and justice despite their precarious living conditions and demonstrate the importance of affect, embodiment and narrative identity. The digital stories by Abeer, Miras, Saddam and Kholoud are not about anger, revenge or resentment; rather, they seek to construct a two-pronged 'otherness' through which suffering, forgiveness and solicitude are recognized as part of what it means to be human. Ricoeur (1996, 191) offers a particularly poignant account of the relations between self and other that is instructive:

> In true sympathy the self, whose power of acting is at the start greater than that of the other, finds itself affected by all that the suffering other offers to it in return. For from the suffering comes a giving that is no longer drawn from the power of acting and existing but precisely from weakness itself. This is perhaps the supreme test of solicitude, where unequal power finds compensation in an authentic reciprocity in exchange, which in the hour of agony, finds refuge in the shared whisper of voices or the feeble embrace of clasped hands.

Although Lajee's youth media projects challenge the dominant narratives of Palestinians and Arabs, what is significant is the ability to produce narratives of memory, belonging and collective identity that present new resources of hope for mutual recognition of suffering, conviviality and dialogue with the other (Bjawi-Levine, 2009). Janette Habashi's (2008) research posits that Palestinian children in the refugee camps in Gaza and the West Bank express multiple dimensions of national identity configured around ideas of self and the other, opening up possibilities of dialogue and reconciliation.[13] Furthermore, the political is realized not in terms of the pedagogic model but in terms of a performative one that is grounded in the subjective and mobilized through somatic and sensual experience.

TRANSLOCAL ENGAGEMENTS

The various media projects—magazine, photography, digital stories and radio podcasts—helped create a space for dialogue and engagement for the youth to interact and collaborate with each other and their adult mentors. An important aspect of the youth media practices are the avenues opened up in engaging with the community within and beyond Palestine. The youth media projects have forged links and connections with other groups locally and globally, in small towns in Australia, the UK, Belgium and the United States, and in larger international venues. Lajee's popular dance documentary featured an interesting mix of Palestinian folk genres such as *dabke* to express the plight and struggles of Palestinian people in refugee camps. Through an innovative use of computer labs across various refugee camps in the Middle East—Palestine, Syria, Jordan, Lebanon—young people at Lajee connected thousands of Palestinian refugees to each other and to their homeland. Lajee's youth media projects exhibit some interesting aspects of translocality, as Palestinians in the refugee camps inside Palestine and in various Middle East countries shared their sense of geography, place, neighborhoods and villages. In doing so, Palestinians brought together individual and collective memories of dispossession and dwelling through their stories and narratives. There have also been several instances of 'virtual' translocality, where young people from Lajee connected with their age cohorts from European towns and cities via videoconference, generating interesting cross-cultural conversations. The high school students from Palestine shared a range of media narratives using email, electronic slide presentations and web videos to continue their conversations and build long-term relationships.

Lajee, sponsored and supported by a wide range of local, regional and international institutions and agencies, constitutes dense nodes of relations between place and spaces, whether they be villages and neighborhoods or virtual environments through which young people engage in media-making. Thus, Lajee can be considered an example of what Appadurai (1996) has characterized as the "translocal," to examine the dialectic mediations between the local and the global. Whereas the idea of locality is useful in describing the way in which young Palestinians deploy media forms to connect and relate with other youth from various other locales around the world, it also complicates their sense of home and dwelling, because they inhabit the spaces in refugee camps. Precisely for this reason, Appadurai (2000, 7) remarked, "We need to avoid assuming that sites are the same as communities or that localities are simply geographical locations. Especially for prisoners, refugees, asylum-seekers, and other highly vulnerable groups, both sites and journeys remain real and difficult." However, processes of globalization have also altered the relations between identity, subjectivity and social imagination and have enabled the rise of translocality among various social actors and groups. And, as Appadurai indicated, processes of globalization, marked by an increasing presence of technological developments, have altered how we 'think' the relations between identity, subjectivity and social imagination.

Lajee's radio podcasts, scripted and produced by children and young people, deal with a wide variety of personal, local and global topics. Although the radio broadcasts are available on the Internet as podcasts, they utilize several low-tech applications through which children and young people produce radio narratives. On most occasions, Lajee's young members bring creative ideas regarding their view of the world that are then united with their right to expression. Interestingly, the young broadcasters do not think of their listeners as passive receivers; rather, in an uncanny way, they seem to dissolve the perceived separation between speaker and listener—a separation that Walter Benjamin (1999) termed the major flaw in the makings of the institution of radio. This offers us an interesting perspective, which on the one hand critiques the institutional epistemology of radio, and on the other hand offers a potential for creating dialogue via the Internet to produce forms of empowering and enabling communication. The motivation to become a radio broadcaster demonstrates that children seek to go beyond merely using media to voice their opinions. Rather, the abiding interest in radio has led numerous children to express their desires to pursue professional careers as civic broadcast journalists. Whereas we may perceive this as an instance of what Appadurai characterized in terms of technologies altering relationships between identity, subjectivity and social imagination, a notable feature of Lajee radio is the production of specific aspects of Palestinian soundscape that become available to other Palestinians living as exiles in the Middle East and other parts of the world. These radio stories via the Internet lead to the possibility of forging a network of translocal relations where place, identity and subjectivity all tie into multiple registers: memories of their homeland, and a longing for return that Edward Said (2004, 133) characterized as having far-reaching pedagogic implications. Similarly, other media projects of Lajee are involved in forging translocal networks of relations. Through such connections and networks, young Palestinians are involved in crafting new forms of political spaces while at the same time archiving their memories of displacement and dispossession. The political spaces—indeed, the very ideas of the 'political'—are grounded in a range of performative acts that become visible in terms of embodied practices.

Ricoeur's hermeneutic approach provides a way forward in exploring identity and selfhood in terms of embodied subjectivities. For instance, the notion of identity and self in the Palestinian context is frequently expressed as *hawiyya*—the identity cards issued by Israel to Palestinians living in the Occupied Territories. The long history of the Israeli occupation of Palestinians' land, the dispossession of their homes, the refugee camps in which they live, the presence of checkpoints around their villages and towns, all are connected with *hawiyya*. Similarly, the notion of self is expressed as *dhat* in Arabic (*dhatiya* for selfhood). Both *hawiyya* and *dhat* defy a linguistic translation; instead, both notions are grounded in symbolic registers and can be better understood as embodied practices. Ricoeur's formulation of identity in terms of ipse- and idem- opens up the possibility of examining identity and selfhood in terms of embodied practices.

CYBERMOHALLA

The Cybermohalla project might be conceived as a group of interlinked and overlapping media practices that combine, appropriate and rework diverse online and offline environments. These environments as networked spaces constitute oppositional media forms enabling the formation of several local and translocal practices. The local–local links within the neighborhoods have sustained and endured over longer durations, particularly through practices under the rubric of 'public dialogues' with members from the localities. Several collaborations between Cybermohalla and other youth-based initiatives from around the world have also opened up avenues for exchange of knowledge and experiences. One such example is its partnership with Bootle Lab from Liverpool, UK. Historically, the Bootle neighborhood in Liverpool has witnessed several centuries of commerce and global trade, yet the inhabitants of Bootle, most of whom are dockyard workers, have remained poor and marginalized. Bootle Lab, set up by a nonprofit organization, caters to the needs of young women and single mothers. Cybermohalla and Bootle Lab began an online exchange of stories and experiences through blogging, which led to exchange of youth media stories as well. The online encounters and conversations between Bootle's and Delhi's youth led to translocal sharing of knowledge and personal narratives of growing up in two distinct, yet interlinked, geographic areas of the world. The bilingual blogs in English and Hindi were printed, localized and circulated in the localities. Another instance of translocality that involved both online and offline contexts was achieved through temporary media labs. The idea of temporary media labs is central to how tactical media operate. A series of performance-based temporary media activities by Cybermohalla involve participants from the Netherlands, Germany and other places. Several Cybermohalla participants were invited by cultural organizations in Germany to the international theater festival Play Mas. Cybermohalla participants converted their youth media stories into short plays that were performed in German cities as well as in Delhi through the temporary media lab. These labs used low-end ICTs and digital tools to create, co-produce and share their stories. Indeed, as one participant put it, the idea behind the temporary media labs is to rework the media production process, where users become producers, and browsers become editors.

Whereas the Cybermohalla project has also been characterized as an alternate educational initiative, it represents a radical pedagogic experiment in terms of how young people refashion diverse media forms to create multiple narratives about personal and social identities. Writing (mainly in Hindi and English) is a critical component of the narrative process, though the audio-visual communicative modalities are equally important. The young people seem to appropriate ICTs as, on the one hand, 'dêtournement'—that is, mixing and using dominant media forms toward revolutionary ends—and on the other hand, as producers and storytellers (à la Walter Benjamin) of a diverse range of narratives from the banal to the serious. Thus, in creating the diverse media artifacts and objects by reusing and incorporating bits and pieces of pre-existing materials through borrowing, hybridity, co-optation, reinvention (bricolage), and mixing old and new media forms and genres (remediation), Cybermohalla practitioners produce new constellations of meanings out of existing and fixed media forms. In many respects the Cybermohalla media narratives represent what Markus Miessen (2007) has characterized as "conflictual" participation, a form of critical engagement that forces itself into existing power relations, enabling participants to become active agents. Such a conflictual participation is visible as pedagogies of estrangement, allowing youth to construct media narratives that are not intended to produce consensus but dissensus.

Ricoeur's hermeneutic approach opens up a range of analytic possibilities that can be used to examine the multilayered narratives and texts of Cybermohalla practitioners. According to Sandy Farquhar (2010, 8), in Ricoeur's hermeneutic philosophy,

> an essential feature of dialogue (and necessary precondition of interpretation) is its ability to distance the subject from the production of the text so that it can be viewed anew from different perspectives. It is the moment the text becomes distant, that its dialectical counterpart of appropriation comes into play. It is in the act of appropriation (keeping the text close) that we respond.

In the hermeneutics of Ricoeur, a narrative modality of dialogue does not seek consensus or impasse, but the act of distancing and appropriation of texts brings diverse perspectives in a state of tension—or as Ricoeur would indicate, a "concordant discordance." The Cybermohalla practitioners complicate Ricoeur's notion of narrative modality by combining various digitextual media forms to produce multilayered texts that are reconfigured in the process of distancing and appropriation. More specifically, the narratives of Cybermohalla practitioners point to a form of 'critical' participation that cannot be interpreted through either a neoliberal framework or Habermasian communication ethics. Through the twin processes of distancing and appropriation of the narratives, the Cybermohalla practitioners infuse newer meanings to the notions of participation and collaboration. An important characteristic feature of this is that these meanings are produced in praxis, not theoretical abstraction. Participation here can be construed as what Markus Miessen has termed "conflictual" as it reaches a political dimension. Rather than seek a consensus through diffusing the tension, what is needed is to provide grounding and recognition of the legitimacy for different perspectives.

Talking about their initial experience at the locality labs, two young Cybermohalla practitioners, Neelofer and Babli Rai, point out how their writing has evolved through a deepening of conversations and relationships with fellow practitioners and peers at the labs, and also reflect on how the process of writing has led them to a greater sense of participation and involvement with their community and neighborhoods. This is indicative of what Bolter argues is the inseparability of formal aspects of media-making and the cultural contexts of its production. Neelofer's (2004) reflections reveal how her embodied subjectivity, particularly the ipse part of her identity, developed through her conversations and relationships. The collective experiences of herself and her fellow participants and members of her community are rendered through diverse media forms:

> The Compughar (Locality Lab) is our own space. We write and share our texts with one another. Conversations, through which we share our ways of thinking and experiences, help expand and deepen our thoughts. Apart from writing, we also do sound recording, digital and analogue photography, and make animations as well on Free Software Image Manipulation Tool, GIMP. We've also learnt a lot about how computers work. We've been working on creating forms that will help deepen the relationship of the lab with the locality, e.g. wall magazines, and now the locality public events. Our locality, i.e. the neighbourhood, is the link between the deepening and strengthening of the lab, and its extension and spread.

Similarly, Babli Rai (2002) explains how creative uses of media forms have enabled a deepening of relationship with her own self, with fellow practitioners and others in the community:

> We have many relationships outside our family—relationship with our selves, with our environment, objects around us. Through writing, we allowed for these relationships to emerge, and to relate with them. Earlier, I used to see the walls of my house, the clock, the fan, the iron, the road. But when I started thinking about them, and writing, only then did I realise the intensity of my relationship with them. When we translate our texts into images, making palimpsests through animations, we feel our texts have also been given a new life. Through combinations of sound and text, text and image, image and sound, we give seriousness to our skills in each—just like an artisan gives form to his skills, an identity to the form, and a name to the identity.

The writings, a mixture of reportage, personal reflections and fragmentary prose, borrow a repertoire of idioms, metaphors and symbols from the colloquial and vernacular contexts. In describing and interpreting their lifeworlds and the neighborhoods, the young people frequently raise questions of social justice and the failure of state and local institutions to provide adequate shelter, health facilities and educational opportunities. A closer look at the narratives indicates that their creative and critical expressions are neither contrived nor forced. Several young practitioners, mostly women, begin to express themselves via the computer screens. A bimonthly magazine, *Ibarat* (Inscription), explored various meanings of work in women's lives.[14] The magazine, published in Hindi and English, is available in digital and printed forms. A series of creative writings in the form of diaries have been published in a book, *Galiyon Se (By-Lanes)*. These are reflections and thoughts on the everyday life in the city. Here is one such reflection on streets and by-lanes:

Figure 2.3 Cybermohalla poster depicting the multiple nodes and networks of new media. Courtesy of Sarai.

> For the last one year now, I have been in regular conversation with the group of young people in Compughar. Amongst other things streets and lanes were discussed many times. Streets make for great conversations. Streets would lead us to think about the harsh and aggressive behaviour of men towards each other and towards women in particular, the total lack of pedestrian pathways or respect towards them, the absence of street lighting, noisy traffic and its uncaring behaviour, or the near-total inaccessibility for disabled people or elder people. Also being amidst strangers, in crowds and moving with crowds.[15]

This young woman's narrative account of the streets of Delhi offers some concrete insights into what has become of public places and spaces. Although this reads as a political critique, there are many more writings that offer some interesting solutions to civic life and public infrastructure in the city of Delhi. Some participants write about daily life around streets, some draw and sketch using graphics software, presenting multiple perspectives on the topic. The digitextual materials produced become available to all participants and are distributed in the neighbourhoods for further commentary and reflections. What emerges here goes beyond content creation to more complex and relevant forms of creative engagement with particular issues and topics that touch the lives of young people. As such, they can be considered important interventions that seek to broaden the terms of political and cultural discourses in some surprisingly innovative ways. For example, the questions of gender insensitivity and discrimination are taken up by various youth members of Cybermohalla in a variety of media forms—texts, collages, graphics, sound recordings, photographs and video. A conversation between two young women practitioners, Azra Tabassum and Mehrunissa, recorded in the form of a Socratic dialogue called "The Zoo," is a searing critique on teasing in Delhi's public places. Shveta Sarda, coordinator at the Cybermohalla, suggests that linking the broader environments of our digital worlds with the conversational worlds of our communities is central to understanding 'publicness':

> The world of the digital surrounds us. In our lanes and by-lanes we live through a dense palimpsest of images, texts and sounds, increasingly accessed and accelerated through the digital—VCDs, CDs, Cable, PCOs, DTP operations (pamphlets, stickers, sign boards), etc. Through our own practice, we are trying to work out an interface between this density and our concerns. We use the digital to create for us a networked platform in our own explorations with texts, images and sounds.[16]

Sixty young participants from three different labs—twenty from each locality—have been involved in sketching ideas around this idea of 'publicness.' Working with a range of multimedia forms such as animations, booklets, broadsheets, HTML, typed and formatted texts, soundscapes, photo stories, written word, audio and visual juxtapositions or narratives, storyboards, etc., members develop innovative perspectives on alleys, corners, *mohallas* and locality—important metaphors for 'publicness.' Visiting the city alleys and corners, meeting disadvantaged children and other dwellers in the poor and working-class neighborhoods, young participants begin conversations with a young girl working in a factory, an old woman sweeping the streets of Delhi, a middle-aged man who runs a photo studio, a shopkeeper, a tea-stall owner, etc. Several young members have produced a collage called "Hamari Dilli" ("Our Delhi").

Cybermohalla practitioners have been engaged in collecting artifacts, documents and objects and then exploring and mapping through these inanimate materials the life trajectories of poor individuals and families who have settled in the various localities over the years. The narratives rendered vis-à-vis such diverse documents as a ration card, land-survey notice and identity papers are poignant accounts and stories of how the power of state and local institutions disrupt the lives of poor migrants. The fragmentary reflections of Cybermohalla practitioners describing their personal family narratives caught up in the phantasmic world of documents, interspersed with several longer discussions, are reminiscent of Walter Benjamin's (1999) philosophical writings. The image and text reflection titled "Paper Waits/

Weights" was presented by the Cybermohalla project at the International Colloquium on Information, Society, History and Politics in Amsterdam in 2007. The reflection states that "documents determine access to formal networks. Documents tell stories. Stories of broken lives, fragile access, combative claims, capacities of negotiation, dreams of mobility and more are part of the hidden transcripts of documents."[17]

The "Walls" project draws upon ideas of publicness and locality to talk about how walls interact with and shape human experience. The experimental multimedia work carried out by young participants connects ideas of dwelling and experience:

> Dwellings are made of walls. Our lived experience shows these walls are testimonies of fractured, fragile, contested stories of the everyday struggle to make life in the city. Fragile lives build themselves and reside along walls. Women gather around walls to share experience, youngsters lean against them to recount the day's stories from other parts of the city, infants rest in their shade.[18]

The Cybermohalla project provides opportunities of self-expression and exploration for young underprivileged people from Delhi. The new and old ICTs not only enable enhanced participation in media but also allow young participants a creative range of possibilities for commentary, critique and dialogue. The approach to cyberspace and the new media as open-ended and globalized forms of communication with the ability to connect with localized forms of communication as embodied in the *mohalla* is an innovative feature. This overlapping of the local and global contexts offers media educators theoretical and practical resources in creating flexible models of media pedagogy. What the young people seem to accomplish here is an important aspect of media engagement that pushes the boundaries of media pedagogy toward eclectic theory–praxis dialectic. Perhaps an apt term would be to call these instances 'pedagogies of estrangement.' Several years ago, Paul Willis (1990, 136, emphasis added) suggested that a great deal of symbolic work by young people needs to be considered educational, particularly when it involves "making (not receiving) messages and meanings in your context and from materials that you have appropriated [it] is, in essence, *a form of education in the broadest sense*. It is a specifically *developmental part of symbolic work, an education about 'the self' and its relation to the world* and others in it."

The narratives produced by the Cybermohalla practitioners, their creative and critical reflections, are marked by particular ideas about the 'political' that seem to question the dominant understanding of terms such as *participation* and *citizenship* and *civic engagement*. As a form of radical pedagogy, these go beyond dominant notions of education. As a form of 'direct education,' they emulate what Paulo Freire outlined through his philosophy of education: dialogical education through interaction with a focus on practice (or praxis). Indeed, this idea of 'direct education' does not imply either romanticizing or privileging young people's experience; rather, experience, following McLaren (1993, 7), "is a way in which individuals confront the contingency of the present, the inevitable alternation of oppression, and the politics of daily living."

The ICTs that the practitioners appropriate also open up potential spaces of dialogue for the young practitioners; discussions lead to collective participation in a variety of multimedia experimental work. It is the idea of the political in the Cybermohalla narratives that maps a more nuanced elaboration of participation and collaboration. This is particularly visible in the numerous writings organized under "Public Domain." Three bilingual books, *Galiyon Se (By-Lanes)* in 2002, *Book Box* in 2003, and *Behurupiya Shehr (Polymorphous City)* in 2007, provide specific inflections to political questions about their neighborhoods, localities and the city. More recently, the young people's work has been published in the form of a book titled *Trickster City* (2007) that includes writings and reflections that offer phenomenological insights into the poor and working-class youths' experiences.

As socio-biographies of their lifeworlds, these writings provide glimpses into 'vital conjunctures' of youth identities as they navigate uncertainties and disruptions in their lives. Yet, in all these and other forms created, there is a strong will to narrate and mediate their subjectivities from the personal to the social in spatial and temporal contexts. For instance, the idea of 'space'—whether as a conceptual abstraction, particularly in the reflections titled "The Edges of Questions" by Shamsher and the response from Suraj, or as concrete reality of their neighborhoods—becomes a central motif of their narratives.

TOWARD AGONISTIC PUBLIC SPACES?

How do we make sense of pedagogic practices of the Cybermohalla practitioners, particularly their notion of participation? The work of Chantal Mouffe (2007, 3) may offer some provisional ideas in understanding the Cybermohalla project in terms of an "agonistic pluralism." While distinguishing her approach from other perspectives, Mouffe outlines her concept of agonistic pluralism in relation to public spaces:

> Public spaces are always plural and the agonistic confrontation takes place in a multiplicity of discursive surfaces. While there is no predetermined centre to this diversity of spaces, there always exist diverse forms of articulation among them and we are not faced with any kind of dispersion envisaged by some postmodernist thinkers. Public spaces are always striated and hegemonically structured. A given hegemony results from specific articulation of diversity of spaces and this means that the hegemonic struggle also consists in the attempt to create a different form of articulation among public spaces.

The Cybermohalla project is engaged in sketching out a form of 'agonistic' public space where participation and collaboration, following Florian Schneider (2006, 572), imply a form of "conflictual" engagement, and where "collaboration is driven by complex and often diverse realities rather than romantic notions of common ground and commonality of interests." The digital and other media narratives on daily life in the *bastis* (slums) and localities provide a nuanced account of larger social and political questions that become visible in terms of affect and embodiment. Young people's narrative identities are complex and multilayered, not fixed and immutable. The above analysis pointed to the relational nature of youth identities shaped differently by their particular socio-biographies and life trajectories.

Through the study of Cybermohalla, I looked at how technology, particularly the old and new ICTs, provided a baseline for an examination of the ways that young people engage the new media forms. Developing media materials in the form of graphics, text, page design and layout, design aesthetics and digital constructions offered interesting opportunities for the young participants to become media makers. The idea of learning through content creation also includes designing the messages in creative and expressive ways. The combinations of media forms enabled the young people to creatively build media materials on a range of personal and social topics. The conversations between young participants revealed that they not only are capable of understanding complex issues but can act on these as well. The dialogues between the young people, their peers, media pedagogues within the initiative, and the larger community pointed to aspects of participation and involvement that would not have been possible in other media and educational settings. Through a series of personal and social narratives, young people pointed to both the problems and prospects in theorizing participation. Young people's interactions within the locality, the ongoing conversations with the community, the engagement with their environment, the coming together of local forms of knowledge and ICTs, point to an interesting exploration of collective identities.

As noted earlier, Ricoeur's work, along with feminist phenomenological writings, remains indispensable to a more substantive understanding of youth subjectivity, one that offers productive avenues for examining youth media practices in terms of the stories, plots and inter-subjective webs of relationships between and among young people and their lifeworlds. Furthermore, as demonstrated in the previous sections, against the poststructuralist theorizations of subjectivity, a phenomenological approach grounds youth selfhood and experience in the here and now. In this concluding section, I offer a comparative discussion of the youth media projects in terms of translocality, imagination and the political. Whereas the congeries of youths' social identities is imbricated differently, class remained an enduring structural dynamic influencing young people's experience of social inequities. It is through their media practices that youth not only confront the inequalities but also produce alternative political imagination. Returning now to Katz's categories of resilience, reworking and resistance, I would like to make the following observations. According to Katz (2005, 240), whereas resilience refers to survival strategies of people, reworking is a practice whereby people respond to social problems around them, and resistance, a still rarer practice, is the capacity of people to effect radical social change. Unlike other approaches to agency, Katz's model enables a better analytic grasp in sketching the material contexts within which political agency unfolds. Furthermore, such a perspective is cognizant of the fact that not all forms of agency lead to resistance.

The discussion of human action in Ricoeur's work and feminist theories points to the creative potential of agency that is expressed through a repertoire of registers—linguistic, cognitive, embodied, performative, etc. The study of the two youth media projects revealed that although poor and marginalized youth lives are characterized by deep historical and structural contradictions, young people are developing strategies to question and, in some instances, to address the underlying causes of pervasive socioeconomic inequalities and domination. Such strategies have taken different forms depending on the contexts and the nature of struggles of youth in Bethlehem and Delhi.

My study of the affective and ideological dimension of youth agency revealed its relational character. More importantly, the dialectic mediation of idem-ipse identities of youth suggested a more complex formation of youth experience, differently shaped by the vital conjunctures in their lives. For instance, the life trajectories of young women in Delhi and Bethlehem were marked by specific personal, familial, historical contingencies that not only shaped their personal and collective experiences, but also marked their gendered identities in unpredictable ways.[19] Thus, a singular conception of agency ignores the variable and multiple youth biographies that are simultaneous and nonsynchronous rather than linear and stage-based. Furthermore, as Kennelly (2009) notes, agency resides in the collective, not in individual action. Drawing on Terry Lovell's (2003) work, Kennelly (2009, 262) refers to the examples of Rosa Parks, Martin Luther King Jr., and other leaders of the civil rights movement who attended the Highlander Folk School in Tennessee, which served as a training ground for civil rights activists.[20] Parks's act of defiance did not emerge as an individual action but in the context of the larger collective. Political agency emerges relationally and is grounded in collective actions. Because youth media practices are carried out through collaborations between and among youth and adult mentors, and within communities and neighborhoods, young people mobilize political agency collectively. Individual accounts of agency obscure the collective actions of people, and they are also politically unsustainable.

The digital narratives of young people from Lajee and Cybermohalla are powerful examples of how such political agency is mobilized in collective contexts. In such instances, what emerged is a 'conflictual' participation that produced dissensus, not consensus. Lajee's youth produced digital stories as acts of resilience. The digital stories are powerful instances of how young people produce narratives of hope and justice despite their precarious living conditions. The photo-narratives provide evocative glimpses into the disruptions in the everyday lives of young people, their families and community. Yet, the young people do not seek the viewer's empathy; rather, they demonstrate *sumud* (steadfastness) and resilience in the face of atrocities. In important ways, the concept of resistance finds a profound meaning in the Palestinian idea of *sumud* that is not only a way of coping with suffering and pain but also an embodied practice of resilience and optimism. Similarly, Cybermohalla's youth are also engaged in several small acts of resilience.

The sort of democratic engagement that the young people advocate through their media practices can be understood in terms of Chantal Mouffe's (2007) notion of agonistic struggle. In contrast to the deliberative model of democracy that is built on the principle of consensus, Mouffe's agonistic model considers 'conflictual' participation an intrinsic aspect of political discourse. Moreover, Mouffe identified a range of artistic and cultural practices as instances of agonistic struggles whose primary aim lies in challenging the consensus-based politics. In addition, Mouffe notes that critical art practices lead to the creation of agonistic public spaces that disrupt the workings of dominant hegemony. Without going into Mouffe's philosophical discussion of the agonistic model of democracy, it is safe to posit that her perspective is able to account for the multiple ways in which several cultural practices articulate the political. Indeed, I argue that several youth media projects exhibit characteristics of critical art outlined by Mouffe (2007, 4), where "critical art is art that foments dissensus, that makes visible what the dominant consensus tends to obscure and obliterate. It is constituted by a manifold of artistic practices aiming at giving a voice to all those who are silenced within the framework of existing hegemony." Therefore, as counter-hegemonic interventions, youth media practices produce a plural political space of engagement. My chapter examined the particular ways in which young people creatively deployed media forms—through the practices of bricolage (as in Cybermohalla) or using a variety of digital tools (as in Lajee)—that enabled them to produce new meanings. Indeed, the youth combined the formal aspects of their work—in terms of 'designers as producers'—with social and political critiques. Ellen Lupton (1998), following Walter Benjamin's formulation of "author as producer," suggests that designers as producers mediate social and material reality where language becomes a raw material, and theory is seen as practice, and writing as a tool for social change. The youth media practitioners produced meanings by appropriating digitextual materials and developing narratives and stories as collaborators.

The plural political spaces created by young people through low-end ICTs and digital tools build local-local and local-global solidarities that I characterized as translocal sharing and the exchange of knowledge and resources to effect social change. Perhaps the most striking feature of the various youth media practices relates to developing a range of networked spaces. What was significant about the networked spaces is that they engendered both offline and online projects designed to disrupt dominant forms of power in different locales. These networked spaces as mobile events produced a wide range of translocal practices that endure and foster long-term solidarities across local-local and local-global contexts (as in Cybermohalla).

Finally, this chapter demonstrated how poor and marginalized youth increasingly appropriate low-end ICTs and inexpensive media to produce a range of media forms and narratives. Lajee constructed the space of the refugee camp as a site of protest. Whereas it is not clear when and how the youth counterpublics might effect social change, by developing such spaces, young people produce their own narratives that are attentive to the shifting configurations of power dynamics in their particular social and cultural environments. Lajee and Cybermohalla's youth media projects were involved in developing a range of translocal practices in offline and online environments that endure and foster long-term solidarities across local-local and local-global contexts. Several collaborations between Cybermohalla and other youth-based initiatives from around the world have also opened up avenues for the exchange of knowledge and experiences. Another instance of translocality that involved both online and offline contexts was initiated through Cybermohalla's temporary media labs that involved participants from the Netherlands, Germany and other places.

ACKNOWLEDGMENTS

Parts of this chapter were adapted from: Asthana, Sanjay. *Youth Media Imaginaries from around the World*. New York: Peter Lang, 2012.

NOTES

1. The Palestine portion of the essay is based on research funded by the Qatar National Research Grant awarded by the Qatar Foundation, Doha.
2. Youth media studies have largely been influenced by representational theories focused on the constructed character of media production and reception, and examined politico-economic and ideological dimensions of youth media, but none broached the complex issues of embodied practices, affect and narrative identity that go beyond the ideological.
3. Any discussion of youth media production should prefigure the political economy of media, institutional and global flows of capital, and consumer culture engendered by the various media forms when analyzing how young people appropriate and construct media narratives. Indeed, one must be alert to what Reguillo (2009, 22) persuasively argued: "Today young subjects face a paradox. On the one hand, globalization jointly with technological development has undoubtedly increased the cultural offers. But on the other hand,

it is equally true that the possibilities for access are reduced or restricted. In this sense, the thinking and analysis regarding the relationship between youth, communication and social change must be precisely located in the tension produced by this paradox."

4. Andrew (1984, 2000) and Stadler (1990), among others, noted this lack of attention to Ricoeur's work in film and television studies. However, there have been some analyses of films that engaged aspects of Ricoeur's work (Andrew, 1993; Rosen, 1993).
5. Indeed, as Valdes (1991, 20–25) argued, Ricoeur and Derrida developed particular strands of Heidegger's philosophy that has given us two faces of post-structuralism: hermeneutics and deconstruction. Whereas there are significant disagreements between Ricoeur and Derrida, they agree on several points. For instance, the making of meaning is accompanied by a pattern of reiteration. Derrida notes the logocentric assumption of fixed meaning; Ricoeur insists on the polysemic nature of language. Both attribute indeterminacy to the inherent polysemic nature of language. Whereas Derrida's work makes a radical break with the metaphysics of Western thought, Ricoeur continues his critique from within such a tradition, noting both the problems and prospects.
6. According to McNay (1999, 322), "A potential objection to Ricoeur's notion of the self is that the imputation of an ontological status to narrative introduces a tacitly transcendental concept of identity. Ipseity, however, is not to be understood as some transcendental essence of self that can withdraw from empirical reality. Rather, selfhood is historical *ab initio*."
7. See also Morny Joy (1993) on Ricoeur's relevance to feminist approaches.
8. The idea of agency developed in Ricoeur's work is grounded in the hermeneutic of experience, and as McNay (1999, 329) notes, this "understanding of the creative dimension of action or agency need not necessarily denote a celebratory populism evident in types of cultural studies or feminist standpoint theory."
9. Since the creation of Israel in 1948, Palestinians have been split into three groups: the Israeli Arabs (Palestinians living inside of Israel), Palestinians living in the Occupied Territories, and Palestinians in diaspora (in Arabic, *Ghurba*), dispersed around the world.
10. www.1948.com.au/2008events/melbourne/DOH/DOH.html.
11. Wiles, *Dreams of Home* (2006, 13).
12. John Cromby (2007, 236) argues that most human actions are rendered as "felt thinking," where feelings and thinking are co-constituted. Although feelings might refer to certain somatic aspects of emotions, they include other affective sensations as well. Indeed, "feelings are phenomenological experiences reflective of the momentary state of our body-brain system as it mediates and enables the flow of our being in the world."
13. Habashi's (2008) work is significant because it directly examines the particular ways in which Palestinian children construct national identity.
14. http://preview.sarai.net/community/cybermohalla/ibarat01/english01.htm.
15. http://preview.sarai.net/community/cybermohalla/book01/bylanes.htm (2002), p. 6.
16. Email communication with Shveta Sarda. For Cybermohalla's notion of 'publicness' and digital practices, see also Lovink (2007) for Sarda's discussion.
17. www.sarai.net/practices/cybermohalla/minor-practices/collecting-documents.
18. https://mail.sarai.net/pipermail/cm_public/2005-September/000045.html.
19. See Jacqueline Kennelly (2014) for a thoughtful analysis of how gendered affect shapes the experiences of young women activists and their participation in anti-globalization, anti-poverty and anti-war movements.

20. Myles Horton founded the Highlander Folk School on the Cumberland Plateau, Tennessee, in 1932. Initially, Horton and his associates developed programs for social action and the mobilization of working-class coal miners and later turned to desegregation issues in the South. According to Horton, discussions of racial inequality needed to address the underlying economic and material injustices. In their splendid series of dialogues, *We Make the Road by Walking: Conversations on Education and Social Change,* Myles Horton and Paulo Freire (1990) offer insights into the relational dynamics of political agency and social change constituted through collective actions. The book provides an account of how Rosa Parks, Martin Luther King Jr., and other civil rights activists participated in Highlander's Citizenship Schools in late 1950s.

REFERENCES

Andrew, Dudley. *Concepts in Film Theory*. Oxford and New York: Oxford University Press, 1984.

———. "History and Timelessness in Films and Theory," in *Meanings in Texts and Actions: Questioning Paul Ricoeur*. Edited by David Klemm and William Schweiker, 115–132. Charlottesville: University Press of Virginia, 1993.

———. "Tracing Ricoeur." *Diacritics* 30, no. 2, 2000. 44–69.

Appadurai, Arjun. *Modernity at Large: Cultural Dimensions of Globalization*. Minneapolis: University of Minnesota Press, 1996.

———. "Grassroots Globalization and the Research Imagination." *Public Culture* 12, no. 1, 2000. 1–19.

Asthana, Sanjay. *Youth Media Imaginaries from around the World*. New York: Peter Lang, 2012.

Bassett, Caroline. *The Arc and the Machine: Narrative and New Media*. Manchester: Manchester University Press, 2007.

Benjamin, Walter. "Reflections of Radio," in *Walter Benjamin: Selected Writings*. Edited by Michael W. Jennings. Cambridge and London: The Belknap Press of Harvard University Press, 1999.

Bjawi-Levine, Laure. "Children's Rights Discourse and Identity: Ambivalence in Palestinian Refugee Camps." *Jerusalem Quarterly* 37, 2009. 75–85.

Bulle, Sylvaine. " 'We Only Want to Live': From Israeli Domination towards Palestinian Decency in Shu'fat and Other Confined Jerusalem Neighborhoods." *Jerusalem Quarterly* 10, no. 1, 2009. 24–34.

Couldry, Nick. *Why Voice Matters: Culture and Politics after Neoliberalism*. Thousand Oaks: Sage, 2010.

Cromby, John. "Feelings and Embodies Subjectivity," in *Citizen City: Between Constructed Agent and Constructed Agency*. Edited by Vasi Van Deventer et al., 232–240. Ontario: University Publications, 2007.

Dillabough, Jo-Anne, and Jacqueline Kennelly. *Lost Youth in the Global City: Class, Culture, and the Urban Imaginary*. New York: Routledge, 2010.

Farquhar, Sandy. *Ricoeur, Identity and Early Childhood Education*. Lanham: Rowman & Littlefield, 2010.

Habashi, Janette. "Palestinian Children Crafting National Identity." *Childhood* 15, no. 1, 2008. 12–29.

Horton, Myles, and Paulo Freire. *We Make the Road by Walking: Conversations on Education and Social Change*. Philadelphia: Temple University Press, 1990.

Joy, Morny. "Feminism and the Self." *Theory and Psychology* 3, no. 3, 1993. 275–302.

Kallio, Paulina Kirsi. "Performative Bodies, Tactical Agents and Political Selves: Rethinking the Political Geographies of Childhood." *Space and Polity* 11, no. 2, 2007. 121–136.

Katz, Cindy. *Growing Up Global: Economic Restructuring and Children's Everyday Lives*. Minneapolis: University of Minnesota Press, 2005.

Kennelly, Jacqueline. "Youth Cultures, Activism and Agency: Revisiting Feminist Debates." *Gender and Education* 21, no. 3, 2009. 259–272.

———. "'It's This Pain in My Heart That Won't Let Me Stop': Gendered Affect, Webs of Relations, and Young Women's Activism." *Feminist Theory*, in press 2014.

Lovell, Terry. "Resisting with Authority: Historical Specificity, Agency and the Performative Self." *Theory, Culture and Society* 20, no. 1, 2003. 1–17.

Lovink, Geert. *Zero Comments: Kernels of Critical Internet Culture*. New York: Routledge, 2007.

Lupton, Ellen. "Designer as Producer," in *The Education of a Graphic Designer*. Edited by Steven Heller, 159–168. New York: Allworth Press, 1998.

Mahmood, Saba. "Feminist Theory, Embodiment, and the Docile Agent: Some Reflections on the Egyptian Islamic Revival." *Cultural Anthropology* 16, no. 2, 2001. 202–236.

McLaren, Peter. "Critical Literacy and Postcolonial Praxis." *College Literature*. Vols. 19–20, 1993. 7–27.

McNay, Lois. "Gender and Narrative Identity." *Journal of Political Ideologies* 4, no. 3, 1999. 315–336.

Miessen, Markus. *The Violence of Participation*. Berlin: Sternberg Press, 2007.

Mouffe, Chantal. "Artistic Activism and Agonistic Spaces." *Art & Research: A Journal of Ideas, Contexts and Methods* 1, no. 2, 2007. 1–21.

Neelofer. "Our Own Space." Sarai, Cybermohalla, 2004. Accessed October 15, 2011. www.sarai.net/practices/cybermoholla/generative-contexts/locality-labs/our-own-space.

Rabinow, Paul. *Reflections on Fieldwork in Morocco*. Berkeley and Los Angeles: University of California Press, 1977.

Rai, Babli. "Text-Image-Sound." Sarai, Cybermohalla, 2002. Accessed October 15, 2011. www.sarai.net/practices/cybermohalla/public-dialogue/books/book-box/text-image-sound.

Reguillo, Rosanna. "The Warrior's Code? Youth, Communication and Social Change," in *Youth Engaging with the World*. Edited by Thomas Tufte and Florencia Enghel, 21–39. Göteborg: Nordicom, 2009.

Ricoeur, Paul. *Time and Narrative*. Vol. 2. Chicago: University of Chicago Press, 1984.

———. *Oneself as Another*. Translated by Kathleen Blamey. Chicago: University of Chicago Press, 1996.

Rosen, Philip. "Traces of the Past: From Historicity to Film," in *Meanings in Texts and Actions: Questioning Paul Ricoeur*. Edited by David Klemm and William Schweiker, 93–111. Charlottesville: University Press of Virginia, 1993.

Said, Edward. *Humanism and Democratic Criticism*. New York: Columbia University Press, 2004.

Schneider, Florian. "Collaboration: The Dark Side of the Multitude." *Sarai Reader* 6, 2006. 70–382.

Skattebol, Jen. "Affect: A Tool to Support Pedagogical Change." *Discourse: Studies in the Cultural Politics of Education* 31, no. 1, 2010. 75–91.

Sobchak, Vivian. *Carnal Thoughts: Embodiment and Moving Image Culture*. Berkeley: University of California Press, 2004.

Soep, Elisabeth, and Vivian Chavez. *Drop That Knowledge: Youth Radio Stories*. Berkeley: University of California Press, 2010.

Stadler, Harald. "Film as Experience: Phenomenological Concepts in Cinema and Television Studies." *Quarterly Review of Film and Video* 12, no. 3, 1990. 37–50.
Thrift, Nigel. *Non-Representational Theory: Space, Politics, Affect.* London and New York: Routledge, 2007.
Valdes, Mario. *A Ricoeur Reader: Reflection and Imagination.* Toronto: University of Toronto Press, 1991.
Wiles, Rich. *Dreams of Home.* Ramallah: Lajee, 2006.
Williams, Raymond. *Resources of Hope: Culture, Democracy, Socialism.* New York: Verso, 1989.
Willis, Paul. *Common Culture: Symbolic Work at Play in the Everyday Cultures of the Young.* London: Westview Press, 1990.

3 Performing Patriarchy

Indian Girls (En)gender a Social Imaginary

Kathleen Gallagher

> Ms. K: The safest place called home is the most unsafe place for them. She's being burned to death for not bringing in enough dowry. She is burned to death because the husband is having an affair. These things, it's very sickening.
>
> (Teacher, Prerna School, Interview January 20, 2012)

Prerna School, founded in 2003, is an all-girl pre-school to 12th grade school, run by a foundation called Studyhall Educational Foundation (SHEF). SHEF began its work in 1986, with the goal of providing quality education to all children in India. Its main area of work has been in Uttar Pradesh, which is one of the largest and most underdeveloped states in India. Currently SHEF reaches out to over 300 teachers, 6,000 children and 14,000 student teachers through its schools and other programs. Prerna serves India's lowest-caste girls. Its founder, Dr. Urvashi Sahni, completed a doctoral degree in drama education at Berkeley University but returned to her homeland to put some of the ideas of drama and learning she had encountered to work. Founding first a middle-class fee-paying school called Studyhall, she used the resources and infrastructure of that school to build Prerna, a school intended to serve those girls working primarily as domestic servants, from urban slums in and around Lucknow, who would be least likely to have access to any kind of education. The Studyhall building at Vipul Khand provides a home for Prerna, which opened its doors in 2003 to eighty students and four teachers but now serves over 600 girls and employs sixteen teachers. Most students undertake domestic servant work during the morning hours and many then go on to domestic tasks in the evening at home. The school, therefore, operates during the afternoon hours of 2–7pm.

Prerna is located in Lucknow, the capital city of Uttar Pradesh (UP). UP is the most populous state of India with a population of more than 199 million, and a sex ratio of 908 women to 1000 men. Lucknow has a population of 2.81 million people. Prerna is located in the area of Gomtinagar, which is a neighbourhood like many in Indian cities, where affluent residential homes are situated alongside very poor slums. The majority of students come from the slums of Gomtinagar, with some traveling from other more distant slums. Prerna has created a space rich in creative learning and critical analysis of the ever-present threats of unbridled patriarchy and the day-to-day abuses of class and caste structures.

From their own website (www.studyhallfoundation.org), one begins to get a sense of the kind of philosophy at play at the school, as well as the pro-social and de-institutionalizing forms of education on offer:

> We believe that schools should be nurturing places where everyone—teachers, students and parents—should feel supported, cared for and respected. We conceive of teaching as an extremely creative and complex process, one requiring much imagination, continuous thinking, caring and commitment. Teachers are all very creative persons, needing the freedom and the opportunity to discover their own hidden depths, which flower and blossom, given a hospitable climate. We try to create an environment that nurtures the creativity and growth of our teachers too, because we believe that only those who are prepared to learn and grow all their lives can teach effectively. We work towards making our school a "community of learners", based upon a foundation of mutual support, caring and trust—one, in which we are constantly learning from each other.

Rhetoric aside, upon arriving in Lucknow and visiting Prerna, we sensed—without yet understanding—the difference that seems to drive this "community of learners"—teachers, students, administrators, founders, community supporters and food-catering mothers alike. Much of our growing understanding came from the day-to-day ethnographic immersion in the space, but also and especially from captivating moments of theatre and performance, which acted both as a form of critical analysis and a space of productive resistance to the gendered forms of subjugation lived out by the girls and women in the school. Prerna school, in Lucknow, is one of five research sites in a collaborative ethnographic project situated in schools in the cities of Lucknow, Taipei, Boston and Toronto. In our work, we have often used drama, methodologically, to set in relief the very real, material, embodied experiences that constitute the lives of youth in such socio-culturally, politically and aesthetically diverse contexts.

That broader study from which this chapter comes is titled, *Urban School Performances: The Interplay, through Live and Digital drama, of Local-Global Knowledge about Student Engagement*. It is a multi-sited and multi-modal ethnography examining questions of engagement and artistic practice in theatre spaces and schools marked by disadvantage. The curricular expectations, and the way drama is positioned in the schools in each of these sites, remains different, as is the kind of drama pedagogy experienced by the students. Between the years of 2008–2013, local drama work in each site was shared across sites via digital video uploading to blog sites. Online collaborative questions and analysis of the digital performance data engaged the researchers across sites in a sustained dialogue about the differences and similarities we noted in the classroom cultures, the social relations, the student (dis)engagement, the drama pedagogies and the theatre-making practices. Over the course of the first three years of the study, we had found ourselves engaged in a rich exchange through blogs, wikis and the digital capture of live performances with the young women of Prerna school, but being there, perhaps unsurprisingly, created new and unanticipated experiences despite the ethnographic knowledge we had gleaned from afar.

Once there and finding ourselves in the room with the young women, sitting next to other bodies in a crowded classroom space, our fears and curiosities and gazes in full view, we in fact found everything changed. Although the previous three years of digital exchange had produced a familiarity, a proximity, even a comfort, in-person performances can make things anew. Being there, watching and influencing the social relations, raised new questions for us about liveness and affect in collaborative ethnographic work with youth. Of course, throughout our research processes we aimed to maintain a collaboration conscious of the power relations across developed and developing world contexts. Towards this end, we asked: What can these research experiences tell us about how the local conditions and practices of patriarchy—experiences compounded by escalating forces of globalization often deceitfully reproduced through discourses of *opportunity*—produce and refract the subjectivities of young Indian girls? In response to these and related questions, the reflections in this paper come solely from my own deeply personal, phenomenological and often existential experiences of entering a space as an outsider and wrestling with its many meanings and one's own social locations and political commitments.

To this book reflecting on phenomenological approaches to understanding the effects of 'asymmetrical globalization' on youth culture, I wish to make two contributions. The first of these speaks to how drama methods and performance, undertaken by young people as forms of communication and resistance, can be understood and richly theorized by phenomenological and affect theory. The second contribution attempts to account for how the researcher/audience might respond to such performances and what resources phenomenology and affect theory can offer to help us do so ethically. The basic premise of the chapter is that experiences that were communicated to us through performance may have revealed aspects of the lives of the young women we worked with that might otherwise have been inaccessible to us. Taking in the abundance of meanings (literal, abstract, symbolic, metaphoric, contextual, subtextual) always present in a performance, we have leaned on phenomenology to understand both how and why theatrical representations of lived lives always say more than they mean and often provoke new and unanticipated responses in an audience. Without romanticizing either the drama methods or the interpretative lenses, I am suggesting that we came to know the young women's experiences in raw and candid ways that demand of us, as researchers, a kind of political astuteness about the many guises of globalization. These experiences also demand an ethical reflexivity about our role in the reception and subsequent interpretation of these young women's stories. The first section of the paper (Performing Patriarchy I and II) will thus explore the use of such theatre methods and phenomenological analytics, and the second part of the paper (The Social and Theatrical Imaginary) will think through the concept of research reflexivity that such methods demand in the context of globalization.

Throughout the chapter, feminist philosophers, social and affect theorists, and performance studies will be called upon to make sense of gender and lived experience, differently inflected by the creative processes of performance. Lorraine Code's (2006) turn to "ecological thinking" and its effects on a social imaginary, as laden with images, meanings, metaphors and interlocking explanations in specific time periods and geographic-cultural climates, is also particularly instructive. Affect theorist Sara Ahmed's (2004) work counters the social psychologists when she holds that emotion does not live in one person or the other but in the way people encounter one another. This assertion brings particular interpretive strength to our research experiences, these encounters being complex interactions shaped by histories of contact and colonizing ethnographic practices. Emotions, according to Ahmed, are not housed inside people but are produced as effects of circulation that occur in social and cultural practice. Finally, Hannah Arendt's ([1958] 1998, 1982) notions of "visiting" Others' stories in order to experience the possibility of "thinking without a bannister" or without preconceived critical categories, are fruitfully brought to bear on the encounters we had with 'strangers.'

These theorists help us make sense of how girlhood is lived as a theoretical and aesthetic condition as well as a set of social relations. References to them will be interrupted throughout by the unadulterated voice of Ms. K, a teacher in the school who engages the girls in weekly 'critical dialogues.' Critical dialogues are a form of dialogic pedagogy initiated from short in-class improvised dramas. Following the collective viewing of such a short script-less drama, the students discuss what they have seen and what questions were provoked for them by the enacted scenes. Ms. K was a kind of guide for us, a team of three researchers from Toronto (myself and two doctoral research assistants), as she welcomed us into the classroom and gave generously of her time in interviews.

PERFORMING PATRIARCHY I: INVERTING THE OPPRESSOR

On our first research trip to Lucknow, India, our research team had occasion to watch two groups of Indian girls perform scenes illustrating patriarchy. One group was in year 12 (16–17 years old), the other in year 8 (12–13 years old). They thought a performance of how they live the relationships of caste and patriarchy might help us understand their world, that is to say, cross great cultural, racial, socio-economic, linguistic, geographic and religious divides to get a greater sense of their lived realities, to somehow 'feel' their world. The older girls, especially, wanted to engage us in a critical dialogue about structures and systems and dreams and desires with an urgency I have seldom experienced as a researcher. The following transcription from our video footage gives some sense of the lively debate in the classroom, as Dr. Sahni attempted to simultaneously translate for us the critical dialogue the girls were having after the performance on the pressures of arranged marriages they experience in their families. The following transcribed video segment explains one of the short improvised performances we watched, with Dr. Urvashi Sahni aiming to translate the scene as it unfolded. Following the scene is the transcribed critical dialogue that followed.

Improvised Performance Class Year 12 January 18, 2012

Ms. K: We will do a short skit, showing one day in an Indian family. The daily routine of an Indian family. They are trying to reflect the different powers that each individual in the family has.

Urvashi: *First introduce yourself. It's a small family where there's a father, mother, two daughters and one son.*

Anne[1]*:* *Three children is small?*

Ms. K: *Yah! Very small.*

[improvised scene begins]

Urvashi: *I must translate: So they say "Why do you only wake us up? Why don't you also wake up our brother? He is also sleeping." This is the wife, she says go give this to your dad. And that's the son. She says, so what should I cook today? She says go ask your dad. The father asks the son "What would you like?" Brother says some peas. Father asks daughter what happened to the money he gave her yesterday. She says that she spent it. He asks on what. She says on sugar and tea. He gives her some more money and says to go make the food. "Make it well! Do it fast, I'm getting late. What is this food? There is this long hair in it, what is this? And the vegetable in some water. I will eat in the restaurant, I cannot eat at home. Here take some money (to the son) and go." Mother says that the girls want to go to a friends' birthday. Father says it's too late and they can't go. Daughter asks "Is our work to be restricted only to the kitchen?"*

Urvashi: *[translating a girl's response] Does this happen in all families? Yes.*

Urvashi: *[translating another girl] So she says it doesn't happen to us because I don't have a father.*

[Urvashi attempts to translate the Hindi exchanges, but there is too much loud talking going on at the same time to hear anything. She then translates about seven minutes of conversation after the scene ended that happened among the girls and teachers]:

Urvashi: *She is silenced. And when she's so silenced, she's never going to learn to speak up and she won't speak up there either. So we asked her who gave the dad this right? So she's saying when women don't speak up, the father automatically takes the right. So then Kavita said, you know, my mother left my dad because of this, because he used to really bully her and beat her.*

Kathleen: *So the mother left?*

Urvashi: *She left. So I said, why could she not have stayed there and taken her rights? She said, because he can beat her. I said, why don't we beat him back?! She said because the papers will really criticize her and nobody will like her if she beats her husband; you just can't do that.*

Urvashi: *[her own thoughts] They are very into that it's a generational thing. That because we treat our daughters like this so they become like that. Nobody speaks up because we treat our sons like this.*

Kathleen: *Do any brothers object and side with their sisters?*

Urvashi: *So Bivi was saying how they were talking about the basic thing that they never learned to speak up against it because they are afraid of being beaten, and second, they have no money. So they don't know how they'd support themselves. There's nowhere to go. You can't go home, your parents tell you you're wrong, you can't leave your husband, go back. Society won't give you any place to stay. So you have no choice but to stay there. So I asked the question: And what happens when men leave their lives, in some cases, or when wives leave their husbands when they just can't bear the beating, you know, their husband is a drunk or something . . .—Do women manage to support themselves or not? They said ya. So how come they manage to do that then? So they said it's actually in their heads that they can't do it. Helplessness is a question of how you feel, and also because you are so darned frightened by the beating.*

Urvashi: *She said 10% of brothers do help.*

Urvashi: *[speaking to the students] Now that children are educated, do you think that that will change anything? Every time I ask this question, "How do we change this?"; it is by education.*

Urvashi: *[translating] So, she's asking the question, during the play, what was wrong with the question? There was a hair in the food—so he threw a fit, went off to the restaurant. What's wrong with that? The girls could have also gone to the restaurant. And I said, the boy is already out and nobody's caring when he is coming back. Nobody stops the boy; nobody even cares where the boys are.*

Kathleen: *They have freedom of movement?*

[Kathleen asks about the education question—whether the girls think that education is the way to change this situation]

Urvashi: *Yes, they all said yes. But they all said that in your education you should be talking about this problem daily. That is when you learn.*

Kathleen: *They are saying it is up to them to change it?*

Urvashi: *Yeah, that they should challenge it. She's saying, (you know, when we get home we can watch it and I will translate all of it for you). She's saying that women train their sons so badly that they grow up and beat their own mothers. I have seen that happen!*

[end]

Critical Dialogue Video file #1: Jan_18_2012_1.mp4

Ms. K: *[speaking in Hindi]*

[girls begin raising their hands and offering responses/answering questions—not clear what they are talking about]

Urvashi: *So, I will tell you what they are all saying. They're saying—so her mother said that she doesn't need to work. As far as the mother is concerned she just needs to study. But she says her dad sometimes says, "Now you've had enough of study, now we need to get you married," but her mother says "She will study as long as she wants to." [points to another girl] She says my mother says "You know I was married at nine so I did not get the opportunity to study, but I want you to have that opportunity. What will you do to fulfill the dream that I had?" [points to a third girl] And she says [clarifies in Hindi], so her mother said "I want you to study and get a job when you finish. And all of this dowry stuff that continues, when you marry, your job will be a dowry in itself." So that will work.*

[another girl speaks]

Urvashi: *Her mother says also "My dream is that I didn't study and I want you to study." She says she wants all her daughters to study as long as they want to. But if someone tells them, she really has no money to make it happen.*

[another girl speaks and everyone laughs]

Urvashi: *She said "It's all the opposite in my house."*

[Urvashi speaking to a student in Hindi]

Urvashi: *For her, there are four sisters and three brothers and her mother wants her to study so that she can take care of her brothers and teach them. Another girl says that she has three sisters and one brother, and her father said I will help you with your studies, but you need to help your brother with his.*

[another girl]

My mother didn't go to school so she wants me to go and learn.

[a girl speaks]

Urvashi: *[translating] My brother and I both can't study. My mother wants us both to study . . . [Urvashi's own comment] Our mothers had it so hard that they don't want to make it so hard for their children.*

[Urvashi tells us that a girl has asked to read her poem]

Urvashi: *[translating poem] In our country*
Our country is a place where a man is in power
And women and children don't break his power.
Every man says you must live by his command,
And if you don't do that, then you can't live in my house.

[end of video footage and end of class]

In these empirical moments, Mathew Ratcliff's notion of a "phenomenological stance" made good sense. In studying experiences of psychiatric illness, Ratcliff (2012) argues that adopting a "phenomenological stance" enables a distinctive kind of empathy. Such a phenomenological stance involves suspending one's habitual acceptance of a shared world, the backdrop against which we typically interpret the experiences of others. 'Radical empathy,' he argues, expands the range of intelligible experiences and makes clear what more 'mundane' forms of empathy fail to accommodate. That is to say, our sense of belonging to a shared world "comes to light as a phenomenological achievement" (ibid., 491) rather than a mere supposition of our insights and interpretations. As audience to their performances and subsequent dialogues, and as researchers, we needed to delay interpretation and any sense of a shared world so that we could see their scenes and their lively discussions in *their own* terms with our own very differently positioned eyes. There was a lot in that first classroom experience for us to think through. The discussion that followed added further personal dimensions to the performance of patriarchy we had witnessed.

When we visited the year 8 students, they were bustling with excitement about sharing a performed piece with us that they had adapted from a textbook, with the teacher's help. It was a scene about a meeting between a potential bride's family and the groom's family. We did not videotape this scene because the students were not participants of our study and we did not have Urvashi to offer the simultaneous translation, but the body language was nonetheless very revealing. The groom's family was inspecting the potential bride (she was thirteen), investigating her suitability to be a bride. How well did she clean? How well did she cook? The girl herself was most proud of her ability to sing but the groom's family, and the groom himself, took this as a bad sign, the sign of an uncontrollable spirit. When she articulated that she wanted to be educated, the groom's family found this entirely unacceptable. We watched the eleven- and twelve-year-old girls play out the role of oppressor with a certain playfulness. There was clearly something delightful about playing out this scenario with each other and for us. The storyline was explained to us by the teacher after we had watched the scene in Hindi. Not understanding the words complicated our meaning-making, but it also allowed us to pay a different kind of attention to their bodies and their sense of play and elation. When the teacher gave us the translation, I remember feeling somewhat surprised that the story of oppression had been presented with such a sense of play, visible in their bodies. They moved in unguarded ways, they smiled at each other, they were enjoying their exaggeration of the menacing family. We could see clearly the 'victim' in the scene but the energy of the scene seemed more focused on the characters playing the oppressors. Some of their excitement might have been about having foreign visitors in their classroom, but I sensed that the playing out of the story itself offered a kind of intoxication. Seyla Benhabib's (1992, 100) insight is particularly relevant here: "All struggles against oppression in the modern world begin by defining what had previously been considered private, non-public, and non-political as matters of public concern, issues of justice, and sites of power." There was a palpable pleasure in exposing this domestic drama, in making public the injustices of their lives.

Theatre scholar Jan Cohen-Cruz (2006) understands this kind of performance power as the social potential of personal story, which for her is "grounded not in particular subject matter but rather in storytelling's capacity to position even the least powerful individual in a proactive, subject position" (13), or as bell hooks (1990) describes it, story made from experience affords a privileged critical location from which to speak. Cohen-Cruz (2006) further argues that storytelling literally *makes* knowledge. She (ibid., 14–15) offers a persuasive interpretation of what was going on in that year 8 room the day we visited:

> To the degree that the teller has a strong sense of identity with an under- or misrepresented culture, the story is personal and cultural; attention to the story is attention to that culture as represented from within. Such stories often serve as counter-histories, which like oral histories make public points of view that were previously 'hidden from history'

(Rowbothan, cited in Perks and Thomson, 1998, p. xi). Through stories that emphasise oppression, people see their struggles in social context rather than as personal limitations, for the larger inequities that underlie their personal experiences rise to the surface.

The pleasure I sensed in the girls' performance and its communication of gendered subjugation kept a hold on me in the following days. Whereas the above-cited theorists helped me to make certain kinds of sense of the scene, I knew I also needed to better understand the broader histories and politics of women's storytelling in India. In the nineteenth century, the stories told about and by women in India were limited by narratives of women's inferiority or their 'natural' domestic character. Some Indian reformers of that time believed that social evils could best be eliminated through education but the concept of education for women was limited to producing good home-makers and perpetuating orthodox ideology (Jayawardena, [1986] 1994). There is a rich history of women's agitation for women's rights in the early twentieth century in India, although much of this was overshadowed by Gandhi's edicts about the 'nature' of women.

> In framing any scheme of women's education this cardinal truth must be kept in mind. Man is supreme in the outward activities of a married pair and, therefore, it is the fitness of things that he should have a greater knowledge thereof. On the other hand, home life is entirely the sphere of women and, therefore, in domestic affairs, in the upbringing and education of children, women ought to have more knowledge.
>
> (M.K. Gandhi, cited by Jayawardena, [1986] 1994, 96)

Later, Jawaharlal Nehru's views were more in keeping with the progressive reformers of his time. In a speech in 1928 in Allahabad, he references Ibsen's "Doll's House" when he insists that the future of India cannot consist of making half the population of a country the mere plaything of the other half or progress would not be made. He claimed to be dissatisfied with the lot of the Indian woman, describing her as the "follower and obedient slave of her husband and others" (see ibid.). From the scene we witnessed in the year 8 classroom, not much seems to have changed a near century later. Nehru's brief reference to 'others' who would also enslave women was elaborately performed for us as girls played out the oppression visited upon the bride-to-be by the in-laws and siblings of the would-be groom's family.

Indian women revolutionaries of the early twentieth century, such as Bhikaiji Cama, Lala Lajpat Rai, Krishnavarma and Vir Savarkar, were regarded as anarchists and terrorists by the British colonizers. By the time of the Second World War, Communist women too had become very active in the nationalist struggle, which was bound up with women's rights across India. Jayawardena [1986] 1994, 106) writes, "At this time, the All-India Student Federation set up a Girl Students Committee to mobilize militant young women.... By 1940 the girl students held a conference in Lucknow." Here we were some sixty years later in a Lucknow school for girls watching 12–13-year-olds on the cusp of adolescence fighting for an education and railing against child marriage. Historian Kumari Jayawardena sums it up best when she concludes that the study of women's participation in political struggles of India in the nineteenth century and the first four decades of the twentieth century gave the illusion of change while women were kept within the structural confines of family and society.

Within the first decade of the twenty-first century, the Indian Parliament passed the Right to Education Act in 2009, but has struggled to fill the financing gap and, therefore, implementation is thwarted. Even with such positive policy changes, entrenched forms of patriarchy and the caste system continue to limit the lives and life chances of young women. Take, for instance, Shivan Vij's (2012) recent exposé in the *New York Times*. The discourse of globalization in India and across the Western world continues to celebrate the advent of a 'new India,' but Vij's editorial speaks of the many Indians being displaced from their low-caste occupations, jobs they are born into but never chose. Those who belong to artisan castes are struggling to adapt to a modern economy, those with technical skills like hand loom weavers or oil extractors have been made redundant by mechanization and imports. Young girls from the Bedia caste, born into prostitution, are now being removed from their families because of an imported morality but have no other means of survival because they require government assistance to shift from such 'traditional' occupations. The greatest barrier though, Vij writes, is the poor quality of public education, which often does not provide English instruction, perhaps the greatest handicap of lower-caste girls in a globalized world. But using drama methodologically meant that we did not need to rely on language alone to communicate across our cultural and linguistic borders. We used the phenomenologically inspired method of theatre to watch the embedded and embodied knowledges of young women, in their context of globalization. This both opened up the possibility for communication but also made clear how globalization is implicated in such methods.

It is impossible to say, with any certainty, why the girls seemed to take such delight and exhibit such playfulness in their performance of gendered oppression. Certainly having Western women in their classroom, keenly interested in their work, was a novelty. There may indeed be many different interpretations of these first shared moments with the young girls at Prerna but I return to a phenomenological stance and our readings of both struggle and pleasure that seemed to saturate our first impressions. Calling up Ratcliff's notion of a phenomenological stance allowed us to feel a kind of 'radical empathy' based not on a shared world but rather dependent on our ability to see this performance in its own terms and to see these young women as constructing these understandings for us. But it is, to an even greater extent, Arendt's sense of the great capacity of human activity that really opened up for us the ability to read this not as simple contradiction but as a powerful moment of beginning, a looking back that propelled a looking forward, the one that needed the other to initiate itself.

In her introduction to Hannah Arendt's *The Human Condition,* in a re-publication forty years after its first original publication in 1958, Margaret Canovan (1998) describes Arendt as a "theorist of beginnings." Whether lamenting totalitarianism or describing a revolution, Arendt's "reflections on the human capacity to start something new pervade her thinking" (Canovan, 1998, vii). Canovan goes on to suggest that dichotomies were too constricting for Arendt's intellectual imagination and so she more often thought about distinctions as threefold, as between labour, work and action, or power, violence and strength (ibid., vii). Whereas the pleasure of performing the oppressor for us and making public their previously private and domestic experiences of subjugation, the scenes prepared for us by both the younger and the older girls may have well been exploring the complicated distinctions between power, violence and strength. Underlying this performance work is Arendt's emphasis—in *The Human Condition* and in many other works—on our human capacity for action. Canovan insists that reminding us of the capacity to act even in the most unlikely circumstances was a central purpose for Arendt. And acting, beginning something new despite their circumstances, was produced in their performances and became a major theme in our subsequent discussions with the young women over the week we spent with them.

Attuned to this contradictory moment in the performance, wherein the real and material realities of oppression for these young girls were on full display for us, yet also perceiving their gratification in sharing that work with us, made us understand more fully Arendt's supposition that each of us is capable of acting and starting something new, whatever the conditions. And starting something new always heralds the potential for change.

PERFORMING PATRIARCHY II: MANIFESTING HOPE

In my experience, storytelling through theatre has been a powerful way to reach strangers. It gets to the heart of Kwame Anthony Appiah's (2006, xxi) critical question: "What do we owe strangers by virtue of our shared humanity?" When we watched the older girls do their improvisation prior to engaging in a critical dialogue on patriarchy, we saw again the performance of gender in ways that seemed unfathomable to a Western, twentieth-century sensibility and political reality. In this scene, the young woman prepared a meal for her father and brother, which they rejected. The mother gave her son money to eat in a restaurant because he had rejected his sister's cooking. The girl felt betrayed by everyone: father, brother and mother, drawn in by internalized patriarchy and the ever-present burden of pleasing the men of the house. Again, bell hooks (1990, 485) states plainly how "sexism is perpetuated by institutional and social structures; by the individuals who dominate, exploit, or oppress; and by the victims themselves who are socialized to behave in ways that make them act in complicity with the status quo." Ms. K captured the larger social context for us when trying to explain how sexism was perpetuated institutionally, forcing the complicity of mothers:

> *Ms. K: Even if she [a mother] goes out of there she hasn't a place to live and she has to take the burden of the children also. So it's very difficult for them [mothers] to come out. There is nothing like economic support for the females. The only thing they have is the jewelry that they get in the marriage. But how long will that continue?*
>
> *(Prerna School, Interview January 20th, 2012)*

The year 12 girls created the improvisation to help us better understand how patriarchy played out in their domestic and everyday lives. They wanted to give us a 'felt' experience of patriarchy. The perennial question asked regularly by teachers in Prerna school was how the theatre work they created might intervene in their realities. We were wondering the very same thing. The improvisation we observed launched the critical dialogue in their classroom on that day. Although we could basically follow the scene from its embodied performance, our collaborator, Dr. Urvashi Sahni, translated from Hindi for us the words of the actor who played the central role in the scene:

> *She's saying that women train their sons so badly that they grow up and beat their own mothers. "I have seen that happen!"*
>
> *(Urvashi translating for a student during the critical dialogue and drama performance, January 21, 2012)*

When one becomes audience to a performance, a performance marked urgent because of the atrocities it speaks, there are important questions to be asked by ethnographers who understand that naturalistic repetitions of trauma can be re-violating, as Julie Salverson (2001) warns, and must therefore be aesthetically transformed so that our perspective as audience can move from consumption to intellectual and political engagement. How, we wondered, could we make something of this shared story so that our presence does something more? After watching the lively critical dialogue that ensued, understanding so little but feeling the power of their shared grounding made manifest through theatre, an inexplicable but powerful buoyancy filled the room. Despite the layers of oppression we witnessed in this short scene, how the girls subsequently engaged with one another, periodically tossing encouraging smiles in our direction, produced in us a startling sense of hope. It was, in part, because we watched the girls' delight as they made their stories known to us and watched their support of, and love for, one another even as they shared, through their critical dialogues, ever more distressing stories about their domestic experiences of abuse and violence. In a later focus group, one young woman struggled to find the English words to explain her sense of the community she felt she was part of at Prerna:

> *Laxmi:* *If someone have a problem in my class we always ask her, "What problem you have, why you are so quiet, and why you are crying?" So, if she only, sometime before, she tells us, so we try to solve the problem and ask her, "How can we help you?" So if she is ready to take help, so we help her.*
> *(Prerna student focus group interview, January 2, 2012)*

In the performance, we were watching bodies play out a present set of circumstances that held little hope. But in the collective creation process we watched, the devising of the work, hope seemed not only a future dream, but also a felt presence in the room. Sara Ahmed (2004, 184), in her text, *The Cultural Politics of Emotion,* fittingly describes a relationship to hope in the following way:

> But hope is not simply about the possibilities of the future implicit in the failure of repetition. . . . I would argue instead that hope involves a relationship to the present, and to the present as affected by its imperfect translation of the past. It is in the present that the bodies of subjects shudder with an expectation of what is otherwise. It is in the unfolding of the past in the present. The moment of hope is when the 'not yet' impresses upon us in the present, such that we must act, politically, to make it our future. If hope impresses upon us in the present rather than being merely futural (see Benjamin 1997), then hope requires that we must act in the present, rather than simply wait for a future that is always before us.

The very emotion of hope keeps something open, she concludes. This notion of hope as a work *in the present* and an emotion that keeps something open is entirely resonant with our sense of how theatre was being put to use by the girls at Prerna, how their bodies were engaging in a rehearsal of hope, a practice they came to embellish with phenomenological detail. This is hope as a political strategy activated through their playful inversion of the oppressor in the first performance and their courage in the face of impenetrable patriarchy and servitude in the second. Although other scholars of affect (Potaminanou, 1997, cited in Ahmed, 2004) argue that such hope can have the opposite effect in that fixations with hope can foreclose transformation or change, Ahmed's positioning of hope as crucial to the act of protest allowed the girls we witnessed, in performance then in dialogue with one another, to open the possibility that what angered them about their lives may have been foreseeable, but was not inexorable.

Before I turn in the next section to the position occupied by 'the researcher,' Arendt ([1958] 1998) offers as a starting point another important phenomenological sense of human activities and the relationship between us the spectators, and the girls, the creators. That world we share, in those performative moments, beckons another larger world and like a table at which we are gathered, that world "relates and separates men at the same time" (ibid., 52):

> To live together in the world means essentially that a world of things is between those who have it in common, as a table is located between those who sit around it; the world, like every in-between, relates and separates men at the same time.
>
> (Ibid.)

The dilemma for research then is in reconciling this idea that without "a common sense" (ibid.), a shared experience, we are merely driven back on our own subjective experiences without the critical possibility of populating one's senses with the perspectives and perceptions of the plural world. Finally, from her analysis of human beings in *The Human Condition* as creatures who *act,* even if those actions can create danger as much as overcome it, one can take the idea that new beginnings are always possible even when societies seem intransigent and culture stagnating. 'Acting in concert,' as the young performers did, remains thinkable.

THE SOCIAL AND THE THEATRICAL IMAGINARY: THE POSSIBILITIES AND RESPONSIBILITIES OF UNDERSTANDING AS RESEARCHERS

Ms. K: *If you come across children who are actually working from six o'clock in the morning until eleven o'clock, twelve o'clock they go back to their homes, finish off their own housework, chores, then they come to school. From school at six o'clock they are going back to their work places, and at nine o'clock, reaching back home. So after nine o'clock I think they hardly find time to study because they are too tired, so, whatever they are studying is within the school day. So, I think if they are attending classes and they give—attendance is good, healthy attendance here—so whatever their academic achievement, I think it's all because of their good attendance, because most of them are working as domestic workers. And it's all physical labour. So they get physically tired. So we can't expect them to, you know, read a lot, and do a lot of homework. So, you know, we try to help them to study well in school; all*

> *expectations that they will not find time at home. I think a few will find one hour, some will study for two hours, but not more than two hours study they can find at home. At times their parents do not allow them to study. They say, "Why are you studying? Why don't you do the household work?" So these types of problems they are facing at home.*
>
> *(Prerna School, Interview January 20th, 2012)*

For Canadian feminist philosopher Lorraine Code (2006), "ecological thinking," or ideal co-habitation, relies heavily on the social imaginary. The social imaginary, she (ibid., 30–31) writes

> is social in the broadest sense: it is . . . about the kinds of habitat and living conditions that are within reach and/or worth striving for; about social-political-economic organization and the just distribution of goods, privileges, power, and authority.

Code remains indebted to Castoriadis, who himself owes much to Aristotle, in juxtaposing the importance of an *instituting* rather than an *instituted* imaginary. An instituting imaginary can interrogate the social structure to "destabilize its pretentions to naturalness and wholeness, to initiate new meaning" (ibid., 31). Code insists that the instituting imaginary is a vehicle of radical social critique; it requires thinking and acting away from received conceptions of knowledge, subjectivity, responsibility and agency (ibid., 33).

Considering the relationship between a social imaginary, then, and a theatrical one, becomes central to the looming question of whether, or how, dramatic and improvisational work bears any significant relationship to the development of a social imaginary that might break open, or alter in any way, the oppressive material social order within which many young women in India currently reside. Bertolt Brecht (1977, 19) asked, in his play *The Measures Taken and Other Lehrstueke*, "Taught only by reality, can reality be changed?" Brecht's own solution was to create a distancing effect, to make things strange and less familiar, in order to use theatre to question reality. Castoriadis talks about shaking epistemology free and preparing a way for a "regenerative imaginary" (cited in Code, 2006, 33). When we watched the girls perform their short scenes, we became obsessed with the question of whether such theatrical exploration could provoke any kind of change at all given the micro-oppressions of their daily lives and the constant assaults on their experiences of gender and caste/class. Now, much depends on what counts as change here. There can be subtle but sometimes also enormous changes in individual girls, their sense of personal strength and courage. There are also changes in their sense of solidarity and community. But none of this guarantees greater social transformation, although it is typically held out as the ultimate goal. We asked Ms. K how she understood the role that drama might be playing in the 'real' lives of the girls:

Kathleen: *One of the other cornerstones of the school is drama, and obviously, the use of drama in socially engaged ways. So what are your perceptions of the role of drama in the lives of these girls?*

Ms. K: *I think they have usually taken up issues, which are very closely related to their lives. They have not taken any play which has not touched any one angle of their life, be it domestic violence, be it early marriage, be it drunken father, be it exploitative father, be it sexual abuse problem—they have almost tried to touch almost all the problems they face, and at times, they are the ones that are writing the script, and then they find those plays very close to them, their lives. And when they are enacting, you can find that it is, you know, the real self that is enacting them.*

Kathleen: *In your experience as a psychologist, would you understand that to be therapy, or therapeutic?*

Ms. K: *It has empowered them. It has really empowered them because you know by enacting the problems, they have enacted the solutions also to it. And from that solution they have actually found solutions to their own problems.*

Kathleen: *Yeah.*

Ms. K: *So it has actually, so it has, it has got some therapeutic values also.*

Kathleen: *So it's like a rehearsal—*

Ms. K: *Yeah.*

Kathleen: *—for the solution that you might enact in your life.*

Ms. K: *For sure. And if they do not find a solution, they try to put suggestions into it as to what they would like. So they really feel like this is what they want in life.*

(Prerna School, Interview January 20th, 2012)

The girls were not, in our observation, relying on distance but on proximity in their drama explorations. They were using stories in order to try out solutions, as Ms. K explains. We knew from conversations that some girls who had attempted to put their dramatic solutions to work in their real lives had encountered further marginalization from family. One young woman, Kushboo, now lives with her grandmother, having been banished from her father's home because of ideas about further education she began to express at home. The risks for such experiments and flights of imagination were great, we learned. But still, the pull towards performing together and critiquing their experiences remained powerful for the young women we spoke with in the year 12 class.

Some further thinking about 'the real' may be useful here. For a long time now, I have been thinking about the place of performance in engendering dialogue and in some instances, performance as an invitation to discuss the unspeakable. Madeleine Grumet (1990, 101) has described the power of art in the following way:

> The artist, on the other hand, admits the relation to the object that the scientist represses. That is the message of Henry James's artist in "The Real Thing" (1893/1979). After struggling in vain to illustrate a text on the aristocracy by working with authentic models, the artist finally has his servants pose, and it is their perception of class difference that strikes the gestures he draws. His canvas depicts a relationship to the phenomenon rather than a display of the thing itself.

The 'real' of what we witnessed with the girls was their illustration of *their relationship* to their lives, not their 'real lives.' Like James's work above, their performances depicted a relationship to, or reflection on, a phenomenon rather than a mere display or reproduction of it. Their own phenomenological experiences were housed inside the performance and we came to speak of reality through those symbolic representations of it. Elin Diamond (1997, 66) describes performance as always "a doing and a thing done." It is both something that describes certain embodied acts in specific sites, but it is also therefore a very complex way to see. In addition, such a performance, through its economy of expression and play with the senses, also points to the politics and contexts beyond its own specificities. The performance always exceeds in the abstract that which it symbolizes in the concrete.

What is further important both to our research and to understanding how performance communicates to an audience is the fact of its collective representation. Collaboratively created and executed, we watched the young women share the storytelling through performance. Cultural theorist Richard Sennett (2012) in his new book, *Together: The Rituals, Pleasures and Politics of Cooperation,* illustrates the power of cooperation and makes the argument that there are models of working, an architecture of cooperation, that may establish political togetherness in the wider public sphere. Using the historical model of the Renaissance workshop, he argues that the nub of cooperation "is active participation rather than passive presence" (ibid., 233), and this demanding sort of cooperation is not a given but *earned* in a rehearsal or theatre-making process. It may also, he further argues, lay the groundwork for complex cooperation later in life. Ms. K's sense of how the girls were manipulating drama to 'try out' solutions made good sense to us; theatre as a rehearsal for real social relations is not a new idea. But our own implication in this process, or the immediate question of how we should ethnographically understand what we were witnessing—and respond in a way that *contributed something*—was never far from our minds.

Many feminist scholars have critiqued empathy, as an emotional or political response. Megan Boler (1997), for example, strongly argues that passive empathy, promoted as a bridge between differences, is not a sufficient educational practice. Educational theatre has a long history of such forms of apolitical consumption of the Other's story in an effort to empathize or even sympathize with the Other, as some moral theorists advocate (see, for example, Smith, 1982, cited in Sennett, 2012). The imagination, in these cases, is often called upon to make a leap so that something that seems so distant, so 'other,' becomes knowable. We were well aware of these dangers, as Western white, privileged women being 'moved' by the plight of raced and classed bodies as they performed their enslavement for us. Deleuze (1988, 126) asks the question before us most clearly: "How can a being take another being into its world, but while preserving or respecting the other's own relations and world?" Although I have also been very critical of empathy as a response, Sennett offers some new (to me) thinking about empathy that may leave open the possibility for critical responsiveness that preserves and respects the other's own relations and world. The politics of power remain intact, of course, as do all the ways in which our responses as human beings and as researchers can go seriously wrong. But the following articulation has made the possibility of productively witnessing another's struggles, across political and cultural gulfs, more imaginable to me.

Sennett (2012, 21) writes, "Both sympathy and empathy convey recognition, and both forge a bond, but the one is an embrace, the other an encounter. Sympathy overcomes differences through imaginative acts of identification; empathy attends to another person on his or her own terms." He goes on to write that empathy is the more demanding exercise and has political application:

> As a philosophic matter, sympathy can be understood as one emotional reward for the thesis-antithesis-synthesis play of dialectic. . . . Empathy is more linked to dialogic exchange; though curiosity sustains the exchange, we don't experience the same satisfaction of closure, of wrapping things up.
>
> (Ibid., 22)

The impulse to engage when we are moved, to respond when others share so unguardedly with us, to contribute something useful, is an understandable one. What purpose might we serve as a presence in the lives of distant others?

Once again, Hannah Arendt offers a critical insight. Her ideas of training the imagination to "go visiting" or populating one's imagination with a cast of characters is tremendously useful here. Arendt's (1982) notion of "visiting" others' stories, as opposed to simply consuming them, provides an opening. The story, she argues, presses its audience to "go visiting"; the visitor is invited to converse with the perspectives he/she finds, to consider how they are different from his/her own, rather than to simply assimilate them (Gallagher, 2011). More importantly, her call to "think without a banister" (Arendt, 1979) is especially relevant to our purposes because it signals a way of proceeding in which critical categories are not imposed on, but inspired by, one's engagement with a phenomenon (Disch, 1994, 144).

Thinking without traditional concepts, or in our case cultural, gendered and racial stereotypes of youth, is seeing past the categories and formulas that are deeply ingrained in our minds (Arendt, 1979). She argues that the world of visiting is twofold: It distances the visitor from the familiar and takes her/him to standpoints that are unfamiliar. This move would be familiar to those who take comfort in traditional understandings of empathy but Arendt further challenges the notion of neutrality or transcendence that such a move might promise. Rather than a presumed and easy slippage into equality between teller and listener, Arendt signals a kind of practical equality of concern. More recently, the work of Stein (1989, 6) defines empathy as "acts in which foreign experience is comprehended." Stein (ibid., 19) stresses that it is not a matter of having the same feeling as someone else and then attributing that feeling to that person. Instead, from the outset, one experiences the feeling *as* hers. As Arendt describes visiting as "twofold," Stein (ibid.) describes the "two-sidedness" of empathy: we have an experience of our own that "announces" another experience as someone else's.

Elizabeth Spelman (1988), in *Inessential Woman: Problems of Exclusion in Feminist Thought*, warns of a "boomerang perception" that erases otherness, making assimilationist assumptions about the other. Arendt, by contrast, is speaking about making an "other" of ourselves. In interpreting her complex notion of "visiting," Lisa Jane Disch (1994) puts forward the paradox of "situated impartiality" (162) in an attempt to name the elusive critical position that is achieved by visiting. Arendt, in various works, speaks of being and thinking as yourself from a place that is not home. Rather than empathy, then, Arendt's visiting, or what Disch has called "situated impartiality" is, as I understand it, a way to not see with others' eyes, or through standing in the shoes of another (as is commonly used metaphorically in the theatre), but attempting to visit, that is, to see someone else's position through your own eyes. In other words, where empathy can conflate difference, visiting makes it central. Arendt helped us to understand that whereas human differences are irreducible, there is still reason to believe that communication can occur. And where communication is successful, change remains possible. The finer points of Arendtian philosophy could be taken much further still than I have begun here, but what this understanding opens up is the possibility for an empathic response that does not erase power imbalances but proposes a justice made more imaginable because of the public sharing of stories across gulfs of understanding, the practical equality of concern.

TO CONCLUDE

Kathleen: *I want to ask if you have any questions for us? Is there anything that you would like to know? About young people in Canada, or Toronto, or drama or about anything at all. Do you have any questions for us?*

Laxmi: Yes, I have question. What have you observed from our school?
Kathleen: From your school?
Laxmi: Yeah.
Kathleen: [laughter] It's a very good question. It will take three hours to answer.
Girls: Three hours!
Kathleen: I think I will say one thing, because I've learned many, many, many, many things.
[laughter]
Kathleen: I think I've learned that school can be a very creative and imaginative and loving place. Sometimes in schools that we go to in Toronto, there are some very good teachers, but the school is an institution. *It doesn't put young people at the centre. And here, we're aware, that you are always the centre, the most important thing; more important than books, more important than curriculum, more important than exams. And at home, sometimes, schools forget that the students are the most important and need to be at the centre of every decision. I think I saw that here. I knew it, before, from conversations, but I couldn't imagine it until I was here. So that's a big observation that I've made, that it's possible; it's possible to do that. And schools in North America, they make excuses in order to not put the student at the centre. They make excuses. And they could do better. They could do what you do here.*
Poonam: *It's the same in India.*
Kathleen: *It's the same in India. At other schools. Yeah. Yeah, I believe so. Now I have an ideal in my head. I have an imaginary. I won't accept it anymore. If the school says, "That's too difficult, we can't do that, we have to do it this way," I will think it's not too difficult to do it that way.*
[The girls speak in Hindi to each other]
Laxmi and Poonam [together]: *Thank you.*
(Prerna student focus group interview, January 21, 2012)

The stories and the dramas that were shared with us at Prerna achieved an amplitude that mere ethnographic information could not have. We arrived with a fair amount of knowledge, but with much less understanding. Hannah Arendt ([1958] 1998, 50), in her many reflections on the public realm, argues forcefully that "appearance—something that is seen and heard by others as well as by ourselves—constitutes reality." She goes on to argue that all of our experiences and senses lead an "uncertain, shadowy kind of existence until they are transformed, deprivatized and deindividualized, as it were, into a shape to fit them for public appearance. The most current of such transformations occurs in storytelling and generally in artistic transposition of individual experiences" (ibid., 50). The performances of the girls at Prerna asked us to enter into their standpoints, as well as the circumstances that had given rise to them. It was also important that this critical thinking on their part and our own remain public. We left with a hope for still greater understanding. We also came away with some new ideas about ourselves, our local Toronto sites, and with a sense of the daunting task of global ethnographic work. Stuart Poyntz (2013, 9), in making the argument that strangers are an inspiring feature of modern democracies, offers a beautiful and relevant insight about these 'stranger' encounters:

> Strangers signify plurality, horizons of otherness through which young people's eyes begin to see more widely. Stranger hospitality invites serendipity into one's world, the promise of surprise that reminds us that things needn't be as they seem. Strangers pull us out of a state of being into a state of becoming because new people and new situations bring different parts of ourselves into view.

We further came away from these in-person encounters with more knowledge of gendered experiences in modern day India, teetering towards some thoughts about our responsibility to those experiences both in the immediacy of the relationships we had made and in the subsequent work our research might do for audiences it would encounter.

Arendt, as I have argued, thought that storytelling helps us to feel less at home in the familiar world. Here, we were in an unfamiliar world, feeling connected in ways we had not anticipated. Yet, there was no way for us to inhabit their world, although drama had called on us to see it in its starkness. The young women we met wished to connect with us, to create an encounter through their stories; they invited us into a world we could not know. Our critical categories were challenged as we were invited to engage with the lives and phenomena we encountered. Always aware of the imbalances of social power, the dialogues we engaged in brought nonetheless a humanity to our work which is not to be underestimated. Experiencing someone else's experiences *as belonging to them* is a radically important conception of humanizing research in the current moment of global social and economic instability and, some would argue, renewed and strengthened forms of imperialism. In her 1968 work, *Men in Dark Times*, Arendt (25) argues that storytelling—talking of our world—is of value because it is

> concerned with the common world which remains 'inhuman' in a very literal sense unless it is constantly talked about by human beings. For the world is not humane just because it is made by human beings, and it does not become humane just because human voice sounds in it, but only when it has become the object of discourse. However much we are affected by the things of the world, however deeply they may stir and stimulate us, they become human for us only when we can discuss them

> with our fellows. . . . We humanize what is going on in the world and in ourselves only by speaking of it, and in the course of speaking of it we learn to be human.

Called then to respond to the girls' accounts of their world—from the Latin respondēre: to promise in return, reply, answer, to pledge—we also re-find ourselves, our humanity, and re-examine our world. As we create knowledge from this encounter and move forward with research ideas, our basic understandings of processes of globalization have been valuably interrupted by the theatrical and social imaginaries of young women who escorted us through their worlds and their rehearsals for imagined worlds. We have teetered between hope and empathy, but a cooler empathy achieved through dialogic exchange, and a hope that grew from our practices of 'visiting,' our 'situated impartiality' that allowed us to see with our own eyes the perspectives and lived worlds of others.

A return to Appiah's (2006) question about our responsibility to strangers is especially appropriate for researchers interested in youth and their phenomenological experiences in a world of growing inequality, economic polarization and social dislocation. The problem of cross-cultural communication, he writes, can seem very difficult in theory when we are trying to imagine making sense of a stranger in the abstract:

> But the great lesson of anthropology is that when the stranger is no longer imaginary, but real and present, sharing a human social life, you may like or dislike him, you may agree or disagree; but, if it is what you both want, you can make sense of each other in the end.
>
> (Ibid., 99)

NOTE

1. Anne Wessels is a doctoral candidate and one of the research assistants on the project.

REFERENCES

Ahmed, Sara. *The Cultural Politics of Emotion*. New York: Routledge, 2004.

Appiah, Anthony Kwame. *Cosmopolitanism: Ethics in a World of Strangers*. New York: W.W. Norton and Company, 2006.

Arendt, Hannah. *Men in Dark Times*. New York: Harcourt Brace Jovanovich, 1968.

———. *Hannah Arendt: The Recovery of the Public World*. Edited by Melvyn Hill. New York: St. Martin's Press, 1979.

———. *Lectures on Kant's Political Philosophy*. Edited by Ronald Beiner. Chicago: University of Chicago Press, 1982.

———. *The Human Condition*. 2nd ed. Chicago: The University of Toronto Press, (1958) 1998.

Benhabib, Seyla. *Situating the Self: Gender, Community, and Post-Modernism in Contemporary Ethics*. New York: Routledge, 1992.
Boler, Megan. "The Risks of Empathy: Interrogating Multiculturalism's Gaze." *Cultural Studies* 11, no. 2, 1997. 253–273.
Brecht, Bertoldt. *The Measures Taken and Other Lehrstuecke*. London: Methuen, 1977.
Canovan, Margaret. Introduction to the second edition of *The Human Condition,* by Hannah Arendt. Chicago: The University of Toronto Press, (1958) 1998.
Code, Lorraine. *Ecological Thinking: The Politics of Epistemic Location*. New York: Oxford University Press, 2006.
Cohen-Cruz, Jan. "Personal Storytelling as Social Intervention," in *Drama as Social Intervention*. Edited by Michael Balfour and John Somers, 12–25. Concord: Captus Press, 2006.
Deleuze, Gilles. *Spinoza: Practical Philosophy*. Translated by Robert Hurley. San Francisco: City Lights, 1988.
Diamond, Elin. *Unmaking Mimesis: Essays on Feminism and Theatre*. London and New York: Routledge, 1997.
Disch, Lisa Jane. *Hannah Arendt and the Limits of Philosophy*. Ithaca and London: Cornell University Press, 1994.
Gallagher, Kathleen. "In Search of a Theoretical Basis for Storytelling in Education Research." *International Journal of Research and Method in Education* 33, no. 1, 2011. 49–61.
Grumet, Madeleine. "On Daffodils That Come Before the Swallow Dares," in *Qualitative Inquiry in Education: The Continuing Debate*. Edited by Elliot Eisner and Alan Peshkin. New York and London: Teachers College Press, 1990.
hooks, bell. *Yearning*. Boston: South End Press, 1990.
Jayawardena, Kumari. "Chapter 6, Women, Social Reform, and Nationalism in India," in *Feminism and Nationalism in the Third World*. Edited by Kumari Jayawardena, 73–108. London: Zed Books, (1986) 1994.
Potaminanou, Anna. *Hope: A Shield in the Economy of Borderline States*. Translated by Philip Slotkin. London: Routledge, 1997.
Poyntz, Stuart R. "Eyes Wide Open: Stranger Hospitality and the Regulation of Youth Citizenship." *Journal of Youth Studies* 16, no. 7, 2013. 864–880.
Ratcliffe, Matthew. "Phenomenology as a Form of Empathy." *Inquiry: An Interdisciplinary Journal of Philosophy* 55, no. 5, 2012. 473–495.
Salverson, Julie. "Change on Whose Terms? Testimony and Erotics of Injury." *Theatre* 31, no. 3, 2001. 119–125.
Sennett, Richard. *Together: The Rituals, Pleasures and Politics of Cooperation*. New London: Yale University Press, 2012.
Smith, Adam. *The Theory of Moral Sentiments*. Indianapolis: Liberty Press, 1982.
Spelman, Elizabeth. *Inessential Woman: Problems of Exclusion in Feminist Thought*. Boston: Beacon University Press, 1988.
Stein, Edith. *On the Problem of Empathy*. Translated by Waltraut Stein. Washington, DC: ICS Publications, 1989.
Vij, Shivam. "A Journey to a Casteless Society." *The New York Times International Weekly* (New Delhi, India), October 14, 2012.

4 Relational Phenomenology and the Politics of Global Urban Youth Research

Clovis Bergère and Lauren Silver

> Such losses generate their own markers, first the telling yellow tape, then maybe graffiti on a nearby abandoned building. As much as they become a part of the local landscape, such signs remain largely invisible to outsiders, whose momentary experience is more likely to come in a fleeting headline than in a physical encounter.
>
> (Howard Gillette, 2013, in reference to the homicides in Camden, NJ)

I cannot forget the image as I peered across the pews. In synchrony, I witnessed several young males, Marqui's classmates, with their palms forming an encasing to rest and cover their faces. Backs crouched and faces laid down in unison. Bowed heads created a predictable absence in rows of bodies pressed closely side-by-side. I could feel the warmth of the young man, who sat beside me, his arm pushed against mine. I recognized this recent high school graduate, even though I did not know him well. Yet here we were, pressed uncomfortably close. His face was also lowered. The weight struck me as heavy, and the shame remained encased in the privacy of self-seclusion amidst community—mourning.

A female student sitting in front of me pressed her tear-stained face into the arm of the girl next to her—gasps and sobs escaped from the young ladies in hurried episodes amidst an exchange of tissues. Somehow, I expected these expressions and they seemed more predictable to me than the hidden faces of the young men. I noticed one female teacher trying to comfort a teenage boy, as she moved into his space and quickly pulled his face up from his hands so that she could embrace him. I wondered whether the intrusion was welcomed or tolerated by the youth.

I have never done this before.

I felt absent and on display, as I looked at Marqui's body—exposed and still, even as it was covered in a fine suit. I paid my final respects, moving through the line. How did I feel? I know I held my hand over my heart but no tears escaped. I was distinctly aware of my whiteness

> and was self-conscious, as I wondered whether I even belonged there. I had never been to a funeral for a youth, let alone a murdered youth.
>
> (Scenario in Camden, NJ, US, recalled by Lauren Silver)

Marqui's life, like the lives of too many youth of color in Camden, NJ, in the United States, had ended through a gunshot. Lauren had come to know Marqui as an ethnographic researcher at the local high school from which he had graduated. "He was in the wrong place at the wrong time," echoed teachers and students in the week that followed Marqui's murder and preceded his funeral. The local media represented the motive as unknown. A male classmate and friend who graduated with Marqui exclaimed in disbelief, "This wasn't supposed to happen to one of us, and definitely not to Marqui." The local media, as well as Marqui's teachers and friends, had recognized him as a youth who showed promise—charismatic and well liked, he was supposed to become a music mogul or an entrepreneur. The two opening pieces, a quote from Howard Gillette and Lauren's recounted scenario, point to an insider–outsider dynamic. The phenomenology of tragedy also reveals tensions and gradations in the encounter. As a researcher with the local high school, Lauren did not know Marqui well outside of the research context. She grappled with whether it was appropriate for her to witness such intense intimacy and pain. She felt like an outsider; yet, school staff granted her with the privilege to witness a community's mourning. Had she 'earned' this privileged sight?

In this chapter, we draw on specific examples from our fieldwork with urban youth in Camden, New Jersey (NJ) in the United States, and Labé and Conakry in Guinea, West Africa, in order to explore what we term the 'politics of encounter' in ethnographic research. In doing so, we are guided theoretically by relational phenomenology, a broadly conceived set of philosophical writings that both foreground our sensitive experience of the world and place our encounter with the world at the center of analysis. To borrow French phenomenologist Emmanuel Levinas's phrase, we are trying to both "account for the unaccountable" (Levinas, 1998, 112) whilst retaining our gazes firmly on the politics and unequal power relations that traverse the worlds we research as well as the research encounters themselves. We use phenomenology as "neither a school of thought nor a set of dogmas" (Jung, 1996, 1) but rather as a set of invitations and theoretically produced openings. In reflecting on the methodological and ethical dimensions of conducting research with young people in environments characterized by extreme urban poverty and inequality, we ask: What can phenomenology tell us about the politics of encounter in global, urban youth research? And, more importantly, how can we somehow do—a little more—justice to those lived experiences we claim to describe?

We organize the chapter theoretically, paying attention to key aspects of relational phenomenology. As such, we begin with a discussion of the contexts of our field sites, and then describe our theoretical encounter with the 'field.' Specifically, we consider how phenomenology invites us to move away from narrowly defined notions of the field to consider a more dynamic relationship with an ever-changing field. Phenomenologically, the research field appears 'in between,' in the relational space that is momentarily constituted between the academic researcher and the bodies, structures and things that make up the 'field.' This phenomenological approach clearly favors the inclusion of both traditional forms of ethnographic narration and invites us to consider less structured ways of writing field notes as well as visual methods of collecting data.

In the second part, we turn our attention to the idea of the "transversal" (Schrag, 1994) in phenomenology and how it can shed new light on the increasingly global assemblages created through doing research. We follow phenomenology's radical invitation to foreground the moment of encounter in order to explore ethical and moral dilemmas of conducting ethnographic research in contexts of inequality. Here Levinas's notion of the "trace" (Levinas, 1998; Kleinberg-Levin, 2009) provides a surprisingly powerful tool for engaging with the complex politics of encounter and the intimate aspects of academic research. We conclude by reflecting on phenomenologically inspired avenues to share our research with the youth participants that have shared with us their daily lives. Here, we problematize the notion of 'giving back' and also propose fruitful ideas on collaboration.

GLOBAL SOUTH AND 'SOUTHERN NORTH': THE SHARED URBANITIES AND EXPERIENCES OF YOUTH

Spanning across the Atlantic, in West Africa and North America, our exploration of research encounters takes a decidedly global turn. On one hand, Camden, NJ (the site of Lauren's research on identities and urban education), is a mid-sized US city situated in the southern part of New Jersey, across the Delaware River from Philadelphia. In recent decades, it has earned a solid and distressing reputation as America's poorest and most dangerous city with violent crime rates more than five times the national average, and rising (CQ Press, 2013). Once a thriving industrial center, home of the Recording Corporation of America (RAC Victor) and the Campbell Soup Company, Camden, NJ, has lost nearly half of its population since it peaked at 125,000 in 1950 (Gillette, 2005). Camden's demographic shift reflects what is now a sadly familiar narrative of 'white flight' and industrial decline in many US cities. On the other hand, Conakry and Labé (the sites of Clovis's research on street corners and informal youth spaces), are two of Guinea's most populous cities with respective populations of 1.9 million for Conakry, the country's capital, and 110,000 for Labé, a rapidly growing urban center at the heart of the Foutah-Djallon highland region in the center of Guinea (Diallo, 2002, 5). Like Camden, NJ, these Guinean cities are characterized by extreme poverty, services dysfunction and increasing insecurity, particularly in the case of Conakry. Yet, their recent demographic trajectories are shaped by different, if equally tragic, forces including colonization and global economic turmoil.

Given the vast historical, geographical and demographic differences between these contexts, our examples might seem to bring together urban settings that are too diverse to be discussed meaningfully together. Yet, when we foreground our sensitive experiences of these diverse locales—and here we are following one of phenomenology's most fundamental invitations—many links can be drawn between these sites (Mendieta, 2001). For instance, driving through Camden, NJ, Lauren observes abandoned and crumbling buildings and urban prairies taking over much of the space outside the main thoroughfares. She experiences the particular ethos of a place that has been siphoned off from the North, so to speak—abandoned by institutions of commerce, culture and education that sustain 'other' global cities. While making her way, she wonders about the daily experiences, hopes and visions of youth who live and grow up in this 'Southern North.'

Experientially, the often seemingly insurmountable divide between the so-called cities of the global North and South are often crossed. This crossing happens both ways: Not only do places in the North assume characteristics more typically associated with the South, including services dysfunction, endemic poverty or the dominance of the informal sector, but the phenomenology of everyday life also reaches across global boundaries from cities in the South to the global North. For instance, looking at photographs taken by Guinean youth of an illegal festival held on the outskirts of Conakry brings to the fore Clovis's own experiences attending illegal outdoor parties in Europe (see Figure 4.1).

Experientially, complex worlds and assemblages come together in 'dialectically enriching' ways: the pounding music, the excitement of the journey out of the city to vacant lots, and the incessant buzz of illegality, bring colliding together two worlds. Holding them in conversation and tension with each other is a way of responding to phenomenology's invitation to foreground our subjective experiences of the world. It can also raise new questions for research. In this case, for instance, new practical and theoretical questions emerged from the global conversation: What can be learned about the changing statuses of youth in urban Guinea and London (where Clovis worked at the time)? What is the role of autonomy in urban reproduction and change? And, more practically, what have the institutional responses been to these illicit gatherings of youth (Bergère, 2011)? In drawing on examples from our research in both the global South and 'Southern North,' we are responding practically to phenomenology's invitation to foreground the increasingly globalized experiences of everyday urban life. We also raise new questions for research that take into account the increasingly global politics of the research process itself.

Figure 4.1 Conakry youth celebrating New Year's Eve 2011. Credits: Clovis Bergère

RESEARCH OUTSIDES: METHODOLOGICAL FAILURES OR MEANINGFUL MOMENTS?

The process of doing urban research in the social sciences is typically implemented as systematic engagements, which include surveys, interviews (whether open-ended or structured), focus groups, or increasingly, various forms of tracking and mapping activities that rely on visual and audio data. Through these methods, anthropologists, sociologists and specialists in urban studies have been able to precisely map, deconstruct or historicize the everyday workings and structural forces that shape the urban landscape. Researchers document the raging inequalities that continue to plague urban residents' lives or explain cities' interactions with global flows of capital, people and information. Yet, when reflecting on the process of doing research, our attention is often drawn outside of these formal and systematic engagements, or at least, these encounters with research participants are recalled in distinct ways from the research monograph. In addition to the objective data and scientific explanations, research activities are made up of more experiential impressions, fleeting moments, smells, hand gestures and textures that somehow linger on long after we have left the field.

Sometimes, when we engage over the long-term, we find ourselves invited to leave our 'researcher' persona and share happy and tragic moments with the community we are studying. Furthermore, scholars note that unplanned events and peripheral relationships can turn out to be highly meaningful moments in the research process (Rabinow, 1977, 143; Thrift, 2003, 125; Simone, 2004, 23; Michael, 2012). In other words, research encounters often throw us into unpredictable situations, as well as ethical dilemmas. These moments may initially appear as failures in research. Yet, it is often in these unplanned encounters that new meanings emerge and our research takes new turns. As such, these events should not be disassociated from the process of research itself. Michael's (2012) work on the anecdote is particularly instructive as a resource here, which foregrounds unplanned—and often catastrophic or embarrassing—research 'failures.' These incidents "seem to demand to be told" (ibid., 26).

The funeral of Marqui in Camden, NJ, recounted above, is clearly too tragic and unfortunately too common an event in this city to qualify as an anecdote. Yet, clearly, similar to an anecdote, it is a story that 'demands to be told,' an image that as researchers we 'cannot forget.' Unplanned, the experience cannot somehow be shaken off, put to the side so that the proper research process can continue. It is a haunting experience that needs to be accounted for. Phenomenological thinking, here, invites us to reflect both epistemologically and practically on ways of accounting for what may appear truly 'unaccountable.' Premised on the distinction—first made by Kant—between 'phenomena,' objects as we come to know them through human sensibility, and 'noumena,' objects as *things-in-themselves* that we cannot directly experience, phenomenology insists on taking into account, even foregrounding, our sensitive and often pre-objective experience of the world. As such, it is in many ways a reaction against the excess of Cartesian rationalism. For instance, for Merleau-Ponty (1964, 147, emphasis in original):

> This rationalism seems so full of myths to us: the myth of *laws of nature* vaguely situated halfway between norms and facts, and *according to which,* it was thought, this nevertheless blind world has been constructed; the myth of *scientific explanation,* as if knowledge of relations, even extended to all observable phenomena, could one day transform the very existence of the world into an analytic and self-evident proposition.

At the heart of this statement is the idea that our engagement with the world cannot be reduced to a dualism between the world as an object and us as subjects. As bodies in the world, our experience of the world is first pre-objective, before it can be narrated or rationally explained. What this points to is a much more dynamic, almost 'kinetic,' relation between the social agent and the world or, by extension, between the academic researcher and the field. Levinas (1998, 166), following Merleau-Ponty, points to a "pre-original reason that does not proceed from any initiative of the subject, an anarchic reason." Bourdieu—perhaps a strange bed-fellow for phenomenology—has also drawn extensively on Merleau-Ponty's notion of a pre-objective level of experience, a notion that posits the body and "practical sense" at the heart of our encounter with the world (Bourdieu and Wacquant, 1992, 19). For Bourdieu, this indicates an "ontological complicity" or "mutual possession" between us as academic researchers and the field. As Bourdieu and Wacquant note, Merleau-Ponty's example of the soccer field is here worth quoting at length:

> For the player in action the soccer field is not an 'object,' that is, the ideal term which can give rise to an indefinite multiplicity of perspectival views and remain equivalent under its apparent transformations. It is pervaded with lines of force (the 'yard lines'; those which demarcate the 'penalty area') and is articulated into sectors (for example, the 'openings' between the adversaries) which call for a certain mode of action and which initiate and guide the action as if the player were unaware of it. The field is itself not given to him, but present as the immanent term of his practical intentions; the player becomes one with it and feels the direction of the 'goal' for example, just as immediately as the vertical and the horizontal planes of his own body. It would not be sufficient to say that consciousness inhabits this milieu. At this moment consciousness is nothing other than the dialectic of milieu and action. Each maneuver undertaken by the player modifies the character of the field and establishes new lines of forces in which the action in turns unfolds and is accomplished, again altering the phenomenal field.
>
> (1963, 168–169, as cited in Bourdieu and Wacquant, 1992, 21)

In approaching the field, we are drawn to certain events and occurrences which, before we can narrate it, we 'pre-recognize' as significant and meaningful. There is obviously something dangerous in presenting our encounter with the field as purely intuitive and smooth. Not all football players are good, and even the best ones have bad days. As the vignette shared above highlights, our engagement with the field is not always through flow and often much more jarring than perhaps suggested in Merleau-Ponty's soccer field analogy. Yet, Merleau-Ponty's quote above also points to a more complex understanding of our relation to the field. First of all, it clearly and powerfully recognizes the extent to which we are as much shaped by the field as we shape it, thus radically debunking the myth of the absolute (non-interfering) methodological design. Review boards and other such institutional controls still all too often promote objective research designs as the only valid option (Stoller, 1997, xiii). Paying attention to our experiential impressions in the field is clearly very important, as is being responsive to those stories and unpredictable events that somehow 'need to be told.'

But the quote above also needs to be read in relation to the specificity of academic knowledge, and the extent to which it shapes—pre-objectively—our perception of the field. Just as the 'yard lines' constitute lines of force that guide the soccer player's actions, so does academic knowledge of social reproduction, institutional racism or global flows of capital constitute lines of force that guide our actions in the field even without our direct awareness. Again, Merleau-Ponty foregrounds the epistemological importance of perception. As Merleau-Ponty explains: "The vision is already inhabited by a significance which gives it a function in the spectacle of the world and in our existence" (1962, 52). Merleau-Ponty shows that a "wooden wheel placed in the ground is not, *for sight*, the same thing as a wheel bearing a load" (ibid.). Similarly, attending a murdered youth's funeral as a researcher with theories of urban inequalities, social reproduction and institutional racism as 'background' for our sense experience is not the same as attending as a friend, local resident or pastor.

In phenomenology, meaning occurs 'in the middle,' in the meeting of consciousness and its object. As such, phenomenology also points to the uniqueness and value of the particular meanings that occur in the encounter of a researcher's consciousness, which includes her or his 'academic' and 'non-academic' consciousness. The line between the two become increasingly blurred at a tragic event such as Marqui's funeral. In other words, academic discourses that give significance to the field also produce new and important meanings. Practically, this invitation to recognize the pre-objective dimensions of academic knowledge is also an invitation to complement more traditional research methods with other perhaps more experimental or experiential approaches. In recounting the tragic event of Marqui's funeral, Lauren chose to use a highly personal and subjective prose. This allowed her to engage with her own feelings and emotions with regard to the event.

Working with youth in Guinea, Clovis found the visual dimension of a photo-elicitation project particularly apt at foregrounding aspects of youths' experiences of urban environments that might have escaped even the youth themselves. He therefore worked with four youths from Labé and Conakry who documented over a seven-month period the spaces where they socialized. Of particular interest to the project was the location of informal meeting spaces and street corners, often ironically referred to as 'bureaux' or office in French. These highly fluid and spontaneously organized meeting spaces form a crucial and important part of Guinean urban youths' social, cultural and economic lives. They strategically invest overlooked parts of the urban fabric with their presence, desires and dreams of economic mobility.

The photographs created as part of the project yielded many surprises, some of them potential failures that turned out to become meaningful moments of research. For instance, one of the participants kept returning pictures to Clovis that represented young apprentices, including woodworkers, mechanics, electricians or welders at work. These photographs clearly were outside of the brief, which was to photograph the place where the young person himself was spending time and socializing. Yet, these pictures led to discussions regarding the changing status of youth, the role of class and continued relevance of traditional models of castes in Guinea. It revealed complex changes at play in urban Guinea where young men from traditionally dominant castes are not allowed to work manually in what is still often seen by elders as demeaning trades. As a consequence, they now find themselves largely unemployed. Photography provided a particularly fluid medium for capturing the young person's experience of the city as he navigated everyday youth spaces. His photographs seemed a consequence of his desire to share a particular aspect of life in urban Guinea. They also opened up many questions regarding generational change and youth employment in the country.

THE RELATIONALITY AND TRANSVERSALITY OF GLOBAL RESEARCH

In thinking about research encounters, American phenomenologist Calvin O. Schrag (1994) shifts our attention to the space of "communicative praxis," a space of meaning that takes shape in between, in the space of encounter with the other. Conceived transversely, research encounters in his work appear not as a succession of experiences but as a "lying across and folding over of a multiplicity of discursive and non-discursive practices" (ibid., 1994, 67). Schrag describes encounters as a coming together, folding into and across different discourses (academic, religious, or institutional), desires (professional, personal or spiritual), bodies, gestures and learned practices.

As a momentarily assembled configuration, the research encounter ceases to be either a vertically organized hierarchy—with one explanation better than the other—or a horizontal collection of particularized and relativized claims. The question moves from what is really going on here to how is it that these different views come to be in relation to a similar problem (ibid., 71). What can be learned from this particular configuration of theories, bodies, desires, practices and modes of thought? For instance, in an effort to document the global circulation of policy agendas, particularly those surrounding urban planning and youth policy, Clovis watched the daily newscast of the Radio Television de Guinée (RTG—November 30, 2010), focusing on a short piece of detailed reporting about a meeting that had just taken place in Labé. As part of an effort to improve the quality of provisions for youth, French aid workers invited the then Minister in charge of Youth Affairs and Sports, Thierno Aliou Diaoune, to meet with local youth workers in a week-long workshop on the 'rights of the child.' During the coverage of the meeting, the Youth and Sports Minister referred loosely to the recent political turmoil as well as to the more generalized issues of rampant inflation and the unaffordability of even basic goods such as rice and electricity. He explained:

> If we had *"animateurs"* everywhere, if we had *"Maisons des Jeunes"* everywhere, if we had spaces of exchanges everywhere, if we had places where young people could talk about themselves, talk about their experiences, talk about their difficulties, I swear that it would have attenuated what we have lived through here. This is why to me this particular training is important. It will enable you to obtain skills, and, within *"Maisons des Jeunes"* to be able to improve not only skills but also to offer more opportunities to young people so that they can exchange but also so that they can acquire positive behaviours.
>
> (Radio Television Guinée, November 30, 2010)

In many ways, this intervention proposed by the Youth and Sports Minister was fairly typical of mainstream policy discourses on African youth. These narratives construct youth as "lacking" (Simone, 2004; Bergère, 2011). What's more, Guineans and Guinean youth in particular rarely follow the daily newscast by the national RTG. They tend to view it as little more than government propaganda. As such, this little noticed report was hardly noteworthy. But it stood out to Clovis, an academically oriented observer of global policy processes and urbanization, in part because it coincided with a research episode, and together these moments became part of a highly meaningful and thought-provoking event.

At precisely the same time as Clovis was watching the news report, he received about twenty-five photographs taken by a young man from Labé as part of the photo-elicitation project described above (see Figure 4.2).

The photographs and subsequent conversations with the youth showed young men gathering, meeting, talking about "politics, women, the problems of society, and linked to these, the problems regarding the future of the country" (Photo-elicitation notes). In other words, these youth were doing precisely what the Youth and Sports Minister had claimed was missing in their daily lives: They had turned this vacant stretch of city into a 'space of exchange.' Ironically, this bureau was located just a few blocks away from where the Youth and Sports Minister was meeting with French aid workers and local youth workers.

This rather uncanny and unplanned research assemblage formed when these two scenarios came together in Clovis's view and responded to each other in interesting ways. This particular instance led Clovis's research into a different direction, as new questions emerged: How are young people's everyday experiences taken into account by the policies that are meant to shape their lives? What is the relationship between institutional desires and youths' everyday lives in the Guinean city? The Youth and Sports Minister was keen to use youth 'bureaux' when political support or bodies at rallies were needed. However, why did he ignore the presence and significance of these informal meeting spaces while planning with youth officials? Did youth simultaneously

Figure 4.2 Informal youth meeting space, Labé, Guinea. Credit: Clovis Bergère

inhabit several parallel times and spaces? How did the informality and fluidity that characterized these 'bureaux' play out in the multiple definitions of youth and the state? These were just a few of the new questions that arose from the particular assemblage at play in this example of visual research.

In a sense, Clovis's academically shaped perception of the field constituted both of these objects in new and meaningful ways, changing what could be known about them had they not been brought together into view. What started as an exploration of youth provision in Labé and Conakry suddenly raised broader questions with regard to the changing statuses of youth in the processes of urban (re)production and with regard to what has been referred to as the "bifurcated" state in Africa (Mamdani, 1996). As Merleau-Ponty (1962, 62) explains, we must not just practice philosophy but "realize the transformation which it brings with it in the spectacle of the world and in our existence."

THE POLITICS OF 'GIVING BACK'

Clearly, working in urban Guinea or Camden, NJ, we conduct research in places that are understood as needing intervention. The question then becomes what to do? Not only the fields themselves, but also the research flows are highly unequal—youth participants opened new ways for us to perceive their social worlds and to understand the effects of globalization. Yet, we have not been as forthcoming in sharing our academically informed meanings, which include structural analyses of conditions that shape both their lives and our own lives. Typically, this has then been framed as: How do we 'give back'? This question is in many ways flawed from the start, presuming a clear-cut and packaged form of academic knowledge that could somehow be gifted back. And typically the answers to this question have oscillated between two equally flawed positions: one known as the 'expert view,' which equates the particularities of the social scientist's view with privilege, and the other, a romanticized 'view from below.' The latter, in refusing the expert view, also ends up negating the specificity, and thus the value, of academic engagement with the world. The issues at stake become particularly clear when thinking about our specific research engagements.

"And the devil is here in Camden," exclaimed the preacher, as his eyes pierced and cut into the space. When Lauren attended the funeral of a murdered youth in Camden, NJ, the preacher declared that if this incident had been racially motivated, we would have been in the streets protesting. But, he maintained, this was one "brother" killing another. She could not help thinking that this indeed was the result of racism. Camden's situation as the poorest city in the United States, and with the highest murder rate, is part of a much broader narrative of racial segregation in America. Today Camden is a city disproportionately younger, poorer and darker than its whiter and much wealthier surrounding region.

Is the problem, then, that the preacher and most of the local residents in Camden, NJ, are so oppressed that they simply cannot see? Should our ethical commitment as researchers force us to 'tell' them? This is obviously the line defended by Bourdieu and also the 'scandal' (Nordmann, 2006) at the heart of his otherwise impeccable exposition of the social reproduction of inequality. For him, "It is because subjects do not know, strictly speaking, what they are doing, that what they do has more meaning than they realize" (Bourdieu, 1977, 175). Yet, there is something profoundly scandalous in positing the social determination not of opportunity but of capacity itself, a long-noted problem in Bourdieu's thought. This is, for instance, at the heart of De Certeau's critique of Bourdieu as evidenced in the quote below:

> In order for coherence to be the postulate of the ethnological knowledge, to be, that is, the place it allocated for itself and the epistemological model to which it referred, it was necessary to put this knowledge at a distance from the objectified society, and thus to presuppose that it was foreign and superior to the knowledge the society had of itself.
>
> (De Certeau, [1984] 2011, 56)

If we cannot accept morally the notion that Lauren's explanation of the situation is 'superior' or a better explanation than the preacher's, do we then have to accept the notion that what we see in Camden, NJ, is not racist because this is the view that emanates locally? If we accept this, however, what then is the role of the academic researcher? Do we limit our roles to 'giving a voice' as has so often been the mantra within our field of Childhood Studies?

There is something clearly implacable in Rancière's assertion that "it is the explicator who needs the incapable and not the other way around: it is he who constitutes the incapable as such" (Rancière 1991, 6). In response to Bourdieu's "sociologist king" (Rancière, 2004, 165), he proposes a pragmatic approach, one that offers to postulate equality in order to realize it. For Rancière, the belief in one's superiority dominates the social body and is at the heart of social reproduction. As he explains, it is not that those in a dominated position are incapable of seeing their positions, but rather that they come to accept their positions, are too conscious of social inequalities to even try to change them, and in response, practice a kind of 'self-exclusion.' As he (1991, 40) famously explained:

> [The] belief in intellectual inequality and in the superiority of one's own intelligence does not belong to scholars and distinguished poets alone. Its force comes from the fact that it embraces the entire population under the guise of humility. I can't, the ignorant one you are encouraging to teach himself declares; I am only a worker. Listen carefully to everything there is in that syllogism. First of all, "I can't" means "I don't want to; why would I make the effort?" Which also means: I undoubtedly could, for I am intelligent. But I am a worker: people like me can't; my neighbor can't. And what use would it be for me, since I have to deal with imbeciles?

Academic discourse then loses much of its specificity and ceases to expose invisible structural or external forces at work in shaping people's lives, but instead becomes a platform, a kind of megaphone. According to Rancière, it is not that urban youth, living in environments of poverty or violence, cannot see the reasons for their situations, it is just that they cannot be heard.

Understood as such, academic works should translate lives rather than offer interpretation. As Rancière (ibid., 9) put it:

> Understanding is never more than translating, that is, giving the equivalent of a text, but in no way its reason. There is nothing behind the written page, no false bottom that necessitates the work of an other intelligence, that of the explicator; no language of the master, no language of the language whose words and sentences are able to speak the reason of the words and sentences of a text.

And so, in many ways, Rancière offers a much more convincing view of philosophy and by extension academic discourse than Bourdieu's 'expert view.' Rancière's position clearly moves beyond trying to legitimize academic discourse as a better or deeper form of understanding, and in doing so, purposely celebrates intelligence everywhere it is found. Rancière challenges knowledge as the reserved domain of science or philosophy.

Still, we ask: Is there not something also overly romantic in pretending that social inequalities can be done away with so easily? And doesn't denying social sciences the right to explicate—not absolutely or totally but partially and contingently—also rid social sciences of any specificity? Here again, phenomenology invites us in complex and multiple ways to think beyond this dichotomous oscillation between the 'expert view' and an 'idealization' of politics offered by Rancière.

Phenomenology, at least as presented by Merleau-Ponty and Levinas, turns our attention dually to the centrality of perception and the experience of the research encounter itself. As we have seen, following Merleau-Ponty and Bourdieu, our research fields are crisscrossed by academically informed lines of force that guide our actions as researchers. But social research is also primarily made up of encounters with others, meetings with research participants. Complex relations and unequal flows of power transverse these encounters. These discrepancies are augmented when research takes place across global settings, in cities often at the receiving end of globalization. When working with children and youth, inequalities based around generational power and 'age class' structures further complicate the politics of the encounter. What then can we learn from thinking phenomenologically about the research encounter and its experience? Levinas's phenomenology of sociality and notion of the 'trace' are particularly instructive here.

At the heart of Levinas's philosophical reflection is the desire to account for the experience of radical alterity that comes from encountering another human being. Just as is Merleau-Ponty, Levinas (1998, 166) is interested in our pre-objective, corporeal and "anarchic" engagement with the world. For him, this constitutes a kind of "passivity incarnate," a sensibility that precedes all reflection, through which an "exigency" (ibid., 112) takes hold of our flesh. In the presence of the other, in coming into contact with her or his face, we are seized in our flesh and become "hostage" to a moral indictment to the other. As Levinas (1998, 166) notes:

> Proximity thus signifies a reason before thematization of signification by a thinking subject, before the assembling of terms in a present, a pre-original reason that does not proceed from any initiative of the subject, an anarchic reason. It is a reason before the beginning, before any present, for my responsibility for the other commands me before any decision, any deliberations.

Capturing this pre-narrative experience of a moral invitation to submit to the absolute priority of the other in many ways also entails attempting to describe that which is indescribable, that which "seems to withdraw from apprehension the closer and more intensely it is approached" (Kleinberg-Levin, 2009, 81). This experience of an un-representable alterity in the encounter with the other is what Levinas attempts to capture through the notion of the 'trace.' In the face of the other, "the face of the neighbor [that] obsesses [us]" (Levinas, 1998, 93), we encounter the "passage of a trace," an enticement to commit morally to the other, to submit to the "absolute ethical priority of the other" (Kleinberg-Levin, 2009, 105).

Thus, when Lauren attends Marqui's funeral and experiences the radical alterity of the preacher, she is at once confronted with the apparent incompatibility of his explanation with her own understanding of the tragic event, and somehow exposed sensibly to the preacher. In this encounter lies a 'trace,' an invitation. As this experience 'obsesses' her, she also feels a moral responsibility not to confront and obliterate his explanation, but to reflect upon and recognize it. What is key here is not to equate the 'trace' with a kind of 'natural benevolence' or 'divine instinct' as Levinas's concept has sometimes been misconstrued. Instead, the passage of the 'trace' requires work. Crucially, as such it does not sit somehow outside of history and society. As Kleinberg-Levin (2009, 112) notes, "Tracework is nothing but an opening," adding:

> It cannot be reduced to the totally present, an object of possession and knowledge, but demands of us an interminable effort to ground our lives nonetheless in an experience of its paradoxical order—a universality that commands its own transcendence in the name of the absolute singularity of the other.
>
> (Ibid.)

So, what might this invitation to work, and to follow our phenomenological experience of the 'trace,' look like on the ground? In Camden, NJ, Marqui had a vision for a youth corridor before his life was ended so abruptly. He had dreamed of transforming a block of abandoned houses into a recording studio, a dance studio and other spaces for youth to occupy and create in during afterschool hours. Such a vision, if realized, would change the experiences and phenomenology of young people living in this blighted part of Camden, NJ. How do we support such practical engagements in the places we research? How does our research contribute or work in dialogue with the actions? Many options could be explored, from raising awareness and funds, and simply lending a hand, all of which would necessarily depend on the particular and singular circumstances of the project and its participants. Yet, again we find ourselves invited to think relationally, as we can confidently suspect that help from the preacher, academic researchers or Marqui's young friends might all be crucially needed.

CONCLUSION

Thinking phenomenologically about the encounters of social research with youth works as a series of invitations that shift our academic senses in subtle and incremental ways, rather than in prescriptive ways. Inviting us to reflect on our embodied and sensed experiences in the research field, phenomenology foregrounds unplanned events as part and parcel of research, rather than as failures that sit outside of systematic methodologies. This forces us to recognize our dynamic engagements with research fields and participants. Of the world, we are both the 'touching hand' and the 'tangible,' to use Merleau-Ponty's famous analogy of the right hand touching the left one. As he (1968, 133) explains:

> [My] hand, while it is felt from within, is also accessible from without, itself tangible, for my other hand, for example, if it takes its place among the things it touches, is in a sense one of them, opens finally upon a tangible being of which it is also a part. Through this criss-crossing within it of the touching and the tangible, its own movements incorporate themselves into the universe they interrogate, are recorded on the same map as it; the two systems are applied upon one another, as the two halves of an orange.

Yet, as we have emphasized throughout this chapter, unequal power flows traverse research encounters in multiple and complex ways. When research takes place with young participants in urban contexts characterized by extreme poverty, failed amenities and disconnected institutional settings, these power asymmetries are inescapable and sharply felt. As such, phenomenological experience cannot be conceived as somehow sitting outside of historical and social processes. Rather in the encounter with research participants, we experience the 'passage of a trace,' an invitation to commit morally and ethically to the other. As Levinas clearly explains, this moral obligation to recognize alterity is not given to us through "natural benevolence" or "divine instinct" (Kleinberg-Levin, 2009, 101). It requires work. Here Schrag's notion of "transversal rationality" seems particularly helpful in thinking through the practical outcomes of a politics of global research encounters. Moving 'transversally' beyond the traditional dichotomies of universalism and cultural relativism, or across spatial divisions of the global North and South, new questions start to emerge. Rather than obliterate and simply celebrate the often extreme and seemingly incompatible diversity of views we typically encounter in the field, 'transversal rationalism' focuses our attention on the reasons why these diverse views have come to be assembled, no matter how fleeting or fluid they may be.

How have the preacher and Lauren's explanations of the murder of Marqui come to push against each other during this tragic event in Camden, NJ? What work does each of these interpretations do? And how can they be put together in a productive conversation? These are the kinds of questions that emerge theoretically and practically from thinking phenomenologically about our social research. What's more, 'transversality' also allows for new global connections to be made. As the experiential aspects of research encounters are foregrounded, and we let ourselves enter a kind of 'ontological complicity' with the field, new kinds of academic 'trespassing' start to occur. In Clovis's research, when everyday cultural practices of youth in Guinea and London join forces and intersect with his academic and practical experience in city government, innovative directions in research emerge. These assemblages invite us to foreground young people's cultural politics to make sense of the urban and the global. What's more, by emphasizing the relational nature of experience, phenomenology invites us, as academic researchers, to work with others, artists, activists, religious leaders and most crucially the youth themselves.

REFERENCES

Bergère, Clovis. "Temporary Autonomy and the Framing of Youth Policy Debates in Guinea." Paper presented at the 4th European Conference on African Studies, Uppsala, Sweden, 2011.

Bourdieu, Pierre. *Outline of a Theory of Practice*. Cambridge: Cambridge University Press, 1977.

Bourdieu, Pierre, and Loic J.D. Wacquant. *An Invitation to Reflexive Sociology*. 1st ed. Chicago: University of Chicago Press, 1992.

Certeau, Michel de. *The Practice of Everyday Life*. 3rd revised ed. Oakland: University of California Press, (1984) 2011.

CQ Press. *City Crime Ranking 2013*. London: Sage Publications, 2013.

Diallo, Ibrahima. "Role d'une ville secondaire dans l'organisation de son espace: le cas de Labé dans la région du Foutah-Djallon." *Les Cahiers D'Outre-Mer* no. 217, Janvier–Fevrier 2002. 105–111. Accessed November 3, 2012. http://com.revues.org/1063?lang=en.

Gillette, Howard. *Camden after the Fall: Decline and Renewal in a Post-Industrial City*. Philadelphia: University of Pennsylvania Press, 2005.

———. "Visions of Camden, Exhibition Catalogue." January 14–March 1, 2013. Stedman Gallery, Camden, New Jersey, 2013.

Jung, Hwa Y. "Phenomenology and Body Politics." *Body & Society* 2, no. 2, 1996. 1–22.

Kleinberg-Levin, David Michael. "Tracework," in *Merleau-Ponty and the Possibilities of Philosophy*. Edited by Robert Vallier, Flynn Bernard and Wayne J. Froman, 79–115. Albany: SUNY Press, 2009.

Levinas, Emmanuel. *Otherwise Than Being: Or Beyond Essence*. Pittsburgh: Duquesne University Press, 1998.

Mamdani, Mahmood. *Citizen and Subject: Contemporary Africa and the Legacy of Late Colonialism*. Princeton: Princeton University Press, 1996.

Mendieta, Eduardo. "Invisible Cities: A Phenomenology of Globalization from Below." *City* 5, no. 1, 2001. 7–26.

Merleau-Ponty, Maurice. *Phenomenology of Perception*. London: Routledge & Kegan Paul, 1962.

———. *The Structure of Behavior*. Boston: Beacon Press, 1963.

———. *Signs*. Evanston: Northwestern University Press, 1964.
———. *The Visible and the Invisible: Followed by Working Notes*. Evanston: Northwestern University Press, 1968.
Michael, Mike. "Anecdote," in *Inventive Methods: The Happening of the Social*. Edited by Celia Lury and Nina Wakeford, 25–36. London: Routledge, 2012.
Nordmann, Charlotte. *Bourdieu/Rancière*. Paris: Editions Amsterdam, 2006.
Rabinow, Paul. *Reflections on Fieldwork in Morocco*. Oakland: University of California Press, 1977.
Rancière, Jacques. *The Ignorant Schoolmaster: Five Lessons in Intellectual Emancipation*. 1st ed. Stanford: Stanford University Press, 1991.
———. *The Philosopher and His Poor*. Durham: Duke University Press Book, 2004.
Schrag, Calvin O. "Transversal Rationality," in *The Question of Hermeneutics: Essays in Honor of Joseph J. Kockelmans*. Edited by Timothy J. Stapleton. Springer Publishing Company, 1994.
Simone, AbdouMaliq. *For the City Yet to Come: Changing African Life in Four Cities*. Durham: Duke University Press, 2004.
Stoller, Paul. *Sensuous Scholarship*. Philadelphia: University of Pennsylvania Press, 1997.
Thrift, Nigel. "Practising Ethics," in *Using Social Theory: Thinking through Research*. Edited by Michael Pryke, Gillian Rose and Sarah Whatmore. London: Sage Publications, 2003.

Section 2

Experience and Meaning-Making

Oneself and the World

5 "When the Soil Is Just Right—It Has to Feel Like This"

Peasant Youth of Northeastern Argentina: Experiences and Understanding

Ana Padawer

This chapter explores the association between knowledge and practice that takes place when young peasants participate in productive agricultural activities in the countryside as part of family reproduction. I analyze fieldwork data from the *Paranaense* forest environment, exploring youth's capabilities of connecting articulated information and tacit understandings about the world. Drawing from Ricoeur's (2006) reflections on the original linguistic condition of human experience, I propose the concept of enskilled translations to explore the associations young people make between their practical experiences and the production of verbally articulated knowledge. In the everyday rural contexts in which they participate, young peasants work and talk about nature in relation to their identifications as settlers and claiming a future linked to working the land.[1]

The concepts of practical knowledge, common sense and practical sense have been used in social science from phenomenology (Schutz and Luckmann, 2009) to Marxist theory (Gramsci, 1986) and cultural sociology and anthropology (Bourdieu, 2007), to refer to ordinary understanding. According to these very different theoretical backgrounds, everyday experience in the world is defined as non-reflexive, but accessible to the subject's reflection. The phenomenological approach was a reaction to Cartesian thought in that pre-objective experience was defined as a condition for the objectification of thought. The Marxist notion of class-consciousness is related to Bourdieu's (2007) notion of habitus, a concept that refers to the embodied recognition of the world, a precondition for explicit understanding where social structure is both prerequisite and result. The concept of habitus was in turn recovered by Ingold (2002), in his formulation of the notion of skill as the bodily knowledge of the subject, practicing expert and person in the world.

There is a common argument in the aforementioned perspectives: What is verbally expressed implies a distancing from practices, which involves deploying doubts about what is taken for granted. In this sense, Ricoeur's contributions regarding the conceptualization of the relationship between language and interpretation are especially pertinent. According to Ricoeur

(2006), language enables social objectivations from a being-in-the-world. This conceptualization of the linguistic mediation of human experience enables me to approach knowledge through doing in the verbalizations of young settlers, where an identification of the subjects in relation to a rural past and future constitutes the references about their own world.

The concept of enskilled translations refers to the verbalizations young generations make about their experiences related to nature. When young peasants connect technical jargon or everyday terminology with sensitive experiences, they are able to construct explicit knowledge about the environment that results from learning by doing. This knowledge is based on socially and historically constructed practices, where verbal statements and reasoning are possibilities of a dispositional understanding: Their occurrence is not necessary, but when they take place they bring specificity to practical knowledge, a brief and relative distancing from the situation of being-in-the-world.

In this chapter, I will explore youth's verbally explicit statements about tacit practical understandings, related to their activities in rural environments. I begin by situating this research in relation to phenomenology and the notion of enskilled translations as the objectification of live experience. The context of the study is then introduced through a brief historical and geographical description of peasantry in the area, in order to understand these young men's everyday practices. The article focuses on two young peasants, Damien[2] (aged 16) and Simon (aged 19), considering how they verbally articulate practical knowledge about nature in relation to agrarian activities conducted outside and inside school.

Simon's family has recently moved to the countryside, where they work on a twenty-five-hectare property. In this case, two generations are virtually novices regarding agrarian work. Although his parents could not transmit practical knowledge on crop growing to Simon, they have had some access to financial credit for technical support, and have been able to pay for their son to attend a private agrarian school, thus allowing him to interact with teachers specialized in rural tasks.

Damien's family, on the other hand, has always lived in the countryside; his parents therefore have practical knowledge about rural tasks. They are not landowners, but live and cultivate in state and private properties, permanently risking being evicted. Because of their class condition as landless peasants, they could not afford to send their children to the private agrarian school, so Damien attends a public generalist school and does not have access to technicians.

Taking into account biographical information and the description of contemporary activities of both families, I will explore dynamics of knowledge mediated by practices among young people, considering contrasting situations of class and access to school. The enskilled translations will be considered as objectifications of young settlers' experiences about the natural world, in their connection with structural dimensions and identifications.

The article is based on ethnographic fieldwork initiated in 2009 in a rural area of San Ignacio, a town with over 6,000 inhabitants located in the province of Misiones, northeastern Argentina. The fieldwork was conducted for periods of fifteen-day stays, two or three times a year for five years. During those five years of ethnographic fieldwork, I gradually constructed a trusting relationship with the families whose children attended an elementary rural school, sharing the children's trajectories as they entered high school. My research involved participant observation and interviews conducted at peasant family plots and at schools. Local authorities and state administrators were also interviewed regarding information on productive activities.

PRACTICAL KNOWLEDGE AND ENSKILLED TRANSLATIONS

Practical knowledge has been problematized in many fields and theoretical traditions within the social sciences. Diverse meanings have been attributed to verbalizations where the experience in the world is non-reflexive but accessible to the subject's consciousness, mediated by language in different ways. Both phenomenology and Marxism, through their influences in cultural sociology and anthropology, provide powerful concepts to understand the objectification of lived experience. In the first case, by reaffirming the importance of language, and in the second case, by including spatial and temporal dimensions of experience linked to social inequality.

According to Schutz and Luckmann, the verbal formulation of ordinary experiences implies a dissection of the unity of natural experience, where a quality arises to attention. When issuing a legitimate verbal statement the subject establishes a degree of sufficient familiarity to a certain situation: The element of knowledge that results will then be applied to a range of similar situations (Schutz and Luckmann, 2009, 145–146).

This phenomenological perspective can be complemented with structural and historical relations analyzed by Marxists, especially with Gramsci's notion of common sense as world conceptions expressed by language itself: "The starting-point of critical elaboration is the consciousness of what one really is, and is 'knowing thyself' as a product of the historical process to date which has deposited in you an infinity of traces, without leaving an inventory" (Gramsci, 1986, 11–12).

Knowledge related to language, social practice and hegemony is thus a key issue for Marxists. Derivations in contemporary cultural sociology and anthropology such as Bourdieu's (2007) perspective problematize the relation between class and knowledge, drawing from certain phenomenological approaches anticipated by Schutz and Luckmann (2009) in a structural theory about practical sense. For Bourdieu, conditioning associated with social class produces habitus, systems of durable and transferable dispositions, structured structures that tend to work as structuring structures, generative and organizing principles of practices and representations (2007, 86). According to Bourdieu, scientific knowledge of human action involves an understanding that can only be achieved by positioning oneself "out of the game," that is, outside the practice.

Giddens (1982) critically draws from both phenomenology and Marxism in considering the meaning of social action in his theory of social structuration. Reproduction of a social system is not a prerequisite but a result of limits in cognition and contingency—unintended consequences of actions. Thus, according to Giddens, everyday encounters must be conceptualized in relation to long lasting institutions: "The most casual exchange of words involves the speakers in the long-term history of language via which their words are formed, and simultaneously in the continuing reproduction of that language" (1982, 11).

From a specific anthropological framework, Ingold works on practical knowledge and language, seeking to combine biological and cognitive approaches with socio-cultural concepts that describe human action as agency, intentionality and imagination. Taking from Bourdieu's notion of habitus, he proposes the concept of skill for the bodily knowledge of a subject as a practicing expert and a person-in-the-world. Skills are not universal capacities assuming particular forms transmitted culturally from one generation to the next: They are rather re-discovered and incorporated in the modus operandi of humans through training and experience in particular tasks, where verbalized information opens a path to knowledge when it is placed in a context of abilities gained through experience (Ingold, 2002, 169).

Ricoeur contributes to the aforementioned approaches analysing the relationship between language and experience. Although a subject's experience cannot be communicated, speech acts communicate a public meaning, producing a mutual comprehension in which misunderstandings can nonetheless take place: words are polysemic, gestures and tone of voice have an unstable codification. The contextual function of speech is thus to sift the polysemy of our words and reduce the plurality of interpretations, which is essentially done through dialogue (Ricoeur, 2006, 31).

The live metaphor existing in discourse refers to emotional evocations that have cognitive value (of predication about reality), that complete denotation. Ricoeur states that metaphors not only have emotional functions but also convey new information about reality. This takes place through the inherent tension of metaphoric expressions that include in themselves two opposite interpretations: "A cloak of sorrow," for instance, does not refer to a piece of cloth (Ricoeur, 2006, 63).

When interpreting metaphors, literal meaning is self-destroyed because it produces a sense of contradiction, which involves the extension of meaning beyond the obvious reference. Continuing with the previous example, we are able to understand the metaphor 'a cloak of sorrow' because we notice the tension between the emotion expressed (sorrow) and the object that represents it (cloak). This metaphor communicates about the world: Its meaning stems from the emotion it conveys.

Ricoeur further distinguishes between substitution metaphors, which can be the object of translation and restoration of literal meaning, as compared to tension metaphors, which can be paraphrased but are not literally translatable. They can't be translated because tension metaphors include innovative meaning that is not exhausted in the literal translation. It is in this way that such metaphors say something new about reality (ibid., 65).

As referential bearer, poetic language shares with scientific language the fact that it only reaches reality through a deviation that denies the ordinary vision and the language normally used to describe it. A metaphor's description of reality is guided by the interaction between the differences and similarities triggered by tension at the level of elocution: The new vision of reality stems from this tensing apprehension that does not take place in ordinary vision, but is attached to the ordinary use of words (ibid., 81). For example: Nature is a temple.

The aforementioned concepts are key to the notion of enskilled translations as objectification of lived experience: Degrees of familiarity (Schutz and Luckmann, 2009) are needed by young generations of settlers in their construction of ordinary expressions about their experiences related to nature. The associations they make between bodily sensations and ordinary terms involve world conceptions expressed by language itself, that are received without the benefit of inventory (Gramsci, 1986), but are not fixed: Their daily casual exchanges in the countryside are part of both social reproduction and agency (Giddens, 1982).

When young peasants connect technical jargon or everyday terminology to sensitive experiences, they are able to construct explicit knowledge about the environment that results from learning by doing. This knowledge is based on socially and historically constructed practices, where verbal statements and reasoning are possibilities of a dispositional understanding (Bourdieu, 2007).

Enskilled translations are not frequent, nor are they indispensable to learn through practice. In informal instruction contexts, where verbal articulations are supplementary to an activity, they take place when the subjects are driven by situation to distance themselves from what they are doing, to objectify their practices. It is important to note that because language mediates all social practices, this dispensability of translations does not make them less inevitable. Hence, I argue that when this "out of the game" position takes place, it brings specificity to practical knowledge, a brief and relative distancing from the situation of being-in-the-world.

When skills are linguistically mediated, the information opens a path to knowledge, placed in a context of abilities gained through prior experiences (Ingold, 2002). Thus, when young settlers explain their ordinary tasks using translations between sensations and an everyday or technical word, they are not merely describing. They can expand knowledge; say something new, because the "live metaphor" implies a tension between two opposite interpretations, an extension of meaning (Ricoeur, 2006).

A CHANGING ENVIRONMENT AND TWO FAMILIES

San Ignacio is in northeastern Argentina, near the border with Brazil and Paraguay. It is strategically located near a national road frequently used by tourists and truck drivers carrying yerba mate (*ilex paraguarensis,* an herb used for an indigenous infusion, widely consumed by non-indigenous population since colonization) and wood, near the province's capital (thirty-eight miles). Along with an indigenous population crossing national frontiers, European settlers populated the area since the end of the nineteenth century.

This rural area—identified as Parana Wood Forest biome—has been significantly transformed in the last three decades, with an increase of land ownership concentration for forest industry production. Additionally, yerba mate crises[3] have forced the settlers to diversify their activities or move to the cities. The *Mbyà-Guaraní,* who lived in this territory before the arrival of the settlers, were also affected by these changes in productive activities: The increasingly difficult access to the native forest consequently impaired family reproduction activities for local indigenous people.

Contemporary settlers and *Mbyà Guaraní* people are heirs to a century-old interethnic relationship in a context of construction of the Argentinean State's frontiers. In northeastern Argentina, both the government and private companies organized colonization by selling the land remaining from a large sale made in 1881 to twenty-seven landowners. Indigenous villagers were scattered, whereas European settlements began to grow in the territory, with a pattern of twenty-five-hectare fractions per family. Settlers grow subsistence and industrial crops, in coexistence with both indigenous people who mainly live off forest resources, and large landowners dedicated to timber exploitation and cattle rearing (Gorosito, 2005; Belastegui, 2006, 87–89; Bartolomé, 2007).

Although there is a significant ethnic component in their identities, researchers define settlers mainly in economic terms, as a category in between farmers and peasants. The two aspects are elements of contemporary common sense: In Misiones the category of settler as a self- or attributed-identity may be used to refer to European migrants and their descendants, and also to describe small producers regardless of their national origin.

In the last thirty years, the development of agribusiness production in the global market has impacted rural regions in northeastern Argentina. Forestry has grown even stronger in Misiones, prevailing over the settlers' yerba mate production. This context has deeply impacted Simon's and Damien's families, which have had to reorganize and diversify their agricultural activities in order to survive. Simon's family now practices greenhouse horticulture, forestry, apiculture, poultry, cattle rearing and crop production (maize, cassava, pumpkin, sugar cane). Damien's family, on the other hand, primarily pursues poultry production and farming activities.

Simon's family represents a generation of new settlers that were born in the city, but have returned to the country where their ancestors used to live.

When I first met him, Simon (the second son of four children in the family) was nineteen years old. His parents had migrated from the city to the countryside ten years before. Although some of his great-grandparents and grandparents 'belonged to the farm,' the current group of children and their parents had only recently begun to learn about working the land.

Simon's family owns fifty hectares, which statistically ranks them as settlers. Their biographical account reveals that upon inheriting the land from Simon's grandfather, who bought it with money made in the city, Simon's mother had to learn to milk cows and manufacture dairies and preserves. Her husband, who had always wanted to live in the countryside, started supplementing his carpentry activities in the city through increasingly diversified production on the farm, which required him to learn how to grow the region's typical crops (maize, cassava, sweet potatoes and pumpkin) and incorporate other less traditional species such as soy, peanuts, and sugar cane.

Besides their vegetable production, Simon's family has taken up husbandry and apiarian activities. They started out with a milk cow, and in a couple of years they obtained around twenty head. In the case of beekeeping, they benefitted from a government plan that provided them with training and the necessary elements to kick off production. Their vegetable garden produces enough food for their own consumption and in 2009 they initiated a new greenhouse program. Simon proposed the idea of covered horticultural production after learning about this in his rural middle school. I return to this development and address it in greater detail below.

Damien's family contrasts with Simon's in many ways. They have been peasants for at least three generations (grandparents, parents and children), although they have never had enough capital to purchase land. As squatters, they cultivate private and state properties: When I first met them, they had permission to use a rural road (designed but not yet open) to build a house and poultry pens. For crop growing (maize, cassava), they sowed the ground between lines of pine trees in a large private plantation, weeding the property in exchange for access to the land.

The family is large. Damien is sixteen and is the second son (just like Simon). He has four brothers and six sisters. Damien's older brother and sister have migrated to the city in search of jobs, so Damien is the eldest son at the house and because of this, he is in charge of crop growing and poultry farming. As his father pointed out: "He is my champion on the farm." The eldest daughter also has responsibilities in the family, mainly caring for the younger brothers and sisters in the afternoons: "She is the main helper on the farm," claimed her father.

Damien's family cultivates and rears poultry mainly for self-consumption. The father has repeatedly tried to obtain bank credits or state aid to diversify production (as Simon's family did, with beekeeping, cattle rearing or covered horticulture), but to no avail because they have no property to mortgage. In order to obtain additional income Damien's father has started supplementing his farming activities with a paid job in a tourist attraction in the city.

The lack of land and the family's consequent strategy of social reproduction—the employment of adults and elder sons in the city—have curbed the members' learning in practice in relation to farming. They grow some of the region's typical crops (maize, cassava, pumpkin) and this knowledge has been transmitted from one generation to another, but other less traditional crops (such as sugar cane) or technology (as covered horticulture)—which would require additional information and capital to proceed—have remained unexplored.

With husbandry the family has faced similar restrictions: As Damien's family does not have legal rights to the land, they have not been able to access state programs for water drilling, nor bank credits directed at improving the production of pig, hen or duck varieties. Moreover, because Damien was attending a secondary urban school, he lacked access to additional ideas about how to deal with watering problems. His situation contrasts with Simon's, who became knowledgeable about greenhouse horticulture production through his agrarian education.

METAPHORS AND ENSKILLED TRANSLATIONS

Through interviews with Simon's mother before visiting their family plot, I learned that—as noted earlier—Simon came up with the idea of greenhouse production on the family farm, as a result of his training in tomato growing at his agrarian middle school. For Simon's mother (an urban woman, only recently living in the country), starting the greenhouse involved an increasing awareness of environmental conditions—preparation of land, insect threats and dosage of fertilizers, as well as construction. This new awareness, in part triggered by her son's school knowledge, was part of a gradual learning process regarding agrarian production carried out by the family at large:

> The first thing we did [when we got to the country] was plant. People here usually plant corn, manioc, pumpkin; we also planted soy, peanut, sugarcane. First of all we did also the vegetable garden, with everything that is planted there: lettuce, cabbage, carrot, parsley, chard, onions. . . . Now we left the garden aside, because as of last year my husband has been working in the greenhouse. After that we started with livestock production, beekeeping. Cows, milk . . . quickly the first thing that we got was a milking cow. We started out with three cows but now we have eighteen I think. We started out with a government plan that helped us. . . . And also with beekeeping, we began on our own and then we also benefitted from a government plan. We took a course. After finishing the course they gave my son all the equipment, the suits. . . . Last

year my husband, Simon and my other son—who also finished school and learned all about gardening—borrowed money from a sister in law, a brother in law . . . and we built a greenhouse, on our own. We planted tomato.

With my son's learning, what he worked on at agrarian school, . . . that's when he started: "Daddy, let's build a greenhouse." When they started to build it, I thought it was about putting a cover on the roof and that was it . . . But no! The manure had to be burnt, **preparing the land, disinfecting it,** and I don't know what else. . . . With the greenhouse we all learned. . . . We learned everything: the medicine, insecticide for the bugs, Simon was in charge of that, or my husband. Or for example, tying the tomatoes. I had no idea; I only know that we had to buy a special strong nylon string. But as the plant grows it has to be tied (in a special way). And the "Triple 15," a fertilizer, and you need to know how much to use because if you use too much it's bad for the plant and if you use too little it isn't any good. . . . And the white fly. . . .

(Interview conducted with Simon's mother, July 1, 2009)

Simon's mother's reference to how they started the greenhouse activity is about how she was educated on the problem of soil use. The enskilled translation emphasized in bold print in the text, is rooted in her everyday terminology as a housewife; this is why she mentions "preparing the land, disinfecting it." Due to her peripheral participation in this particular activity on the farm (led mainly by her husband and her sons) her technical vocabulary is limited. Therefore, although she was instructed about a fertilizer brand and she learned about dosing through practice, she is unaware about the debate on the use of chemicals in agrarian production that agribusiness has sparked in recent years. Simon does refer to this debate and it is also mentioned (in a general way) in the accounts of interviewed male members of different families, who are usually in charge of production in greenhouses.

Previously it was mentioned that verbalized information opens a path to knowledge when it is placed in a context of abilities gained through experience. As will be shown next, Damien and his siblings learned about plants and animals through their progressive involvement in agrarian tasks. It all began with walking, learning to focus on where the sprouts were, carrying seeds, bringing water to animals. When I visited the family plot for the second time, I observed this education of attention between brothers and sisters, where the more experienced children pointed to isolated sprouts between lines of pines and novices tried to identify unnoticed specimens:

We walk by lines of pines; there are cassava sticks on the ground, already prepared to 'spring up.' At the centre of the irrigation channels there are lines with settled seeds. Four of the youngest children of the family are walking with Damien and Inez [the eldest brother and sister], slipping in the wet soil and laughing.

Martina says [one of the youngest girls]: Look the cassava! [Pointing at some sticks to me.]
Ana [researcher]: Why do you plant between the pines?
Damien: **Here the soil is prettier.**
Ana: How many lines of cassava do you have?
Damien: Nine
Ana: Do you have a vegetable garden?
Inez [the elder sister]: At the bottom we planted lettuce, cabbage, carrot and beet, but the water took it all. Watch out! Don't step on sticks! [To her little brothers and sisters.] We used to have maize [pointing to black sticks, dry, on the floor]. They were taller than pine!
Damien: Here there is maize [pointing to a green maize plant standing alone].
Inez: And what is this plant called, Damien? [Pointing to a small sprout.]
Damien: Melon. Papa planted it with mama.
Inez: Watch out for the little plant, you! [To Carlos, the youngest boy, already stepping on the melon, while we all continue walking.]
Damien: Over there **I cleaned the [green] onion**, it's there since last year. We pulled the shrub out and three or four weeks later it comes out again. And over there is maize that we planted, three months old.
Martina: There are beans over there . . .
Ana: And how do you work with the [green] onion seed, do you save it?
Damien: It comes from the flower, when it falls off, it dries up and the seed is left.
Inez: [Taking a flower, she rubs with her fingers and detaches the seeds.] **It looks like rice . . .**
Ana: And the bean, how does it sprout?
Damien: That one spreads out, we put up sticks on the side, like this [he forms a triangle with his hands], **like a little shack** and it tangles up there. . . . A pod comes out.
Inez: There was lettuce over there, but the rain dragged everything away.
Ana: And how do you plant them, intermingled?
Inez: Between each onion, there's a bean, and in the middle row, lettuce. [Martina picks up a dry green onion flower and she throws it back down. Inez watches her throw it and says]: Take that to the house.

Carlos:	Look Inez; there is another one over here!
Inez:	Take it also.
Damien:	[A bit further away from us.] There is pumpkin over here.
Inez:	Is there fruit?
Damien:	Not yet.
Inez:	It has the flower. The fruit is coming next.
Damien:	**No, it's not that.** [They look up close and ruffle the leaves.]
Inez:	Oh, **I thought it was** [the flower] **because I saw something yellowish.**
Damien:	This is trunk pumpkin and that is the pumpkin that works as a guide, iron skin pumpkin. **That kind of pumpkin grows in the shrub, and the other one grows with the guide.**
Ana:	Do you have to build the guide, like with the bean? . . .
Damien:	It spreads out . . . **like the isipó** *(aristolocchia triangularis)*, **we only have to make room for it.** Just right now I have to clean everything. . . .
Sylvie:	And there is parsley over there.
Inez:	Wow, there is more over there! . . .
Patrice:	**You stepped on it!**
Damien:	**No, that's weed. . . .**
Sylvie:	**Careful! Look Martina. . . .**

(Observation made at Damien's family farm, November 4, 2010)

This excerpt illustrates how skill comes from following what other people do: Novices watch, touch, and listen to experts' movements, seeking through repeated trials to bring their own bodily movements into line with those they pay attention to, so as to achieve the adjustment of perception and action inherent in fluent performance. When walking by the crop rows, this day young children are trained to see sprouts of melon, while they point to other crops such as green onion or cassava that they already know. To identify the sprouts they must pay attention to the shape and colour of leaves and stems, but this remains unsaid, it is done through attentive walking.

It is harder for the children to identify the plants because there are no defined limits to crop areas in this squatter's farm: They are "between the pines." The activity is not a formalized one, the children are running around the farm, jumping and playing, in a way that knowledge grows as a re-discovering: "Watch out for the little plant, you!" "Careful!" or "You stepped on it!" Verbalizations do not stem from mental representations conveyed from one child to another, but from ordinary activities like avoiding a place to step on, where visual identifications are expressed by certain basic language denotations, such as "I saw something yellowish."

Damien is the expert in this group; he nevertheless uses colloquial terms when explaining the cultivation process ("the soil is prettier," "I cleaned the onion") probably because he has no access to technical support or specialized education about agrarian tasks that would enable him to manage scientific concepts.

Just like Simon's mother, Damien uses metaphoric substitutions, such as when he says, "I cleaned the onion" in reference to weeding. But there seems to be a subtle difference between both substitutions (Simon's mother on disinfection and Damien's on cleaning) on the one hand, and Damien's utterance about the "prettier soil," on the other: Because the boy is mainly responsible for farm activities when his father is away, he is trained enough and uses a live metaphor that compares the attributes of land with a beautiful person. There is a surplus of meaning referring to humidity and soil consistency that is metaphorically evoked.

The lack of technical terminology in Damien's explanations also illuminates how, in the aforementioned fragment, comparisons or similes are used. Thus, everyday language is a resource for relating visual and tactile images through which features of the plants are appreciated by children: "It looks like rice"; or human interventions for their development are described: "We put up sticks . . . like a little shack," "It spreads out like the *isipó,* we only have to make room for it."

THE AWARENESS OF TRANSLATION

As already noted, language information opens a path to knowledge when placed in the context of skills gained through prior experiences. When Simon's mother mentions the preparation of soil as "disinfection," or when Damien mentions "pretty soil," they are using colloquial terms to refer to processes or features that have precise terminology in technical agricultural services.

According to this, the next excerpt from a visit to the greenhouse shows how through technical jargon and everyday language, Simon was able to refer to the prototypical cycles of plants, although his knowledge is founded in skills synthesized from contexts of activities conducted following the paths of others:

> Simon is working in the greenhouse. We arrive from school with his mother and sister. They take me to see him and say goodbye as they follow on home to prepare lunch. We say hello to each other and Simon invites me in to see the plants. We go into the greenhouse and he walks along the planted rows while I follow him a few steps behind. After a few seconds, he leans toward a tomato plant, examining it, and tells me:

Simon: Here the flower is coming out now. **Exactly two months from now, the fruit will mature. This type has to yield ten crowns,**

approximately. Each crown makes five to seven fruits, so it has to give over two kilos per crown. This is known as the round tomato or the colossus variety.

Then he stands up and begins to follow the line of shrubs:

Simon: It is watered through a line that drops water every 15 centimetres.

He stops and takes a black plastic tray from a pile. "**It is planted on 'bandejas' or seedling,**" expressing the word in both languages. This introduction of a word in English surprises me, and makes me ask:

Ana: What did you say?
Simon: The seedlings have 128 cells each. It is planted this way because the tomato's seed is too small—one seed is added to each cell and the whole earth lump is transplanted. This is the way of ensuring plant growth.
Ana: And how do you have to care for it?
Simon: Now I'm pruning. These are **suckers, sprouts, which come out in each bud leaf.** This has to be removed [he cuts off a sprout while he speaks], or it will grow, even faster, than the shoot. **What this would cause is too much volume and no fruit,** or a fruit that is too small, **it is not commercial.** So instead of it being a benefit—having **several sprouts, several tips,** it is a loss.

Simon takes one of the strips of thread that work as a tutor for the plant, and he tangles it around it.

Ana: If you don't tie them, what happens?
Simon: That one over there has not been tied and [the plant] is about to fall. The problem when it falls is that once it touches the ground it is more prone to diseases. **The fruit that touches the ground is stained or just rots.** The leaf that touches the damp ground rots. It's a problem in winter; in summer there is an area in La Pampa, Córdoba, Santa Fe [areas with milder temperature in the centre of Argentina] where tomato is planted **and** tutoring is not used. But **that tomato is no good for the table, it's only for industry,** for sauce, tomato puree.
Ana: And how is it best to tie it?
Simon: It is tied really low, from the thickest leaves. It is done quite big. **If you do it too small, you strangle the plant,** and if it is too big, it comes out. Any of both extremes is bad. . . .

(Observation made at Simon's family farm, July 3, 2009)

In his explanation about greenhouse work, Simon talks to a person that recognizes herself as a novice (the researcher) and that asks him about his work procedures. Because he has carried out his secondary studies in an agro-technical school, Simon fluently manages a repertoire about planting methods composed mainly of technical propositions. In the first sentence, for example, he anticipates the number of "crowns" that will grow, explains the correspondence between them and the quantity of fruits produced, and expresses it also in weight. In the entire excerpt the young man uses an impersonal tense and passive voice: "It is known as . . . , " or "What this would cause is too much volume and no fruit," or "The fruit that touches the ground," producing an instructional mode that evokes school teaching or technical exchanges instead of referring solely to his particular activities. This knowledge is presented explicitly as knowledge that transcends locality: Simon mentions other areas, other producers, and anticipates consequences of pruning and tutoring.

Simon however was not in a class or a technical office, but verbally explaining practices in his covered garden where these contexts are recalled by at least three specific linguistic translations from the previous excerpt. In the first he mentions the colloquial name of the tomato variety ("round tomato") as well as its technical name ("colossus"), conveying his awareness of the translation from an everyday term to a scientific one (by the expression "it is known"). In the third translation this same procedure is done directly in the same phrase, with a brief pause: "These are suckers, sprouts." The second translation implies the use of an English word ("seedling") immediately after the Spanish expression (*"bandejas"* or trays). Here the switching of language seems to reinforce the translation: A more technical and English term is used as a substitute for an everyday Spanish term.

Through the translation of technical jargon and everyday terms Simon can give details and communicate additional information beyond perceptual experience, focusing attention on the size of tomato pits that the seedling trays require, or the varieties of tomato selected by performance and purposes, or a seemingly paradoxical procedure, such as the trimming of new sprouts. In explicit verbal translation there is a position "out of the game" that is recalled by the subject, taking a technical/scientific distance from his practice in dialogue with the novice (the researcher).

When translating terms that refer to a technological device or a variety of crops, the experience in which this knowledge is based is objectified. But it is important to note that such translations between technical jargon and everyday terminology are nevertheless founded in sensitive experiences as a core of knowing in situated learning. This knowledge, which is not fully verbalized but constructed in experiences developed in communities of practice, enables naming a device as *"bandeja"* or perhaps as "seedling" according to context, situations and interlocutors.

As I have demonstrated, these contexts, situations or interlocutors do not correspond exclusively to daily life in one institution or another: Although scientific jargon is predominant in certain social spaces of practices, such as laboratories, agrarian schools and technology agencies, it is also present in certain situations in the productive space, mediating the objectification of processes, perceptions and experiences.

THE INCOMPLETENESS OF TRANSLATION

Reference to one's activities, processes, perceptions and experiences can always be articulated linguistically, on occasions with technical concepts, or with daily ones. However, inasmuch as the knowledge implied is based on practices, some aspects will remain in corporeal sensations. I will show this incompleteness of enskilled translations with two references to the activity of irrigation, a core activity in gardening.

Irrigation is a theme taught at agrarian school and featured in technicians' brochures, and also an important topic in domestic everyday conversations. A document developed by the local station of the INTA (National Institute of Agrarian Technology), where Simon occasionally participates in training activities, is dedicated to this topic:

> Setting up an irrigation system, even in small gardening, demands the comprehension of the hydrologic requirements of cultivation, of how to supply water and knowledge about the equipment's components. The aim of this guide is to assist technicians with the calculus, design and installation of small watering systems. . . . Soil, apart from providing an anchor for the plant, is the reservoir of water, oxygen and carbon dioxide that will be absorbed by roots. **In its structure there are very small particles, which constitute the deposit for nutrients**, which interchange with the soil's solution and facilitate the absorption through the plant's roots. . . . **There are different ways to express the soil's content of water, but the most frequent one is gravimetric humidity, which is expressed as water's mass in relation to dry soil's mass (gr./gr.)**. It is calculated as the weight difference between a sample of damp soil and a sample of oven dried soil at 105°–110°, until constant weight. . . . Right watering aims at preventing the decrease of soil humidity content under a value that would affect plant growth. In horticulture, humidity levels must be maintained in field capacity, with the objective of decreasing the energy consumed by the plant to absorb water. **Even though there are technical instruments to determine the moment when water must be replenished, generally horticulturists can solve this through experience without inconveniences.**
>
> (Villafáfila and Wyss, 2009)

As expressed in the information sheet, the document is quite technical, not intended for farmers themselves, but for its use in training activities, where professionals assist them. The language includes scientific jargon ("nutrients," "energy," "mass"), chemical elements ("oxygen," "carbon dioxide"), calculus formulae ("gravimetric humidity"), and precise measures ("105º–110º"). But it is also written in a colloquial tone, as expressed in phrases like "very small particles" and the closing explanation recognizing that, other than the technical information, horticulturists can solve the irrigation problem through "experience." The "humidity level" is also recalled in Simon's explanation about his tomato greenhouse, during the walk presented previously, when some minutes later the next situation happened:

> Simon moves to the left side of the greenhouse, where there are no sprouts yet and one can see only the pipes that drip water on the soil.
>
> *Simon:* Here it is all ready. . . .
> *Ana:* How does the irrigation system work?
> *Simon:* They are watered once a day, and the soil is almost always checked. That is, the watering amount is not fixed per day. If one digs a little and sees that it is somewhat dry . . .
>
> Then he bends and lifts a piece of moist soil, closes his hand and opens it several times, while talking.
>
> *Simon:* **Now for example, it's just right. When the soil is just right—it has to feel like this, no dripping. Humidity is perfect.** From here, a little more may be possible, but the problem is when you overdo it and the soil gets full of puddles and water drips, then it is too much water. [He throws the soil down and grabs another handful, beginning to open and close his hand again.] **If you press the soil—for example this up here—and it crumbles, then it lacks water. This is the simple technique for every plant.** Although there are plants that take much less water. Decorative plants, for example, need much less water than this. You barely moisten the soil. **But a garden plant, almost all horticultural plants need this point of humidity in the earth.**
>
> (Observation made at Simon's family farm, July 3, 2009)

In the briefing of this activity, Simon used the instructional tone already mentioned to refer to his practices of watering. In addition, he added tactile and visual images about soil ("dripping," "crumbling"), and he closed the idea with a technical recollection about "humidity point," also written in the brochure). Simon learned about watering necessities mostly in terms of sensations regarding stickiness, both tactile and visual stimuli, but he can refer to them in a specialized jargon that is present at school and professional offices during specific circumstances.

Although he can talk about soil conditions and draw comparisons between ornamental and horticultural plants, this knowledge remains mainly nonverbal, thus when asked to explain the logic behind irrigation, such sensorial perceptions were also evoked with everyday terms and their equivalent in technical ones. The incompleteness of enskilled translations does not derive from the practical status of young settlers' knowledge but from the impossibility of communicating experience itself. This is why, in the technical brochure, "determining when water should be replenished" refers to professional equipment, and also to "experience" as a way of knowing that is effective in most cases.

CONCLUSION: ON ENSKILLED TRANSLATION AND SOCIAL STRUCTURE

During my visit, Simon told me about his problems regarding tomato disease control methods, for which reason they had needed to consult—not without certain obstacles—a government technician. Although more noticeable for Damien's family, both domestic groups have social-structure-derived difficulties in accessing specialized knowledge: Here it is possible to see the limits of learning in practice regarding power relationships in a professional field of activities.

Far from an ideal situation in which these young men learn through and from their environments, there are structural limits set by the families' class positions, also conditioning their chances to overcome those limits. For this reason, Simon's and Damien's families do not enjoy easy access to agricultural chemicals and treatments for greenhouse plants, or an irrigation system based on technical studies. The socio-historical situation has restricted apprenticeship relations to certain interlocutors and state agencies, where enskilled translations occur under conditions that subjects are not quite able to change.

As settlers, Simon and Damien follow the paths of prior experiences to rediscover the plants on the farm, or to determine the humidity of soil, learning mainly from a skilled practice experienced on family land. In Simon's case, the agrarian school and technicians constitute a wider community of practices where he can share ways of doing horticulture, providing a scientific terminology that he articulates with embodied knowledge.

Simon's participation in these broader communities of practice is directly linked to the position his family occupies in the social structure: As a young settler he has been able to register in an agrarian secondary school and access credits and programs that foster rural production. However, his participation is also linked to a future plan connected to the land that explains why Simon has urged his parents to start a greenhouse, and why he has continued to informally learn about crops even beyond high school.

In Damien's case, the community of practice rarely surpasses the family plot, and whereas he is the main person in charge of the farm in the domestic group, future plans linked to the country seem more uncertain: his family does not own the land they work on, his older siblings have already migrated to the city and his secondary studies are also urban-oriented. These conditions explain why, even when Damien has shown interest in rural areas, he does not plan a rural future where his agrarian activities would be renewed through the contrast with other ways of doing.

The idea of enskilled translation, which I have suggested in this article, points to interpretation of sensory experiences into colloquial or technical jargon made by young settlers in their everyday practices. Enskilled translations are the live metaphors used and derived from the structural position of subjects. But awareness of translations in relation to such conditions involves the possibility of creating a situation "out of the game" through dialogue, that inevitably includes the incompleteness of translation derived from embodied experience. The aforementioned theoretical perspectives, especially Ricoeur's (2006) concept of live metaphor, shed light on the role of everyday activities and language of ordinary people in the study of the production of social knowledge.

These casual conversations entail a long-term history of social relations in rural contexts, where verbal legitimate statements imply a degree of familiarity but at the same time, the opportunity to explicitly express doubts about what is taken for granted. How can the "humidity point" be determined? Governmental agency brochures recognize the simplicity and the complexity of that everyday task proposing two apparently opposite ways: by measuring and through experience. This article aims to show that both are sides of the same process that does not occur in isolation or in people's heads, but through participation by bodies in social events.

NOTES

1. In northeastern Argentina, both the government and private companies organized a colonization process at the end of the nineteenth century, attracting European migrants from more than ten different countries. These migrants engaged in horticulture, farming and industrial crops (yerba mate—*ilex paraguarensis*—tung, tobacco and tea), activities that their descendants continue nowadays. I will return later to expand this definition.
2. Pseudonyms are used throughout the article to protect the identities of participants.
3. In Misiones, settlers went through several economic crises during the 1960s and 1970s, partly triggered by overproduction and devaluation of the yerba mate *(ilex paraguarensis)* price. A significant number of them were forced to sell their land and migrate to cities (Bartolomé, 2007).

REFERENCES

Bartolomé, Leopoldo. *Los colonos de Apóstoles: estrategias adaptativas y etnicidad en una colonia eslava en Misiones*. Posadas: Editorial Universidad Nacional de Misiones, 2007.

Belastegui, Horacio. *Los colonos de Misiones*. Posadas: Editorial Universidad Nacional de Misiones, 2006.

Bourdieu, Pierre. *El sentido práctico*. Buenos Aires: Siglo XXI, (1980) 2007.

Giddens, Anthony. *Profiles and Critiques in Social Theory*. Berkeley: University of California Press, 1982.

Gorosito, Ana Maria. "Liderazgos guaraníes, breve revisión histórica y nuevas notas sobre la cuestión." Paper presented at the 4th Anthropology Meeting of MERCOSUR, Universidad Nacional de la República, Montevideo, Uruguay, November 16, 2005.

Gramsci, Antonio. *Cuadernos de la carcel. El materialismo histórico y la filosofía de Benedetto Croce*. Mexico: Juan Pablos, (1948) 1986.

Ingold, Tim. *The Perception of Environment*. London: Routledge, 2002.

Ricoeur, Paul. *Teoría de la interpretación*. Buenos Aires: Siglo XXI, (1976) 2006.

Schutz, Alfred, and Thomas Luckmann. *Las estructuras del mundo de la vida*. Buenos Aires: Amorrortu, (1973) 2009.

Villafáfila, Eduardo, and Fabio Wyss. *Riego en Horticultura*. Posadas: Instituto Nacional de Tecnología Agropecuaria, 2009.

6 (Re)scripting Barbie
Postphenomenology and Everyday Artefacts

Naghmeh Nouri Esfahani and Victoria Carrington

INTRODUCTION—BARBIE™ AS AN EVERYDAY ARTEFACT

Few 'real' individuals have had their changing fashion, style choices and impact on culture as intensely scrutinized as has Mattel's Barbie™. Since her introduction to the market in 1959 she has reigned supreme as a popular culture icon, and reflecting her status, an entire academic and publishing industry, particularly within cultural, feminist and gender studies, sits alongside the marketing and distribution juggernaut that is Barbie™. Whereas the range of dolls that sits collectively under the Barbie™ banner has grown over the years alongside the range of markets in which she is distributed (over 150 countries), the Caucasian blonde, tall, thin, blue-eyed, pink-lipped, tanned Barbie™ has remained a shared point of reference. As an artefact, Barbie™ represents an era of plastic mass manufacturing and molding technologies, and as such her plasticity is historically and culturally significant. According to Toffoletti, "Plastic is the definitive symbol of the mid-twentieth century, a period characterized by 'artificiality, disposability, and synthesis' " (cited in Fenichell, 1996, 5). Its indeterminacy also situates it within the territory of the postmodern, marked by the destabilization of hierarchies such as authenticity versus reproduction, and high versus low culture (Jameson, 1991). Whereas her iconic status as a cultural reference often encourages us to speak of Barbie™ as a singular object, she has had more than 50,000 separate design changes to her vinyl body and hair since her original moulding in 1959 (Van Gelder, 2009). Reflecting her essential plasticity, over time her body shape has been altered, her face shape and the size of her forehead have changed, her eyes have changed shape and directionality and her eyebrow shapes have followed the latest fashion. At the same time, her hair has become thicker, longer and more pliant, her skin colour has diversified, her lips have become fuller, and make up trends have come and gone. Originally marketed as a successful model (Weissman, 1999), Barbie™ has been positioned throughout her history and design evolution as a role model for young girls (Boomen, 2009; Mandeville, 1992). Her many plastic selves have included model, teacher, librarian, nurse, veterinarian, astronaut, NASCAR driver, babysitter and presidential candidate, each restyling a response to the changing aspirational values of the girls and their mothers who purchased the dolls.

The dolls also demonstrate the workings of a global manufacture and distribution model. Spade and Valentine (2008, 241) have argued that as "a product of the global assembly line, Barbie™ dolls owe their existence to the internationalization of the labour market and global flows of capital and commodities that today characterize the toy industry." From a cultural studies perspective, Barbie™'s plasticity has been the focal point of a great deal of theorizing, often in relation to the potential for endless transformation (Toffoletti, 2007), a launch point for commentary on cosmetic surgery in contemporary culture (ibid.) and as a link to the increasingly cyborg nature of individuals as plastic prosthetics are used in medical procedures (ibid.). Spade and Valentine (2008) argue that Barbie™ reflects a cultural imperative for women to remain ageless and lean, to consume, and to be unfailingly feminine and happy.

The millions of mass-produced Barbie™ dolls are ubiquitous contemporary artefacts in the lives of families and young girls. She has proved to be immensely popular across time and place, emblematic of contemporary manufacturing and global distribution, and deeply embedded in the cultural landscape of modernity and in everyday use in homes around the world. Barbie™ can, without doubt, be considered a significant everyday artefact in the lives and homes of many young girls, and as this paper will describe, even those who do not share the Western middle-class cultural background embedded in the cultural assumptions displayed by the dolls' design, narrative and fashions.

VERBEEK'S POSTPHENOMENOLOGY OF ARTEFACTS: A BRIEF OVERVIEW

Building from, and moving beyond, Heidegger's theory of technology and his view of its alienating characteristics (Verbeek and Slob, 2006), Verbeek works from a postphenomenological stance to re-theorize technologies as artefacts, reinforcing their materiality most particularly in terms of their mediating role in everyday life. Initiated in the work of Ihde (1990, 1993, 2009), postphenomenology pays attention to the mediating role of technology in the construction and experience of everyday realities. Ihde (2009, 5) reframed classical phenomenology as *post*phenomenology to "reflect historical changes in the twenty-first century," which allows a focus on the specifics of individual technological artefacts rather than technology as a general category. Where the alienating influence of technology was emphasized in the classical approach, where technology was considered to be an obstacle in relations between human beings and the world, Ihde (1990) shifts the focus towards individual technological artefacts and their role in the mediation of everyday life. Verbeek (2005, 2006, 2007), in turn, has continued this shift in focus from technology towards the role of artefacts. This postphenomenological perspective asks how subjects and objects mutually constitute each other (Verbeek, 2005). Whereas technology is conceptualized as a category of existence in classical phenomenology, Verbeek (ibid.) discusses it as single, culturally situated pieces of human product. In a pivotal shift, he emphasizes the co-constitutive nature of this relationship in praxis. Verbeek has worked to analyze the role of human made artefacts as material culture rather than reducing them to their meanings or considering their function as signs and symbols (Ihde, 2009). As Ihde (ibid., 5) notes, postphenomenology as a "modified, hybrid phenomenology" was developed to provide a better understanding of the role of artefacts in humans' lives. Verbeek shifts the focus of technology towards individual artefacts and examines the social, personal and cultural influence of these artefacts in context. This philosophy was expanded through emphasis on the co-constitution by human beings and artefacts of human relationships with the world (Verbeek, 2005). This approach highlights the "coshaping" (ibid., 181) nature of the relationship between human beings and their world. It focuses on the impact of artefacts on human praxis from an existential perspective; how artefacts mediate human actions and influence the way humans behave (Latour, 1992). Central to this view is the argument that, in addition to their role in the development and maintenance of social relationships, our material surroundings co-shape our experience of the world (Verbeek and Slob, 2006).

Verbeek's (2006) focus is on action. More specifically, Verbeek's notion of behaviour is as the product of a co-relationship with our surroundings (Verbeek and Slob 2006). It is Verbeek's (2006) central point that as artefacts facilitate our life and actions, they influence and 'co-shape' our behaviour. For Verbeek, artefacts are not neutral objects. Rather, they are active and complicit in the ways in which social practices are formed and play out. Artefacts "help to shape a situation which would have been otherwise without the artefact" (Verbeek, 2008, 95). To explain this role Verbeek draws upon and expands the notion of 'script.' Latour (1992) and Akrich (1992) used 'script' for the first time to emphasize the characteristics of artefacts that might determine human action. However, whereas Akrich's (1992) emphasis is on the technical characteristics of artefacts and the role of the design features in influencing use, Latour (1992) focuses on the artefacts' physical form and meaning. Latour (1992) believes that it is not enough to consider the script just as something that is prescribed in the design process, rather the script should be analyzed in the use-context according to the users' reactions and behaviour and their relationships with the surroundings. Verbeek (2005) argues that Akrich's and Latour's notions of script limit the concept to an instruction manual and technical functionality. Verbeek (ibid., 362) argues that "scripts transcend functionality: they form a surplus to it, which occurs once the technology is functioning. When technologies fulfill their functions, they also help to shape the actions of their users." He refers not only to connections between the intentions and values of the designer and the user's experienced world, but also to the co-construction of this world as the outcome of this link. Verbeek (2007, 91), however, is keen to differentiate a script from the basic functionality of an artefact, arguing that artefacts, with their material intentionality, "cannot be entirely reduced to their designers' or users' intentions." Verbeek's emphasis is on artefacts' praxis and materiality, that is, on the artefact in use. The influential role of artefacts in the relationship between humans and their world, and the ways in which artefacts influence the organization of human life has been termed "mediation" (ibid., 123). As Verbeek (2005, 208) states, mediation "is not a product's function, but rather a by-product of its functionality." As a result, artefacts mediate action and the concept of mediation is central to interpreting the interaction between artefact, script and user in everyday life.

Verbeek integrates the materiality of artefacts with the mediating aspect of postphenomenology in which the world is always experienced and humans become what they experience in a world influenced by artefacts. In his new version of postphenomenology, there is neither pre-existing world nor pre-existing human being; all factors 'co-shape' the relations between human beings and their world, finding their specific meaning in a specific context as artefacts create a specific form through which the world-reality is experienced (Verbeek, 2005). Importantly, the relationship between human beings and the world is understood to be an iterative one in which both human beings and their surrounding (world) are continuously revealed in response to each other (ibid.). In this view, the act of interacting with artefacts has implications for the ways in which we each engage with and understand the world around us.

We use Verbeek's framework for this study because it incorporates mediation of action and script into postphenomenology, making the case that artefacts and individuals actively co-construct the world as they experience it. Specifically, the notion of script and its practical role in shaping our relations with the world has been given serious attention in Verbeek's work. This brings us back to the choice of artefact in this paper. As noted earlier, Barbie™ has been analyzed predominantly from a cultural studies and feminist studies perspective. Here, the focus has been on the cultural positioning and implications of the dolls for consumption, gender and identity. Our desire in this particular chapter is to take a different view and attend closely to the ways in which this particular material artefact influences the co-construction of the worlds of young girls and as a consequence, to begin to unpack the complex interactions between artefact and user in praxis.

THE STUDY

The study was comprised of a set of six case studies focused on young girls aged 5–9 living in an Australian capital city. The research was designed taking an ethnographic, participant observation approach that followed the ways in which young girls interact with, narrate and redesign Barbie™ fashion dolls in home-based play. Specifically, it involved the close study of doll play by young girls in order to develop an understanding of this activity as an empirical application of Verbeek's postphenomenological theoretical frame in a contemporary context. The main tools for data collection were participant observation, interviews, photography and in-depth field notes.

The particular case described here is a part of this larger ethnographic study. This paper reports on the home-based, everyday engagement of one young girl, Nava,[1] with her set of Barbie™ doll artefacts. Nava was eight years old at the time of the study and the only child of the family. Nava's family was living in a two-bedroom unit in a suburban area. Most of the observations took place in her room and on one occasion in the lounge room. The data described here was drawn from three visits conducted in a period of three months in 2009. All study visits occurred after school hours when Nava was usually interested in playing with her dolls. The intention was to observe and interpret Nava's interactions with the dolls by being a part of her context. Consequently, Nava was free to ask the researcher to participate in her play to avoid any impediment to the natural process of play that could occur through inserting the researcher artificially. In this way the possibility of inquisitive participation was limited to maintain the play with the dolls as naturally as possible (Hongan and Greene, 2005). Mostly the researcher was asked to be a partial participant—a participant-as-observer—by Nava and not a full participant. Asking questions during the process of play and being involved in conversations wherever possible allowed the researcher to build a rich and in-depth data set from the field.

In what follows we weave together descriptions of Nava's everyday doll play with an analysis that makes use of Verbeek's postphenomenological lens with particular reference to the notion of script. Through this examination we analyze the interactions between Nava's collection of Barbie™ dolls, their scripts and Nava herself. In the particular instances described here, the interactions around Nava and her Barbie™ dolls' hair, body, dresses and accessories receive close examination.

Nava's actions have been considered in relation to her interpretation of the dolls' physical characteristics in order to show how the script was transferred and taken up by her, that is, the ways in which our participant's actions have been organized through the dolls' physical characteristics. Whereas Nava's interactions with the dolls are holistic, for clarity of analysis, we analyze this interaction from two different angles. The first approach takes as its focus the application of Verbeek's notion of script and how Barbie™ dolls navigate Nava to specific types of interaction and identification of Nava's action in relation to Barbie™ dolls; the second focuses on Nava's influence on this relationship. We suggest that this analysis provides a powerful example of the potential for postphenomenology in practice.

NAVA AND THE DOLLS' SCRIPT

Mattel's market research on girls playing with Barbie™ dolls revealed the appeal of the doll's hair for young girls (Thomas, 2000). Mattel, as a consequence, has considered hair-play to be a key design concept for its designs targeting girls less than ten years of age (Sarasohn-Kahn, 1998). The hair of a Barbie™ doll, then, has a quite direct script embedded by designers. This script finds form in the hair's pliability, which is the result of both physical (length and colour) and material (softness) characteristics.

Reflecting the influence of the script embedded in the doll's hair, the main focus in the physical interaction between Nava and her dolls was around the hair. Styling the hair was an important activity for her. She plaited and also made bunches and ponytails with the dolls' hair. Figure 6.1 and Figure 6.2 represent the way that Nava styled her dolls' hair. Touching, brushing and styling the hair were the most often repeated manner of interaction in Nava's play activities as she interpreted the script.

In all research visits, Nava's role in her individual play was the hairdresser, which we would suggest reflected the power of the hair script. She

Figure 6.1 Nava is trying different hairstyles on a particular Barbie doll to make the doll ready for the party. Photo credit: Naghmeh Nouri Esfahani.

Figure 6.2 Nava styles the dolls' hair to make them ready for a party. Photo credit: Naghmeh Nouri Esfahani.

acknowledged this preference in the second visit as she was asked about her role:

> *Researcher:* What is your role, Nava, in this story?
> *Nava:* I'm a hairdresser. Do you remember?

Researcher: OK, I thought this is a new story.
Nava: No, I'm always a hairdresser.

In another occasion of play while Nava was touching one of her Barbie™ doll's hair she admitted, "I like black hair. I will never dye my hair because my mum says if I dye my hair it will not be soft anymore. Like these (dolls), they don't colour their hair." Saying this, she showed her appreciation of the doll hair's material characteristic and linked it to her personal experience of hair. In another play activity, Nava altered a doll to make her ready to attend a party and stated that "I have to get my hair done [on behalf of the doll to hairdresser], Nava; you don't have to style it, just tie it."

Nava's interactions revealed the ways in which the dolls' script invited her to touch and play with the hair. Nava appreciated the softness and texture of the doll's hair and asked the researcher to touch the doll's hair, saying,

> It's smoother [after she applied moisturizer to the doll's hair]. Do you feel how smooth it is?

The physical and material characteristics of the Barbie™ dolls' hair led to Nava's close interactions with the dolls. The dolls' hair characteristics, most particularly softness, pliability and length, formed a script about touching, playing and styling, encouraging particular types of interaction, and following Verbeek, the co-construction of a mediated 'world' in which both doll and child were participants.

Nava identified each Barbie™ doll's body as another key point of interest. Observations revealed this to be an area revealing high levels of repeated interaction. Barbie™ dolls' distinctively female body shape invited Nava to replay her everyday life experiences in a range of scenarios. Through her interactions with the dolls' bodies, Nava discovered and explored the range of potential movements, all of which were designed specifically by the dolls' designers to form a script embedded in the dolls' physical characteristics. In her use of the dolls, Nava attempted to discover what the dolls were able to do and how versatile the dolls' bodies were. Nava moved the dolls' hands and legs and also bent the bendable parts, such as the knees. In all research visits Nava posed the dolls differently according to the role they played in the play scenarios. At times this included being seated, walking or even, at times, flying. In one of her play sessions Nava was trying to manipulate the dolls as they do their daily exercises. One of her selected movements proved impossible within the physical limits of the script. Nava responded by saying, "Mum cannot open her legs completely. She is old, that's why she cannot do it." Here, the dolls' script encourages Nava to accept the limitations of the design but to simultaneously accept the form as human-like. Specifically Nava interprets the script to be adult, female and human. Her acceptance of this script enables the dolls to take a role in Nava's play scenarios and to become a tool in her mediation of everyday life.

The material nature of the dolls' bodies invited Nava to engage in physical interactions with them. The smooth, plastic body of the dolls, along with the particular features of the hair, in terms that Verbeek gives us, are features that form a script. According to Toffoletti (2007, 70), "The very material and symbolic ambiguity of plastic [is what] allows us to generate an alternative understanding of the relationship between the body, technology and representation as transformative." Toffoletti (2007) argues that plastic as a material that constitutes Barbie™ is an important factor that creates balance between Barbie's™ fluid nature and her rigid feminine appearance as a cultural icon. The combination of hard and soft plastic that constitutes Barbie's™ body, alongside the weight and shininess of the plastic create a fluid nature for the doll. Whereas on one hand plastic as material means that Barbie's™ body appears rigid and fixed, on the other hand, its robustness and plasticity adds flexibility to the doll's body.

Nava interpreted and practiced her relationships with people around her through her interactions with the dolls. Having an adult body shape appeared to influence her towards play that involved the Barbie™ dolls taking on grown-up roles that reflected the everyday life experiences of Nava.

This interpretation of the script was reflected across all of the activities created around the dolls. In all research visits the general scenario was the story of a mother and her daughters who were going to school or shopping and were busy with everyday life activities such as piano lessons and studying. Nava happily interpreted the dolls as human, assigning human roles to the dolls in her play interactions, using them to replay and reinterpret experienced and imagined everyday events. There were no signs of Nava focusing on the dolls' hyper-feminine shape or Westernized beauty ideals. Instead, Nava interpreted the dolls' physical features in the context of her own everyday interactions.

In one instance of play activity when Nava was playing with her dolls, she kissed one of the dolls as if the doll was a real person and said:

Nava: I like to kiss them.
Researcher: You like to kiss your dolls?
Nava: Yea.
Researcher: Why?
Nava: I just like to kiss them. Every night I kiss them and I say goodnight when I go to bed.

Nava's decision to treat the doll as she would a human led to her delivery of the goodnight kiss in a reflection of her own experience of bedtime. Nava effectively linked the dolls' world to her experience of being kissed by and kissing others in her lived world. In other words, this artefact helped the co-construction of Nava's relationship with her world: The doll's human-like features encouraged Nava to act in particular ways around it; one of these actions was to repeat the goodnight kiss scenario of her own life. In the doll-related good night kissing scene, however, Nava took on the role of the adult where in her own life, she was predominantly the recipient of an adult's goodnight kiss. In this interaction we can see another example of the doll's scripting working to facilitate particular actions and replaying social events from different perspectives. On some occasions Nava played the piano for her dolls when she placed the dolls on the couch and pretended that the dolls were watching her similar to *American Idol* and *Australia's Got Talent* shows.

When Nava used the dolls and assigned the role of mother and daughters to the dolls to play the scenario of a day in her life, she used the dolls to interpret her relationship with her teacher and friends. It seems that the possibility of assigning different roles to the dolls helped Nava to reflect upon and to practice her relationships with her mother and the other people who influenced her day-to-day experiences. When Nava was playing the story of a beauty queen, she switched to her and her friend's experience in relation to the boys at school and her mother's feedback on such a relationship and explained it:

Nava:	Look, it is a secret, I'll tell you but in real life at school it happened to me as well. With a boy and me. [She was whispering so her parents would not hear her.]
Researcher:	So it's a real story?
Nava:	Yea but in my school. . . .
Nava:	My friend at school, there are three boys they love her and there are four boys they love me.

These examples address the script embedded in the human body shape and the material characteristics of the dolls' bodies and hair. Through assigning both human roles and enacting scenarios from the world around her, a postphenomenological analysis suggests that Nava and the dolls co-construct the world in which they coexist. The analysis of Nava's engagements with the physical nature and feel of the dolls provides evidence of the co-construction of everyday lifeworlds that Verbeek anticipates (Verbeek and Slob, 2006).

Fashion—with its interchangeable dresses and accessories—is another physical characteristic that attracted Nava. Dressing and undressing of the dolls is the script that positioned the dolls as *fashion dolls*. Being detachable, removable and replaceable, the dolls' dresses and accessories embed the general message: *dress me and undress me*. Undressing and dressing the dolls is the script that is embedded in the characteristics of the dolls' body shape and physical characteristics. Reflecting the power of this script, the research visits found that Nava regularly left dolls naked, necessitating a dressing sequence before she started playing. The selection of accessories and clothing was an important feature of the play scenario. In the first research visit all Nava's dolls were naked sitting on the shelf in Nava's room. These dolls' slippery surface and the smooth surface created by the plastic allow the dresses to easily slide on and off inviting her to dress and undress them. The size, texture and detailing of the clothing and accessories themselves encouraged this process. During the play scenarios, Nava revealed many instances of swapping dresses and jewellery among the dolls. Wearing jewellery such as earrings, necklaces, bracelets and rings was another script prescribed by the combination of the dolls' physical body and the characteristics of the accessories. The earring holes and the ring hole in the dolls' fingers invited her to use doll-compatible jewellery with her dolls, and in different visits the dolls wore different jewellery from the previous study visit. Through dressing and undressing and using the accessories, Nava co-constructed her daily experience and understanding of dressing and undressing.

EXTENDING VERBEEK: NAVA'S RE-SCRIPTING

To this point, we argue that the script embedded in the dolls had an influence on the ways in which Nava used them. Nava interpreted the embodied script and used it to build scenarios and actions that mediated her experience of the everyday. However, the data collected across the research sessions also showed that Nava did more than actively interpret. There were multiple instances observed where Nava's interactions went beyond the capacity of Verbeek's notion of script to account for. Nava physically reshaped the dolls. In effect, she *re-scripted* them.

In one visit, Nava showed two of her dolls to the researcher and mentioned that she does not like to play with those dolls anymore as she "cut one of the dolls' hair one day to make fringe for her [the doll]." On another occasion, Nava changed the colour of a doll's hair. To do this, she used colourful powders from a temporary hair colour kit to colour the doll's black hair for a rock party, saying, "I want to make it red, purple and mix of colours." Nava physically altered the script of the hair in order to retool the object to her particular needs. When Nava finished colouring the doll's hair she was very excited, emphasizing her pleasure at the results with a "Wow."

In one play event, Nava enacted the scenario of the prettiest girl in the country. As part of this scenario she made a specific mixture of different moisturizers to create a smoother skin for the doll and make the doll ready for the competition. Nava referred to the usage of the same mix for her own skin in our conversation:

> *Nava:* I think they are going to a competition about who is the prettiest? The prettiest girl in the country.

She mixed the powder and cream together and rubbed it on the dolls' skin.

Figure 6.3 Nava uses colourful powders to change the doll's hair color. Photo credit: Naghmeh Nouri Esfahani.

Nava: This is milk [body lotion] and some perfume in it.
Nava: Touch it. It's smoother. Do you feel how smooth it is?
Researcher: I like it, it's so smooth.
Nava: I just made it up and ended up with something good.

Interestingly, she only used the mixture for one doll that won the competition. In this case Nava actually replayed the lived experience of interacting with her skin and possibly her interpretation of her mother's experience of using cosmetics to create smooth skin and the cultural link between smooth skin and female beauty. She even suggested that

> these two [she pointed to another cosmetic bottle which was moisturizer] for skin will be great. If you put a little bit of this on your hair and then put a bit of this, your hair and skin will be very smooth.

Nava re-scripted the dolls' skin to be able to project her experience of the smoothness of skin and her knowledge of how to achieve this. Her interest

Figure 6.4 Nava is making a specific mixture of different moisturizers to create a smoother skin for the doll. Photo credit: Naghmeh Nouri Esfahani.

in changing the skin was sustained. In another of the research visits Nava described how she tattoos and decorates her dolls with her mother's lip liner. Whereas other girls in the study permanently tattooed their dolls, Nava consciously used a non-permanent marker as she did not like to "damage the dolls." She used the lip liner as a tool to apply her desired temporary modification.

In the examples addressed in this section, Nava created a new version of doll to fit in her individual context. In other words, the artefact Nava was interacting with was the physically modified and re-scripted one. The analysis undertaken here clearly shows that the process of interacting with the dolls involved more than a singular response to or interpretation of the script. Whereas the object and Nava did work to co-construct a world and to interpret it, the script embedded in the artefact did not necessarily direct this construction. Nava was not a passive recipient of the dolls' scripts. Instead, she actively and constantly looked for connectivity, trying to discover or recall the links between herself and her dolls, interpreting the script while replaying events from her daily life or drawing on popular culture. Importantly, she actively redesigned the artefact to more closely control the co-constructed world in which she and the object operated.

Verbeek's initial discussion of script accounts well for some of these activities. On one level, Nava's interactions can be seen to be guided by the roadmap of the script. She and the dolls work together to mediate the world. However, as shown here, Nava's actions with the doll extend beyond this. Nava *re*-scripts and redesigns the dolls: she colours the dolls' hair; she creates new physical features; she smooths and polishes the plastic skin. Nava effectively interrupts and then changes the script. And this changes the mediation. Importantly, the data gathered and analyzed indicates that Nava does this iteratively. Nava and the doll appear to be in an iterative relation of change. The material changes made to the doll happen over time, and each new alteration builds on the previous re-scriptings. Nava's iterative re-scripting activities enable the doll to better reflect Nava's needs as a young girl.

CONCLUDING COMMENTS

It is doubtful that Verbeek had small girls like Nava or their dolls in mind when developing his conceptual frame. However the focus of this paper on the everyday interactions between a young girl and her everyday artefacts has something important to tell us about the co-construction of everyday worlds and perceptions. Whereas Verbeek tells us that artefacts and the people who interact with them co-create lived realities in praxis, he assumes a single directionality: from artefact to user. In this interpretation, the artefact, through its script, has intentionality, or purpose, and this in turn mediates the perceptions and practices of the individual. However, Verbeek has less to say about the artefact altering, redesigning and re-scripting carried out by Nava. We suggest here that Nava tells us something important. Her iterative re-scripting of her dolls evidences the power of individuals to retool artefacts in ways that move outside the embedded scripts. In other words, she used these alterations to co-construct her lived experiences in ways that are agentive and work to interrupt the embedded, original scripts.

Based on the data collected and our analyses, it is our position that the notion of a static, unitary script as understood in postphenomenology does not, by itself, reflect the ongoing interchange between users and artefacts. The co-construction of the lived world is more complex. Rather than passive recipients of the embedded scripts of artefacts, Nava shows that we are surrounded by our own re-scripted artefacts and worlds. Nava's interactions with the dolls are also iterative. Once a doll has been re-scripted, the altered artefact then interacts with the girls in new ways, leading to more changes. The notion of re-scripting describes this iterative process between user and artefact, attempting to capture the dynamism and fluidity of the lived worlds that are co-constructed.

Our interest in this paper has been to take an everyday object in the life of a child and seek to understand, from a postphenomenological perspective, how that young person interpreted the embedded script. What we found was that this young child read and used the embedded scripts of this global fashion doll, but also that she agentively re-scripted the dolls, effectively repurposing them to allow her to build scenarios and lifeworlds that reflected her own cultural and lived experience. As we argued early in the paper, Barbie dolls are particularly emblematic of plasticity and change alongside their connection to culturally specific gender roles. It seems that in this case also, Barbie's plasticity is informative. Her ability to absorb redesign and re-scripting makes her a powerful everyday object in the life of this young girl, but it also allows us to develop a more nuanced understanding of the close interaction between artefact and individual in the co-construction of everyday lives.

NOTE

1. To keep the participant anonymous, we chose a pseudonym name for our participant and call her Nava in the paper.

REFERENCES

Akrich, M. "The De-scription of Technological Objects," in *Shaping Technology/Building Society: Studies in Sociotechnical Change*. Edited by W. Bijker and J. Law, 205–224. Cambridge: MIT Press, 1992.

Boomen, M. "Hacking Barbie in Gendered Computer Culture," in *Doing Gender in Media, Art and Culture*. Edited by R. Buikema and I. Van Dertuin, 193–206. New York: Routledge, 2009.

Fenichell, S. *Plastic: The Making of the Synthetic Century.* New York: Harper Business, 1996.

Hongan, D., and S. Greene. *Researching Children's Experience: Methods and Approaches*. London: SAGE, 2005.

Ihde, D. *Technology and the Lifeworld: From Garden to Earth*. Bloomington: Indiana University Press, 1990.

———. *Philosophy of Technology: An Introduction*. 1st ed. New York: Paragon House, 1993.

———. *Post-Phenomenology and Technoscience. The Peking University Lectures*. Albany: State University of New York Press, 2009.

Jameson, F. *Postmodernism: Or, the Cultural Logic of Late Capitalism*. Durham: Duke University Press, 1991.

Latour, B. "Where Are the Missing Masses? The Sociology of a Few Mundane Artefacts," in *Shaping Technology/Building Society: Studies in Sociotechnical Change*. Edited by W. Bijker and J. Law, 225–258. Cambridge: MIT Press, 1992.

Mandeville, A. G. *Contemporary Doll Stars: 40 Years of the Best, Featuring Fashion Dolls: Barbie*. Cumberland: Hobby House Press, 1992.

Sarasohn-Kahn, J. *Contemporary Barbie Dolls: 1980 and Beyond*. Dubuque: Antique Trader Books, 1998.

Spade, J. Z., and C. Valentine. *The Kaleidoscope of Gender: Prisms, Patterns, and Possibilities*. 2nd ed. London: SAGE Publications, 2008.
Thomas, J. "Ride 'Em Barbie Girl: Commodifying Folklore, Place and the Exotic," in *Worldviews and the American West: The Life of the Place Itself*. Edited by P. Stewart, S. Siporin, C. W. Sullivan and S. Jones, 65–86. Logan: Utah State University Press, 2000.
Toffoletti, K. *Cyborgs and Barbie dolls: Feminism, Popular Culture and the Posthuman Body*. London: Tauris, 2007.
Van Gelder, L. "A Barbie World: No Wonder Barbie Looks So Great at 50—The Ultimate Blonde Bombshell Has 25 Hair and Makeup Pros on Call." *Allure*. 2009. Accessed January 10, 2010. www.allure.com/beauty-trends/how-to/2009/a_barbie_world.
Verbeek, P.-P. *What Things Do: Philosophical Reflections on Technology, Agency, and Design*. University Park: Pennsylvania State University Press, 2005.
———. "Materializing Morality: Design Ethics and Technological Mediation." *Science, Technology and Human Values* 31, no. 3, 2006. 361–380.
———. "Morality in Design, Design Ethics and the Morality of Technological Artefacts," in *Philosophy and Design: From Engineering to Architecture*. Vol. 1. Edited by P. Vermaas and P. Kross, 91–103. London: Springer, 2008.
Verbeek, P.-P., and Slob A.F.L. "User Behavior and Technology Development: Shaping Sustainable Relations between Consumers and Technologies," in *Eco-Efficiency in Industry and Science*. Edited by P.-P. Verbeek and A.F.L. Slob, 385–399. Dordrecht: Springer, 2006.
Weissman, K. N. *Barbie: The Icon, the Image, the Ideal: An Analytical Interpretation of the Barbie Doll in Popular Culture*. New York: Universal Publishers, 1999.

7 Armed Insurgency, Young Women and the Feminization of Resistance in the Niger Delta

Paul Ugor

> Among the important lessons taught by the literature on women's resistance is that African women are not passive victims waiting to be "saved." Clearly, they are political actors affected by powerful economic, political, and social structural forces over which they may appear to have little or no control. However, these very powerful forces may also be influenced by how women define their interests and the actions they take (Gordon 1996). In other words, women are active subjects. They are part of a dynamic process of constituting and being constituted by society.
>
> (December Green, 1999, 10)

INTRODUCTION

One of the most explosive eruptions of youth in the public sphere in contemporary sub-Saharan Africa, which reverberated both locally and internationally, was the insurgency waged by at least fifty different armed youth groups in the Niger Delta region in southeastern Nigeria, beginning in 2006 and lasting until June of 2009. Operating under the aegis of a loose umbrella organization known as the Movement for the Emancipation of the Niger Delta (MEND), almost 50,000 young men and women in the oil-rich Niger Delta region mobilized themselves and took up military weapons against the Nigerian state and powerful multinational oil corporations like Shell, Chevron, Agip, Total and other oil-servicing and construction companies operating in the Delta area. The armed youth, allegedly agitating for self-determination and a fair share of the oil wealth belching forth from the rich wetlands in their backyards, kidnapped foreign expatriates working for transnational oil companies, vandalized oil installations belonging to both the Nigerian state and international oil companies, attacked security institutions and their personnel, and a host of other violent activities that crippled oil production in the region for almost five years, reducing Nigeria's crude oil production at some point by about 7,500 barrels per day.

A fairly dense body of scholarship has already taken shape around the Niger Delta armed youth rebellion. Although the real social roots of the violent crisis that engulfed the region for seven years remain unclear, scholars generally concede that whereas the insurgency may have been hijacked by unscrupulous criminal elements for selfish interests (Ikelegbe, 2011), the violence that erupted in the Delta could realistically be linked to a long-standing history of corporate exploitation. This is what Michael Watts (2007) calls a prolonged history of "accumulation by dispossession," in which the huge earnings from the crude oil explored in the delta region have been used mainly for the benefit of people outside of the area, leaving over thirty million inhabitants in the oil region in chronic poverty and unimaginable social and economic dislocation (Okonta, 2008; Peel, 2008; Shaxson, 2007; Watts, 2008a). Although the oil-rich Delta region is literally the main fiscal oxygen for the modern Nigerian state, with oil wealth from the region amounting to 80% of government revenue, 96% of foreign exchange earnings, 96% of export revenue and almost half of GDP (Watts, 2008b, 61), "the villages and towns in the region are still locked in a cycle of extreme poverty, widespread unemployment, environmental pollution, and social injustice" (Rowell et al., 2005, xiii). Instead of a life of prosperity, wealth and development/modernity, what the Niger Delta people have experienced in the past fifty years of oil exploration in the region is "a tale of terror and tears" (Watts, 2001, 196). It is these sordid conditions that triggered the youth violence between 2003 and 2009.

At the end of the Niger Delta insurgency in June 2009, a total of 20,192 young men and women were officially demobilized and registered into the presidential amnesty programme commissioned by the federal government of Nigeria. Out of this total number of youth supposedly involved in the Niger Delta insurgency, approximately 1,500 (possibly more) were said to be young women and girls, mostly between the ages of 17 and 40 years. This official figure is a far cry from the actual number of young women who were directly or indirectly involved in the militant activities during the insurgency in the Niger Delta. It is perhaps fair to suggest that out of the estimated 50,000 armed militants involved in the Delta insurgency, at least 5,000 were young women. In spite of the bourgeoning literature on the Niger Delta crisis, however, scholars have rarely acknowledged that these women were directly engaged in the armed conflict and resource struggles in the region. This systematic erasure of the story of female insurgents in the history of the Niger Delta struggle is in part traceable to the public rhetoric of the male militants themselves, who have rarely openly acknowledged the invaluable role played by women in the resource struggles in the region since 2000. This absence of stories of female insurgents in the broader history of the Delta insurgency is significant and indicative of the tripartite dimension of oppression being experienced by women in the region. As Oluwatoyin Oluwaniyi (2011, 150) has observed, Niger Delta women generally not only struggle against state repression and the exploitation and threat posed by multinational oil corporations, but also oppression from a high-handed patriarchal male elite, "resulting in their impoverishment and disempowerment." Oluwaniyi argues, then, that "far from being undifferentiated, the struggle for resource control and self-determination by the ethnic minorities of the [Delta] region is gendered" (ibid.).

My own field research and some documented evidence indicate that not only were young women directly involved in armed encounters with the Nigerian military and other security personnel in the murky creeks in the Delta during the insurgency years, they also took part in the organization of protests, the gathering of intelligence and the siphoning of weapons from the outside world into the creeks. Other activities by the female insurgents included the generation of funds that sponsored the armed protest, the invocation of ancestral powers to protect the young fighters from enemy attacks, and the organization of groceries and other foodstuff used for cooking in the bush camps established by youthful insurgents across the Delta region (Ikelegbe, 2005; Oriola, 2012; Oluwaniyi, 2011; Turner and Brownhill, 2004). The young women involved in the insurgency functioned as armed foot soldiers, spies, informants, couriers and sacred protector/guardians. In some cases, they acted as baits to lure their expatriate-lovers working for multinational oil corporations to vulnerable locations where they were ultimately kidnapped for huge ransom payouts by the MEND militants. These and many other brave and 'invisible' roles and responsibilities by female insurgents helped give teeth to the popular revolt across six years of active military battle with the Nigerian state and transnational oil conglomerates. The huge gap, both in the popular narratives by the male militants themselves and the intellectual discourse around the Niger Delta insurgency, sheds significant light on the prolonged and subtle but powerful ways in which female agency and subjectivity in both colonial and postcolonial African struggles have been (and continue to be) glossed over, diminished, and at times, deliberately erased, thus obfuscating the complete picture of the history of popular struggles for social, political, civic and economic rights and resources in Africa.

In this chapter, then, I present the lives of some of the women who were directly involved in the Niger Delta insurgency and reflect upon the sociocultural and discursive ramifications of their involvement in the Delta rebellion for a new sociology of youth that grounds itself in the layered voices and lives of young people themselves. This concern with female agency and social activism in the context of the armed political protest in the Niger Delta is not an idealistic attempt that trivializes or obliterates horrific experiences such as rape, physical brutality, deaths, unthinkable poverty and many other ghastly crimes inflicted on African women in the pervasive contentious geographies that have engulfed the continent since the 1970s. But I do want to build on and contribute to the growing literature that highlights gender subjectivity and the active differential politics now played by young women in the history of armed struggles for social and economic rights across sub-Saharan Africa.[1] Undoubtedly, the Niger Delta uprising in general was a spontaneous response by an angry and frustrated youth generation to a prolonged history of structural violence and marginalization. And I use the term 'structural violence' specifically in referring to the systematic hindrance of the potential growth or development of an individual or collective entity, constrained by the conditions of the relationship, particularly by the skewed distribution of power and resources (Galtung, 1975, 80). But mainstream historiography on the Niger Delta revolt has been gendered, to say the least. It has been consistently framed as a male-dominated rebellion to social and economic injustice, thereby ignoring both the harrowing experiences and the invaluable roles played by women in that collective struggle.

This strategic 'silencing' of women's rebellion against global capital and postcolonial brutality in many ways engenders further inequities within the already charged unequal socio-economic terrain in the marginalized Delta region. Thus, drawing heavily on the individual biographies of the lives of three young women who participated in the armed insurgency, I offer a phenomenological account of the feminization of popular resistance in the Delta. I demonstrate how young women became significant non-state actors, renegotiating power relations between them and the Nigerian state and global corporate forces, rather than vulnerable social subjects waiting to be protected and rescued by supposedly powerful men in their communities. In many ways, therefore, this chapter complements the mounting body of literature on gender and identity politics in the politically charged geographies in postcolonial Africa, sign-posting the extraordinary ways in which women in contemporary Africa are not necessarily always 'victims,' but increasingly featuring in accountability struggles that challenge the unequal power relations between small and big powers—whether local or transnational, political or economic, religious or ethnic. I begin by setting up the particular research context, methodology and theoretical framework that shaped my critical engagement with some of the female ex-militants in the Delta. I then present the lives and voices of three young women who participated directly in the Delta insurgency, and end with a reflection on individual memories as an important site of gaining access to the lived experience of young people engaged in collective social struggles against powerful forces of globalization.

RESEARCH CONTEXT, METHODOLOGY AND THEORY

I began my research work in the Niger Delta in July of 2010 as part of my postdoctoral research on the "Politics of Youth Culture in Nigeria," a project that examined and reflected on the ways in which marginalized youth in Nigeria reinvent their identities under precarious social and economic conditions. It is this research project that led me to the National Youth Service Orientation Camp in Obubra, Cross River State, where the Nigerian federal government, through a special Presidential Amnesty Committee, was running a Demobilisation, Disarmament, Rehabilitation and Reintegration program for the initial 20,192 ex-militants shortlisted for rehabilitation/retraining after the declaration of amnesty by the Nigerian government for the armed Niger Delta youth by Late President Yar 'Adua in June of 2009.

I visited and stayed at the Obubra amnesty camp from 18–30 of August 2010, where I spent time with about 650 ex-militants from three different states, including Delta, Edo and Bayelsa. The ex-militants had been mobilized for the rehabilitation/non-violence training program organized by the Nigerian Federal Government and run by an NGO, the Foundation for Ethnic Harmony (FEHN), in conjunction with the Centre for Conflict and Peace Studies of the University of Rhode Island. My time at the camp was spent interviewing and interacting with over sixty male ex-militants, attending some of their lectures, watching them undergo Para-military training, and engaging them in discussions about everything from what happened before, during and after the insurgency years to petty chit-chats about their families and even personal relationships with wives and girlfriends. It was in the course of my fieldwork at the NYSC camp that I heard of a batch of about 750 girls involved in the insurgency who were due for their own training at the camp in December of the same year. But I had to return to Canada in early September for the fall term and thus missed that particular training session for the female ex-militants.

I returned to the Delta region again in February of 2011 and had no luck tracing any of the young women that participated in the DDRR program in December of 2010. In August of 2011, I returned again to the Delta for the third time, and this time, I was fortunate to meet the last batch of amnesty training at Obubra, which included some 200 young women. Most of the girls were either unwilling or scared to talk to me openly about their role in the Delta insurgency. Although I interviewed about thirty of them in camp, most of the interviews were unhelpful as the girls evaded my questions and often gave surface answers that shed little light in relation to their roles and responsibilities in the context of the Niger Delta uprising. I initially thought the female ex-militants were wilfully silent because they were uncomfortable with me as a male researcher from the United Kingdom. I was later to learn that the girls thought I was a CIA agent or that I was working for an international cable network like CNN or the BBC and wanted to broadcast their stories on international television, thus destroying their public image as 'decent women.'[2]

As I reflected on this 'strategic silence' or evasion, it reminded me of Ann Fujii's thesis that silences in research work, especially in conflict and post-conflict zones, can be "polyvalent. Their meanings can be multiple and contradictory. They can both hide and reveal" (Fujii, 2009, 158). Indeed, as Alcinda Honwana (2006, 18) points out in her perspicacious work on child-soldiers in Mozambique and Angola, we cannot afford to ignore "informants' agency" in post-conflict research because "even within the constraints inherent in their situation, they can choose what messages they wish to convey to the world and how they wish to communicate them." This is like an internal surplus, as Ricoeur might say, inside the words left behind in the interviews.

I maintained a close relationship with some of the female ex-militants I interviewed at the NYSC Camp, which ultimately led me to the three female ex-militants whose social activism I examine in this chapter. As I maintained contact from abroad over a one-year period, making frequent calls to some of the female ex-militants I interviewed both within and outside the camp, the relationships solidified, trust was developed and more details of their activities emerged, leading to an incredible world of female activism and agency during the struggle for environmental justice in the oil-rich Delta.

Phenomenology, both as a continental intellectual movement and a radical mode of interpretation, is essentially a twentieth-century European scholarly tradition. But how might this deeply Euro-American intellectual movement yield productive insights for an engaged analysis of society, culture and politics in the so-called developing world? Specifically, how might phenomenology be useful for any radical re-reading of youth, gender and identity politics in the context of political violence in contemporary Africa? I raise these questions from the experience of hindsight: On occasion, I have been asked in conferences by Africanists and non-Africanists alike about the appropriateness of the so-called European theories for making sense of 'uniquely' African socio-cultural and political processes.

Although grounded in a vast expanse of Euro-American scholasticism stretching from Germany to France, and later, the United States, the real essence of phenomenological research transcends its European pedigree. Indeed, as Dermot Moran (2000, 3) reminds us, phenomenological research does not cohere into one single "agreed method, or accept one theoretical outlook, or one set of philosophical theses about consciousness, knowledge, and the world." Still, as a radical and unconventional way of doing philosophy and social science, phenomenology "emphasizes the attempt to get to the truth of matters, to describe phenomenon, in the broadest sense as whatever appears in the manner in which it appears, that is, as it manifests itself to consciousness, to the experiencer" (ibid., 4). In regards to youth studies, for example, this invites attention to youth in the exact ways they present themselves to the world, not an interpretation that seeks to speak on behalf of such youth. Both as an anti-traditional method and an iconoclastic academic movement, phenomenology shifted philosophical inquiry from somewhat elitist abstractions to an intellectual concentration on what Husserl saw as "the lived-world, the world of ordinary, immediate experience" (Stewart and Mickunas, 1974, 12), especially as felt and perceived by the thinking subject. Phenomenology's main contribution, then, as Dermot Moran (2000, 21) reminds us, has been "the manner with which it has steadfastly protected the subjective view of experience as a necessary part of any full understanding of the nature of knowledge." This primacy and emphasis on what Edmund Husserl termed "the things themselves" is perhaps an urgently needed intellectual remedy in youth research in general. Whereas the discourse of globalizing processes and their ramifications for young people's lives has flourished in the global field of the sociology of youth in the past decade, the exact ways in which social change has impacted youth and how they are processing those changes, *particularly from the perspective of youth themselves,* remains largely foggy. This ungroundedness in the global sociology of youth perhaps accounts for Steven Miles's critique: that it is not enough to just suggest that the world is changing and that young people are changing with it. What matters is the answer to Miles's question: What form does "the link between . . . young people and social change actually take?" (Miles, 2000, 66). It is in order to contribute in response to this question that I have chosen to focus squarely on the 'subjective experiences' of the young women themselves in this chapter. Rather than collate and interpret a string of activities supposedly undertaken by young women in the context of the Niger Delta crisis, I have chosen instead to focus on the voices of 'the young women themselves' who were directly involved in the political conflict and violence in the Delta, and to work with those texts through a blend of the biographical method (grounded in anthropology) and phenomenological analysis.

LIFE STORIES, PHENOMENOLOGY AND YOUTH RESEARCH

The life stories or oral method, Tamsin Bradley (2011, 35) observes, "literally involves asking people to orally recount either the whole story of their life or a period of it or even one particular experience." As in phenomenology, life stories centralized the perception(s) of the subjective voice in its analysis. The real value of this methodological choice is that it "seeks to destabilise the power relations between the person who shares their experience and the researcher who records and later analyses it" (ibid., 35). As a distinctive way of gathering in-depth social data, the life stories approach "enables much closer insights into the complexities of people's life experiences than other techniques allow" (ibid.). Similar to phenomenology, life stories often turn to "the content of consciousness itself—to the phenomena . . . [to describe] the essences of phenomena, the explication of the various levels of meaning of phenomena, and their interrelationships" (Stewart and Micunas, 1974, 8). Doing so involves a process of individuation, which Sajama and Kampepinen (1987, 3) describe as the process whereby "a thing is distinguished by a subject from all other things." Individuation can be achieved in two ways: "either qualitatively, by describing the object so precisely that the description applies to only one object, or spatio-temporarily, by indicating the unique location of the object in space and time" (ibid.).

In what follows, I have combined both approaches. I use a qualitative method of individuation, focused on attending to three distinct subjective experiences of gender activism in the context of the Delta insurgency. I do so in relation to specific thinking subjects who are responding in diverse ways to an outer world marked by all kinds of social, economic, political and cultural forces and inequities. I recount a subjective experience, in other words, but this "is not a description of something purely 'inner,' but of their involvement with a world which exists independently of [their] experience of it" (Mathews, 2006, 20). I have located my analysis of gender and youth activism in the Delta region within the context of a prolonged history of structural violence perpetrated by the Nigerian state and transnational oil corporations in the Delta. My critique combines subjectivism with objectivism, drawing heavily on the voices of the young women themselves, but casting specific interpretations around such voices as a way to foreground and accentuate the significance of certain actions, thoughts/ideas, perceptions, logics, rhetoric(s) and other forms of human entanglement that weave together the lives of the young women in this article.

In the next segment, the layered voices of the girls appear in their own words and on their own terms. Whereas the female ex-militants I interacted with were merely responding to questions and issues raised by me, and thus shaping the direction of our discussion in many ways, I have tried to ensure that the core of the discussion by each interviewee is left intact. The value of such an approach is that it allows "women to explore, record and give voice to their experiences, positive and negative . . . " (Bradley, 2011, 1), without any extraneous mediating influences (like translation) that often claim to give direction and depth to such subjective experiences.[3]

FEMALE WARRIORS IN THE DELTA CREEKS: GENERAL EGBERIMA, HOPE EBIKIRIAMA AND LILLIAN KIAGBODOR

As part of this research project, I interviewed over thirty female ex-militants whose ages ranged between 17 and 35 years. The women were directly or indirectly involved in the Niger Delta armed conflict between 2005 and 2009. Unlike other studies of women and violent conflict in Africa, however, all the young women I interviewed were not forced or tricked into becoming part of the violent struggle for environmental justice in the Delta by armed group(s) operating in the region. Almost all the women said they had joined MEND voluntarily, without threat or coercion by any person or constituted authority, whether communal or otherwise. Initially, some of the girls had gone to the bush camps set up by the male militants as petty traders to sell groceries like cigarettes, soft drinks, bottled water, toiletries or local delicacies. Others went there as partners to visit loved ones. There are others who first encountered the Para-military camps set up by the MEND insurgents as community emissaries carrying food, money, prepaid phone cards, information and other everyday resources for young male militants scattered in camps all over the Delta creeks. The shift in identity from petty traders, lovers and community messengers to actual combatants or 'Freedom Fighters' was a spontaneous but conscious action that happened mostly after the women witnessed the acute suffering and pain experienced by those from their local communities in the bush camps.

I begin with General Egberima, perhaps the fiercest female fighter during the Delta insurgency, and then follow with two other women who belonged to two different MEND camps. Apart from Egberimama, who expressed explicit interest in having her name featured in the research, I have used pseudonyms for the other two ex-militants to protect their identities. All three women speak individually about themselves and analyze the specific contexts that shaped their actions as young people responding to both local and global forces shaping their individual and collective lives. Although I have prefaced the bios with short introductions, the introductions have been gleaned directly from my interactions and interviews with the women.

GENERAL EGBERIMA/MA—LEADER OF THE NIGER DELTA AMAZON FORCE

Although popularly known in the whole of the Delta region as General Egberimama, her real name is Cyril Hart (named after her father), and she hails from Gbile Kingdom in Usoka, Degema, the oldest local government region in Rivers State. She was born and raised in Port Harcourt in Rivers State and completed her secondary school education in June 1985. Egberima's father died very early, leaving her mother, a poor trader, with nine children. She herself has one daughter and told me she had begun to train her to be as brave as herself. When I interviewed General Egberima in 2011 she was thirty-six years old, and had joined the struggle for self-determination in the Delta in her late twenties. She worked with Chief Alhaji Mujaheed Asari Dokubo, leader of the Niger Delta Peoples Volunteer Force (NPVF). She was the only woman who fought alongside Asari Dokubo during the armed insurgency and had in fact volunteered to take over from him as commander of the NDPVF group in case he was arrested by the Nigerian security agencies. She told me Chief Tompolo, the fiercest MEND commander alive, knows her. She had visited his notorious Camp 5 at Gbaramatu in Delta State during the heyday of the insurgency. She also lost her younger brother to the insurgency; he was a fighter with Tom Ateke's group. Almost everybody around the Niger Delta knows about General Egberimama's exploits as a woman warrior during the armed struggle.

Currently, she runs a small restaurant close to Kidney Island, at Abonnema Warf, in Port Harcourt, Rivers State. The amnesty program promised to sponsor her to go to the United States for training, but it was not exactly clear when that will happen. Egberima's plan is to establish a catering school where she will teach young women in the Delta how to use the culture and food of their people to make money and support themselves. According to her, "If we cannot make money and have a better life from oil wealth, we can do so from other things. Our people were extremely rich even before Shell and other big oil companies came to the Niger Delta to destroy our land and make our people lazy, so why should we now depend on only oil?" Below she talks about how and why she came to join the Delta insurgency.

> My involvement with the Niger Delta struggle began when I joined the Ijaw Youth Council (IYC) in the late 1990s and was trained in the use of weapons by my late uncle, Chief Okoboro at Elemama in the ancient town of Kalabari in Rivers State. I saw my uncle training some young men on how to use guns and I went there and tried what they were doing. I turned out to be a pretty good shot and I just stayed with the group; nobody invited me and I wasn't asked to leave by anyone. I was the only woman amongst 197 people trained by my uncle to help in the Niger Delta struggle. Unfortunately, today, people who have benefitted from the struggle do not remember people like my uncle again. It was a very rigorous training for one year. That is when I saw bravery, sincerity of purpose and genuine actions aimed at delivering the Ijaw nation from exploitation and extermination by the Nigerian government and greedy oil companies. We had very little money, food and other material resources, but we were determined to speak truth to power. We shut down oil wells, fought Nigerian soldiers and policemen to a standstill and we helped educate local women through propaganda. Some women who did not take up weapons like me provided advice, money, food, water, and prayers, especially through the power of Egbesu. I was actually infused with the powers of Egbesu during the struggle; no bullet from any gun could penetrate my body. That is the power of Egbesu, the Ijaw god of war and justice. While we were fighting, I had no fear of death. I knew we were right, that we were fighting for our ancestral land, and that our forefathers were behind us and will protect us. The Ijaw gods don't support an unjust war, so I knew we were on the right path of history.
>
> The Nigerian federal government and the oil companies created the war in the Niger Delta. The federal government has done nothing for us since they started drilling oil here more than fifty years ago. Oil companies connive with 'big men' from our local communities to exploit our people. The oil companies not only use 'force men' [security officials] to intimidate aggrieved youth protesting against exploitation and injustice in our communities, they use a lot of our young men as cheap labour, paying them peanuts for long hours of work. This is why some of us women joined the struggle. Some of the women just helped the boys with information [intelligence]; others went to the camps to sell water and food; and others went there to help the boys avoid 'homosexuality'. But today, the Niger Delta Development Commission (NDDC)

recognises only male ex-militants, but they don't remember the sacrifices of women like me. They give contracts to men, not women. When the federal government granted amnesty to the Niger Delta militants in June 2009 they invited only men to go and submit their weapons, but what of women like me who carried dangerous weapons too to fight for our people? Why wasn't I invited to bring my own girls and submit our own guns? That is why in February 2010 I went to the Niger Delta Development Commission (NDDC) office and stripped myself naked in protest against the injustice done to the women of this region who suffered for the freedom of the Niger Delta people. I even smeared faeces on the walls of their offices. That should teach them a lesson not to take Niger Delta women for granted. And I'm ready to do more if they don't listen to me. I paid such a high price for our struggle against the oil companies because now I can't even marry and have my own husband, yet, I'm not being recognised for my efforts to free our people from bondage. That is our country for you!

Today, I advise the young men and women in the Niger Delta against cultism and senseless violence, especially against each other. They should concentrate on the struggle and nothing else. That is what will attract international journalists and academics like you to pay attention to our cause. That is why I oppose the kidnapping of foreign expatriates working for oil companies. Kidnapping is a 'personal race, not the community struggle'. I see kidnappers as a shame to the Ijaw kingdom. I ask the Niger Delta youth to love one another and stop betraying one another and the struggle. In fact, if that happens, I see a more powerful generation in the future that will exceed the exploits of Egberimama![4]

HOPE EBIKIRIAMA ALIAS "AKPURUKA BABE"

I first met Hope at the Royal City Comfort Hotel at Odogunyan, in Ikorodu, Lagos State in February of 2012. She and other female ex-militants were there for training as caterers, sponsored by the Nigerian Federal Government as part of the amnesty program for the Delta ex-militants. Hope is from Okrika Local Government Area in Rivers State, one of the leading oil-producing states in the Delta region. She is a professional caterer by training and is now married to a young man she met in Camp during the Niger Delta struggle. Her husband is a young man from Akwa-Ibom State, another core oil-producing state in the Delta region with prime offshore oil wells mostly owned and run by the transnational oil conglomerate, Mobile. Hope had already given birth to their first child when we met in Lagos. As Hope herself told me,

The Niger Delta conflict was not just about violent conflict and war; it led young people to find love and happiness, to gain a clear sense of the meaning of life, to start their own families, and be responsible citizens. Fighting and suffering alongside each other opened our eyes to many things and made us ask ourselves important questions about the meaning of life. Now we're looking forward to the future with hope and determination.

In the following excerpt she talks about her involvement with the armed insurgency in the Delta, the stifling social conditions in the oil region, the challenges women face there and the politics of violence as a weapon for young people resisting global economic forces.

I joined Tom Ateke's group about five years ago when I was about 29/30 years of age. We were about one hundred girls in the camp and no one was forced to join; people just came to the camp on their own. And my choice to join the militant struggle in the Delta was not because I am a bad person or that I naturally like violence, but because of the extreme suffering we have experienced here for years. If you finish from college as a young person in the Niger Delta, you have no work, no business, or any other thing to turn to. Just nothing! I am a professional caterer by training, but I have no job or money to open my own business. If you apply to oil companies even for small contracts to supply food and drinks to their canteens as a caterer, they will not give you the job. Instead, they give the jobs to outsiders, i.e. Hausa and Yoruba people. In some exceptional cases, you may be considered for a position in the oil companies, but some senior supervisor in the company will ask you to bribe him with a huge sum of money before you are given the job. But because you don't have money to pay, you'll be denied the position. That is how some people in the oil companies exploit even ordinary people who have nothing.

It was because of all this suffering that we decided to join our brothers to fight for our freedom. Outsiders have been taking away what belongs to the Niger Delta people for years, bringing suffering and pain to the entire region. On top of that, they'll still come to our communities and burn down houses and people's property when we complain. My friend Tombiaba hails from Tombia town here in Rivers State and she doesn't have her certificates again because soldiers went to her village and burnt everything down for no just cause. We have been suffering in the Delta for a long time; no jobs, no money, no food, no hospitals, no tarred roads, and so on. I cannot even count the problems we deal with everyday in this place. And this suffering is caused by our corrupt leaders at the top who take everything including those meant for common people. So for us the women, joining the armed insurgency was about survival. Ateke Tom treated us like a father and took us like his own children, and is still nice to us even till today. He is a good leader. He fed us, gave us money to open bank accounts and protected us. Generally men in the Niger Delta don't empower women in any way so it felt good to be empowered to live our lives the way we wanted and with our own earnings. So we joined the movement and supported him because he wasn't fighting for just his personal gain, but because of our collective interests. It was a fight for our future and the future of our children. I am about to have my own child and I don't want my children to go through the same pain I went through in Life.

I am not one hundred percent proud of what I did as a woman, but I can tell you that violence was necessary in the Delta. It was violence that created the opportunity for government to train us in various careers, so people don't walk around jobless because they have no handiwork or training of any kind. It is because of our agitation that the government sent us to Obubra for 14 days where we had training in non-violence. I have that certificate to show. We later went to Ikorodu in Lagos State to do the training in catering services. All these things came about because we fought the Nigerian government and oil companies to a standstill. Nobody would have listened to us without violence. Now we even have a son of the Delta as President of Nigeria. Do you think these things will have been possible without violence? That is the only language that the government and oil companies understand. Since I was born here in the Delta I have been hearing of the Niger Delta people going to different courts, writing petitions and leading delegations to governments all over the world, but those strategies have never helped our people. So I have no regrets about what I did as a young woman to save our people. When my child grows up, s/he will hear of what I did as a woman for our people and how I fought to save his/her future. The battle hasn't ended, but at least, they now know that we are capable of fighting back and will be careful in the way they treat us. I am proud to be part of the movement that created that awareness. Because of our efforts, I don't think anybody in this country will take us for granted again, at least not blatantly.

It was not easy in camp, I tell you. Detractors wanted our leader (Tom Ateke) and people around him dead. Government was against him. Soldiers and other security agents were looking for him and his followers. So it was quite difficult for us, especially as women. Living in the creeks with no electricity and decent accommodation was tough for everyone, but we knew we were fighting a just cause so we stuck to our guns. We managed whatever we had in camp and prayed to our gods to help our struggle. And I think this is where we must thank a lot of our women. Although not all took up weapons to fight, they supported the struggle spiritually, using the power of Jesus and Egbesu. They invoked the gods of our land to protect us and shield us from our enemies. Some women even gave up their business capital to support the struggle. Things haven't changed completely, but at least, there have been some changes and there's more to come, I believe.

Now that the violence is over, I hope they don't forget us, especially the women. We have voluntarily submitted to the amnesty program and have undergone two phases of the training program. The government should follow-up appropriately by providing us the requisite funds to open our own businesses. After the training, the government should get us jobs. They should try and fulfil their promises because the boys might go back to the forests if they deceive us. The government should help because it is their responsibility to take care of its people.[5]

TIMINIMI KIAGBODOR

Timinimi (aged 34) hails from Ukporoza kingdom in Gbaramatu Local Government area in Delta State and came to the Amnesty camp under the auspices of General Tompolo, the infamous ground commander of MEND in the Niger Delta during the insurgency years. She completed her high school education years back in the late 1990s but could not proceed further with her studies due to lack of funds. Timi told me there are thousands of young people like her in her community in Gbaramatu, both men and women, who share the same story: young people whose lives have been messed up by a nonchalant Nigerian state and "greedy" oil companies that don't care about the future of the immediate communities where they generate stupendous wealth. For Timi and others in her cohort, they joined the Niger Delta struggle "out of frustration." Below she talks about this life of "frustration" and uncertainty for people in her generation and the particular methodologies of resistance employed by women in her community to resist global corporate forces in the form of multinational oil companies:

When I say we joined the Delta struggle out of frustration, I mean a series of things that happened to us even within our own local communities, things done by our own leaders that have left a lot of people sad, bitter and angry. Now, you know this whole crisis started with the ethnic crisis in Delta State, particularly between the Itsekiri and the Ijaw people. There is a long history of oppression between these two ethnic groups. The Itsekiri have always oppressed us the Ijaw nation because they have people in high places; 'big men' at the top that speak for them and protect their collective interests. We the Ijaw have often been treated like people who do not know anything. So the ethnic crisis was the main trigger for the larger crisis, particularly when they forcefully took away the headquarters of the newly created local government of the Ijaw from Ogbijor to Ogidigbe in 1996. Since then, we've been 'setting our blows' and waiting for action. It was from that ethnic crisis that things exploded and expanded to embrace the Nigerian army and other issues in the Delta.

You have just noted that the reason for your interest in us young Niger Delta women is because it is only men that scholars have written about when it comes to the Niger Delta struggle. But I must note however that as far as I know, no woman has been directly involved in 'carrying guns' [fighting]. They know nothing about it really; I haven't even heard about it in our communities. But crisis generally affect us as women, even as we walk around pursuing our everyday life. When insurgents and the army begin to burn and destroy things, it does affect us too. Even if you go to the Delta yourself to see how people live in that area it will affect you. So for most women, even just their prayers, prayers that result from acute suffering and pain, can become a serious weapon in the hands of helpless and defenseless women. You have also just mentioned that some women have been associated with black magic and juju, but our women were not involved in those things. But any woman who has given birth to a child and doesn't want that child to go and die in a deadly battle, and holds her breasts as 'caretaker' of her child to ask God to protect her son from harm's way, God will surely answer. So in Tompolo's camp women never had anything to do with black juju [black magic]. If there was any such thing, only the men were privy to it. For most women, it was just prayers and peaceful protests to create awareness about the evils by government and oil companies on our people. A good example in this regard will be the one event when the Joint Task Force (JTF) went to Gbaramatu and burnt down the whole community. A lot of people died, some fled to surrounding bushes and forests, and many people didn't even know where family members were. So we the women, mostly those in Warri, mobilised ourselves in a peaceful protests against the government with placards and went over to the DBS office. We wanted to create global awareness of what was happening to our people. We wanted to show the pain oil companies have brought to our communities. So when it came to mass mobilization and civic protest to create global awareness about our conditions and even amongst our own people, I was always there. Women in our area were not directly involved in armed conflict with soldiers or the police. Some might argue that women's blood may not have been spilled directly in battle fields, but our women have lost sons, husbands, children, relatives, farms, and many other things that have in many cases led to their own deaths. How else should women spill their own blood for the freedom of the Niger Delta? So we are victims too. But we have also been warriors, fighting in our own unique way to help protect our land and our people and we are not ashamed of that history.

You've also asked me about the specific conditions around the area where I live in the Delta. I come from Gbaramatu in Delta State, but I have no way of explaining how things are there other than to say where I live, there's truly plenty of suffering, I mean real suffering. We lack many things. We have no other way of surviving apart from fishing. But now as we speak, even fishing has become a serious problem because of the pollution wrought by multinational oil companies on the water bodies in our communities. And in the Delta we don't have enough land for farming which will produce food adequate for both local subsistence and for commercial purposes. Even when we manage to plant a few things, the crude oil spilling from oil pipelines still destroys them. So that's our dilemma in the Delta. And we have no jobs in the Delta. Even those who have managed to get an education, there are no jobs for them. There's Chevron and Shell right by our community, but its only people from other tribes that you find working there. Parents who scrounge all their life to help their children graduate from the university and other colleges in the hope that they'll get jobs with the oil companies and help the family are often left with heavy disappointments because their children cannot secure jobs with the oil companies. We don't even get good education in the Delta. We struggle to do so many things as young people that by the time you get to school, it's already 10am or 11am when classes have far gone in the day. So it's really terrible how we live in the Niger Delta and you can understand why a lot of young people around there are angry with the government and oil companies.

Has anything changed in the Delta since the end of the insurgency? I can only tell you that there's relative peace in the area because people move around without fear, otherwise, nothing has really changed. I know that Shell and Chevron, mostly on account of the struggle by MEND, have now instituted scholarships to support young people in school. But even that is way far between and really small; maybe five people in this community and then five for another community the next year. So they rotate the whole thing. And we have a sizeable population so the funding is grossly inadequate for the helpless people waiting in line to get the support they need to enable them get an education so they can support themselves and their families. And the funding itself is so modest you can barely use it to rent a house in an expensive city like Warri. So what happens if you use the meagre funding you've been given to rent only a house? How do you pay your tuition, buy books and survive on a daily basis? During the crisis, oil production stopped completely in our communities. But with the amnesty, production has resumed and it's business as usual. Oil companies still spew crude oil destroying our land, plants and animals.

So I want the world to know that young people and their parents are suffering here in the Delta. Our biggest problem is lack of employment for our people, especially the youth. Even those who have completed their studies are sitting at home without jobs. Some few have been lucky to secure jobs, but a majority are still jobless. My own brothers have graduated and are at home without jobs. And this is affecting us terribly. If young people have jobs they could help support the extended family, but that is not the case now. My hope is that the amnesty program will help address the crisis of unemployment in the Delta. A lot of us were concerned about coming here because we were told that it might affect us in the future, especially as women. But we've damned the consequences and I do hope that government and oil companies will fulfil their promise to do right by the Delta people from now onwards. I don't know what will happen if they fail to keep their promises, but I can tell you that even as I don't like violence, one might never foreclose possibilities of future violence, especially if young people feel betrayed.[6]

SUBALTER MEMORIES, YOUTH ACTIVISM AND FEMINIST POLITICS IN AFRICA

In the introduction to the second edition of his now famous book, *Why Men Rebel,* Ted Robert Gurr (2010, ix, emphasis mine) notes that: "I was convinced then, and am convinced now, that to build a more peaceful and secure world, we need to *begin by analyzing the minds of men—and women—who oppose bad governments and unpopular policies. But equally we need to know about the societies in which they live, their beliefs and cultural traditions, and the governments they oppose."* Following this well-beaten tradition blazed by Gurr, what this essay offers is a phenomenological route into 'the minds' of the young women who took part in the political protests against oil capitalism and ruthless postcolonial governance in the Delta region in southeastern Nigeria. I use the term 'minds' cautiously only in so far as it designates a certain perspective of complex events and history as understood and recounted by the interviewees. The significance of this approach is that it allows us to gain indirect access into the societies in which these young people lived through their 'voices,' which carry the individual and collective identities of non-state actors. For as Gurr (ibid., xiv, emphasis mine) suggests, among the new guidelines for anyone interested in seeking to understand popular discontent, is the constant need to not only understand "the sources of people's grievances by examining their status and treatment by government and by other groups," but also what the *"people say, not just what others say about them."* Chela Sandoval (2000, 3) stresses the same point when she argues that "[i]n identifying the practices that constitute the differential mode of resistance, it is necessary to stipulate the inner and outer technologies, the psychic and social processes required of practitioners of differential social movement." The power of such an approach, Sandoval (ibid.) argues, is that "one constructs an alternative and dissident globalization in place of the neocolonizing forces of postmodernism." Thus, any phenomenological account of young people involved in oppositional consciousness and social movements such as was the case in the Delta region demands that we speak to and hear from the young rebels themselves to gain insights into the surplus sociality and violence being experienced by the mass of young people left bitter and frustrated by the insensitive governments and global corporate forces that rule contemporary Africa.

The voices of the young women whose experiences we recount here are indeed poignant for many reasons, and precisely so because they describe in very powerful ways what Nelson Maldonado-Torress (2008, xiii) has eloquently described as "subalter memories," that is, "memories of suffering and displacement, but also of happiness and hope in the midst of challenges to human existence by repressive and inhuman social orders." But such "subaltern projects," Maldonado-Torress (ibid.) further observes, whether aimed at achieving emancipation for a whole people or liberation for individuals or groups, all "refer to forms of resistance and transformation that seek to undo dehumanizing practices and suffering that ensues from them." Although speaking as individual participants within a larger youth movement that sought to contest and rework all sorts of political, social and economic asymmetries between them, local patriarchal political elites and late-capitalist oil capitalism, their accounts in many ways represent a shade of history recounted by members of an entire generation of women who rose in unison against corporate and postcolonial oppression, using both passive and active strategies of resistance that have so far only been recounted in a few essays (see Ikelegbe, 2005; Oluwaniyi, 2011; Oriola, 2012; Turner and Brownhill, 2004). Their actual voices have not, however, really been heard.

This essay offers us a new phenomenological account of youth activism in the Delta that not only creates a social and analytical space to hear directly from the young women who were involved in the self-determination struggles in Niger Delta themselves, but also functions as a global social lever from which these young women address the world, recounting not just their actions, but also their motivations, reasons and thoughts within specific stifling postcolonial conditions. By recounting their experiences of 'war created by government,' oil pollution wrought by multinational oil companies, unrelenting unemployment, excruciating poverty, individual and collective traumas, ethnic rivalry and other forms of social tensions and inequities, these young women tell us directly not only about their lived lives, but also how they and their various communities have borne, processed and resisted powerful social and economic forces that are all linked to relentless globalizing processes. Such personal narratives undoubtedly shed strong light on why young people all over Africa who survive on the margins are now increasingly constituting themselves into what Achille Mbembe calls "alternative sovereignties" that are poised against constituted authority. This emphasis on young non-state actors themselves, rather than what others say about them, is indeed an urgent imperative in youth studies, especially the studies about contemporary African youth, for it offers us a new avenue and reliable heuristic for a productive engagement with what is often labelled as 'senseless' and 'mindless' violence by young people in the pervasive contentious geographies of modern-day Africa.

For the thousands of girls in the Delta creeks who ignored family warnings/threats and transgressed entrenched social boundaries to join the violent struggle for the hydrocarbon resources from their homeland, therefore, the armed insurgency was about the search for justice and social and economic rights taken away from them and their communities as citizens of the Nigerian state. Ebinabor Frank, another young woman who was a member of the Farah Dagogo group, puts it rhetorically: "How can you not support somebody who has realised that his people have been cheated and is trying to reclaim that which was stolen from the people to give back to the people? Even in the Bible, it is stated that you claim what belongs to you by force."[7]

Here we see how young people mobilize all kinds of oppositional rhetoric to not only rationalize their actions in the face of institutionalized corporate violence, but also to beckon us to the social consciousness and conscience of young people in postcolonial Africa. We begin to see here how young women in oppressed communities all over Africa are not only thinking subjects acutely aware of their social environments, but also social beings who are influenced by and in turn influence both local and global events unfolding around them and act accordingly in search of redress, whether such problems are political, economic, socio-cultural or even philosophical. Thus, sociality, especially as privileged in these young women's accounts, embodies a constellation of complex, interwoven and sometimes contradictory web of forces swirling around the Niger Delta as a geo-political entity, which ultimately leads to processes of co-optation, exclusion and domination on the one hand, and the struggles for social belonging and equity, on the other. Such active responses and reactions by young women in contemporary Africa are poignant reminders that African youth are not just passive global entities waiting to be rescued by whatever forces exist outside of their own world. They, like their counterparts all over the world, are aware and interested in tracking and resisting what Sandoval (2000, 9) describes as "the imperializing nature of transnational capitalism"; i.e., its ability to cross borders, to colonize, subjugate and subjectify people. But the contentious politics of young people in the Delta and elsewhere in the African Postcolony indicate how a restless youth generation is now acting in very proactive ways to redefine the course of both local and global histories that have implications for their own personal lives and the future of their immediate communities. The young women featured in this research speak for themselves in terms of their motivations, inner thoughts, actions and reading of both local and global forces whirling around their lives. By so doing, I do not, whether as researcher or privileged male figure living in the heart of the global metropolis, speak about or on their behalf. Put differently, whereas I acknowledge my role in shaping the discursive outcome of the materials collected and interpreted in this chapter, the work was not mainly invested in an indulgent effort to "give voice to the voiceless." Rather, by collecting, sifting and encouraging the interpretation of specific accounts of the Niger Delta insurgency by these women, I aim to provide a better understanding and knowledge of the complicated web of tensions and power renegotiations that accompanied the Niger Delta youth rebellion.

NOTES

1. See for example, Caroline N. Moser and Fiona Clark, eds., *Victims Perpetrators or Actors? Gender, Armed Conflict & Political Violence* (London: Zed Books, 2001); Chris Coulter, *Bush Wives & Girl Soldiers: Women's Lives through War and Peace in Sierra Leone* (Ithaca: Cornell University Press, 2009); Cindy Ness, ed., *Female Terrorism and Militancy: Agency, Utility and Organisation* (Abingdon: Routledge, 2008); Laura Sjoberg, *Gender, War and Militarism: Feminist Perspectives* (Santa Barbara: Praeger, 2010); Melissa Leach, *Rainforest Relations: Gender & Resource Use among the Mende of Gora, Sierra Leone* (Edinburg: Edinburg University Press, 1994); Meredith Turshen and Clotilde Twagiramariya, *What Women Do in Wartime: Gender & Conflict in Africa* (London: Zed Books, 1998).
2. In a recent phone call to one of the girls I interviewed at Obubra, she told me that most girls who registered for the amnesty program are now seen as "prostitutes and criminals" and are often being discriminated against by their communities.
3. Although the interviews were conducted mostly in Nigerian Pidgin English, and in formal and informal situations, I have rewritten the interviews in Standard English for the purpose of non-Nigerian readers who may not understand Nigerian pidgin. The outcome is a much firmer documentation and portrait of the complexities around how young women in Africa confront and process personal and collective struggles, especially in the face of straitened circumstances.
4. Based on two personal interviews I conducted with General Egberima at Udeme Hotel in Yenogoa, Delta State on September 30, 2011, and at Pend Hotel in Port Harcourt on October 3, 2011. I have also followed up the interviews with personal visits in Port Harcourt and frequent phone calls from Birmingham, UK, and Hamilton, Canada.
5. Based on personal interviews I conducted with Hope Godwin at the Royal City Hotel in Odoguyan in Ikorudu, Lagos State on February 23, 2012, and at her home in Okrika town in Rivers State on August 4, 2012.
6. Based on a personal interview conducted at the NYSC camp Obubra, Cross Rivers State on September 22, 2011.
7. Personal interview at the Royal City Comfort Hotel, Odogunyan, Ikorodu Local Government, Lagos State on February 23, 2012.

REFERENCES

Bradley, Tamsin. *Women, Violence and Tradition: Taking FGM and Other Practices to a Secular State.* New York: Zed Books, 2011.

Coulter, Chris. *Bush Wives and Girl Soldiers: Women's Lives through War and Peace in Sierra Leone.* Ithaca: Cornell University Press, 2009.

Fujii, Lee Ann. "Interpreting Truth and Lies in Stories on Conflict and Violence," in *Surviving Field Research: Working in Violent and Difficult Situations*. Edited by Chandra Lekha Sriram et al. Abingdon: Routledge, 2009.

Galtung, Johan. *Peace: Research, Education, Action. Essays in Peace Research*. Copenhagen: Christian Ejlers, 1975.

Green, December. *Gender Violence in Africa: African Women's Responses*. Basingstoke: Macmillan, 1999.

Gurr, Ted Robert. *Why Men Rebel*. 40th anniversary paperback ed. Boulder: Paradigm Publishers, 2010.

Honwana, Adeola. *Child Soldiers in Africa*. Philadelphia: University of Pennsylvania Press, 2006.

Ikelegbe, Augustine. "Engendering Civil Society: Oil, Women's Groups and Resource Conflicts in the Niger Delta Region in Nigeria." *Journal of Modern African Studies* 43, no. 2, 2005. 241–270.

———. "Popular and Criminal Violence as Instruments of Struggle in the Niger Delta Region," in *Oil and Insurgency in the Niger Delta: Managing the Complex Politics of Petro-Violence*. Edited by Cyril Obi and Sirir Aas Rustad, 125–135. London: Zed Books, 2011.

Maldonado-Torres, Nelson. *Against War: Views from the Underside of Modernity*. Durham: Duke University Press, 2008.

Mathews, Eric. *Merleau-Ponty: A Guide to the Perplexed*. London: Continuum, 2006.

Miles, Steven. *Youth Lifestyles in a Changing World*. Buckingham: Open University Press, 2000.

Moran, Dermot. *Introduction to Phenomenology*. London: Routledge, 2000.

Okonta, Ike. *When Citizens Revolt: Nigerian Elites, Big Oil and the Ogoni Struggle for Self- Determination*. Trenton: Africa World Press, 2008.

Oluwaniyi, Oluwatoyin. "Women's Protests in the Niger Delta Region," in *Oil and Insurgency in the Niger Delta: Managing the Complex Politics of Petro-Violence*. Edited by Cyril Obi and Siri Aas Rusted, 150–165. London: Zed Books, 2011.

Oriola, Temi. "The Delta Creeks, Women's Engagement and Oil Insurgency." *British Journal of Criminology* 52, no. 3, 2012. 534–555.

Peel, Michael. *A Swamp Full of Dollars: Pipelines and Paramilitaries at Nigeria's Oil Frontier*. London: I.B. Tauris, 2008.

Rowel, Andy, James Marriott and Lorne Stockman. *The Next Gulf: London, Washington and Oil Conflict in Nigeria*. London: Constable and Robinson, 2005.

Sajama, Seppo, and Matti Kamppinen. *A Historical Introduction to Phenomenology*. London: Croom Helm, 1987.

Sandoval, Chela. *Methodology of the Oppressed*. Minneapolis: University of Minnesota Press, 2000.

Shaxson, Nicholas. *Poisoned Wells: The Dirty Politics of African Oil*. New York: Palgrave, 2007.

Stewart, David, and Algis Mickunas. *Exploring Phenomenology: A Guide to the Field and Its Literature*. Chicago: American Library Association, 1974.

Turner, Theresa, and Leigh S. Brownhill. "Why Women Are at War with Chevron: Nigerian Subsistence Struggles against the International Oil Industry." *Journal of Asian and African Studies* 39, nos. 1–2, 2004. 63–69.

Turshen, Meredith, and Clotilde Twagiramariya (Eds.). *What Women Do in War: Gender and Conflict in Africa*. London: Zed Books, 1998.

Watts, Michael. "Petro-Violence: Community, Extraction and Political Ecology of a Mythic Commodity," in *Violent Environments*. Edited by Nancy Lee Peluso and Michael Watts, 189–212. Ithaca and London: Cornell University Press, 2001.

———. "Petro-Insurgency or Criminal Conflict? Conflict and Violence in the Niger Delta." *Review of African Political Economy* 34, no. 114, 2007. 639–660.
———(Ed.). *Curse of Black Gold: 50 Years of Oil in the Niger Delta*. Brooklyn: PowerHouse Books, 2008a.
———. "Anatomy of an Oil Insurgency: Violence and Militants in the Niger Delta, Nigeria," in *Extractive Economies and Conflicts in the Global South: Multi-Regional Perspectives on Rentier Politics*. Edited by Kenneth Umeje, 51–74. Aldershot: Ashgate, 2008b.

8 Phenomenological Passports
Youth and Experiences of Place, Mobility and Globalization

Leslie Robinson, Maria-Carolina Cambre, Andrew Jackson Obol, and Cathy Mashakalugo

Culture, they say, is a two-way street.

—Langston Hughes

The time is out of joint.

—*Hamlet* (I, v, 189)

PREAMBLE

It was constructed to be, among other things, a gateway: a very special gateway for an event, an experience, one of a series of exhibitions, or 'World's Fairs' as they came to be known, which were later to be understood as milestones of global integration (Young 2008), claiming to "put the world—or at least what its organizers deemed the most important parts of it—on display (342). At a time of intense European empire building, and promising the world (whose world?) to visitors, the 1889 Paris Exhibition "attracted 28–30 million visitors and an average of 175,000 per day" (ibid., 341). At the foot of the iron latticed gateway, visitors were met with France's exuberant and detailed display of recent acquisitions, rather colonies; "the Algerian and Tunisian pavilions, complete with dome and minaret; the Vietnamese pavilions of Annam and Tonkin; and the Angkor Pagoda for Cambodia, modelled on the recently excavated ruins of Angkor Wat," complete with reconstructed "primitive dwellings" from Asia, Africa and early Europe (ibid., 348 and 350). Simulations of distant lands and cultures, complete with imported inhabitants instructed to perform dances or daily "routines," were expressed as a panorama of readily viewable exhibits compressing time and space and "altering the terms of contact between Western and non-Western cultures" (ibid., 354).

Entry to this bustling fair signalling progress and industry, optimism and anxiety, grandeur and folly, was accessed by way of the new Tower of Babel (Conley, 2010). Yet this very marker, to the surprise of Exhibition organizers who had endured it being ridiculed as a "useless and monstrous blot on the skyline" (ibid., 765), was visited by nearly two million people during the fair. Somehow it quickly accrued meanings as the symbol of "modernity, of communication, of science or of the nineteenth century, rocket, stem, derrick, phallus, lightning rod or insect, confronting the great itineraries of our dreams" (Barthes, 1997, 1).

The poet Huidobro was equally enthralled and asked whether there is anyone who has not heard its song, famously describing it as the 'Guitare du ciel' (sky's guitar) (Conley, 2010, 770). For Spanish Dadaist Guillermo de Torre it was a station on the celestial route of an interplanetary railroad (ibid.). A physiological study done the year it was built showed that "hearts beat faster there" (Harriss, 2009, 64). At its debut this 106-story tower of riveted girders became the world's tallest structure and at the same time the subject of so many and varied representations, whether visual or verbal, that they defied cataloguing (Conley, 2010). Beyond its transmission, within a decade the tower quickly became a transmitter with its wireless signal extending to Moscow, Madrid, New York and Prague, transgressing "geographic, national, and linguistic boundaries" (ibid., 765–766). And as Conley (2010) astutely observes, it calls people to it, it is "absorbent" and at the same time "projective," travelling via visual reproduction, circulation and the conditions of an emergent global consumer culture. By now you may have an image of the iconic monument we are referring to in your mind's eye. Do we need to name it?

Celebrated by international artists, for Roland Barthes (1997, 7) it is the first "obligatory monument; it is a Gateway, it marks the transition to a knowledge." But what conditions must exist for visitors to feel obliged to make their way to it? What kind of knowledge is promised, proscribed or authorized? Where does it take viewers and what is it that this tower marks? Barthes maintains there is nothing, a "zero degree" and empty monument, "there is nothing to see inside the tower" (ibid., 4). He wonders, "Why then do we visit?" (ibid.).

And 'we' do visit. Crowds continue to flock with about seven million visits per year, making it the most visited and most photographed monument worldwide (Harriss, 2009). But the question must be asked: Is it in fact, as Barthes (1997) claims, "present to the entire world?" Is it part of "the universal language of travel?" (1). Does it actually attract meaning "the way a lightning rod attracts thunderbolts" (2), for everyone? American writer Joseph Harriss (2009) recalls his own "epiphany" occurring one evening as he strolled down the street not far from his apartment. He found himself below the tower and glanced up. He (2009, 64) writes,

> Above me the gigantic, intricate tracery of crisscrossing girders soared more majestically than the columns and vaults of any Gothic cathedral. I was held, fascinated—awestruck is not too strong a word.

Harriss feels himself *held,* the size and complexity of the structure itself awe him, exerting some sort of fixating spell. And yet what is the dream or myth in which he participates that makes the experience take on an enchanted quality? Is he not already one of those whom this tower was meant to interpellate? Is he not already positioned to pass through the Gateway and transition to "a knowledge?" Perhaps prior knowledge of the tower and its haunting fame, gained through print, televisual and electronic media, sets the stage for experiences such as this one.

INTRODUCTION

We had travelled to Paris for a cultural studies conference. Three of us travelled directly from Uganda, and the fourth from Canada.

> *I think it was our first evening. . . . Mashaka and I decided to head out to look for something to eat. It was late but our perception of time was a bit off since there was still so much light and we had some jetlag. It was July yet Mashaka was wearing a puffy black jacket that looked better suited for early winter. I recall passing by a touristy shop and Mashaka pointing energetically . . . "What is this funny thing I keep seeing everywhere?"*

Noticing the never-ending reproductions, Mashakalugo was compelled to ask, "What is this funny thing?" Given its illustrious history and its role in the Western imaginary, many may be unprepared for the possibility of arriving at this monument or images of it without any predetermined ideas. It may be the case that such an incident indicates that what is meant when the monument is described as a global icon is not, in fact, the entire world. So what 'world' is implied? We might wonder what words like 'global,' 'worldwide,' 'globality' and 'globalization' *mean* when they are used descriptively or in terms of lived experiences. How might someone without preconceived notions of the tower experience it? Javanese dancers were presented as part of the 'viewed' world to the 'viewing' world in 1889, which was clearly an-other one, performing as part of the Paris Exhibition during the tower's inauguration. What might *they* have made of the Eiffel's engineering marvel?

Do our understandings of globalization include assumptions about how such iconic monuments should be experienced by travellers? What is the relationship between a certain kind of knowledge and notions of globalization? Mashakalugo's question was met with disbelief:

> *I stopped walking in that moment. Could she possibly not recognize this iconic structure? Didn't she know Paris was the city of love? "Mash, are you serious? That's the Eiffel tower!" I said, immediately recognizing a tone of amazement in my voice. I regretted what I said and the way I said it.*

Some have never seen the Eiffel tower and many do not know it exists. Yet, it feels like everyone is supposed to know that it is in Paris, the city of love, that it is famous and iconic, but the news of this must-see monument is not, as Barthes would have it "present to the entire world" after all. Leslie regrets her reaction, but how many of us assume that knowing something about this monument is "common" information and that we must *all* know that the Eiffel tower is a symbol of Paris and of France. In certain spaces, not knowing this is often simply seen as ignorance. In other words, it is required knowledge. But what geographical knowledge is deemed indispensible and for whom?

Like many in the Westernized world, Leslie's knowledge of the tower has been absorbed vicariously over time through media representations of various kinds. It was her first visit too, but for her, there was the presence of a knowing-how-to-see the tower. Access to this knowledge is unequal, it is simply not available to all, but assumed to be essential on some level.

Leslie muses:

> *As we continued walking my mind went back to Uganda as I was trying to compare my own experiences to what I thought Mash might be experiencing. I pictured Gaddafi's mosque, the Kasubi Tombs that recently burned down, both of which I have seen from afar but neither of which I have actually visited. . . . Images of Idi Amin and Joseph Kony followed. I regretted conjuring up such negative images of Uganda, the country I have chosen as my second home.*

And Obol reflects:

> *I am saddened that when Leslie was thinking of Ugandan icons that the first things that came were Idi Amin and Joseph Kony. In Paris, I felt that most people didn't know Uganda exists and those who do, know about Idi Amin and "Kony 2012," that movie I didn't like. Everyone out there seems to think we are in a war zone and it's a sad situation because if you actually come on ground you see that there is so much peace. I blame the media for how we are represented. Or maybe I should blame it on the government for not doing enough to clean up the country's image. Uganda is a peaceful place, a nice place to stay. Its good that Leslie calls it her second home, its very hospitable here.*

The images presenting themselves to Leslie's mind involve places/people some might consider famous but that she had never encountered. On some level they are stereotypes or clichés. The reality may be that the significant places/people Leslie is actually reaching for are unknown because they are somehow deemed unimportant. Obol "blames the media" for this unfair and unequal communication, resisting the presentation of Uganda as a "war zone." He also feels "most people" don't know Uganda exists. Who might most people be for him here? On whose terms are so-called iconic events/things created and how is access to understanding, or even knowing of the existence of what is understood by mainstream Western media, to be globally significant, permitted or denied? Despite visual and verbal representations of the Eiffel tower beyond number and always increasing exponentially through ceaseless processes of reproduction, circulation and consumption, and its pre-eminent fame as something so globally recognizable that it can be used as a cipher, this is not exactly the case. The experience of the monument is in this case a rupture with the known rather than a progression in some kind of relational transaction. What can we learn then, through our experiences about globalization? In what follows we will explore experiences that can be said to fall under the rubric of globalizing forces that, like the spellbinding force of the Eiffel tower, draw people into their rhythms and logics. We critically ask in whose image/interests do stories of globalization function and serve? What is at stake, and who is forgotten, in projecting globalization as a universal and universalizing phenomenon?

WHY PHENOMENOLOGY?

Hermeneutic phenomenological reflection orients both research and researchers to the components of both descriptive and interpretive perceptions of a lived experience. In other words, it is about how people go about understanding the world in which they live (Gadamer, 1998; van Manen, 1997). The process involves investigating the experience as lived in the lifeworld, allowing essential themes to emerge, while writing and rewriting to feel out the essence of what is often overlooked, maintaining a strong relation to the phenomenon and repeatedly stepping away to examine how the parts inform the overall experience. This approach demonstrates a will not to explicate but rather to describe, in the spirit of a commitment to the nature of lived experience (van Manen, 1997). The four existentials of spatiality, corporeality, temporality and relationality are used because they are fundamental structures of the lifeworld and are grounded in the way that all human experience occurs (ibid.).

There are many schools of thought in phenomenology, or "accents" (Lyotard, 1991), and many ways to write phenomenologically, but one thing on which it is generally agreed is that it is not a social science method or technique, rather it is a way of being/seeing the world. Jean-François Lyotard (1991, 34) does not mince words regarding the shortcomings of the social sciences: "Given the objective experimental methods, modeled after physics, that are used by psychology, sociology, etc., are these fields not radically inadequate? Will it not prove necessary to at least begin by making clear the diverse modes according to which consciousness is 'interwoven with the world'?" Many scholars have attempted to systematically examine human experience through phenomenology, and there is no agreement on what in the end phenomenology actually is. In *Phenomenology,* Lyotard (ibid., 34) wrote that it is "a step in 'European' thought and has understood itself as such, as Husserl showed in the *Crisis.*" And that "there are presently *many* phenomenologists, and since its meaning is still in process, it is unfinished precisely because it is historical. Despite the different 'accents' . . . there remains a common phenomenological 'style' " (ibid., 34). As Gayle L. Ormiston (1991, 2) notes in her foreword, Lyotard shows that for phenomenology, analysis is always beginning and never finished: "Lyotard's phenomenological analysis demonstrates the extent to which phenomenology always and already has been involved in seeking radically new beginnings."

So Why Phenomenology?

The term signifies a study of 'phenomena,' that is to say of *that* which appears to consciousness, *that* which is 'given,' in the place of the traditional consciousness, which 'digests,' or at least ingests, the external world. Phenomenology reveals a consciousness which "bursts outward . . . *a consciousness in sum, which is nothing if not a relation to the world*" (Sartre, in Orniston, 1991, 7). In this approach, phenomenological meaning is never conclusive: truths and essences are profiled, but never quite fully discernable. The phenomenological researcher does seek decisive ends, but works to open up to the phenomenon and the surprises it reveals (ibid., 8). Thus engaging in this process means that "with every thinking there is a rethinking, a re-collecting that modifies the parameters of the debate . . . by the very fact that the issues or the contentious points have been (and will have been) re-contextualized, recited, and recalled for a particular purpose . . . [with the recognition that] every reconstruction . . . involves a 'rupture in the order of things' " (ibid., 9).

As we approach experiences of globalization by reengaging with particular moments before, during and after a trip to Paris, essences of experience emerge and in turn, trigger our reflections on the context of asymmetrical globalization. We operate from the understanding that, as Merleau-Ponty (2005, 28) writes in *Phenomenology of Perception,* "the phenomenological world is not pure being, but the sense which is revealed where the paths of my various experiences intersect, and also where my own and other people's intersect and engage each other like gears."

The lived experience described herein—all in relation to a shared yet divergent set of experiences in Paris—are guided by the Dutch phenomenological school of thought represented most prominently in Canada by the work of Max van Manen. We also draw on "Africana phenomenology" (Henry, 2006), particularly drawing inspiration from Franz Fanon's and W.E.B. DuBois's works, both explicitly poetic and anti-colonial.

Our processual and emergent approach allows us to engage in phenomenological sense-making from "a comparative cultural perspective" (Henry, 2006, 1). Exploring non-Western/marginal experiences, we work toward de-linking from the Western universal claim to reason and its embeddedness in European culture. In so doing we "do not attempt to subsume culturally distinct philosophies under the categories of another" (ibid., 21), accepting incongruities and contradictions in sense-making as necessary and unavoidable. Rather, as students/learners we aim to glean insights that respond to Paget Henry's (2006, 21–22) call to invent new hybrid approaches to comparative phenomenological analysis, which "seek to create bridges, partial points or areas of complementary convergence, meta-philosophical discourses and communicative groups between . . . culturally distinct philosophies."

Thus, we four authors work in the spirit of decolonizing our sense-making through a commitment to inter-cultural and inter-epistemic writing processes that are both creative and collaborative. Our work draws from and is shaped by our intersecting experiences in and around a trip to Paris as a crystallizing event. As co-authors—two Ugandans, one Canadian and one Argentine immigrant to Canada—we work to open up new expressive potentials through phenomenological explorations and analysis where 'youth' co-author a collaborative meaning-making process. Mashakalugo and Obol, both in their mid-twenties, contribute as epistemic partners in knowledge-making and creative processes (Papastergiadis, 2011). We note that, in the Ugandan context, young people up to and even beyond thirty are considered youth. Mashakalugo is a Ugandan citizen of Rwandese and Tanzanian origin. A volunteer youth centre coordinator and HIV/AIDS counsellor and member of numerous youth groups, she is also a first-year University student. Mashakalugo describes her social position as falling into the lower class. Obol, from Northern Uganda's Lira District, has spent most of his life residing and schooling in the country's Kampala capital. With a degree in industrial, fine art and design from Makerere University, majoring in illustration, he works as a freelance illustrator. Obol describes his social position as lower-middle class. Carolina and Leslie, both over thirty, participate in the Western institutional academy as students and researchers and reside primarily in Canada. The lived experiences of the four travellers involved in the research represent their expertise, while all four are also artists and activists.

Following Fanon, our collaborative partnership is shaped by an ethical commitment to those whose existence is subordinated and systemically excluded from traditional academic discourse in general. Philosopher Nelson Maldonado-Torres (2008, 158–159) tells us that vision for liberation takes its point of departure in the "preferential option for the damnés" where subjectivities, otherwise institutionally condemned, can contribute critically to the new humanity Fanon called for. Thus, our collective stance has the de-colonial aim of 'making visible the invisible' through lived experience descriptions that manifest "the mechanisms that produce such invisibility or distorted visibility in light of a large stock of ideas that must necessarily include the critical reflections of the 'invisible' people themselves"

(Malonado-Torres, 2007, 262). In this way we work to improvise a new relational ethics for knowledge generation and sharing. In particular, Ugandan youth such as Obol and Mashakalugo can be seen as being out of their *proper place* in any conventional academic milieu and may then be well placed to make subversive entries into knowledge dissemination—at the interplay between creative, spontaneous and poetic expression and (Western) scholarship.

OUR PHENOMENOLOGICAL PROCESS

All four authors contributed lived experience descriptions as we re-collected our memories of the trip to Paris six months later. We focused on preparation, critical travel moments and the return. Following our shared commitment to art/artivism,[1] we took an *any medium necessary* (Asante, 2008) approach including poetry, drawing, journaling and oral recordings. The process involved continuous reworking of reflections and stories with an emphasis on encouraging deep reflection and wondering and sitting with the stories. Whereas our roles varied in terms of recording, transcribing and translating our experiences, the ordering and stringing together of pieces was undertaken by the Canada-based travellers with checking and approval from the Ugandan travellers. This means that one of the limitations of this piece is that the words written by those of us outside the discourses of the Western academy have had a measure of translation in response to an academic paradigm where in order for these words to be taken seriously they need to be framed and "articulated, always, in relation to European categories of thought, whether conservative or progressive, whether from the Right of from the Left" (Mignolo, 2011, 240). The challenge of honouring multiple modes of enunciation while being conscious of what might be *permissible* in academic writing comes through in Leslie's journal:

> *As I began to read Mashaka's words I recognized the need to settle myself and slow down my pace: "world of opposites," "psychological torture" and "witch traitors" drew me in. . . . It became clear to me that I would need more time to grapple with words that struck me as coming from a deep and mysterious place. As an only partial sense of her writing impressed upon me I felt a tinge of worry invade my burgeoning and distracted sense of intrigue. I thought her writing was probably too cryptic, too creative, too random, too analytical. . . . I folded the papers up neatly and placed them in my laptop case, for a later time and place where I could sit with them and see what to do.*

Drawing on the work of Merleau-Ponty, Max van Manen understands every expression of meaning as always already marked by suppositions. We thus constantly questioned these beginning suppositions marking the collaborative process. As students of phenomenology, working at times side by side in either Uganda or Canada and other times independently across time zones and through cyber space, our enunciation and translation work was necessarily iterative and emergent. We continuously wondered how certain constraints and liberties around time, technology and space—different for each of us—impacted our inter-cultural, inter-epistemic collaboration. We were conscious that our very collaboration was in itself an expression of globalized communication and asked how globalizing forces were enhancing or inhibiting our goal of equitizing power relations. As we grappled with ambiguities, we maintained an ongoing effort to gain traction in negotiating our asymmetrical relations through reciprocity; with artistic/poetic and youthful enunciation transforming our scholarship while our scholarship informed the artistic and youthful.

SPACE/TIME/BODY/RELATION

If we accept Giddens's (1991, 21) understanding that the processes of globalization concern the "interlacing of social events and social relationships 'at distance' with local contextualities," where does it leave us, with regards to the "*specific experience* of globalization" (Tomlinson 1994, 150)? Giddens (1991, 187) asserts that "the transformations of place, and the intrusion of distance into local activities, combined with the centrality of mediated experience, . . . radically change what 'the world' actually is." Although everyone lives a local life, phenomenal worlds for the most part are truly global. Giddens's theory of 'time-space distanciation' explains how he sees the transformation of place and time in modernity. Once time was measured with clocks, rather than with context-specific markers like the altitude of the sun in the sky, or the length of one's shadow. The lifting of time out of space set the stage for the "globalizing tendencies of modernity" (Tomlinson, 1994, 151). Whereas global capitalist markets may shape the economic flows in local neighbourhoods, everyday experiences are "*structured* by forces which are, ultimately global . . . does this imply that our phenomenal worlds are global?" (ibid.).

Giddens's formulation of the concept of 'mediation' as something that also distances, and his understanding that all experience is mediated, at least through language, are linked by Tomlinson to the arguments Giddens makes regarding global experiences.

To draw us closer to the (im)possibility of global words, we derived a set of indigenous themes from the phenomenological accounts and our consequent reflection upon them. Experiences of standardized asymmetrical travel, (mis)represented and (mis)placed identities, and pain and betrayal prompted our further exploration orienting ourselves around the salient literature on youth and globalization.

1. ASYMMETRY AND STANDARDIZATION PARADOX

Obol posits:

> *Take the dilemma of whether to go slow or fast: either the developing countries who move a bit slow should catch up, or the developed countries should slow down for the rest to catch up, could it ever come to that? If globalization is to work in this colonial system would that mean that there must always be a certain order from the top to the lowest?*

At the same time that Carolina feels pressure around her behaviours in the Metro, her navigation of the Metro system succeeds:

> *Although I had used the Metro in Paris before, it still seemed like a maze with all its connections and long winding passageways between different trains where the advertisements kept repeating themselves. I found myself learning where to look for signs of which way to go and practicing my instructions for how to get from one place to the next. I felt hyper aware of my movements. In my small notebook, I recorded the exact moves to make . . . "take the mustard line 10 in the direction of Pont de St-Cloud at Cluny la Sorbonne for one stop to Odeon and transfer to the reddish purple line towards Port d'Orleans and get off at the last stop." All the details of direction and colour were necessary so that I could walk confidently.*

Obol approached it differently:

> *Upon entering the metro I felt as though I was in a Giant maze full of hyper people. Overwhelmed and anxious I adjusted my speed to a much faster pace just to keep up. . . . Moving in all directions and up and down twisting stairways left me dizzy and in a sweat. At least the colour codes helped us to move faster, like everyone else.*

How often do we question our efficient and mechanic-like movements? Should every 'body,' every village, every nation be moving at the same pace?

Carolina continues:

> *Standing in line to buy tickets, I studied with a sense of urgency how the people in front of me managed the ticket machine. I did all I could to avoid attracting any attention from impatient commuters, who were so impatient that they would sometimes leave the line and speed over to the turnstiles and jump over them.*

Obol comments:

> *I am just like smiling at how Carolina wanted to show that she is not a tourist [laugh] as I felt the same way. I thought asking around for directions would deem me vulnerable while inconveniencing others. When desperate enough I would put much effort in to looking for the friendliest face to approach.*

What are the conditions that drive us to fit in? What are we really afraid of as we avoid "inconveniencing others" or simply being spotted as someone who just doesn't know the way? How many of us, like Carolina, may appear to be managing the system, yet are internally panicking in an effort to mimic the movements of those around us? And where do the fastest ones, those that "jump" the turnstiles, fit in the hierarchy? Are they beating the system?

Carolina takes us further:

> *This particular day Mash was trying to insert her metro ticket but the machine was not responding. Normally it would vacuum it up and spit it out while unlocking the turnstile, but the machine kept refusing her ticket. It seemed as if we were all just standing there lost not knowing how we were going to get through and stay together. Yet, we did not say anything or have any suggestions for Mash, it was as if we were all stuck in some kind of time lag. Persisting, she turned towards the rest of us, shrugging her shoulders as a rush of commuters arrived. I learned quickly that these Parisian commuters will not wait, and do not really care how they get through, they must keep going.*

As our movements become increasingly mechanized, do our tolerance thresholds for those out of sync change too? Will there be a moment when a certain pace is expected no matter where you are?

> *As the tension rose with Mash in front of that one turnstile and people rushing towards her, a large middle aged man wearing a suit with the jacket opened, strode right up to Mash, and with his big belly he briskly walked right into her, pushing her forward as she hopped and jumped to keep in front of him. Being so tiny, Mash practically disappeared from sight in that instant without the man even acknowledging she was there. He swiped his Metro pass swiftly not missing a step, using his belly to drive Mash through without so much as a word or a glance at her. Trapped, she bobbed forward arms waving in the air, with a bit of a yelp with eyes wide calling for help! But there was no time to react. It was like watching someone get swept away by a sudden swift current. Suddenly the man was gone, and Mash was on the other side*

of the turnstile, it was so comical and unexpected that I had to laugh. A new meaning came to me for the phrase "taking it in stride" and it seemed we were all united in our surprise, with a chorus of "Oh my goodnesses" and "Did you see that?"[echoing] at this shocking moment where a perceived obstacle suddenly dissolved.

Obol recalls:

Carolina and Leslie stood just looking helpless on the other side of the turnstiles. That moment and place put people from the different continents together, separating Mash and I. Well Mash was stuck in the middle, trying to get to the other side. Is using these turnstiles meant to be so hard? People like that French man with the big belly, I guess he was used to it and he saw this small girl who could go through with him. I guess he helped a lot.

John Urry (1996) describes the *tourist gaze:* it is projected by visitors to a given place around their expectations of the inhabitants, and in turn, reflected back by the locals to the visitors. This performative behaviour has countless adverse effects on residents and visitors alike who are swept up in an economic system which prioritizes certain cultural attributes while those that can't easily be commodified/standardized are stereotyped, marginalized or lost, such as the slower pace Obol is accustomed to. Urry (ibid., 116) recalls how the reconstruction of Paris in the mid-nineteenth century created the conditions for *la vie Parisienne* as the "quintessentially modern experience" enhanced by unprecedented capacities for seeing and being seen. Urry (ibid., 118) suggests that the anonymity of the crowd creates space for "those on the margins of society to move about unnoticed, observing and being observed, but never really interacting with those encountered." Perhaps there is something about Paris, where the visitors far outnumber Parisians, that accelerates and isolates us all, marginal or not? As strangers in the city, how do we encounter each other: Do we address and help each other, shrug our shoulders, or just grumble and go on our way?

Returning Home

Returning home after those two weeks was difficult for all in the sense that our stories of travel were met with varying degrees of non-acceptance. In Carolina's case she didn't even attempt to share her experiences:

I did not really talk to anyone about the trip. No one asks about my travel and when they do it is really out of courtesy and not actual interest.

How many of us have felt some kind of resistance to hearing about someone's time abroad? Leslie recalls:

> *"So how was Paris?" a friend asked me, shortly after my return to Canada. My mind immediately went to my stockpile of stories much less about Paris itself, but fixated instead on the shared adventures of navigating the trip alongside my two close friends and colleagues, both first time travellers from Uganda. "It was a miracle really, how we managed to pull it off—so many hurdles!" I told her.*
>
> *I summarized the trouble we had convincing the airline attendant that Mashaka's ticket was legitimate and later in Addis Ababa how she was accused again of not having a proper ticket and was interrogated until the last moment, until finally she was the very last to board the plane . . . how after searching for Mashaka and Obol for hours, I received a panicked email from the Parisian lady who was to host us explaining how she had received a call from the immigration police who were holding my colleagues for interrogation. My friend at first seemed surprised to hear the stories, though her attentiveness quickly faded.*

Obol reflects:

> *When asked about my journey I didn't share very much as some people just ask it as a formality, to seem like they are interested . . . but as you speak they are not even paying attention. So I learned not to discuss a lot about the travelling unless it's very important.*

If one were to assess the collective intensity of our desires to tell travel stories against people's general unwillingness to hear them, might we also learn, like Obol and Carolina to keep them to ourselves? Are there unspoken social cues that lead people to ask about travel experiences through "courtesy and not actual interest" as Carolina puts it, or as Obol suggests "as a formality"?

Leslie concludes:

> *She cut me off eventually, exclaiming that she had "challenges at airports, but nothing that bad." I remember thinking "of course she wouldn't have had anything 'that bad' with her Canadian passport and bright white skin."*

Obol reflects:

> *Leslie, a Caucasian, is talking about white skin and privileges that give her friend (and herself) easy go through at airports. I guess it has always been like that but being conscious about it adds a lot of credible value to what one says. I think that for many Westerners it's very easy to use*

> *the airport, it's an everyday thing. Yet for someone like Mashaka, it is a one-time thing, it can even demoralize someone to travel again. The reality is, like Bob Marley said, "I have no chains around my feet but I am not free." Its like this illusion of freedom, but when you look deep it's not true. This is coming from Leslie: If in your passport your photo is white, there are some privileges you have for yourself.*

Both of these travellers connect the source of the travel issues to skin colour. Leslie felt her listener did not understand that travel was much different for someone from Uganda—the blackness is taken for granted. Obol notes a view of Westerners having "ease" at airports. But is this only a skin colour issue, or is it more complex? Is it not much easier for a Black American to pass through an airport than a White Colombian? It is not just that Leslie's listener had white skin, but also that she had a Canadian passport? How many of us have noticed a hierarchy amongst passports and that some passports seem more valued than others?

For Mashakalugo this trip was a "one-time" thing and demoralizing. For whom is travel made so upsetting and humiliating to the point where they are disinclined to travel again? Those who travel will eventually have issues: baggage may be lost, seats may be switched, flights delayed and cancelled. We may encounter rudeness or poor service where we will personally blacklist an airline, but won't most of us travellers travel again?

In Mignolo's (2011) construct of the colonial matrix of power, he charts our modern/colonial world order extending Anibal Quijano's (2000) earlier work on the coloniality of power. The colonial matrix unveils how racism and patriarchy (and the authoritative and economic power of nation states) manifest as the modern conditions for constructing and controlling knowledge and subjectivity. Through this frame we can see that "those who classify often forget that those who are classified do not and that being out of place in the set of regulations points to the existential condition of coloniality of being" (Mignolo, 2011, 45). Overlooking the fact that passports are also culturally overdetermined is an indication of what Maldonado Torres (2004) describes as the constitutive feature of modernity, the *forgetfulness of damnation*. When a Canadian arrives in Uganda and pays her fifty US dollars for a visa stamp on her passport, how often does she think of the medical tests, the interviews and the waiting game that a Ugandan might endure simply for aspiring to get a Canadian travel visa?

2. (MIS)REPRESENTATION

What is it like to experience travel abroad for the first time as a twenty-something Ugandan: to cross the colonial divide over to a city that represents the epitome of postmodern globality? In some senses the voyage has the potential to alter or re-configure one's sense of personhood. With a

Figure 8.1 Calling me "French buoy."

broadened imaginary for seeing and interpreting the world, does a young Ugandan like Obol or Mashakalugo return home with a heightened sense of self, or rather a further complicated one? For fellow peers, whose circumstances deny the chance of travel, bearing witness to the intercontinental experience of another is fraught with conflicting emotions. How might attaining a first stamp on one's passport become a marker of an altered identity and sociability for a youth upon returning to the "underside"?[2]

Obol expresses his experience of returning home through sequential art along with anecdotal descriptions:

> *Back from Paris, about one week, I went one cool easy evening to see my friends at my former hostel. There I found them all seated in our favourite hideout spot behind the hostel smoking the good stuff, chatting and laughing off their escapades as usual.*

Obol's story evokes a sense of comfort and familiarity, setting a "cool and easy" tone. With a feeling of belonging and emplacement he readily approaches the "favourite hideout spot," eager to assume his membership among friends "as usual." The tone of his account contrasts with another scenario, one where he was among a crowd of new friends while in Paris.

> *Me, Paul and some other friends were hanging around outside the conference room waiting for the bus to take us to the Sorbonne. My friends*

> *were sharing experiences, while I was busy listening. I felt like everyone had so much to share about themselves, while I shied away. Since there was a big number of people from all parts of the world I was just looking around at people, different dress codes, hair styles, skin colours. I didn't feel like I fit in. I felt like I was in the midst of a group so far away from my state of mind.*

With these contrasting *hanging out* moments in mind we may wonder if Obol will find his friends back home in a "state of mind" closer to his own.

> *Everyone was surprised to see me because I was humungous. I remember my friend David said "Uh OJay you look so big, look at your arms." I wasn't surprised at their reactions because I was conscious of my physical weight. My other friend Elijah kept calling me "French buoy."*

The anticipation of returning to chats of their "escapades as usual" was met with a seemingly inflated search for a physical marker of change, a sign of a new man. Being called "French Buoy" reflects a change in the eye of a friend: Has Obol been somehow contaminated by 'Frenchness'? He was given a nickname, and in a teasing way his difference, largely invisible though marked by weight gain, was noted and underscored.

> *Everyone laughed at that name, even me, but in my mind I didn't want the name to stick. I didn't want people associating me to that wealth and money stuff. It felt like I am bragging because I have travelled around the world. It is a common thing that happens to people who have come back from outside as everyone thinks that they have a lot of dollars on them.*

In the almost impossible feat of interpreting what international travel could have been like for Obol, his friends made assumptions. The social relationships 'at distance' with local contextualities called for negotiation. This mutual impact in the relationship appears to be more than a Giddensian "interlacing" of social events. Even the notion of 'time-space distanciation' seems to be inadequate in the experience of change in the social milieu that is more akin to a time-space mash-up. For Tomlinson (1994, 153), "the experience of place in modernity is not one of alienation, but of ambivalence. People 'own' their local places phenomenologically in a sort of provisional sense, always recognizing the absent forces which structure this ownership," and the awareness of the influence of capital, "wealth and money stuff" from afar, including its geographical connections.

Renowned creative writer Ngũgĩ wa Thiong'o (2012), attentive to the lived experience of identity formation, offers us an entryway into the absent forces that recondition Obol's ownership of his locality. He (ibid., 15–16) writes: "The colonial process dislocates the traveller's mind from the place he or she already knows to a foreign starting point even with the body still remaining in his or her homeland." In the symbolic world "behind the hostel" and in the presence of those who "come back from outside the country" it seems as though one's travel experience earns "bragging" rights along with a re-jigged identity. Yet for Obol, the proposed identity transformation is unwelcome and he resists playing along as "French buoy." Travel can mean different things, but is often linked to "a lot of money or dollars." With this assumption, people ignore funding alternatives, enabling travel without one personally acquiring wealth. The colonial process mitigates alienation from one's base through "a continuous process of looking at oneself from the outside of self or with the lenses of a stranger . . . that is from another self toward oneself, rather than the local being the starting point, from self to other selves" (ibid., 15–16). Obol, now associated by his peers with wealth, is in reality no wealthier than he was two weeks earlier.

But a specific kind of travel marks Obol's alienation:

> *If I were coming back from Kenya or Rwanda it may not be that way, but the fact that I was from Paris, it was obvious to them that I must have a lot of money. The mood was nice though, they were all happy to see me, welcoming me.*

Obol recognizes an implicit hierarchy of destinations revealed through his friends' responses. His particular experience of mobility resulted in a virtual shift as his friends looked at him as if transformed, and for signs of increased wealth. In his dissonant encounter with this, Obol's own views appear to have changed.

Fanon (1963) takes us further into how *alienation from the base* manifests in the social and political context at play in this moment among friends. For him a colonial system denies aspects of humanness among the people it dominates, continually forcing one to ask the question, "In reality who am I?" (ibid., 250). Obol makes it clear for us who he feels he is not: someone associated "to that wealth and money stuff." For Fanon (1967), in the colonial context ordinary life is overdetermined by the political to such an extent that abnormal turns normal. Obol's *travel around the world* and his consequent representation by his peers became overdetermined by the political and distorted by *a foreign starting point*. Was the mood "nice" because the modern world somehow, in that moment, returned with Obol?

Obol continues:

> *I was uncomfortable with the fact that they wanted me to shoot them beers to celebrate the moment. I was broke, I think I had about 20,000 shillings (about eight dollars), but I understood why they were hoping I would sponsor them some drinks. My reaction was polite; I bought some spirit sachets and one "U.G." (a very famous Ugandan spirit). So*

> *those passed around as I shared some more experiences. It felt good to be back home.*

Obol feels simultaneously "uncomfortable" and glad to be home, suggesting how our prevailing modern/colonial world system maintains "a field of gravitation that makes aspirations for humanity collapse into aims for inclusion and projects of assimilation based on the ultimate value of the master's kind of life" (Maldonado-Torres, 2008, 131). Obol negotiated his discomfort amid his welcoming friends because he "understood" the (mis)conception into which he was inserted. Why does he not say he is broke? Instead he spends his last shillings "to sponsor them some drinks" and maintain the illusion. Perhaps for Obol in that moment it was a small price to pay "to celebrate the moment" of coming home. Had he not "passed around" spirits would he have faced rejection? Does his reaction attest to Tomlinson's (1994, 160) assertion that "local exigencies maintain a certain priority even in a lifeworld opened up to the global?"

By considering the complex ways in which meanings are assigned to the human acts of giving and receiving we might move toward a better understanding of how colonial contexts work to mediate relationships in Obol's encounter. Modernity/coloniality works to impair the possibility of reciprocal interhuman contact, maintaining generosity as an expression reserved for the exclusive use of the dominator (Maldonado-Torres 2008). When Obol finds his friends at the hostel *as usual* his re-entry into that world seems to emerge as a paradox: Is he one small step closer to the *ultimate value of the master's kind of life?* Or is he one step back, facing possible dismissal by his peers? *In reality who is Obol?*

3. PAIN AND BETRAYAL

> *Hello, to open minded people and change lovers for betterment. As I was sharing my experiences in a world of opposites I learnt that in this world people will never see, perceive, act or think in the same way. This testifies to the fact of difference and uniqueness in people. And this makes me believe more strongly in the Artivist way of using all possible medias to reach, teach, learn and change for a better world, responding to Asante's call in one of his books.*

Mashakalugo's greeting to "change lovers for betterment" invites people of a certain bent/calling to collaborate in an artivist (artist/activist) way. She calls out to "open minded people." Is there something that connects us all? Her opening address incites reflection on one's own position on the spectrum of open-mindedness: Open according to what terms, whose terms?

"A world of opposites" is Mashakalugo's articulation of difference, as she experienced it in relation to her Paris *aller-retour*. Thinking back to a shared experience walking to the Eiffel tower, an image reformulates: Mashakalugo wanders slowly and cautiously in her black winter jacket as a cluster of seemingly carefree girls dash by in mini-shorts. The magnetic force that seems to draw so many of us to the 'city of love,' to return to share our stories of the view from the top, evokes an alternative response: *"In this world people will never see, perceive, act or think in the same way."*

Kjeldgaard and Askegaard's (2006) research on the *Globalization of Youth Culture* explains how the assumed to be uniform consumption habits of young people (clothing styles, music tastes and media habits), as purported by marketing and popular business literature, has caused youth to be seen as the ideal example of a global segment (see Hassan and Katsanis, 1991; Marketing News, 2002: Moses, 2000; Tully 1994). As noted by Lukose (2005, 915), "A short-hand way to mark the advent and impact of globalization is to point to the evidence of 'global' youth consuming practices." Often, signs of a global youth culture are all too readily treated as obvious evidence of a homogenized group of consumers. Yet "myth is exactly such a naturalization of a social set of signs (Barthes, 1973). The myth of a global youth hence constitutes an ideological explanatory framework for practices observed in social reality" (Kjeldgaard and Askegaard, 2006, 231).

Mashakalugo's own calling to "change for a better world" is reminiscent of African American scholar and artivist M.K. Asante's (2008, 205) vision "to create and to have a palpable impact in the real world." Her commitment to the "artivist way" is reinforced by her observation abroad, "the fact of difference and uniqueness in people." In Mashakalugo's symbolic imaginary, what *different* and *unique* symbolic world stood in lieu of the packaged and sold *rêve de Paris*?

Upon her return from Paris, Mashakalugo reunited with her friends:

> *The reactions I received from the people I used to call my people as I shared these experiences are unbelievable to me. . . . My friends in need and indeed, the people I would recommend to be my next of kin, they blew me like sand at the coast. Blown in no direction the wind instead makes the sand meander, not meeting or reaching its destiny, kept at the coast all the time though in the motion of movement. Even at this moment I still feel the pain and the psychological torture put on me in struggling to get the answer to the question of whether it was worst or best, right or wrong, to accept the call and respond positively to world developers and well wishers.*

Mashakalugo's voyage somehow functioned to interrupt and reset a sense of time and awareness of space as she attempted to reconnect with her people. In a way it is as if by travelling a long distance, we bring that distance with us. Returning to the trip, perhaps to some of the experiences Mashakalugo would have liked to share, we recall an unforgettable moment when she stood up in front of an audience during a session on HIV/AIDS research in Uganda. She brought two professors up to date on current realities in her own community as they frantically took note. It was surprising that these so-called experts were so disconnected. Later, the excitement of tasting strawberries for the first time and her desire to share them by packing a few to take home, vaporized in the shadow of feeling *blown like sand in all directions and going nowhere*. Somehow the going 'somewhere' became worse than staying in place. Mashakalugo experienced a deep and violent rejection and betrayal by "people I used to call my people," but what, in actuality has changed?

Excerpts from a letter Mashakalugo wrote to the organizers of the cultural conference that brought her to Paris recall her pre-trip aspirations:

> *At the conference I hope to contribute my views to help big people*[3] *better understand the nature of young people, especially in Uganda and elsewhere in Africa. . . . Upon coming back I hope to share up with my fellows alternative ways of handling issues that I will learn from people from across the globe. . . . I hope to get inspiration as I have plans of joining up with others in related disciplines to advocate for combating youth unemployment (February 26, 2012).*

But back home there is a tangle of contradictions to get caught up and "kept" in, as her hopes to "share up" and "advocate" are met with indifference or perhaps even malice. Thiong'o's work on the decolonization of African memory can offer an entry point into the complex and layered psychic terrain of Mashakalugo's post-travel suffering. For Thiong'o (2009), Africa's contact with Europe, since the onset of modernity/coloniality, manifests through enactments of dismemberment whereby the colonial subject's memory severs from her own individual and collective body. "Colonialism attacks and completely distorts a people's relationship to their natural, bodily, economic, political, and cultural base. And with this base destroyed, the wholeness of the African subject, the subject in active engagement with his environment, is fragmented" (ibid., 22). Paradoxically, in the "motion of movement," Mashakalugo fits this description as she is held hostage by haunting visions of betrayal as her *plans of joining up with others* are derailed. Through the legacy of colonialism and its systemic assault on African memory unity is broken: "There is no healing, no wholeness; only a dislocation of the national psyche, for in not remembering the past, there are no inherited ideals by which to measure the excesses of the present" (ibid., 46). Mashakalugo asks if it was "right or wrong, to accept the call and respond positively to world developers and well wishers?" For those of us who are scholars, who called upon Mashakalugo to join forces in our efforts toward *world development*, this question begs more questions. Were our efforts to bring artivist Mashakalugo to the world stage to speak on her own behalf about youth concerns just another case of good intentions gone wrong? Despite only one year of University education, her conference 'performance' elicited lavish encouragement including invitations by professors to supervise her graduate studies. What are the conditions that led such "well wishers" to suppose that our encouragement will indeed help her? Or were we really thinking of helping our own agendas? Did our adherence to the universal (according to whom?) claims to higher (Western) education overlook "the question of whether it was worst or best" to entice Mashakalugo to join our *calling*? The aftermath of Mashakalugo's trip to Paris evoked "pain" and "psychological torture," yet what called forth this misery?

For Maldonado-Torres (2007, 256) modernity/coloniality reveals a coloniality of Being, evinced first by the cry, "not a word but an interjection . . . a call of attention to one's own existence. . . . And the cry points to a peculiar existential condition: that of the condemned." Failing to comprehend the connections between our past, present and future, the strategic antagonist of our global age has become our amnesic and distorted sense of self (ibid.).

> While other people were showing the contentedness, curiosity and hopefulness with their eye turned straight on me questioning me and waiting for sweet replies and maybe to learn or not from them there was a chick of gung starts (do not ask what they do anyway). They roamed around like lost cats in the desert, tried to hide like icebergs in oceans. But their hearts were black with burning fire. They used to change places on hearing conversations looking at me on angle 45 degrees opening and closing their eyes often like disco lights. Whenever my face would meet theirs they would turn their five heads down and sideways as if they were dodging their eyes from wind or water.

Like "lost cats in the desert," the treachery of friends is signalled. The travelled Mashakalugo stirs up fractured memories. Her international travel (and the staying behind of her young friends) evokes hearts "black with burning fire." Is it threats of future change or domination—*blowing in like wind* or *charging like water*—that her "friends in need and indeed" are "dodging"? For Thiong'o (2009, 46) memory of colonialism has become "shut up in a crypt, a collective psychic tomb" through denial and the lack of collective mourning. The five heads "down and sideways" in shameful gesture avoid eye contact in contrast to the others with eyes "straight on." They do not allow a connection and do not validate the teller's tale. By extension, the teller herself is denied. Focusing on the structures of our social fabric that distort and bury collective memories allows us to acknowledge the complexity of subjectivity formation and the subtle, dispersed and unpredictable ways that pain manifests in the ordinary sphere of life. Veena Das (2007, 62, our emphasis), attentive to the lived experience of social suffering, asks:

> What is it to bear witness to the criminality of the societal rule that consigns the uniqueness of being to eternal forgetfulness through a descent in everyday life—to not simply articulate loss through a dramatic gesture of defiance but to inhabit the world, or inhabit it again, in a gesture

> of mourning? *It is in this context that one may identify the eye not as the organ that sees but the organ that weeps.*

Das's (2007) work nuances the notion of resistance by conceptualizing agency in ordinary life as multi-faceted, fragmented and mobile. For her, some subjectivities are formed through the complex relationships between originary moments of pain and the bleeding pain that endures, creating a psychic and corporeal terrain that can no longer be accounted for by one particular outside force. As the structures of social control infiltrate, the assault on the individual multiplies, disperses and fractures, becoming difficult to identify and name. But the pain becomes a place inhabited.

Mashakalugo continues:

> *However much these witch traitors didn't want to listen, the truth remains the truth and no man shall ever bury the truth. At least one day in a lifetime it will be dug up and known by the world. A good thing remains good whether in dark or light. As the clouds cover the sky, rain falls, the sky darkens but the sun will never cease to shine. I felt bad but it made me stronger.*

Mashakalugo's truth refuses to be buried and forgotten, it "remains," it "will be known," it is good and is as sure as the unseen sun shining behind the rain: It is resilient. What kinds of resilience are required to confront the subtle rejections based on non-acceptance of some kind of perceived privilege? Following Das, the excessiveness that is the pain is not just extraterritorial but creates its own territory where one can gain traction.

As pain is marked into the everyday, transforming subjectivity, an opening can yield to yet another self, the subject that *re-becomes*. Within this opening, wounds can make possible new forms of agency as human subjectivity transforms (ibid.). Mashakalugo, simultaneously vulnerable and powerful, seems to occupy a terrain where "both the limits of insanity and the possibilities of emancipation are born out of the same horrors of subjugation" (Sandoval, 2000, 85). To "respond positively to world developers and well wishers" is sacrificial pain that makes her stronger. With a nod to her affinity to African orature, Mashakalugo testifies that "creative imagination is one of the greatest of remembering practices" (Thiong'o, 2009, 28). The non-concrete but real world of pain accompanies these experiences made possible through 'globalization': a micro-fracturing of selves, worlds and a re-suturing of subjectivities.

CONCLUSION

Our goal was to explore avenues for liberating subjectivities and forms of sociability in the context of Western globalization and its modern/colonial structure, particularly in relation to the agency/invisibility of Ugandan youth perspectives and our/their entry into engaged scholarship. Through reflection and dialogue around a set of lived experiences that intersected, diverged and fragmented in relation to a trip to Paris, the standardizing mechanisms of asymmetrical globalization were brought to the fore, provoking many more questions. Mashakalugo asks:

> *Do we not still follow colonial orders only indirectly? Aren't the two systems of colonialism and globalization now intermarried? Has the work of the colonizers, now difficult to recognize physically, only manifested through the operational wiring of the same logic through machines and regulations?*

We questioned the very notion of globality—and the conundrum of its impossibility if it is meant to include everyone, if everyone can include a pluriversity of ways of knowing, doing and being. Utilizing the lens of modernity/coloniality positioned us to consider how marginalized epistemic subjectivities are disallowed to make claims about the human condition and how dominant knowing subjects categorize and map the world in their/our own image. Wondering about the ways that differentially placed agents (mis)interpret/(mis)represent what it means to be 'global' in our shared *world of opposites,* we were besieged by the multiplicity of perspectives. As Mashakalugo observed earlier, we can at least agree that "in this world people will never see, perceive, act or think in the same way." This attitude is consistent with de-colonial thinking, which, rather than claiming to be the only option, accepts being one option among many, epitomizing "the horizon of pluriversality as a universal project" (Mignolo, 2011, 44).

Through our wondering about our journey, moments that re-emerged as representations of self and other were shattered and pieced together again in unexpected ways. Our accounts of subjectivity transformation also revealed a shared sense of hope embedded in the synergy that emerges through working together as epistemic partners toward justice. By taking youth perspectives and artistic/poetic enunciations seriously, we move towards an inter-cultural and inter-epistemic imaginary for rupturing the apartheid of knowledges in Western scholarship, making space for subaltern forms of expression.

Philosophically, phenomenology attends to lived experiences while at the same time recognizing that these very experiences can never be portrayed in their original form. The focus is on reflective understanding, always situated yet engendering a consciousness that allows the world to appear. Merleau-Ponty (2005, xii) writes,

> Reflection does not withdraw from the world towards a unity of consciousness as the world's basis; it steps back to watch the forms of transcendence fly up like sparks from a fire; it slackens the intentional threads which attach us to the world and thus brings them to our notice.

The phenomenological stance recognizes our situatedness in space and time and the plurality of influences on our human condition. In many ways this attitude is in line with Mendieta's (2001, 2007) formulation of a phenomenology from below; one that works fragmentarily as globalizations (both adverse and beneficial) intersect and manifest unequally. Such a view of the global condition allows us to witness how, "as participants in globalization, we experience and witness only aspects of it. As agents conditioned by it, we may be acted upon by planetary forces and tensions, but differentially" (ibid., 18).

The planet is globalized, indeed, but not all in the planet are globalized in the same way. As different actors move into globalized *spatio-temporal configurations* (Giddens, 1991), they enter a terrain *already* organized to disable certain subjectivities from exerting their rights with the same degree of power and competence as more privileged others. As it appeared to us in the scenario of the Paris metro *turnstiles,* the ways we come to understand our relationships to space and time, and thus conceptualize our world, are reflected in the way we see ourselves and other selves as human beings being in the world. Whereas some may see or be seen moving *swiftly* through globalized configurations, placed to *help* an-other along the way, others may be held momentarily, *stuck in the middle* or *standing helpless on the other side*. Yet, as affected agents in and of globalizations, we have come to share the view that rethinking experiences of place, mobility and globalization demands a rapport that works "fragmentarily and by way of fragments" (Mendieta, 2007, 17) through the inclusion and valorization of subaltern perspectives and means of expression.

NOTES

1. Artivism is embodied art that acts in the struggle against all forms of oppression and is epitomized by all artist/activists working at the interstices of creative expression, social/political change and self/community empowerment (Asante, 2008; Sandoval and Latorre, 2008).
2. Following de-colonial thinkers such as Mignolo (2011), the "underside" points to the colonial divide and the understanding that modernity is contingent on coloniality.
3. In the Ugandan context 'big people' is an expression commonly used to denote people who occupy positions of power such as professors, policy makers and political leaders.

REFERENCES

Asante, M.K. *It's Bigger Than Hip-Hop: The Rise of the Post-Hip-Hop Generation.* New York: St. Martin's Press, 2008.

Barthes, R. *Mythologies*. Translated by Annette Lavers. London: Paladin, 1973.

———. *The Eiffel Tower and Other Mythologies*. Berkeley: University of California Press, 1997.

Conley, T. " 'Hive of Words': The Transnational Poetics of the Eiffel Tower." *Modernism/Modernity* 17, no. 4, 2010. 765–777.

Das, V. *Life and Words: Violence and the Descent into the Ordinary.* Berkeley: University of California Press, 2007.

Fanon, F. *The Wretched of the Earth.* Translated by C.L. Markmann. New York: Grove Press, 1963.

———. *Black Skin, White Masks.* Translated by C.L. Markmann. New York: Grove Press, 1967.

Gadamer, H.G. *The Beginning of Philosophy.* New York: Continuum, 1998.

Giddens, A. *Modernity and Self-Identity: Self and Society in the Late Modern Age.* Cambridge: Polity Press, 1991.

Harriss, J.A. "Still Standing Tall." *American Spectator* 42, no. 6, 2009. 64–65.

Hassan, S. S., and L. P. Katsanis. "Identification of Global Consumer Segments: A Behavioral Framework." *Journal of International Consumer Marketing* 3, no. 2, 1991. 11–28.

Henry, P. "Africana Phenomenology: Its Philosophical Implications." *Worlds and Knowledges Otherwise* 1, no. 3, 2006. 1–23.

Hughes, Langston. "Cultural Exchange," in *Langston Hughes: Poems.* Classic Poetry Series. Accessed March 29, 2012. www.black-success.com/langston_hughes_2004_9.pdf.

Kjeldgaard, D., and S. Askegaard. "The Globalization of Youth Culture: The Global Youth Segment as Structures of Common Difference." *Journal of Consumer Research* 33, no. 2, 2006. 231–247.

Lukose, R. "Consuming Globalization: Youth and Gender in Kerala, India." *Journal of Social History* 38, no. 4, 2005. 915–935.

Lyotard, J.-F. *Phenomenology.* Translated by B. Beakley. New York: State University of New York Press, 1991.

Maldonado-Torres, N. "The Topology of Being and the Geopolitics of Knowledge." *City: Analysis of Urban Trends, Culture, Theory, Policy, Action* 8, no. 1, 2004. 29–56.

———. "On the Coloniality of Being: Contributions to the Development of a Concept." *Cultural Studies* 21, no. 2–3, 2007. 29–56.

———. *Against War: Views from the Underside of Modernity.* Durham: Duke University Press, 2008.

Marketing News. "Global Youth United: Homogeneous Group Prime Target for U.S. Marketers." October 28, 2002.

Mendieta, E. "Invisible Cities: A Phenomenology of Globalization from Below." *City: Analysis of Urban Trends, Culture, Theory, Policy, Action* 5, no. 1, 2001. 7–26.

———. *Global Fragments: Latinamericanisms, Globalizations, and Critical Theory.* Albany: State University of New York Press, 2007.

Merleau-Ponty, M. *Phenomenology of Perception.* Translated by C. Smith. London: Routledge, 2005.

Mignolo, W. *The Darker Side of Western Modernity: Global Futures, Decolonial Options.* Durham: Duke University Press, 2011.

Moses, E. *The $100 Billion Allowance: Accessing the Global Teen Market.* New York: Wiley, 2000.

Ormiston, G.L. "In the Midst . . . Multiplicities . . . Always Beginnings: An Introduction to Lyotard's Phenomenological Episodes," foreword in *Phenomenology* by J.F. Lyotard, 1–25. Translated by B. Beakley. New York: SUNY Press, 1991.

Papastergiadis, N. "Collaboration in Art and Society: A Global Pursuit of Democratic Dialogue," in *Globalization and Contemporary Art*. Edited by J. Harris, 275–288. Oxford: Wiley Blackwell, 2011.

Quijano, A. "Coloniality of Power, Eurocentrism, and Latin America." *Nepantla: Views From South* 1, no. 3, 2000. 533–580.

Sandoval, C. *Methodology of the Oppressed*. Minneapolis: University of Minnesota Press, 2000.

Sandoval, C., and G. Latorre. "Chicana/o Artivism: Judy Baca's Digital Work with Youth of Color," in *Learning Race and Ethnicity: Youth and Digital Media*. Edited by A. Everett, 81–108. Cambridge: MIT Press, 2008.

Shakespeare, W. *Hamlet* (Act I. Scene v. Line 189). Edited by A. Thompson and N. Taylor. Plymouth: Northcote House, 1996.

Thiong'o, N.W. *Re-Membering Africa*. Nairobi: East African Educational Publishers, 2009.

———. "The Education of the Colonial Bondsman," in *Globalectics: Theory and the Politics of Knowing*. E-book. New York: Columbia University Press, 2012.

Tomlinson, J. *Globalization and Culture*. Chicago: University of Chicago Press, 1994.

Tully, S. "Teens: The Most Global Market of All." *Fortune*. May 16, 1994. 34–41.

Urry, J. "Tourism, Culture and Social Inequality," in *The Sociology of Tourism: Theoretical and Empirical Investigations*. Edited by S. Leivadi, Y. Apostolopoulos and A. Yiannakis, 115–133. New York: Routledge, 1996.

Van Manen, M. *Researching Lived Experience: Human Science for an Action Sensitive Pedagogy*. 2nd ed. London: Althouse Press, 1997.

Young, P. "From the Eiffel Tower to the Javanese Dancer: Envisioning Cultural Globalization at the 1889 Paris Exhibition." *The History Teacher* 41, no. 3, 2008. 339–362.

Section 3

Embodiment and Temporality

Oneself and Time

9 Sex Education, Bodily Orientations and the Northern Territory 'Intervention'

Mary Lou Rasmussen

'The intervention' is shorthand for what is formally known as the Northern Territory Emergency Response (NTER) in Australia. An ongoing initiative, announced by the John Howard Liberal[1] government in August 2007, and continued by the Rudd and Gillard Labor and now the conservative Abbott government,[2] it is a plan for addressing—among other things—alleged child abuse[3] in Aboriginal Northern Territory (NT) communities. It is a highly controversial measure that has drawn criticism and support from within and outside Indigenous communities. Anthropologist Elizabeth Povinelli claims that "since 'the intervention,' sexuality has become a general *stain* on Indigenous culture in the sense of a smear and defecation of cultural pleasure" (2011b, 34). In making this claim, Povinelli draws our attention to the ways in which bodies, pleasures and emotions are marked by the spaces they inhabit, what Sara Ahmed terms 'bodily orientations.' I see the ongoing intervention as a key social and political object that permeates the spaces that Indigenous people in remote communities in the NT must inhabit. Specifically, I turn my attention to how 'the intervention' operates to locate Indigenous people in remote areas as specific sorts of sexual subjects inhabiting spaces that are depicted as culturally backward, sexually dangerous and particularly problematic for children and young people. What might it mean for bodies to be oriented in this way by such a project?

Ahmed's (2006) idea of bodily orientations is partially underpinned by the phenomenological thought of Husserl *(Ideas)* and Merleau-Ponty *(Phenomenology of Perception)*. In particular Ahmed (2006, 38) argues that phenomenology focuses attention on the background: "It might do so by giving an account of the condition of emergence for something." Consequently, temporality is seen as crucial to phenomenological analysis. A phenomenological approach "helps us explore how bodies are shaped by histories, which they perform in their comportment, their posture and their gestures" (ibid., 552). An approach that is cognisant that bodies are not fixed in space and time is crucial to understanding how Indigenous cultures and sexualities have been affected by the intervention.

Rosalyn Diprose, in her (2008) article "Biopolitical Technologies of Prevention," brings together Foucault's 'political technologies of bodies' and

Merleau-Ponty's ideas regarding 'temporality and the intercorporeality of bodies' to analyze biopolitical technologies of disease prevention. The NTER has been rationalized essentially on the grounds of concerns over the health and well-being of Indigenous people,

> including concerns for the health of children and families in remote Indigenous communities. The immediate catalyst for the NTER, the *Little children are sacred* board of inquiry, was primarily focused on child abuse. The inquiry recognised that poor access to health care was one of the factors which led to child abuse and neglect—alongside alcohol and drug abuse, unemployment, gambling, pornography, poor education and housing, and general loss of identity and control.
> (Povinelli, 2011b, 207–208)

A Foucauldian approach is attentive to the negative impacts of such pre-emptive policies, such as those enacted through the technologies of the intervention. Diprose argues that the implementation of biopolitical technologies of disease prevention cannot be read outside the logic of other types of interventions (since September 2011) that are motivated by pre-emption against a future risk that is incalculable.

Analysis of such technologies also needs to consider how "power operates at the micro-level of the body's movements, spatiality, and temporal rhythms to realign the body's forces and powers" (Foucault, 1979,136–138, in Diprose, 2008, 145). For Diprose (ibid., 148), Foucault is well complemented by Merleau-Ponty in this task because

> as Merleau-Ponty (1962) puts it, however sick or subjected a body is, it never loses its futural orientation toward its material, social, and meaningful world and the unpredictability this implies. Unless it is dead. A body subjected to paternalistic, infantilising, totalising modes of governance will try to emerge from the sense of timelessness that such governance can effect and re-orientate itself toward an undetermined future. It will do this by reaching for material at hand, most likely what has worked before to punctuate time.

In understanding 'the intervention' it is also necessary to attend to how communities and bodies re-orientate themselves, with and against the timelessness of such modes of governance.

The first section of this chapter provides some background to the politics of 'the intervention,' specifically focused on the grounds used to justify this extraordinary set of measures. In the second section I read Indigenous peoples' orientations toward 'no pornography' signs, erected as part of 'the intervention,' as a perverse form of public sexuality education. Here I elaborate on Povinelli's argument about sexuality within remote Indigenous life-worlds being stained since 'the intervention.' In the final section, I introduce

Povinelli's 'politics of recognition' and place this alongside Kate Senior and Richard Chenhall's (2008) " 'Walkin' About at Night': The Background to Teen Pregnancy in a Remote Aboriginal Community." Senior and Chenhall's study uses longitudinal qualitative research to understand young women's experience of youth cultures and sexuality. This ethnographic study was conducted by Senior in the period prior to 'the intervention.' It is also the only study I have been able to locate that is situated in a remote community in the Northern Territory that draws specifically on young women's experiences of sexuality, and includes young people living in these communities that have become subject to the NTER. In crafting this analysis, my aim is to juxtapose these young women's bodily orientations and disorientations within and against the 'politics of recognition' playing out before and after 'the intervention.'

It may seem odd to juxtapose these two stories, because they are not synchronous, and both rely on data not collected by the author. In taking this approach it is worth prefacing this paper with a few comments about how I conceptualize method in this queer phenomenological approach. Johanna Oksala (2011, 220), in a study of Foucault, phenomenology and feminist theory, writes that phenomenology

> is 'a philosophy of the subject' in the sense that it subsumes the objective under the subjective. The intersubjective conditions of experience, for example, must and can be disclosed through a description of the subject's structures of experience.

By contrast she argues that Foucault had a different relation to experience, to her mind he

> maintains the irreducible correlation between the constituted and the constitutive and resists all foundational recourse to experience. But he does not contest the ontological or even epistemic indispensability of subjective experience.
>
> (Ibid., 220)

For Oksala (ibid., 218), such an approach recognizes that "bodies always assume meaning through a complex process in which competing discourses, conceptualizations, and cultural practices intertwine with private sensations, pleasures, and pains." In order to undertake a phenomenological study of sexuality education, bodily orientations and 'the intervention,' it is thus important to attend to multiple sites of data analysis "through different ontological registers, ranging from textual forms, such as novels and newspapers, to forms of subjectivity adumbrated in citizenship and stranger-sociability, as well as to multiplex cultural formations called *the nation* and *the public sphere*" (Gaonkar and Povinelli, 2003, 395, emphasis in original). And we also need to "ask what happens to meaning as it is borne across the chasm of two language codes, of genre, of one semiotic mode to another, say the movement from oral forms of repetition to written forms of iteration" (ibid.).

In this chapter I endeavour to access stories that people have told directly in response to public signposts that denote rules relating to consumption of pornography in remote communities: one initiative of 'the intervention.' Alongside this data I consider scholarship and popular commentary which comments on these signposts. I also draw on Senior and Chenhall's study of young women's sexuality in remote communities prior to the intervention, because anxieties about the sexuality of young Aboriginal people were used by the nation to rationalize the implementation of this set of biopolitical technologies. Attention is also given to the meanings applied to sexuality, shame and young women's pregnancy, endeavouring to think about how these meanings are borne across cultures, temporalities and logics of freedom.

'BODILY ORIENTATIONS' AND THE NORTHERN TERRITORY EMERGENCY RESPONSE

In "Orientation: Toward a Queer Phenomenology," Sara Ahmed (2006) focuses her attention on the significance of orientation, focusing specifically on sexual orientation, in order to consider the relationship between how we reside in space, how we inhabit spaces, and who or what we inhabit spaces with. This is significant, she argues, because spaces are sexualized. Spaces inhabited by Indigenous people living in remote communities have been sexualized in very specific ways in the context of 'the intervention':

> The policy focus is increasingly on only 66,000 out of 517,000 Indigenous people, some 13% of the total Indigenous population. The Australian Government's public views are increasingly defined in terms of the remotest dwelling Aboriginal people. On the other hand, this focus is justified by a fiction that these locales are where things are *really bad, especially on emotive issues like child abuse. This is simply untrue, as Ian Anderson and Peter Botsman have pointed out using Australian Institute of Health and Welfare sex abuse notification data published earlier this year.*
>
> (Altman, 2007, 4, my emphasis)

Sexuality, sex education and Indigenous people in remote communities have been threaded together within the context of 'the intervention' in contemporary Australian politics to profoundly shape bodily orientations in a very specific and deleterious set of political manoeuvres. In 2008, Australian Bureau of Statistics data suggests that 24% of Indigenous people were living in remote (or very remote) areas. Remote communities in the Northern

Territory and in Cape York have received the most publicity; both are the subject of "escalating and increasingly ideological conservative rhetoric" (ibid., 2). These communities are also dogged, Slater (2008, 11) notes, by a "narrative of dysfunction [which] suggests that the social body of remote Indigenous communities is moribund; no dialogue is required." Historically, Eva McRae-Williams and Rolf Gerritsen (2010, 2) note, such communities were "established principally as a means of administering Aboriginal welfare policies . . . [and they are] not economically sustainable."

First it is important to elaborate on how 'the intervention' has been manufactured and rationalized. A Board of Inquiry into the Protection of Aboriginal Children from Sexual Abuse, commissioned by the government of the NT, Australia, commissioned a report that was publicly released on June 15, 2007. The report was entitled *Ampe Akelyernemane Meke Mekarle (Little Children Are Sacred)* (Wild and Anderson, 2007). In response to the publication, the Howard Federal Government (in which our current Prime Minister served as a Minister), announced that it would be undertaking an intervention in remote Indigenous communities in the NT. The authors of the *Little Children Are Sacred* report, Rex Wild and Pat Anderson, have both sought to distance themselves from 'the intervention' with Pat Anderson stating, "There is no relationship between the Federal response and our recommendations. We feel betrayed and disappointed and hurt and angry and pretty pissed off at the same time" (Sweet, 2007).

The Racial Discrimination Act was suspended so that 'the intervention' could be rolled out in seventy-three remote communities in the NT. The Federal government assumed control of these communities and their assets, increased police and ministerial powers, and authorized take over of community finances and licensing of community stores. Logistical support has been provided by the police and the army. Teams of medical practitioners were sent into communities to conduct health checks for Aboriginal children. There has been quarantining of welfare payments, as well as prohibitions on alcohol (in some communities that had already implemented such prohibitions) and on pornography. NT government statistics demonstrate the number of substantiated cases of child abuse in Indigenous communities is very low. In fact "the number of people arrested or summonsed for sexual abuse offences against Indigenous children in prescribed communities has decreased from 39 in 2006–07 to 26 in 2007–08. The number of adults arrested for physical assaults against children in prescribed communities has increased marginally from 8 in 2006–07 to 9 in 2007–08" (Attorney General's Department, 2008, 116). Whereas 'the intervention' has many components, sexual abuse of children has been a central and often repeated justification underscoring this biopolitical project.

In a discussion of statistics specifically related to cases of substantiated child abuse among Indigenous Australians, Peter Botsman (2007) demonstrates that at the time 'the intervention' was announced the targeting of remote communities was difficult to reconcile with government statistics on child abuse:

> There were 319 substantiated instances of Indigenous child abuse in the Northern Territory (NT) in 2004/5. This compared to Queensland 1,186, New South Wales 1,642 and Victoria 770. Perhaps the Commonwealth and other states should be sending an army of bureaucrats to study why the Northern Territory has a comparatively good record for looking after Indigenous children.
>
> (Botsman, 2007, 7)

Botsman seeks to illustrate the illogicality of targeting particular populations of Indigenous people where there was no evidentiary basis for such a strategy.

Elizabeth Povinelli (2011a) is critical of the way in which the Howard Government utilized Wild and Atkinson's study to conflate child sexual abuse as somehow intrinsic to Indigenous people living in remote communities and their continued relationships to land, culture and kinship networks. She (ibid., 296) notes that Wood and Anderson's report

> was careful to dispel five myths about Indigenous sexual abuse (Aboriginal men are the only offenders; Aboriginal law is the reason for high levels of sexual abuse; Aboriginal law is used as an excuse to justify abuse; Aboriginal culture is the reason for underreporting; and Aboriginal men do not have an important role to play in preventing child abuse). Yet it was in terms of such myths about the cause of Aboriginal sexual abuse that the federal government and the national media made sense of the abuse.

As Povinelli suggests above, the media response to 'the intervention' tended to reinscribe an understanding of remote Aboriginal communities as unsettling places beyond the immediate gaze of settler communities. These communities have been produced as particularly pathological places (also see Baird, 2008).

Povinelli (2006, 10) wants to turn the gaze away from myths about Indigenous communities and turn the focus towards how "the dialectic of individual freedom and social bondage is distributed geographically, how social phenomena that contest this distribution are made commensurate with it, and how discourses that arise from this distribution circulate, are localized, and are contested." When, where and who is seen to conform to liberal politics of recognition, which insists that individual freedom is a universal good? Who is placed outside this frame and for what purpose? Further, what strategies are enacted to ensure that bodies fall into line? And, what happens to bodies and practices that are produced as incommensurate through the politics of recognition enacted through 'the intervention'? In the context of a phenomenological understanding of children, young people, sexuality and 'the intervention,' Povinelli's work is a means by which to apprehend how particular relationships between sovereignty, freedom and place are knitted together and "made commensurate." For Povinelli (2011b,

88), this apprehension is linked to phenomenology because "understanding as interpretation is part of the comportment of everyday life. . . . [This] does not mean such understanding is outside language and consciousness, or that it is within the individual subject." Rather, like Oksala's (2011) discussion of Foucault and phenomenology in feminist theory, governmentality is taken up as a way of conceptualizing experience that is always informed by knowledge, power and subjectivation. Knowledge, power and subjectivation cannot be understood as commensurate in this way of seeing; for Povinelli (2011b, 91), this incommensurability provides "a potential field of maneuver for Indigenous and non-Indigenous subjects supporting and opposing 'the intervention.' "

In a discussion of governmentality and 'the intervention,' Deirdre Tedmanson and Dinesh Wadiwel (2010) classify the biopolitical technologies associated with this event as constitutive of a "new race/pleasure war." In this context they examine data relating to child abuse in Australian Indigenous communities as well as underscoring the long history of reporting (by Indigenous people) of systematic neglect of Indigenous communities in Australia in regards to social support services and housing and economic opportunities. There is recognition that child abuse is part of all communities, and can generally be expected to be more prevalent in communities that experience social and economic disadvantage. Tedmanson and Wadiwel (2010, 10) are careful to note that the *Little Children Are Sacred* report "specifically rejects the notion that Aboriginal culture is the reason for the under-reporting of child abuse" and they conclude that

> the intervention functions not as a means to address child sexual abuse but as a set of coordinated mechanisms that enable the governmentalities of power to mask violent domination, racialization, and economies of pleasure. These same powers organize, sustain, legitimate, and give effect to 'white' sovereignty.
>
> (Ibid., 12)

In writing about queer phenomenology, Ahmed notes that phenomenologists develop an awareness of what is happening nearby. This might include the repetition of actions, and, I would argue, the repetition of "myths about the cause of Aboriginal sexual abuse" in Aboriginal communities. The changing landscapes and rhetorics, at once brought about and justified by 'the intervention,' have been significant in shaping the worlds of people living in remote communities. Paying attention to an understanding of our surroundings is critical from a phenomenological perspective because "we are not only directed toward objects, but those objects also take us in a certain direction. The world that is around has already taken certain shapes" (Ahmed, 2006, 545). The queer phenomenology I am attempting, in relation to sex, education and 'the intervention,' attends to expert knowledges that have rationalized and critiqued 'the intervention'; relations of power, specifically with regard to ideas of sovereignty in late-liberalism; and subjectivization. The study of subjectivization is integral here as it describes the processes by which people come to think of themselves as subjects. In such an approach sexual subjectivities are not distinct from 'the intervention'; rather, 'the intervention' is a powerful discourse that has the capacity to produce particular understandings about the relationship between sex and Indigeneity. The biopolitical technologies of 'the intervention,' and people's responses to these biotechnologies, require critical scrutiny because they are now a part of the process of becoming a sexual subject.

I have dedicated specific space to this elaboration of the background of the event that has come to be known as 'the intervention.' A phenomenological analysis requires a rich description of the space in which the analysis is to take place. This background must be attended to because "a background can be what explains the conditions of emergence or an arrival of something as the thing that it appears to be in the present" (Ahmed, 2006, 549). I am arguing that a detailed description of 'the intervention' must form part of a phenomenology of young teen sexuality within remote Indigenous communities in the Northern Territory. This is not to say that sexuality would become absent but for 'the intervention,' but that it would appear differently, outside the background of 'the intervention.' In short, the orientations of 'the intervention' impact much more on specific bodies. For instance, in my discussion of the blue signs below it is possible to see some quite different interactions with these signposts. A signpost is not just a signpost; it accrues meanings based on numerous factors. A phenomenological account attends to where the signpost is physically located, on who might see the signpost, and on how frequently they might see it—Is it part of daily life, or a curiosity for a passing eye? What does the signpost say? Why is it there? Who has had the authority to decide that the signpost belongs at the entrance to particular communities, and not others? What can we learn from the way that the signpost is defaced and written about? Beyond the physicality of the sign itself, the queer phenomenology I am attempting here also seeks out evidence of emotions and conversations that are provoked in relation to the signs. I gather this evidence because together it helps me to better understand this one element of this ongoing biopolitical technology, known as 'the intervention.'

BLUE SIGNS, PORNOGRAPHY AND SEX EDUCATION IN REMOTE COMMUNITIES

> Throughout the Northern Territory large bright blue or yellow signs were erected at the entrance of Indigenous communities announcing that pornography and alcohol were banned and in the process publicly branding Indigenous communities as spaces of perversion and decay.
>
> (Povinelli, 2011a, 297)

Figure 9.1 Blue road sign in Tennant Creek, Northern Territory of Australia, warning against importing liquor and pornography. Photograph copyright Jagath Dheerasekara, 2010.

These blue signs were erected at the entrance to seventy-three Northern Territory Indigenous communities. The pictures of these blue signs (see Figure 9.1) were taken by Jagath Dheerasekara; many images of these signs have also appeared on the Internet. Clearly these signs appear as something out of the ordinary to locals and tourists alike. Whereas they may be a mere curiosity to some, many people living in these communities abhor these signs. Why have such signs been erected, and what lies behind the blue sign? As a researcher in sexuality education, and in the context of this discussion of bodily orientation and young people living in these remote communities, my particular interest in these signs is in the encounters that they stage, within the context of 'the intervention.' The blue signs were removed by the Australian Government Department of Families, Housing, Community Services and Indigenous Affairs (FaHCSIA) in 2012. A press release issued in January 2013, related to the removal of the signs, states:

> As people in the Northern Territory would be aware, the Australian Government has responded to community concerns about signs and is working with the Northern Territory Government, Indigenous communities, land councils and the Local Government Association of the Northern Territory *to make signs more respectful.*

> All 250 of the blue signs notifying alcohol and pornography restrictions have been removed across the Northern Territory and replaced with 49 redesigned, more respectful highway signs, strategically positioned on borders, major highway intersections, airstrips and barge landings. Government Engagement Coordinators and Indigenous Engagement Officers are actively engaging their communities to redesign community signs, replacing text with community agreed wording, including local Aboriginal artwork.[4]
>
> (My emphasis)

Justifications for the signs by government representatives at community consultations about 'the intervention' refer back to the *Little Children Are Sacred* report (Nelson et al., 2009, 129) and perceived connections between consumption of pornography and grooming of children for child sexual abuse. Following on from this report, these signs have come to very publically orient people within these communities with associations to pornography and alcohol abuse. This can be read as an act of public sex education by which people (tourists, community members, visitors to communities) come to know these communities as troubled by alcohol and pornography. This situation continues, even as substantiated cases of offences related to consumption of pornography and of child abuse remains incredibly low in these communities.[5]

Drawing on Husserl and Butler, Sara Ahmed (2006, 551 and 553) argues that

> Orientations involve at least a two-way approach, or the 'more than one' of an encounter. . . . It is precisely how phenomenology exposes the sedimentation of history on the repetition of bodily action that makes it a useful resource for feminism. What bodies 'tend to do' are effects of histories rather than being originary.

The bodily orientations associated with these signs involve strangers and community members encountering these signs. Strangers might encounter a sign once, though this one encounter is clearly enough to provoke some to interact further with the sign, to take a photo for readers of a blog, for example. For community members the orientation to these signs is more mundane, each trip to and from the community repeats the association with pornography and alcohol, educating people in the communities about the perceived problem of pornography that lies within. If what bodies tend to do is about what they are oriented towards, then the frequent encounters with these signs surely also sediments particular understandings about sexuality, pornography and its place within these communities. This sedimentation has the potential to affect people living in these communities, as well as those who transit through.

Phenomenology "asks us to be aware of 'what' is around. After all, if consciousness is intentional, then we are not only directed towards objects, but those objects also take us in a certain direction" (Ahmed, 2006, 544).

Figure 9.2 Road sign in the Northern Territory of Australia warning against importing liquor and pornography. Photograph copyright Jagath Dheerasekara, 2010.

The direction in which these signs orient people in these communities is often towards shame. This is apparent in transcripts from community consultations undertaken to evaluate the progress of 'the intervention.'[6]

FS2 (FaHCSIA Staff) (Manager of Government Business Managers):

Those big blue signs, they're a shame job.

Richard Downs (RD) (Spokesman for the Alyawarr Nation):

They're a shame job.

FS2: They make people think that there is a big problem in communities when there isn't?[7]

As Tedmanson and Wadiwel (2010, 16) indicate, in the context of the NTER it is possible to see "[s]hame as a technique designed to undermine the possibility of enjoyment for the shamed becomes a new apparatus of domination." Shame is not a discrete orientation, standing alone, only marking particular bodies in the community. There is a strong sense in the transcripts of shame associated with a sense of indignation, that these signs marked all the community as perverse.

In the *Social Justice Report 2011* of the Aboriginal and Torres Strait Islander Social Justice Commissioner for the Australian Human Rights Commission, Mick Gooda (the commissioner) observes the damage caused by the blue signs. He writes:

> Each of the Intervention communities had big blue signs erected outside them which, amongst other things, loudly proclaimed restrictions on alcohol and pornography—as if everyone living behind those signs are alcoholic, perverts and perpetrators!
> I invite the residents of Yarralumla, Redhill, Woollara, Mosman and Toorak, to name just a few well-known, middle-class suburbs, to contemplate how they would feel with similar signs erected at the entrance to their communities.
>
> (Commissioner, ATSI Social Justice, 2011, 80)

The Commissioner goes on to point to the ways in which the signs negatively impact the social fabric of the communities in which they are erected:

> The approach typified by the blue signs damages our communities and reinforces negative stereotypes; stereotypes which we sometimes use as weapons to turn on our own through lateral violence.
>
> (*Social Justice Report,* 2011, 80)

In the context of the discussion of young people and teen pregnancy later in this chapter, these associations with shame, and the undermining of the possibility of enjoyment, are particularly salient. Shame and sexuality are continuously interwoven through the compulsory sex education imposed by the blue signs.

This interpretation is reinforced in excerpts below taken from *Will They Be Heard?—A Response to the NTER Consultations June to August, 2009.* This report was prepared by Alastair Nicholson, Larissa Behrendt, Alison Vivian, Nicole Watson and Michele Harris, under the auspices of the Research Unit, Jumbunna Indigenous House of Learning. Nicholson et al. strongly critique the consultation process undertaken by the Department of Families, Housing, Community Services and Indigenous Affairs (FaHCSIA) and argue that the consultations were "insufficient to qualify as indicating consent by Aboriginal people in the Northern Territory" to 'the intervention' (Nicholson et al., 2009, 9). The consultation process, officially entitled *Future Directions for Northern Territory Emergency Response* is critiqued

Figure 9.3 Ampilatwatja in the Northern Territory. Photograph copyright Jagath Dheerasekara, 2010.

by Nicholson et al., who also argue that feedback from communities involved in the consultation process reflects, among other things, "resentment about the intervention signs which imply that Aboriginal people use pornography" (ibid.).

The conversations reported below took place during a consultation in Ampilatwatja in the Northern Territory. Ampilatwatja has a population of approximately 350 predominantly Alyawarr-speaking People, and is situated 325km North East of Alice Springs.[8] The transcripts are taken verbatim from the community consultations conducted by FaHCSIA on August 12, 2009, as reported in *Will They Be Heard?*

> **RD:** That blue sign, the pornography, you know, it's pointing the community, at each community, each outstation, you know. As if we involved in all that and we not. Not out in the remote areas, nothing.
>
> **FS2:** So it gives the impression to people that it's a problem?
>
> **RD:** That we have a pedophile problem—that we have a sexual abuse problem, alcohol problems and we don't!
>
> **RD:** And I haven't heard one apology from any of the ministers, so, Brian, you got to understand, I mean that's how we feel. We're put down. We're pushed down. . . . But we been pushed aside, we are outcasts, we're labelled. Yet the white society across Australia are pure,

Figure 9.4 Blue sign—Alice Springs in the Northern Territory. Photograph copyright Jagath Dheerasekara, 2010.

appear to be clean [language], they got no sexual abuse happen nothing yet they are the ones that's starting.

FS1 (FaHCSIA Staff) (General Manager in charge of the intervention in the NT):

That's not true.

RD: It's out there, but we are the ones that get targeted. And . . . that's like me accusing you of something else and you're trying to tell me it's not me and such and such and that's how I feel and you got to understand that too.

These signs are perceived by members of these communities as marking them in particularly onerous ways. They understand themselves as being clearly set apart from the white society in Australia through the installation of such signs at the boundaries of their communities. In this community consultation this speaker emphasizes his feeling that the signs are accusatory, despite strong protestations otherwise from his interlocutor.

Similar sentiments were presented at a consultation that happened the following day in Arlparra/Utopia in the Northern Territory. Rosie Kunoth-Monk, President of Urapuntja Council and Barkley Shire President, stated the following:[9]

Rosie Kunoth-Monk (RKN): I've just come back from listening to the Top End communities in the Arnhem Lands, and people are dissatisfied with what's at the front of our Sacred Lands, those blue signs. I have spoken to Jenny Macklin's advisor. I have asked them to remove that.

RKN: There is this morning on the news, just for your information, sly grog running between Geelong and Ballarat. Why hasn't the intervention signs gone up there? Now I would imagine it is a little bit more than just the grog, sly grog, selling. I would imagine there is pornography there, I would imagine there are drugs there.

RKN: If there's one rule for black people, and one rule for white Australia, who are our brothers and sisters? There is a division being created, and these are some of the questions that are going around. The other thing is, when you said, or Rex Wild and Pat Anderson put out, *The Little Children Are Sacred.*

This perception of the negative effects and bad feelings associated with the blue signs is echoed in Tedmanson and Wadiwel's (2010, 15) discussion of the place of 'the intervention' in orienting broader Australian imaginaries of Aboriginal communities:

> There is a correlation between the governmentalized regimes of controls on pleasure [blue signs] and the prurient, sexualized, and intensely moralizing national public discourse about 'the intervention.' The gaze of the Australian public, reflected in the media reporting at the time of 'the intervention,' portrayed Indigenous communities as generically (and, by inference, 'genetically') 'dysfunctional' spaces where rampant and out-of-control bestial sexual transgression was the norm rather than an exception, despite statistical evidence (as previously cited) to the contrary. . . . To collectively penalize a people is to treat them as a group that is second-class or less than human. It effectively severs the social contract of reciprocity between that collective group and the state.

In the excerpt from the transcript of the community consultation above, the speaker's experiences of these signs as accusatory is palpable. Protestations to the contrary provide no comfort. The signs orient public and private discourse, feelings, media debates, and young people's experiences of themselves as sexual subjects within these communities.

These signs also license a broader understanding of Indigenous people, and especially of Aboriginal people living in these communities, as at once abject and distinct, in need of special education measures. If bodily orientations are performative, as Ahmed (2006, 555) suggests, then the politics of the signs and the ways in which they set precise bodies apart is particularly concerning from the perspective of sex education because these signs orientate people in these communities toward an association with pornography. Even as they are promoted as a means to protect children, they ineluctably orient these children towards objects that they previously knew nothing about.

This sexualization of Indigenous lifeworlds was of great concern to Indigenous people living in these communities. This is evident in the following transcript where government representatives echo the feelings of people about the blue signs:

> **FS1 (FaHCSIA Staff) (General Manager in charge of the intervention in the NT):**
>
> Thank you for that and I've got the message very clear. This is something—Aboriginal people have been complaining that the signs make out that all Aboriginal people have something to do with pornography. And this has really been very dreadful I think to many people, and I'm sorry. And that the signs make out that Aboriginal people somehow or other are not worried about protecting their children from this rude material, and I know that that's not the case.
>
> The government is thinking about making a change to the pornography ban, the ban on pornography. They want to—they are going to look at the signs again. I said this morning, a lot of people have said they don't like the signs, but I have to say to you, some people, women, for example, even yesterday, said to us they thought the signs have actually helped. So not everybody says that the signs are bad.[10]

High levels of concern among Aboriginal people are at once accepted and refuted, evident in the phrase "not everybody says that the signs are bad." This flies in the face of the overwhelming evidence in the transcripts from the community consultations evaluating 'the intervention' that people living in these communities felt that the signs were a 'shame job.'

Three years into 'the intervention,' bipartisan support for the measures continues though in 2012 the blue signs were removed in response to community protests. There is evidence of a continuing belief, at least among politicians, in the liberatory capacity of 'the intervention.' Elizabeth Povinelli elaborates on the types of thinking that sustain such faith. She (2011a, 297) argues that there is a belief that 'the intervention' would:

> liberate countless Indigenous children who were languishing in rural communities—worse, being raped in these sealed-off spaces, their abuse aided and abetted by childless advocates kowtowing to the sanctity of a perverse traditional law and refusing to accept the irrelevance of customary sexuality and gender to modern life.

The signs are clearly not oriented toward modern white Australians who, it is implied, know how to care for and protect their children. Rather, the signs orient readers' gaze toward understandings of Indigenous children living in premodern conditions, outside the protection of the state, and at the mercy of tradition. This orientation toward the myth that Indigenous people in remote communities are somehow especially negligent in the protection of children is also apparent in contemporaneous press accounts (see Hagan, 2009). What is crucial here is the suturing together of an understanding of Indigenous people *living in remote communities* as premodern and sexually perverse (a perception clearly not borne out by government statistics on child abuse).

Critically, these associations with perversity efface continuous failures of governments to close the yawning gap in disadvantage between Indigenous Australians and the broader community. In order to elaborate the rationale for the continued focus on remote communities within the politics of 'the intervention,' Povinelli turns to the work of Peter Sutton (2009), an Australian anthropologist whose influential book on Indigenous Australia has been used in support of the aims of 'the intervention.' Povinelli (2011a, 298) encapsulates Sutton's argument below:

> Forget problems of structural racism and state neglect; the central cause of Indigenous impoverishment, ill health and educational stagnation was Indigenous people's 'ancient need to pursue family loyalties over essentially foreign ideologies such as the doctrine of the common good' and to cling to 'traditional medical beliefs and practices' that blocked 'certain preventative and curative health measures.'
>
> (Sutton, quoted in Povinelli)

In this reading of the politics of recognition, a clear division is established by Sutton between the "common good," which is a marker for modern liberal individualism versus the backwardness of tradition, kinship and customary practices. Within this frame of recognition, 'the intervention' is constructed as compassionate and necessary, because what other hope is there for people who fail to embrace the liberal dream of their own volition?

The type of thinking espoused by Sutton above is increasingly becoming accepted wisdom in the context of debates about Indigenous education. Echoes of this style of thought are apparent in a recent report prepared by the Menzies Foundation (2010), *Closing the Gap in Indigenous Education: Workshop Report.* The workshop, conducted in July 2010, brought together key Australian bureaucrats and academics, Indigenous and non-Indigenous, to consider strategies for *Closing the Gap* in educational advantage between Indigenous and non-Indigenous students. In imagining how the gap might be closed, the report stated that "many Indigenous people in remote communities are unaware of the basics of the Western economy, and the expectations that apply in mainstream society" (Menzies, 2010, 17).

Logically, therefore, *Closing the Gap* is tied to young people's acceptance of mainstream values. This conflation of remoteness, criminality, sexual perversity and educational disadvantage—and their link to the rejection of mainstream values—is well demonstrated in the following quote:

> Young people in remote communities are negotiating life between two cultures . . . over recent generations, many young people in remote communities have also rejected the authority of elders, leading to a breakdown of traditional values, initiation rites and paths to cultural knowledge, but often without the leavening influence that would have followed from a knowledge and acceptance of mainstream values. Vulnerable individuals have been caught up in petrol sniffing, gunja use, alcohol abuse, violence, and in sexual liaisons that cut across accepted skin groups. The situation is complicated by TV and videos from mainstream Australia that often feature the lowest common denominators of celebrity culture, violence or pornography.
>
> (Ibid., 6)

It is possible to see here how a particular, and increasingly irrefutable, equation is manufactured in which *remoteness is constituted as pathological, the solution to this pathology then becomes the acceptance of mainstream values*. A phenomenological perspective inspired by Diprose is instructive here: Through this frame the manufacture of such equations can be conceptualized as technologies of the body. Such technologies, Diprose (2008, 145) argues, enframe material life; these "ways of thinking are paradigms involving a chiasmic relation between socio-political meaning, technical devices, and human beings and so reorder the world that produces them" (ibid., 145). One example of how such logics reorder the world that produces them is the production of the blue signs, which are meant to encourage the acceptance of mainstream values in the face of the 'breakdown of traditional values.'

But such technologies of the body "reorder the world that produces them," thus the bodily orientations associated with the signs incorporate children and young people living in these communities:

> It was also suggested that the signs had the unintended consequence of raising awareness of pornography among children and heightening young people's curiosity about it. . . . People (especially children) now ask what pornography is when they see the signs. This is embarrassing for parents who now have to explain what the sign means.[11]

As English is a second or even third language in many remote communities, English literacy skills vary significantly in these communities. The 2011 NTER evaluation reports suggest that at least some parents living in these communities could not read the signs, and, if they could, they might not know what the term pornography means. The Northern Territory Emergency Response Evaluation Report (2011) cites a survey conducted to inform the evaluation. In the survey, the prohibitions placed on pornography were referred to as "new rules for sexy pictures" (2011, 14). This rephrasing was presumably implemented in the survey because of perceived difficulties that people living in these communities might have in interpreting the language used on the signs. It is foreseeable that in these circumstances some young people are educating their parents about the meaning of the signs.

The excerpt from the 2011 NTER evaluation report above also suggests that parents found themselves discussing pornography (a topic many parents would avoid) with children and that this was the cause of some discomfort. Given young people's reported curiosity about the signs, there is no doubt that if they did not know what the signs meant when they were first erected, the meaning behind the signs would have been swiftly communicated between them. There is something truly perverse about these blue signs being countenanced in these communities as it is inevitable that they will expose very young people to conversations about the idea of pornography, with parents and/or peers. Importantly, this is perverse not because there is something wrong with talking to young people about sexuality. What I find most concerning about such exchanges is not that families might be talking about sex, but that the touchstone for such conversations are these biopolitical technologies which enmesh Indigeneity, sexuality, shame and perversion. Clearly young people are sexual beings, but in Australia "the education of children about sexuality has always been considered a controversial issue that warrants strict regulation and surveillance in terms of policy, content and procedures" (Robinson and Davies, 2008, 222). The warrant for such an approach speaks to the size of the sex panic that is continuously used as a moral justification for 'the intervention.'

The signs, I would argue, also stand out as a particularly confronting mode of public sex education, especially when put side by side with often repeated controversies about sex education and age appropriate messages. For instance, in September 2012 Catholic parents and schools successfully lobbied the Australian Curriculum Assessment and Reporting Authority (ACARA) to "back down from its plan to explain puberty to children as young as seven [in the proposed national curriculum], over concerns the kids might 'freak out' " (Bita, 2012). So parents in remote communities might be expected to engage in conversations about pornography with any curious child or young person who happens to notice the large blue sign that has been erected at the entrance to their community, whereas ACARA baulks at young people learning about puberty in years 3 and 4 at primary school. The politics that seek to orient bodily orientations related to sexuality are, it appears, often inconsistent. It is important to draw attention to these inconsistencies, and to the politics that lie behind these different ways of framing public sex education. Such inconsistencies help account for the histories that shape what it is perceived bodies can do.

'WALKING ABOUT AT NIGHT' AND THE POLITICS OF RECOGNITION

" 'Walkin' About at Night': The Background to Teenage Pregnancy in a Remote Aboriginal Community" is an article based on an ethnographic study of young Aboriginal teen mothers[12] in a remote NT community undertaken by Kate Senior in 2002–2003, prior to 'the intervention,' but published (with Chenhall) in 2008, in the thick of its implementation. Goldstein notes that "Povinelli asks her readers to develop a 'critical theory of recognition' so as to better understand the cunning involved in the conflation of politics of culture with the culture of capital" (2010, 17, citing Povinelli, 2002). In undertaking this analysis of "Walkin' About at Night" my focus is on how Senior and Chenhall's observations can speak back to the cunning conflation of culture and capital manifest in 'the intervention,' a conflation in which young Indigenous people's sexuality is too often pathologized.

In "Walkin' About at Night," Senior and Chenhall explicitly focus on young women's cultural and sexual practices and their bodily orientations, against the backdrop of settler colonialism. I draw on Senior and Chenhall to consider how an ethnographic perspective constructs experiences of bodily orientations and sexuality in remote communities. I read this ethnographic study against the present politics of 'the intervention' to try and apprehend young women's experiences of sexuality from a perspective that is informed by participant observation. Senior and Chenhall's (2008) analysis conveys myriad bodily orientations related to Indigenous young women's 'walkin' about at night.' This activity could be described as a euphemism for sexual activity, but as Senior and Chenhall (ibid., 174) note:

> The activity which is coyly known as 'walkin' about at night' is, for many youth in the community, one of the defining acts of being a teenager. It flouts parental rules, and creates a group who replace the family as central pivots in an individual's life. The after-dark world of the River Town[13] teenager is full of drama. Parents and relatives are evaded and there is romance, intrigue, gossip and fighting. There are relationships between different groups of youth to be negotiated: with boys; with rival groups of girls; and with the petrol sniffers. 'Walkin' about at night' is not a spontaneous or random activity. It requires careful planning. Young women arrange together to slip out of sight from adults at the end of the movies, discos and basketball games. Some young women point out that being out at night is an event in itself and is important in maintaining a position within a peer group.

Sexuality and teen pregnancy are often parts of this practice, but to read "Walkin' About at Night" just through this lens is, as Senior and Chenhall's analysis suggests, reductive. This practice is about joy, drama, spending time with friends, avoiding boys, meeting up with boys, a passage to adulthood and some financial independence (via government payments for children if girls do get pregnant); it is about competition (sometimes violent) between girls for the attention of boys. It is also about freedom, and about its loss.

The practice of 'walkin' about at night' is clearly intrinsic to high rates of teen pregnancy in River Town and associated problems of poor maternal and child health. However, Senior and Chenhall (2008, 279) do not think that the way to respond to these issues is via the production of more prophylactics in the form of contraceptives and sexuality education. Rather than simply conceptualizing young people or Aboriginal lifeworlds as a problem in need of fixing, Senior and Chenhall, like Larkins et al. (2011), are careful to point to "larger structural inequalities, resulting from colonisation, poverty, and a history of exclusion from participation in economic, education and governance processes, [which] has resulted in very few options for young people, other than leaving the community altogether" (Senior and Chenhall, 2008, 279). From the perspective of queer phenomenology, such analysis is critical because it focuses not simply on bodies, but on bodily orientations.

By contrast, the politics of recognition countenanced via 'the intervention' resulted in prohibitions on pornography and a politics that operated to mark specific bodies as shameful. In the passage below, Povinelli (2008) elaborates specifically on the politics of recognition that she perceives to be at play in 'the intervention':

> The hegemonising force of Howard's speech act and subsequent legislation internally split indigenous activists roughly into supporters of state intervention . . . and critics claiming that the Act was a land grab, a new form of paternalism. . . . However, these critics were continually asked the rhetorical question: 'What about the children?' The charge of sexual abuse could not be dismissed. It had to be answered, countered, and debated. This is why sex panics have been so important during large-scale political and economic transformations. They are the equivalent of screaming 'Fire!' in a movie theatre; no one is going to stop to ask: What's going on here? . . . By characterising the problem as the sexual assault of children in the rural aboriginal world the Howard government was able to link its conservative programme to certain progressive romances of the culturally robust rural aboriginal person.

For Povinelli, 'the intervention's' foundation in allegations of widespread and systematic child abuse in remote communities is a purposeful and powerful political story that is difficult to refute. Barbara Baird (2008, 294) notes that those who question the politics of 'the intervention' are characterized as mad and pathological. Opponents of 'the intervention' characterized it "as a coercive attempt to enforce assimilation onto Indigenous people in remote communities" (ibid., 291). Indigenous people living in remote communities are already set apart from the wider Australian community in terms of kinship and cultural practices, and through continuing practices of colonization, poverty, poor housing, education and health care. These people are constructed as out of time, and out of place (and simultaneously timeless); thus they have come to serve a particular role in the Australian popular imaginary, "that of the culturally robust rural Aboriginal person" (Povinelli, 2008, no page).

The sexualization of Indigenous people in the production of 'the intervention' means that apprehending the sexual lives of young people outside this hegemonizing framework has become more difficult. What Senior and Chenhall demonstrate is that the cultural practices related to teen sexuality, pregnancy and parenting in River Town are not equivalent to those in the broader Australian community. Older women in the community did voice some concerns about young women's parenting practices (Senior and Chenhall 2008, 277), but for Senior and Chenhall (ibid., 276) 'ambivalence' is the term that most aptly captures the mixture of emotions expressed by community members in relation to teen pregnancy:

> Having a baby in River Town is an important step in being considered as an adult in the community. It is how a young girl progresses to becoming a woman.

From a queer phenomenological perspective, bodily orientations in River Town profoundly affect what young women do with their bodies, when and where. 'The intervention' points to ways in which this spectrality of sameness provides an impetus for government policy, guided by a liberal politics of recognition in which becoming 'independent' is considered to be a universal goal that all good Australians might share. But clearly not all Australians can share in this becoming 'independent'; young women's futures are severely constrained by their context, a context that provides little hope of financial independence outside state assistance. This helps to explain the ambivalence of community members towards young women's teen pregnancies.

The ways in which we perceive these young people's sexuality in River Town must therefore resist "the spectrality of sameness" (Ahmed, 2006, 549). The conditions of emergence that pertain to these teen mothers means that many young women in this community will become parents much earlier than young white Australian women.[14] But these young women's experiences as teenage mothers will not just be shaped by the decisions they make as biological parents, but by complex webs of relationships and responsibilities in a community and place where becoming 'independent' is anathema to the interdependence that orients bodies within the community. Within the liberal politics of recognition that are at play within 'the intervention,' the policy focus is inevitably on the individual and their capacity to thrive, as an individual, within a society that perceives good subjects as self-authorizing subjects. Tedmanson and Wadiwel (2010, 8) reinforce this idea in their study of governmentality, race, pleasure and 'the intervention.' They argue that "this racialized agenda was accompanied by coercive administrative processes that aimed to 'normalize' Indigenous peoples and force incorporation into the 'mainstream' neo-liberal market economy."

Reading and responding to the experiences of these young women through the lens of this self-authorizing subject, the experiences of the young women in River Town appear more fractured and disorienting. But such a conclusion fails to see that in these remote communities this type of self-authorizing subject is not the primary condition of subjecthood. Drawing on Povinelli, Elspeth Probyn (2008) seeks to trouble the way in which choice is apprehended in relation to the sexual lives of young women. She (ibid., 234) notes that "choice is always sexualized when it comes to women" and goes on to ask:

> What defines the conditions of possibility in which women come to make sense of their subjecthood and thus the ground from and in which to make choices? . . . The promise of liberalism was and is that of freedom, of subjects released unto their own making. Choice . . . operates within this frame to demarcate cultures of constraint versus those of freedom.

In the frame of liberalism, the young women of River Town might be understood as deciding to become young mothers because they have no other options. Senior and Chenhall (2008, 279) perceive teen pregnancy in River Town as partially explicable through this frame:

> Young women's motivations to have sexual relationships and to get pregnant are heavily influenced by their need to pursue activities that heighten their self-esteem and give them a sense of control over at least one aspect of their lives; however they do so in a socio-economic framework where their range of options from which to choose is very limited.

For Senior and Chenhall, sexual activity is a way of exercising choice in a context in which young people have few opportunities because of colonization and structural and economic inequalities.

Another way of thinking about the constraints experienced by young women is offered by Probyn (2008, 240), again drawing on Povinelli:

> In distinction to liberal Anglo-European discourses of self-making, Povinelli draws on her extensive fieldwork and relationships with Aboriginal people to explore what she sees as 'maximally embodied social relations' or 'thick life.' ... This is to say that constraint here should be thought of not only as a form of subjection to power. It is also a constraint that demarcates different forms of power as generative of deep meanings.
>
> (Povinelli, 2006, 45)

'Walkin' about at night' is not unproblematic in the lives of these young women, as Senior and Chenhall's research suggests. But Probyn and Povinelli help us to think about their orientations toward teen pregnancy as something more than a 'form of subjection to power,' or as a way to 'heighten their self-esteem.' These orientations are also embedded in 'thick life,' in social relations. A similar point is made by Senior and Chenhall (2008, 278) who note that:

> Young Indigenous peoples' understandings concerning pregnancy are also framed by the value placed on family in such communities as River Town, where the connections between people and their environment has a great influence on how individuals construct their own identity. In reviewing Indigenous youth research, Harris states that "Growing up means learning about their 'interdependence' within a complex matrix of kin and environmental relationships and responsibilities—rather than becoming 'independent.' "

In the context of 'the intervention,' Indigenous communities in Australia continue to be constructed as in need of saving; being Indigenous and living in a remote location has been conceived as somehow commensurate with risk and perversity. Being outside the frame of liberal recognition is construed as the problem, especially for children. Drawing on Senior and Chenhall, and Povinelli, I have tried to draw attention to different ways of conceptualizing bodily orientations in Indigenous communities, analytics that attend to histories of people and their place in their communities, in order to think differently about sexuality and young people in Indigenous communities.

CONCLUSION

> Potentiality and enjoyment are never outside specific social orderings even if they cannot be contained within any particular social ordering. . . . Every moment of enjoyment emerges from the specific and differential way that a social order apprehends bodies and subjects. Enjoyment is separate from the social order only from an analytic point of view.
>
> (Povinelli, 2011a, 290, 291)

Drawing on Deleuze, Povinelli thinks about enjoyment as affect, as a space of potential for new ways of being and becoming, and argues further that it is not possible to think about enjoyment as outside 'specific orderings.' Povinelli wants to emphasize this particular reading of enjoyment because she believes that enjoyment is not contained by the social order, nor can it be separate from this order. A queer phenomenology helps to grasp how potentiality and enjoyment are constrained and contained in differential ways. Such an approach understands that affect and related experiences are informed by, but not commensurate with, knowledge, power and subjectivation.

Inspired by Povinelli, I argue that Indigenous people living in remote communities experience sexuality, or sexuality education, with and against 'the intervention'; as a consequence, young people's experiences of sexuality and sexuality education are always betwixt and between Indigenous lifeworlds and liberal politics of recognition. Tedmanson and Wadiwel (2010, 18) go further, arguing that 'the intervention' is

> based in a deep 'moral panic' about the savagery of 'others,' a tension [that] is exposed between envy and disgust that oscillates from the lust for the power to control Indigenous 'others' to the desire to 'take care' of the perceived vulnerable by regulating and containing sexual and other 'pleasures'—itself a perversely gratifying experience for the dominant.

If one concurs with Tedmanson and Wadiwel, then this leaves little way of speaking back to those biopolitical technologies that endeavour to eliminate Indigenous lifeworlds, nor does it provide young people with a means to negotiate the economic, political and social losses that continue to adhere to the remote communities in which they live.

Povinelli (2011a, 305) suggests young Indigenous people seek "not to be sexualized or spiritualized, not to be the perverse or sanctified other to settler culture, but rather not to have this as their choice." Yet what Senior and Chenhall's study of young women suggests is that settler colonialism cannot govern the proliferation of sexuality, pleasure, pain and desire in remote communities. Whereas this study was conducted in the period before 'the intervention,' after 'the intervention' young Aboriginal women continue to record high rates of teen pregnancy. To my mind, this suggests a clear gap between fantasies of domination, and young people's experiences of sexualities in remote communities.

Colleen Bryant and Matthew Willis, in a report entitled *Pornography Awareness: A Process of Engagement with Northern Territory Indigenous Communities* (2009, 58), note that engagement with Indigenous communities through sexuality education in the context of 'the intervention' may cause

> [problems to] arise when aspects or beliefs from one culture are combined with, or clash with, the beliefs of another culture. There is a need for ongoing and non-judgmental discussion about the nature of differing belief systems regarding sex and sexuality and how young people can effectively negotiate a healthy sexual identity. This process can be assisted by focusing on unifying concepts or beliefs such as respect and rights and responsibilities that largely exist irrespective of culture.

There is at least acknowledgement here of the significance of culture in the recognition of how people negotiate sexuality; what is concerning is a belief in the possibility of non-judgmental discussion within the framework of 'the intervention.'

Using a queer phenomenological approach, I have tried to capture how sexuality education and young women's experiences of sexuality must be apprehended alongside specific bodily orientations, spaces, temporalities and histories. I have also shown how the biopolitical technologies of 'the intervention' seek to dominate and impose particular styles of sexual subjectivity, always imagining a 'becoming independent' that is at odds with sexual cultures that are experienced and enacted by young women in places like River Town.

ACKNOWLEDGMENTS

I wish to thank Stuart Poyntz and Jacqueline Kennelly for their support in editing this paper. I also want to acknowledge the photography of Jagath Dheerasekara. I found Jagath's images while researching this chapter and he granted me permission to use them. Jagath is an Amnesty International Human Rights Innovation Fund Grant recipient for his "Manuwangku, Under the Nuclear Cloud" project. Jagath's human rights activism led to his persecution and exile in France as a political refugee. He returned to Sri Lanka in the mid-1990s following the change of regime. On returning home, Jagath began a career in telecommunications and his second spell of photography. As time went by, both his personal and commissioned photography took an increasingly larger role. He settled in Australia with his family in 2008. In Australia his photography and activism chiefly focus on Aboriginal people's rights, refugee rights and rights of communities whose livelihood and environment in which they live are endangered. Jagath has presented his work in a number of solo exhibitions, selected group exhibitions and festivals. His work is held in both institutional and private collections. He is a passionate educator/facilitator for photo media driven community/participatory art projects. A two-time university drop-out, Jagath holds a master of science in information technology from the Keele University, UK. He lives and works in Sydney.

NOTES

1. The Liberal Party is considered to be more conservative than Labor in the Australian context.
2. In June 2010 the Federal Labor government, with bipartisan support, extended 'the intervention' for another ten years.
3. This paper should not be construed as in any way condoning child abuse. Rather it is an attempt to understand how sexual politics within the context of 'the intervention' has implications for depicting all Aboriginal sexuality as problematic, and particularly sexuality involving children and young people.

4. See www.fahcsia.gov.au/sites/default/files/documents/02_2013/attchment_c_drfat_imp_plan_29_jan_2.pdf. Accessed June 13, 2013.
5. According to the NTER evaluation report, "Across Australia in 2009–10 a total of 165 defendants (both Indigenous and non-Indigenous) were prosecuted in magistrates' courts for a principal offence involving child pornography. This represented 0.03 per cent of the over 500,000 Indigenous and non-Indigenous defendants prosecuted in that year, indicating that child pornography offences are relatively rare compared with many other offence types" (2011, 186).
6. Individual speakers were not named in the transcripts of the consultations, but the communities from which they came are identified.
7. Ampilatwatja, NT—Part 2, Department of Families, Housing, Community Services and Indigenous Affairs (FaHCSIA) Consultations: *Future Directions for Northern Territory Emergency Response,* August 12, 2009 (Nicholson et al., 2009, 145).
8. See http://barkly.nt.gov.au/our-communities/ampilatwatja/. Accessed June 10, 2013.
9. To over 1,200 Alyawarr- and Anmatyerre-speaking people, this area is 'Utopia,' a population that can boast a slightly improved health status in comparison to the national average for Aboriginal people. Arlparra is the main community providing a range of services to the other fifteen homelands in the region. Collectively the sixteen homelands is better known as 'Utopia.' Arlparra is located some 260kms northeast of Alice Springs in the Sandover Highway. See http://barkly.nt.gov.au/our-communities/arlparra. Accessed June 10, 2013.
10. Arlparra/Utopia, NT—Part 2, Department of Families, Housing, Community Services and Indigenous Affairs (FaHCSIA) Consultations: *Future Directions for the Northern Territory Emergency Response,* August 13, 2009 (Nicholson et al., 2009, 192).
11. See www.fahcsia.gov.au/our-responsibilities/indigenous-australians/publications-articles/closing-the-gap-in-the-northern-territory-including-northern-territory-emergency-response/report-on-the-northern-territory-emergency-response-redesign-consultations?HTML#p2t3 (updated June 14, 2012; accessed September 20, 2012).
12. "In 2009, Indigenous Australian women had a teenage birth rate of 79 per 1000 per year compared with an overall Australian teenage birth rate of 17 per 1000 per year. . . . There are many factors other than age (such as family, individual and socioeconomic characteristics) that contribute to these outcomes . . . many outcomes are the consequences of pre-existing disadvantaged circumstances" (Larkins et al., 2011, 551).
13. Senior and Chenhall (2008) use the name River Town as a pseudonym for the town in which Senior did her study, a remote community in the Southeast of the top end of Australia's Northern Territory that has "about 900 Aboriginal people and 60 non-Aboriginal people. . . . There are very few opportunities for local employment, and most people are dependent on Government welfare payments. Poor educational outcomes and low levels of employment form an important background for the consideration of the situation of young people in River Town, as these factors influence their experience and their expectations of what constitutes a normal life. Normality for most young women in River Town is motherhood . . . data for pregnancy begins at 13 years old and shows a marked peak by the age of 15" (273).
14. In a study of female Aboriginal and Torres Strait Islander high school students in Townsville, in far north Queensland, Larkins et al. (2011, 553) report that students said the ideal age for commencing a family was "between 20 and 25 years of age, although a small number thought 18 or 19 years of age would be preferable. One young woman from a focus group reported: "I don't want to be 26 with grey hairs when I start having kids. . . . I don't want to be no old lady."

REFERENCES

Ahmed, Sara. "Orientations: Toward a Queer Phenomenology." *GLQ* 12, no. 4, 2006. 543–574.

Altman, Jon C. "The Howard Government's Northern Territory Intervention: Are Neo Paternalism and Indigenous Development Compatible?" *Centre for Aboriginal Economic Policy Research,* Topical Issue no. 16, 2007. 1–19.

Attorney General's Department. *Northern Territory Emergency Response, Report of the NTER Review Board (October).* Canberra: Attorney General's Department, 2008.

Baird, Barbara. "Child Politics, Feminist Analyses." *Australian Feminist Studies* 23, no. 57, 2008. 291–305.

Bita, Natasha. "Schools in Sex Education Revolution." *The Courier-Mail.* September 17, 2012. Accessed September 20, 2012. www.dailytelegraph.com.au/news/sex-educaction-gets-physical/story-e6freuy9–1226475402901.

Botsman, Peter. "Putting Indigenous Child Abuse in the Northern Territory into Perspective." Working Paper, June 30, 2007. Accessed September 22, 2012. www.workingpapers.com.au/papers/putting-indigenous-child-abuse-northern territory-perspective.

Bryant, Colleen, and Matthew Willis. "Pornography Awareness: A Process of Engagement with Northern Territory Indigenous Communities." Canberra: Australian Institute of Criminology, 2009.

Commissioner, ATSI Social Justice. *Social Justice Report 2011.* www.humanrights.gov.au/social_justice/sj_report/sjreport11/index.html.

Diprose, Rosalyn. "Biopolitical Technologies of Prevention." *Health Sociology Review* 17, no. 2, 2008. 141–150.

Gaonkar, Dilip Parameshwar, and Elizabeth Povinelli. "Technologies of Public Forms: Circulation, Transfiguration, Recognition." *Public Culture* 15, no. 3, 2003. 385–397.

Goldstein, Ruth. "Talking Drums and Ethical Conundrums." *Anthropology Matters* 12, no. 1, 2010. November 9, 2014. www.anthropologymatters.com/index.php?journal=anth_matters&page=article&o =view&path%5B%5D=189&path%5B%5D=310.

Hagan, Stephen. "Kids Having Kids." *ON LINE Opinion—Australia's E-journal of Social and Political Debate.* March 10, 2009. Accessed September 22, 2012. www.onlineopinion.com.au/view.asp?article=8631.

Larkins, Sarah, and R. Priscilla Page, Kathryn S. Panaretto, Melvina Mitchell, Valerie Alberts, Suzanne McGinty and P. Craig Veitch. "The Transformative Potential of Young Motherhood for Disadvantaged Aboriginal and Torres Strait Islander Women in Townsville, Australia." *Medical Journal of Australia* 194, no. 10, 2011. 551–555.

McRae-Williams, Eva, and Rolf Gerritsen. "Mutual Incomprehension: The Cross Cultural Domain of Work in a Remote Australian Aboriginal Community." *The International Indigenous Policy Journal* 1, no. 2, 2010. 1–27. November 9, 2014. http://ir.lib.uwo.ca/iipj/vol1/iss2/2.

Menzies Foundation. *Closing the Gap in Indigenous Education: Workshop Report.* Melbourne: Author, 2010.

Nicholson, Alastair, Larissa Behrendt, Alison Vivian, Nicole Watson, and Michele Harris. *Will They Be Heard? A Response to the NTER Consultations June to August 2009.* Sydney: Research Unit, Jumbunna Indigenous House of Learning, 2009.

Northern Territory Emergency Response Evaluation Report 2011. Accessed September 20, 2012. www.fahcsia.gov.au/sites/default/files/documents/05_2012/nter_evaluation_report 2011.pdf.

Oksala, Johanna. "Sexual Experience: Foucault, Phenomenology, and Feminist Theory." *Hypatia* 26, no.1, 2011. 207–223.

Povinelli, Elizabeth. *The Cunning of Recognition, Indigenous Alterities and the Making of Australian Multiculturalism.* Durham: Duke University Press, 2002.

———. *The Empire of Love: Toward a Theory of Intimacy, Genealogy and Carnality.* Durham: Duke University Press, 2006.

———. "Doing It for the Kids." *Mute* 2, no. 7, 2008. Accessed September 20, 2012. www.metamute.org/editorial/articles/doing-it-kids

———. "The Part That Has No Part: Enjoyment, Law, and Loss." *GLQ* 17, nos. 2–3, 2011a. 287–308.

———. *Economies of Abandonment: Social Belonging and Endurance in Late Liberalism.* Durham: Duke University Press, 2011b.

Probyn, Elspeth. "Troubling Safe Choices: Girls, Friendship, Constraint and Freedom." *South Atlantic Quarterly* 107, no. 2, 2008. 231–249.

Rasmussen, Mary Lou. *Closing the Gap in Indigenous Education: Workshop Report.* Melbourne: Menzies Foundation, 2010.

Robinson, Kerry, and Cristyn Davies. "Docile Bodies and Heteronormative Moral Subjects: Constructing the Child and Sexual Knowledge in Schooling." *Sexuality & Culture* 12, 2008. 221–239.

Senior, Kate, and Richard Chenhall. " 'Walkin' About at Night': The Background to Teenage Pregnancy in a Remote Aboriginal Community." *Journal of Youth Studies* 11, no. 3, 2008. 269–281.

Slater, Lisa. " 'Aurukun, We're Happy, Strong People': Aurukun Kids Projecting Life into Bad Headlines." *Borderlands E-journal* 7, no. 2, 2008. 1–14.

Sweet, Melissa. "Not a Single Voice in Support of Intervention." *Crikey.* August 7, 2007. Accessed September 20, 2012. www.crikey.com.au/2007/08/07/not-a-single-voice-In-support-of-intervention/.

Sutton, Peter. *The Politics of Suffering: Indigenous Australia and the End of the Liberal Consensus.* Melbourne: Melbourne University Press, 2009.

Tedmanson, Deidre, and Dinesh Wadiwel. "Neoptolemus: The Governmentality of New Race/Pleasure Wars?" *Culture and Organization* 16, no. 1, 2010. 7–22.

Wild, Rex, and Patricia Anderson. *Ampe Akelyernemane Meke Mekarle—Little Children Are Sacred. Report of the Northern Territory Board of Inquiry into the Protection of Aboriginal Children from Sexual Abuse.* Darwin: Northern Territory Government, 2007.

10 Past, Present, Future Encounters

Bodies That Travel, Bodies That Stay

Yvette Taylor

INTRODUCTION

This chapter is based on ESRC funded research *From the Coal Face to the Car Park? Intersections of Class and Gender in the North East of England* (2007–2009), which charts the gendered, generational transitions from the industrial landscapes of one or two generations ago, to a current present and 'regenerated' future (Nayak, 2003; Taylor and Addison, 2009, 2011). In aiming to capture manifold intersections of history, geography and economy, a multi-dimensional approach is adopted to explore middle-class and working-class women's lives between the ages of 16–85 years in the context of de-industrialization and the transition to a post-industrial economy, where processes of 'fitting into place' are subject to contestation (Taylor and Addison, 2009; Taylor 2012a). The project involved in-depth interviews and focus groups with ninety-seven women across class backgrounds living in a range of urban, suburban and rural locales across the North East (see Taylor and Addison, 2009, 2011; Taylor, 2012 for more thorough methodological detail). This chapter explores the lived and reported realities of *young* women within the North East of England, who composed approximately one-third of the sample.

In line with comparable youth studies (Kubicek et al., 2009; Yip et al., 2011), the project initially defined young adults as 16 to 24 years of age (n=11). However, 'youth' is a contested term. It can signify a very wide age range, and the experiences and meanings associated with it are socially constituted, varying both cross-culturally and historically (e.g. Savage, M. et al. 2005; France, 2007; Green, 2010; Khattab and Fenton, 2009; Leccardi and Ruspini, 2006; Therborn, 2011). In an age of austerity, it is common for young adults to have a protracted period of dependency on their parent(s), with record numbers not leaving the parental home until their early thirties (*The Guardian,* June 1, 2012). The same slippages when defining young adults can be seen in youth studies more generally: Valentine et al. (2003, 481) recognize that even when young people leave the family home it "continues to be the site through which many of their individual biographies and expectations are routed" beyond the tidy age of twenty-four. Here, I explore the lived and reported realities of young women within the North East of England, including participants under 35 years; those 16–24 years ($n = 11$) and those 25–35 years ($n = 19$).

Put simply, the research argues that change differently impacts on people and places: Such changes occur and are contested over time and across space, affecting overlapping arenas such as labour, leisure and residency, all spheres in which young women can be rendered 'out of place.' Change impacts on feelings of belonging, in moving forward or being 'left behind,' as desires, hopes and resentments intersect with material (im)possibilities. The broad concern is with the reconfiguration of class and gender inequalities in relation to spatialized urban–rural 'publics,' which open up and close down encounters between those who 'travel' and those who 'stay.' Where 'future selves' are constructed in specific settings, managed and negotiated as people live out shifting geographies and temporalities, this process of mobility and fixity does not simply refer to journeys in between place, for example, movement from one neighbourhood to another. Rather, to 'travel' or to 'stay' evokes a sense of access, entitlement and even accumulation of space as a resource functioning across time to propel certain 'fitting' bodies forward (Charlesworth, 2000; Haylett, 2001; Hewitt, 2005; Taylor, 2012a). In this project, women across the age range very differently responded to, took up or 'lost out' in the regeneration of the North East of England. Often processes of change were framed as a *degeneration* when attached to working-classed subjects and spaces, where "in contemporary Britain, geographical referencing is one of the contemporary shorthand ways of speaking class" (Skeggs, 2004, 15).

Shorthands, substitutes and 'surplus' abound in the literature on class and in wider classed representations, intersecting with, for example, race, sexuality and gender (Taylor et al., 2010). 'Displacement' has become a significant trope with regard to working-class *masculine* 'crisis,' depicting, yet containing, all that is changing if not lost, in relation to forms of employment, community and belonging. Recently, for example, Nayak (2003) suggested that working-class boys in the North East still perform traditional working-class masculinity, even in the absence of traditional jobs, subjectively making claims to a class inflected 'Real Geordie' North East identity (Coll and Lancaster, 1992). Nayak traces how boys negotiate the transition from heavy industry, as the main employer of the preceding male generation, to an unstable economic future. This is seen to leave young working-class masculine identities fractured, caught between the past and the future: "The 'Real Geordies' were like flies in amber, having become petrified in the hardened solution of an older period from which their values descended" (Nayak, 2003, 63). Industrialization has been supposed as good (for men) and de-industrialization bad (for men and, following Nayak, boys) and there has been little attention to women's positioning within economic regeneration/degeneration, representing an assumed fit into a 'feminized' labour force (Adkins, 2002; Armstrong, 2010; McRobbie, 2009). Working-class masculinity, in the context of de-industrialization, receives increasing academic attention (Charlesworth, 2000; Strangleman, 2004) and popular culture representation (e.g., the much screened film and musical *Billy Elliot,* 2000). In contrast femininity is positioned as a reserve, a labour market supply, which can now be capitalized upon, even as this has been named as a classed resource (Skeggs, 1997; Taylor, 2007).

This chapter blends insights from feminist phenomenology and cultural geography to explore factors structuring spatial, gendered and classed experiences. My use of experience—an analytical category situated in data—benefits from the insights of feminist phenomenologists who argue that experience is interpreted via these social positionalities. These experiences do not happen on a random basis to individuals, but are structured by the norms that govern public space; those who do not fit in with these norms are often positioned as 'out of place' or as not belonging. Embodiment is a salient lens through which experiences and perceptions can be understood, as evidenced in many studies, whereby the body is interpellated in relation to dominant sexual and gender ideals (Holland et al., 2001; McRobbie, 2009; Tolman, 2002; Turner, 1984; Young, 2005). Theorists have paid attention to how the body is socially constituted, and how one experiences life through the body, where 'embodiment' signals "the physical and mental experience of existence" (Cregan, 2006, 3). As Jackson and Scott (2010, 146) discuss, 'A body can never be just a body abstracted from mind, self and social context," highlighting the proximities—and social distances—that are created between bodies; meaning is generated through the "social context, which profoundly affects how we experience our own and other's bodies" (ibid., 149).

Drawing on feminist phenomenological theories of community, I argue that communities cohere around particular identities (including place or social group identities) and simultaneously are 'unworked' by processes of differentiation that involve and place 'bodies' and inhere in identity formation (Secomb, 2000, 140–142). Ahmed (2006), in *Queer Phenomenology: Orientations, Objects, Others,* uses the word 'offline' in the sense that bodies are disoriented in space, not following directing 'lines' automatically. Ahmed also uses the words 'angle' and 'slanting' to convey a sense of not fitting in with a straight alignment, developing an account of the 'orientation' of experience in relation to sexual orientation. As we always are in space through our bodies, our bodies can be the starting point to locate ourselves in relation to others. In contrast to orientation, or being at home or feeling 'in place,' disorientation occurs when people are uprooted, the objects around them change, or they are unable to 'take up space.'[1]

The North East is the empirical fieldwork site used to discuss 'bodies that stay, bodies that travel.' It is a fraught location at once propelled into the future, through residents' and policy-makers' claims of regional resiliency, and economic and cultural capacity, while being 'stuck' in the past. It is frequently positioned as behind the times, out of place and caught up in old redundant legacies as a sharp Northern point on the UK North/South divide.[2] Generational dynamics of 'now' and 'then,' 'here' and 'there,' pull young bodies forward when these are seen as 'fitting' middle-class trajectories and regional potentials; other young bodies are situated as wasteful and even 'redundant,' unable to locate, accumulate and fully claim a presence. Here I am concerned with encountering the *young* bodies that 'travel' and the bodies that 'stay,' viewing this as not so much an incidental stumbling upon space or subjects, but rather as complexity structured and contested across the past, present and (imagined) future.

Those who always belonged were frequently pitted against those who never had or never would, the 'new arrivals' with limited histories: To be 'young' was often sufficient enough to be positioned as 'new.' Yet such divisions were generationally fraught with young people both making claims upon a history that was not wholly experienced as theirs and refusing the 'old' landscapes in a 'new' North East. Older women who had experienced the harsh climates of past times, particularly in rural ex-mining and shipbuilding communities, were at times keen to discard this weighty past and hope for a new future: Yet this hope was not easily transferred or actualized in their material environments. Instead, hope was itself often left behind as (another) North East was re-presented as 'up and coming,' failing generational claims of both younger (and older) interviewees. Some are able to appropriate and propertize the past, present and future, where placed personhood is read on the body (Gidley and Rooke, 2010; Skeggs, 2004). Processes of reading bodies in and out of place makes and limits entitlements, "enabling some groups to *propertise their personhood* and others to be beyond appropriation as the foundational ground of valuelessness from which others can mark and know their distinctions" (Skeggs, 2004, 26). Distinctions occur in time and place, meaning some cannot easily 'move forward' or travel to a 'new' future place as imagined through neoliberal urban governance, regeneration, gentrification and an appropriation of specific 'pasts.' The subject of phenomenology is a body-subject, focusing on embodied experience—processes of normativity and differentiation in young women's experience are situated here using empirical data.

WHOSE FUTURE? REGISTERS OF TIME AND PLACE

Questions of the future of cities, residents and city-subjects pose who, where and when questions: Who is 'stuck' in the past, who is capacitated as taking 'us' forward, and what embodied, spatial and material collisions occur in these renderings of past-present-future? As some are recognized as activating their own future landscapes, others are condemned as failing, irresponsible and out of place (Allen and Taylor, 2013; Paton, 2010). Issues of poverty are 'placed' as residing in places/people often without attention to structural economies: "Policies designed to bring about changes in economically disadvantaged lives constitute a cultural process through which class positions and identities are partly created. That process signals inextricable relations between cultural and economic aspects of the way society works, expressed in the daily practices of social life and in observable social differences and inequalities" (Haylett, 2003, 56).

Young people in particular are imbued with a regenerative/degenerative (in)capacity seen as bringing forward or failing certain placed-based futures (Taylor and Allen, 2011; McRobbie, 2009; Taylor, 2012b). Young people's present educational and employment success is also seen to secure and safeguard an older population's future/life (where young people's own pensioned futures are in crisis): Such presences are awkwardly placed and of heightened significance in the North East which has a higher than average UK unemployment rate as well as a higher aged population (National Statistics Office, see www.statistics.gov.uk). At the same time, young people are often outside of the official measures of 'becoming' regenerated/capacitated (situated on sites of cultural capital—museums, art galleries, restaurants—and residential property). The movement of young people *away* from some neighbourhoods and communities was felt as a loss for some older interviewees, whereas the existence of young people *within* these same places was also felt as excess as communicated by older residents. Some bodies get to 'travel,' to become mobile global city-subjects, whereas others are seen to stick and stall community-regional and (inter)national progress: Their 'stay' in place is seen as a lag and a lack. Impermanent and vulnerable claims on the past, present and future sit in opposition to a mobile claim that transcends and accumulates time and place as one's own.

Different registers of time and place collide in troubled and insecure financial times of vast public sector cutbacks. Navigating the differential impact of 'crisis' and 'ways forward' for particular communities involves attention to the situatedness of experience and the intersections of generational, gendered and classed (dis)locations. Many parts of the North East (both urban and rural) are still heavily coded as masculine and 'working class,' given the legacy, both materially and culturally, of male-orientated heavy industry (particularly coal mining and shipbuilding) and the loss of these registers of time/place (Nayak, 2003; Taylor, 2012a). Despite an often assumed 'fit' within a 'feminized' economy, it is working-class women who will bear the brunt of the UK government's cuts to welfare and public services, whether as users of public services or as public sector workers (Kenway and McLeod, 2004). Recognizing the gendering of austerity measures is thus an essential corrective against 'can do girl' discourses (Harris, 2004; McRobbie, 2009).

Many feminist researchers highlight the gendering of social futures, as women are welcomed and celebrated as now included in the worlds of work and education, supposedly becoming unstuck from family cares and all-consuming parental practices. Young women in particular are called upon to be present, to be new future subjects standing in as visible signs of gender equity (McRobbie, 2009). At the same time, many have queried this celebrated post-gender arrival, given that inequalities *move about* rather than *disappear* within the still profoundly gendered sites of family, education and employment (Armstrong, 2010; Evans, 2010). As some women are recognized as activating their own (and their families') futures, others are condemned as failing, irresponsible and out of place (Parker, 2010). This is a distinctly classed process. In these encounters, class 'sticks' as waste and as wrong, as a past residue attached to those behind the times and without worthy futures (Taylor and Allen, 2011). Certain bodies 'stick' (Ahmed, 2006) in these shifts, where the corporeality of women's lives exemplify the embodiment of different gendered identities as daughter, young woman, mother, grandmother (see Taylor, 2012a). Ahmed urges consideration of the normative effects of "the repetition of bodily actions over time, which produces what we can call the bodily horizon, a space for action" (Ahmed, 2006, 66). This repetition and inculcation is influenced by social position, so that it depends on context whether or not one will feel out of place. Generational, gendered and class meanings inscribe the ageing of women's bodies and embodied sensations, as the (mis)placed and (dis)located body navigates the right and wrong time/place as 'travelling' and/or 'staying.' To state this is to acknowledge generational (dis)continuity rather than to position young people in a snapshot of time.

In mapping the past, present and imagined future encounters of younger respondents, it is important to carve out a claim for plural futures, where these can also be reorientated as pragmatic, practical and as 'getting by' in the everyday 'here and now,' rather than as necessarily accumulative and re-productive of normative (middle-class) futures (Armstrong, 2010; Gillies, 2006). Not everyone can flexibly cast themselves through trajectories of future potential. But a dystopian side-step away from negotiated futures to 'failed futures' ignores intersecting dimensions of agency and constraint. I make a case for the importance of class within the attention to 'future subjects' as part of a continued conversation about which futures are celebrated and which are marginalized: Who can travel? Who can stay? The risk in leaving privileged lives unproblematized is that these are understood as fitting, standard and chosen; as the trajectories of agentic and capable future-orientated subjects now able to take full advantage of regenerated or even 'global' cities, while being injured by others' lack, failure and culpability. Middle-class subjects often respond to temporal and spatial shifts with ease, confidence and entitlement, in contrast to vulnerable and pragmatic 'making do' orientations of working-class subjects (Armstrong, 2010; Evans, 2010; Gillies, 2007; Taylor, 2009, 2012c). What would it mean to be responsive to those not identified as future subjects/workers/citizens and not capacitated as 'coming forward' into place? To 'stay' is not necessarily to feel 'stuck' and to 'travel' does not often bring forward that which it promises, taking only the individual travelling subject, rather than the collective city/citizen, forward. Drawing on phenomenology helps attend to the 'body-in-situation' experiences in particular places, and on embodied experience and emotions.

In mapping socio-temporal shifts, it is important not to collapse different spaces as now included on the map of the good sociologist, who simply extends her own reach by racing forward in researching and consuming more space, now on her map. Pressing classed intersections reside in, and are reproduced through, new-old labours, research projects and academic productions (Taylor, 2012d; 2012e).[3] Where others have pointed to the 'stickiness' of race (Ahmed, 2002; Tolia-Kelly, 2010) as a blockage and a stopping, or curtailing, of futures, I point to class as also bound up in 'sticking,' 'blocking' and facilitating futures. The accounts that I tell are themselves 'sticky'; they are retold by me through my particular empirical and theoretical stances (class is also 'stuck' to me as biographical realities and points of dis-identification) (Taylor, 2012c). These collide as intersectional, slippery and lived-in concerns rather than as points which can be neatly added to constitute the future subject.

Diprose (2003) deploys the work of Merleau-Ponty in viewing meaning as 'inherited' and 'pre-reflective,' arising through 'habituated dwelling.' These inheritances shape the 'horizon of social meaning,' which is also embodied. One doesn't just inherit 'ways of being' from one's original community or location but rather one may be marked as different even in the 'same' community because of physical appearance, habits or other factors. There are histories of 'past encounters' that travel with and between us in occupying space, where it takes time, energy and resources to move (Adkins and Skeggs, 2004; Bourdieu, 1984; Taylor, 2012d). Many researchers have turned to the concepts of 'habitus,' 'field' and 'capital' (Bourdieu, 1984), as a framing which opposes a free-floating mobile version of chosen selfhood, speaking instead to how particular paths are shaped as directions, resources, senses and everyday maps, with signposts and sidelines to classed, gendered and racialized terrains (Erel, 2009; Reay, 1995; Reay et al. 2007).

Habitus can be understood here as interplay between past and present, permeable and responsive to settings but setting limits upon 'travelling' through place. Territorial proximities and distances are embodied by those in and out of time and place, who are differentially (dis)advantaged due to classed and gendered locations. Certain places and certain people are not meant to 'become' or arrive in place, whereas some are able to acquire and accumulate place as their own: This is a classed mis-fit, felt intimately and embodied through the rhythms, sounds, smells and sights of past and contemporary landscapes—where some are unable to grasp, feel or embody new selective future orientations (Pini et al., 2010; Walkerdine, 2009). There are a myriad of ways that senses of past, present and future are sustained and fractured through "multiple space-times" (Tolia-Kelly, 2010), and many have posed the question of what it would mean to open up communities to these registers (Amin, 2004; Massey, 2004; Thrift, 2004) that shape daily interactions and habits in place. This chapter contributes to this collection's focus on historicity, temporality and inter-relationality, invoking the past-present-future in and through everyday encounters, embodied in those who can and cannot move through shifting times and places.

PLACING THE NORTH EAST OF ENGLAND

> One North East believes the biggest asset of the region is its people. This is a region where exceptional creativity and innovation takes place. . . . It is a region whose people are imaginative, resourceful and ready to face the challenges of the future.
>
> (Passionate People, Passionate Places; www.onenortheast.co.uk/page/ index.cfm)

Like other UK regions, the North East of England has faced enormous transformation in response to global change, impacting upon the urban landscape, old manufacturing towns, ex-shipbuilding communities and rural mining villages (Parker, 2010; Paton, 2010). Where the region was once built upon shipbuilding, coal mining and heavy engineering, it now relies on service and knowledge-based employment. Manufacturing, business services and the public sector are dominant sectors of the contemporary North East economy (see Colls and Lancaster, 1992; Nayak, 2003; and Taylor and Addison, 2009 for a more thorough description and historicization of regional change). There has been long term economic underperformance in some rural areas of the region, which are defined as 'lagging behind' in relation to the South of England. Yet the main cities of the region have undergone considerable redevelopment with tourism becoming important and Newcastle city centre increasingly represented as *the centre:* The proximity between urban and rural destinations is highlighted in marketing locations such as the Pennine Hills, the Cheviot Hills and Northumberland National Park as touristic draws.[4]

The quest for culture, employment and overall 'liveability' is based on attracting and retaining the middle classes, instigating a 'coming forward' by the responsible active citizen with the right capacities and potential to regionally regenerate. Working-class residents are implicitly—and sometimes explicitly—coded as residue, the source of place-based problems, waste and regional lag (Clavering, 2010; Paton, 2010; Walkerdine, 2009). Regeneration and gentrification have been woven more tightly together with city competition, welfare and workfare policies, as part of neoliberal urban governance. Within such logics, areas and their inhabitants have been deemed in need of 'place shaping' in order to become part of a future and saved from a failed past or social-spatial 'death' (Taylor and Allen, 2011). This is evident in policies of city councils acting as 'place-shapers,' actively seeking to rebrand and 'place-shape' the North East as a place of *'Passionate People, Passionate Places.'* The structural politics of territoriality are signalled in the calls for regional competiveness that seek to strengthen the (right kinds of) attachments, but which actually bring forth further regional-local disparities (Taylor, 2012a; Thrift, 2004). In these policies, (adult) residents are responsibilized as active citizens, through, for example, Neighbourhood Watch Schemes (Gidely and Rooke, 2010; Paton, 2010). The appraisal of 'those who can' move forward and improve place frequently implies that some cannot: Residents are accordingly implicated in their own decline and responsible for their own 'degeneration'—and young people are entirely left off the map in this centering of residents and consumers, only existing as potential 'future citizens' (Parker, 2010). The 'local' comes to stand for cosmopolitan potential as well as an anti-cosmopolitan regionalism signified by and embodied in travelling/staying. Such mis-placement resonates with long-standing discourses that pathologize the poor as irresponsible, beyond (self)help and at odds with contemporary 'city publics' done by desired citizens who are able to activate, claim and improve space (Haylett 2001; Taylor and Addison, 2011; Watson, 2006).

ENCOUNTERING, TRAVELLING, STAYING

> *Gaby:* People have got no airs and graces . . . it's like a belief in where you come from, isn't it, and just . . . people are down to earth and people want to make friends with each other. I feel in Newcastle people don't put up boundaries all the time, whereas in other places, they do.
>
> *Jody:* But then in Jesmond they do. That's kind of one of the differences, isn't it? Because I'm from Newcastle and I've been here all my life but I don't feel at home in Jesmond. . . . Someone who lived in Jesmond would be a professional and have that job and have already that sort of, 'I'm a little bit better than you' attitude. Because I know people—yes, Geordies[5] like their fun and you can have a drink and have a laugh—again it comes back to maybe that class thing? 'Yes, they're quite common, they're not going to be brain surgeons or anything like that, but they're nice warm people that you would like to have as your friend.'
>
> (Gaby, 24, and Jody, 26)

Questions of identity, belonging and (mis)placement quiver with the 'affective energy' of the past, present and future (Thrift, 2004). As Gaby and Jody signal, regional value is recalled, utilized and capitalized upon by differently classed subjects in claiming ways in and out of time and place (by, for example, 'putting up boundaries' or dismantling these through affective practices such as 'having a laugh'). Evocative 'vocabularies of place' (Massey, 2004) exist in accounts of being and belonging in place, and in expressing territorial versions of home, community and change.

Alignment with regional re-framings can propel spaces and subjects forward, framed as (urban, middle-class) becoming, rather than backwardness. This can be contrasted against a sense of being 'stuck' in past-places often characterized negatively as (rural, working-class) residue. Affective geographies do not just exist 'out there' in the authentic resident addressed by local agencies; rather these forms of residency and articulation are appropriated, marketed and circulated, re-materializing who can and cannot 'fit into place.' Class, race and gender are crucial parts of such emplacements—and displacements—serving to ground 'affects' as emerging from somewhere (Ahmed, 2000; Tolia-Kelly, 2010). Laura invokes a North/South economy of belonging as she attempts to reclaim value and 'travel' in managing her embodied performance through accent as a return to and escape from place:

> London is used to having people who are young and ambitious and moving around all over. It's been . . . I think Newcastle sort of had a period of time where there's been a huge swathe of people who have left and not come back. I was quite shocked by that at first and I've got used to it and I kind of have ways round it now. I do have to really make an effort not to, you know, my voice not to be too girlie or to really make sure that I make a comment that can't be laughed off or people don't take you seriously. And I presume that will change. I think it will. Well, it'll have to.
>
> (Laura, 26)

As with Laura's fraught articulation of the 'young and ambitious' who go—and the others who stay, yet have to change—various geographies of affinity and distance were invoked demarcating who was 'like us' and who was decidedly different—both 'then' and 'now.' These everyday temporal–spatial segregations challenge and verify 'insider' and 'outsider' inhabitants, evoking 'fellow feelings,' empathies and hostilities, in classifying residents, neighbours, locals, investors, 'Northerners'/'Southern ers'/'Strangers' (Ahmed, 2000; Dillabough and Kennelly, 2010; Savage, 2010; Tolia-Kelly, 2010).

As with Laura's 'too girly' embodiment, Sophie and Lauren discuss value exemplified through (in)appropriate expressions of femininity, in two very different places. Both places—and performances—are subject to mockery, with perhaps more sympathy conveyed for 'rough' women who are still 'really nice though.' The mother figure becomes a loaded symbol for community (dis)investment and (dis)identification (Byrne, 2006, Gillies, 2006). Here 'poshly-spoken' women in Jesmond are described as 'more classy,' yet they are still subject to ridicule situated against their Byker counterparts. Nonetheless, this evaluation is partly one of recognition and proximity, where Sophie is keen to retrieve some of the associations that do attach to—and are claimed by—her:

> *Sophie:* But the lassies from Byker are like on a different level. They're in your face, loud, scary and this.
> *I:* Why do you think there are those differences then?
> *Lauren:* Because of the different upbringings that they have. Obviously the ones in Jesmond have been brought up with a silver spoon shoved both ends. [Laughter.] And the ones in Byker have had a hard upbringing and their Mam's have been like calling them 'bitch,' 'slag,' 'slut' and everything else. They've grown up to be hard and streetwise.
> (Sophie, 25, and Lauren, 25)

Readings of women do have material effects, as certain areas are avoided, known as troubled, where this sticks to the bodies of those from 'over there,' as a fixing measure of difference and disorder. The politics of identification come into play as the "place called home" (Massey, 2004) is articulated in intimate, familiar currencies and in proximities and distances of (un) relatedness: "The identities in question, including those of place, are forged through embodied relations which are extended geographically as well as historically" (ibid., 5). This is a question of time as well as place, where the temporal dimensions of representing place are apparent in feelings of 'coming forward' or being 'left behind.'

In exploring the territory of affect, Pini et al. (2010) call for 'more politically aware emotional geographies that attend to differentials of power in the processes and practices of affect' (Pini et al., 2010, 560). The economies of emotions and landscapes, as they are known, claimed and carried, highlight demarcations of difference/distance that operate at various scales, encompassing local, regional and national maps, trajectories and histories. The situatedness of local currencies endures as different 'locals' are positioned at a distance, with the emotionally charged politics of place involving complex regional and (inter)national claims. In order to open up to registers that shape interactions and embodied feelings, the next section "Moving Forwards: 'Then' and 'Now' " captures classed, gendered and generational lamentation and celebration as the past, present and future are differently imagined, lost or recuperated.

MOVING FORWARDS: 'THEN' AND 'NOW'

Within interviewees' accounts, and indeed in official policy discourse about 'moving forwards,' the region is repositioned temporally, pointing at the future place of innovation and tradition in reconstituting class and gender, region and nation. The landscape of the North East—and the respective class status of 'Geordies'—was discussed in terms of future-orientated potential, as well as current losses from past times. Some had lost out whereas others felt times/places were improving. Such sentiments highlight spatialized tensions in being 'out of place' and 'behind the times,' where the region is seen as both moving on and stagnating (depending on where one stood). Regional changes were often declared as the sweep of history and geography, from the coal face and shipyards of the past, to a still changing landscape mapped out in residential, leisure and work places. Many interviewees wrestled ambivalently with the pull of the past, and the distance between 'now' and 'then,' refusing a neat repackaging through upgraded urban landmarks. These are the embodied gateways in (not) 'arriving.'

Young people's ability to stay in place is frequently positioned as a projection of future worth and investment, against a loss and escape to other locales—they are 'weighty bodies,' weighed down by positive expectations

Table 10.1 Young Person's Focus Group Illustration: 'Then' and 'Now'

Then	
Good	**Bad**
Old Geordie words like 'hinny'	Coal mining
The World Cup	Unhealthy
Horses	Old
Old English	Dirty
Talking and writing	Clothes that had to cover you
Northumberland Street [in Newcastle]	It was sad
Vickers [factory]	Wars
Trusting	Shillings
Safer back then	
Lots of smoke and industrial	

Now	
Good	**Bad**
Still places to remind you of the past	Expensive
Swearing	Crime has increased, there's more trouble
Common speaking	Underage sex
More freedom	Teenage pregnancies
Underage smoking	Trampy areas
Shorter skirts	Drinking
Better football team	People and places are disrespectful
Better tram lines	Unsafe
Better monument	Dangerous
Healthier people	Posh
Better education	Immigrants
It's fun	Scary
	No smoking

and negative associations (which are differently felt, claimed and rejected by young people themselves).[6] The complexity of place, and place-based identifications around 'tradition' and 'innovation,' are captured by one focus group with young people whose members were mostly from working-class areas. The images and descriptions produced by the young women highlight how, over time, young people make place their homes without necessarily fully knowing or experiencing histories as 'theirs' (Back, 2007; Taylor, 2012a). Thoughts were listed as 'Now' and 'Then' on a sheet of A3 paper which also signalled continued histories and the intersection of linguistic, political, economic, embodied and emotive place-based (dis)identifications.

These young working-class women's accounts highlight a complex re-evaluation as they try to assert some claims on space. Devalued common words ('hinny'), practices and places are claimed as 'good' with contemporary times providing some gendered movements and opportunities, to be carefully navigated alongside new 'dangers' ('teenage pregnancies') and presences ('immigrants'). What these accounts also show is the multifaceted placement of young people in the 'here and now,' as they provide and follow maps through different urban and rural landscapes across time (Skelton and Valentine, 1997). Young middle-class women did not have to negotiate danger or vulnerability in the same way as their working-class counterparts, where classed histories (e.g., of industry) were not necessarily remembered or recounted.

Another young women's focus group conveyed the distinctions within and between spaces, in expressing their hopes, and desired and imagined futures manifest in the desire to be a 'top ender.' The question of 'what,' asked in relation to future educational and employment hopes, quickly turns into a question of 'where,' as different distances are evoked in getting away and staying put:

Donna: I'm gonna live in Seaham all my life. I will live in the top end like though—the posh end.
Sonia: Definitely away from here like.
Karen: I'm gonna be a top ender.
I: What does that mean?
Karen: Top of the Ave instead of the bottom of the Ave.
I: So what's a top ender though? What does that mean to you?
Sonia: It's just a kind of, like the Bykers, the Walkers, that kind of thing.
I: So I mean, would that change things? Would the house be different?
Sonia: No. The houses and that are pretty much the same really.
Karen: Top end houses have got to be better than bottom end ones what ya on?
Donna: I'll be living in Seaham all my life, me like.
Sonia: Nah, I want to move away like. Definitely.
Karen: I'll live in Seaham and I'll live up the top end!

(Donna, 16; Karen, 16; and Sonia, 16)

In the spatial scales evoked in the above account from young working-class women, the local terrain of the 'right end' of the street is both near and far, desired and yet impossible. This is in sharp contrast to the physically removed 'global' terrain seen by Suri (16), as a young middle-class woman, as possible and perfectly plausible as she expresses her desire to "live in the States, somewhere in America so I will probably end up there." Suri already imagines herself as a future global citizen: She occupies a space of choice and seemingly effortlessly anticipates the actualization of future becoming (Horton and Kraftl, 2006; McRobbie, 2009; Skelton and Valentine, 1997; Vittelone, 2008). Plans were made against contrasting firm expectations and hopeful crossed fingers whereby the young working-class women in another focus group expressed being 'stuck' in residential locations, while negotiating educational trajectories into the future workplace *if* GCSEs[7] could be passed (Evans, 2010). The sense of more demanding journeys, of 'escape' rather than 'choice,' is captured in the phrase 'on the run':

> *Sophie:* Used to live in Cowgate and then I moved to Byker and then I moved . . .
> *Jo:* You've missed Arthur's Hill out.
> *Sophie:* Aye, I moved to Arthur's Hill, which was posher, but that was bad as well. Me next door neighbour got murdered and she was like my best friend, and then we had to move to Byker and then moved back over here. So . . . we've been on the run.
> (Sophie, 16, and Jo, 16)

This being 'on the run,' although perhaps used for dramatic effect, is obviously different from a sense of security, expectation and entitlement. For many interviewees, much history and presence was invoked through generational association rather than as individual biography alone, though there were classed differences in navigating these associations as 'fixing' and static or chosen and mobile. Time and space were bound up in the narration of (not) belonging as told through what had been, accounted with regret as well as disavowal; 'old' geographies and histories were recuperated as signalling a continuity between landscape and inhabitants, whilst also being renounced as failing to capture complex movements and contradictions in who could 'fit' both 'then' and 'now.' Having a history was evidenced in the connection to place, through heavy industries, material objects and artefacts, as well as subjective senses (the remembered sights, sounds and smells of places) (Pini et al., 2010).

To 'have a history' could be (dis)orienting, but also be claimed as a demand for visibility, permanence and residency, and an entitlement to place (Savage et al., 2005; Tolia-Kelly, 2010). Such articulations featured in personalized histories of childhoods, combining real memories and imagined 'myths' where communities, families and workers had disappeared off the (gendered) map, to reappear in a deficient form from the 'good old times.'

The juxtaposition—and suggested continuity—between the past, present and future is embodied in Laura and Sheila's narration of history and place. Here, Laura and Sheila remember times and places now gone, recalled through their granddad's and uncles' 'stories.' For both young women these stories serve to create a fixed sense of place where absent people and places are rewritten into the landscape, fostering a sense of belonging, a commitment to stay 'in place,' to stay 'out in the sticks.' Indeed, Laura refuses the promise of (urban) mobility, stating that she would "never move to a city":

> *Sheila:* I think the mining . . . there has been some kind of mining villages, so like all my granddad and uncles and things. . . .
> *Laura:* [whispers] Miners!
> *Sheila:* So all the stories that I've heard, when I was little, is about the mining and the pit and even now, at the cricket club, where I go, one of the lads will say, 'Oh, I'm just a pit lad, me.' They make it out like it's a lower level or whatever but . . .
> *Laura:* I think it's nice.
> *Sheila:* It's nice to have that kind of . . . that history.
> *Laura:* My granddad's from Coffrey and he talked about, 'When we were lads, we used to go swimming here and that was all the quarry and they were the mines.' It's really nice to listen to it. I would never ever move to a city. Never. I like living out in the sticks. Right, there's nothing to do—it's what I like.
>
> (Laura, 26, County Durham, and Sheila, 26, County Durham)

Changes are variously anticipated, rejected, desired and capitalized upon. Alongside the (re)positioning of the past, present and future existed a sense of the speed of change, as right-in-time or out-of-control and racing ahead (or stuck, frozen in time): People and places were seen as more or less able to capitalize upon future directions. Capacities, mentalities and dispositions were spoken of as a future orientated mood, conveyed in place, and in people who could 'aspire' and look to the future, whereby dispositions become spatialized, and spaces become embodied. Gaby and Jody's orientations, as young middle-class women, are towards a more recognizable service-cultural sector as saviour, taking the North East out of its smog-filled industrially polluted past (Colls and Lancaster, 1992; Nayak, 2003; Miles, 2005):

> *Jody:* And I think as well, the history, not just Newcastle but the North East, everyone sort of thinks, 'Oh, it's grey, it's mining,' you know, and it's not particularly like a nice glamorous place, like historically, but I think that's changing and when people come up, they're like, 'Oh God, this is actually really nice.' And you've not lost what it was, but it's like putting new things on it.

Gaby: And saying it's not like stuck in the past, like it's . . . I love the law courts, as well, on the Quayside.
Jody: Oh yes, they're gorgeous.
Gaby: I think they're fantastic.

(Gaby, 24, and Jody, 26)

As young *middle-class* consumers of centralized urban space, Gaby and Jody note the beauty of certain historical presences, which they walk through, remark upon, as they take up their urban space, noting too that "there's a lot of history here." History is available to them in their present travels through the city.

Writing on iconic images of the Angel of the North, the Baltic, the Sage and the Millennium Bridge, which exemplify North East regeneration as celebrated by Gaby and Jody as well as more widely (see, e.g., Hollands and Chatterton, 2001; Nayak, 2003), the young working-class women in one focus group commented on the "beautiful," "coolest bridge in the world," as *viewers,* whilst also feeling unwelcomed as potential *visitors* ("never been," "rubbish art but good view"). Yet this didn't stop one young woman commenting on its "ugliness" and "posh slug" likeness (of the Sage concert hall). When asked about the Sage the young women replied, "It's just too posh for me," becoming a space in which they didn't belong, "I feel like an outsider. They're like, 'Aaah!' " (Jenny). This feeling was endorsed both internally ("Because . . . I don't like art. Just like 'What the hell?' . . . But I've never been, I just think I'd feel like an outsider" [Jo, 16]) and externally by staff and other visitors who asked the young girls outright, "What are you doing here?" Sophie goes on to explain their reactions to their feelings of exclusion: "The Baltic? It's so tight, like if you do something like start laughing then you get told off for it! And we're like, 'Yeah? Do you have a problem?' " The following extract highlights their material and cultural exclusion, within such a space, where the young women prefer instead to use the lift and view the external rather than internal surroundings:

Jo: Everyone looks you up and down.
Casey: There's always old grannies in it and we don't like it so we just gan there to play in the lifts! . . . And running round and taking the mick and dancing. . . .
Sophie: It's dead expensive, as well.
Jenny: The café, like four quid for a drink. . . .
Jo: We had fish and chips, me and my friend went for some chips, and the chips were like £2.20 for medium chips and the large were like £2.50. It's like, 'No. . . .' It's three quid for a muffin.
Casey: I know.
Jo: You get your chocolate muffin and a cup of coffee and it comes to about £4.50 or something. . . .

I: Who are the kind of people that go there do you think?
Jo: Old people.
Jenny: Tourists.
Casey: I hate tourists.
Jo: Lots of kids go there for. . . . And you go in and you get these old women going 'Sshhh.'

(Sophie, 16; Casey, 16; Jo, 16; and Jenny, 16)

It is not simply the expense that is exclusionary, but also the literal and imagined silencing presence of others, whose gaze ("Everyone looks you up and down") the young women challenge, if not completely redirect; these young women may well "hate" those who exclude, but this sentiment in itself is unable to displace the structural dynamics by which their own exclusion is reproduced. Such articulations cast light upon classed sentiments as a structuring feeling where "categories of class operate not only as an organizing principle which enable access to and limitations on social movement and interaction but are also reproduced at the intimate level as a 'structure of feeling' (Cf. Williams, 1961, 1977) in which doubt, anxiety and fear inform the production of subjectivity" (Skeggs, 1997, 6). The significance of habitus as embodiment, the social in the body, is evident in these senses of place as bodily perception, incorporation and responsiveness, expressed as ways of 'standing, speaking, walking and thereby of feeling and thinking' (Bourdieu, 1990, 70). These bodies are embedded in social environments rather than standing apart from these, and they are steeped in past memories which are transmitted to present bodily surfaces and felt intimately as being 'at home' (or not). Emplaced emotions offer connections to the past, challenging a binary between 'now' and 'then,' whereas 'corrections' to the past both cemented and undermined spatialized claims to ownership and belonging (Bondi, 2005).

The speed of change was connected to spatialized divisions between areas that were on their way to 'becoming,' as against those off the map, as backward, redundant and not quite as developed. Such assessments frequently intersected moral and material geographies, as residents and inhabitants of certain classed spaces were seen as 'stuck,' responsible for decline and lacking a future orientation (Evans, 2010; Gidley and Rooke, 2010). The linearity of improvement is implied in looking 'lower down' the socio-spatial scale, where value is attributed and denied in becoming developed and capacitated in specific ways:

> Like Byker, even I would say, it's like a world apart, from Jesmond. In Jesmond, there's big houses, big cars, private schools, private hospital, nice bars. . . . Byker represents the old Newcastle, it's not quite as developed, even the city centre. . . . Byker's a lot lower down than the city centre, the people there are still . . . like the houses are old fashioned.
>
> (Gaby, 24, Jesmond)

The trailing off of Gaby's comment "the people are still . . ." hints at the judgment of people and places as somehow unfinished, incomplete and behind *middle-class* regenerators. At the same time, the lack of movement could be valued as a retention of history, value and special difference, to be not forgotten within the urban market. In some places a parody of a former past was claimed as an 'alternative' capital now available to the middle-classes in occupying traditionally working-class areas. The past could be 'stripped' of value and re-presented selectively for a new kind of presence.

As witnessed, things carry differently: Past constellations shape present/possible futures and the kind of 'Northerner' you can be. Questions of who 'fits' in changing place raises concerns about the ability to move within and between spaces, where to claim space as a geographical range rests upon specific classed resources and histories which travel into the present. Class and gender are bound up in these negotiations and reclamations of the past, present and future even as they are disguised as personal 'choice,' individual extensions and regional expansions.

CONCLUSION

In seeking to strengthen and capitalize upon local attachments, a particular North East character and regional resilience is presented as regenerative; in times of austerity the good (future) worker/resident/consumer is positioned as responsible for riding out tough economic times. The region is presented as a place for emotional and material investments; this is witnessed in recent calls of a particular North East 'resilience' where the good worker/resident/consumer can ride out tough economic times (Bristow, 2010). This chapter has explored what subjects and spaces are imagined and materialized via investments in regional competitiveness and (ambivalent, Northern) cosmopolitanism, concluding that official registers of region and nation disconnect women's emotional attachments and registers of place.

Official registers of region interpellate young women as future-orientated and mobile but young women's experiences of place are coded and understood through classed and gendered embodiment and experience that 'sticks,' as well as 'moves.' Class intersects with gender to shape access to and experience of place and acts as a (dis)orientation through past-present-future encounters. The temporal dimensions of (re)generation disrupt a linear chronological experience of space as class and gender impact on the ability to travel through, orientate and claim space as one's own as a 'fit' with (regenerative) futures, as opposed to a misfitting (degenerative) 'failure.' Being, doing and living via a 'global reflexivity' and as a 'cosmopolitan' space/subject (Giddens, 1991) involves a narrative of competitiveness suggestive of a socially inclusive regional togetherness, while effacing different claims and configurations of spatial compositions.

In mapping the past, present and imagined future encounters of younger respondents, it is important to carve out a claim for plural futures. Not everyone can flexibly cast themselves through trajectories of regenerative potential, 'properly' orientating towards residential-consumer space—and not everyone wants to. I made a case for the importance of class and gender in consolidating and diminishing the chances of becoming 'future subjects,' asking who can travel through and make space their own? Who can stay and who is stuck in place? What would it mean to be responsive to those not identified as the 'right kind' of future subjects/workers/citizens and not capacitated as 'coming forward' into place? These experiences do not happen on a random basis to individuals, but are structured by the norms that govern public space; those who do not fit in with these norms are often positioned as 'out of place' or as not belonging. Bodies are interpellated in relation to dominant sexual and gender ideals (Holland et al., 2001; McRobbie, 2009; Tolman, 2002; Turner, 1984; Young, 2005) and embodied identities and emotions are salient lenses through which experiences and perceptions can be understood.

Not everyone can flexibly cast themselves through trajectories of future potential in taking up space for themselves. I have made a case for the importance of class within the attention to 'future subjects' as part of a continued rather than ended conversation, about which futures are celebrated and which is marginalized. The risk in leaving privileged lives unproblematized is that these are understood as fitting, standard and chosen; as the trajectories of agentic and capable future-orientated subjects while being injured by others' lack, failure and culpability. Past constellations shape present and possible futures and the kind of 'Northerner' or 'Geordie' that young *women* can and cannot become.

NOTES

1. Ahmed's notion of taking up space, or extension, draws on Iris Marion Young and Frantz Fanon's development of Merleau-Ponty's concept of motility, as the ability to extend one's body freely into space (Young [1990] naming this as an 'I can' comportment). In Fanon's development of black experience, however, it is the 'I cannot' of the body being unable to extend itself, unable to complete an action because it is blocked, that is salient (cited in Ahmed 2006, 139).
2. For example, there have been recent debates on the relevance of the UK North/South divide as the North generates more wealth ("North–South Divide 'Set to Widen,' " *The Guardian,* August 13, 2005; "Renaissance for Cities of the North," *The Guardian,* December 31, 2005; "North Just as Prosperous as the South, Survey Finds," *The Guardian,* December 8, 2005). In such accounts, specific landmarks (such as the Millennium Bridge, the Angel of the North, the Baltic concert hall and the Sage art gallery) are often foregrounded, while others, both real and imagined, are dispelled and minimized. (City) space is regenerated and rebranded to feature on a global stage with 'culture' as a form

of capital-building by way of a regional economic strategy, endorsed by the regional development agency One NorthEast to improve 'international competitiveness' (see Taylor and Addison, 2009, for a discussion of the impact of these strategies on young people's sense of place).

3. In empirically and theoretically turning to classed lives, I both take seriously the necessity of 'intersectionality' while refusing a reduction of class analysis, and classed lives, as never enough (Taylor, 2012d; Taylor et al. 2010). Middle-class lives, futures and even 'failures' are worthy of comment, rather than being left simply unstated, obvious or celebrated (see Taylor, 2009): Many have pointed to the worth of interrogating normative identities and positioning (such as whiteness, able-bodiedness, heterosexuality), and I hope to join this conversation on a level that is empirically plausible and which places class in framing futures.

   Many have argued for a more intersectional framing of class, with McDowell (2008) claiming that any re-focus on class must not marginalize gender, or sexuality; it must not make claims to a simple return-to-class as abandonment of intersectionality and other lines of difference (see Binnie 2011; Taylor, 2012a).

4. Unsurprisingly, the ex-mining coalfield community of Easington Colliery is not packaged as part of the new tourist potential, with the last coal mines closing in 1993, bringing drastic changes to its economy, community and housing stock.
5. 'Geordie' is a loaded descriptor used by—and to refer to—people from Newcastle. It has positive *and* negative connotations and these remain very gendered, with men using this to signal *their* industrial heritage, as grounded, real and down-to-earth, whereas it is often attached to women to signal a gendered and sexual inappropriateness in being excessive, brash and out of place (particularly in leisure and nighttime spaces). That said, women did reclaim the positive value of this term, often ambivalently so; for middle-class women it could be a way to deflect class privilege through asserting a local valued authenticity/ordinariness.
6. Strathern (1992) claims that generational differences between parents and children can provide an analogy through which to think about the place of tradition and innovation in English social life (see also Tyler, 2004). This claim can be expanded beyond a familiar frame as regions, neighbourhoods and communities intersect with familial 'inheritance' (see Taylor, 2012e).
7. General Certificate of Secondary Education.

REFERENCES

Adkins, L. "Reflexivity and the Politics of Qualitative Research" in *Qualitative Research in Action*. Edited by T. May, 332–348. London: Sage, 2002.

Adkins, Lisa, and Skeggs, Beverley. (Eds). *Feminism after Bourdieu*. Oxford: Wiley-Blackwell Publishing, 2004.

Ahmed, Sara (2000). *Strange Encounters: Embodied Others in Post-Coloniality*. London: Routledge, 2000.

Ahmed, S. "This Other and Other Others." *Economy and Society* 31, no. 4, 2002. 558–572.

Ahmed, S. *Queer Phenomenology. Orientations, Objects, Others*. Durham: Duke University Press, 2006.

Allen, K., & Taylor, Y. "Failed Femininities and Troubled Mothers: Gender and the Riots" [Special issue: Austerity Parenting]. *Studies in the Maternal*, 4, no. 2, 2013. http://www.mamsie.bbk.ac.uk/back_issues/4_2/index.html.

Amin, A. "Regions Unbound: Towards a New Politics of Place." *Geografiska Annaler* 86, no. 1, 2004. 33–44.

Armstrong J. "Class and Gender at the Intersection: Working-Class Women's Dispositions towards Employment and Motherhood," in *Classed Intersections: Spaces, Selves, Knowledges*. Edited by Y. Taylor, 235–253. Aldershot: Ashgate, 2010.

Back, L. *The Art of Listening*. Oxford and New York: Berg Publishers, 2007.

Binnie, J. "Class, Sexuality and Space: A Comment." *Sexuality and Class,* Sexualities Special Issue, no. 14, 2011. 21–26.

Bondi, L. "The Place of Emotions in Research: From Partitioning Emotion and Reason to the Emotional Dynamics of Research Relationships," in *Emotional Geographies*. Edited by J. Davidson, L. Bond and M. Smith, 231–246. London: Ashgate, 2005.

Bourdieu, P. *Distinction: A Social Critique of the Judgement of Taste*. London: Routledge, 1984.

———. *In Other Worlds: Essays toward a Reflexive Sociology*. Stanford: Stanford University Press, 1990.

Bristow, G. "Resilient Regions: Re-'Place'ing Regional Competitiveness." *Cambridge Journal of Regions, Economy and Society* 3, 2010. 1–15.

Byrne, B. *White Lives: The Interplay of "Race," Class and Gender in Everyday Life*. London, England: Routledge, 2006.

Charlesworth, S. *A Phenomenology of Working-Class Experience*. Cambridge: Cambridge University Press, 2000.

Clavering, E. "Betwixt and Between: Managing Marginalised Classed Identities," in *Classed Intersections: Spaces, Selves, Knowledges*. Edited by Y. Taylor, 117–135. Aldershot: Ashgate, 2010.

Coll, R., and Lancaster, B. *Geordies*. Edinburgh, UK: Edinburgh University Press, 1992.

Cregan, Kate. *The Sociology of the Body: Mapping the Abstraction of Embodiment*. Thousand Oaks, CA: Sage, 2006.

Dillabough, J. A., and J. Kennelly. *Lost Youth in the Global City*. New York: Routledge, 2010.

Diprose, R. "The Hand That Writes the Community in Blood." *Cultural Studies Review*, 9, no. 1, 2003. 35–50.

Erel, U. *Migrant Women Transforming Citizenship*. Aldershot: Ashgate, 2009.

Evans, S. "Becoming 'Somebody': Examining Class and Gender through Higher Education" in *Classed Intersections: Spaces, Selves, Knowledges*. Edited by Y. Taylor, 53–72. Farnham, UK: Ashgate, 2010.

France, Alan. *Understanding Youth in Late Modernity*. Maidenhead: Open University Press, 2007.

Giddens, Anthony. *The Consequences of Modernity*. Stanford, CA: Stanford University Press, 1991.

Gidley, B., and A. Rooke. "Asdatown: The Intersections of Classed Places and Identities,' in *Classed Intersections: Spaces, Selves, Knowledges*. Edited by Y. Taylor, 95–116. Farnham: Ashgate, 2010.

Gillies, V. "Working Class Mothers and School Life: Exploring the Role of Emotional Capital." *Gender and Education* 18, no. 3, 2006. 281–293.

———. *Marginalised Mothers: Exploring Working-Class Experiences of Parenting*. London and New York: Routledge, 2007.

Green, Ken. *Key Themes in Youth Sport*. Milton Park: Routledge, 2010.

Harris, A. *Future Girl: Young Women in the Twenty First Century*. London: Routledge, 2004.

Haylett, C. "Illegitimate Subjects? Abject Whites, Neoliberal Modernisation, and Middle-Class Multiculturalism." *Environment and Planning D: Society and Space* 19, 2001. 361–370.

———. "Culture, Class and Urban Policy. Reconsidering Equality." *Antipode*, 2003. 56–73.

Hewitt, R. *White Backlash and the Politics of Multiculturalism*. Cambridge: Cambridge University Press, 2005.

Hollands, R., and P. Chatterton. *Changing Our Toon: Youth, Nightlife and Urban Change in Newcastle*. Newcastle-Upon-Tyne: University of Newcastle-Upon-Tyne, 2001.

Horton, John, and Kraftl, Peter. "Not Just Growing Up, but Going On: Children's Geographies as Becoming; Materials, Spaces, Bodies, Situations." *Children's Geographies*, 4, 2006. 259–276.

Jackson, S., and Scott, S. *Theorizing Society*. Milton Keynes, UK: Open University Press, 2010.

Kenway, J., and McLeod, J. "Bourdieu's Reflexive Sociology and 'Spaces of Points of View': Whose Reflexivity, Which Perspective?" *British Journal of Sociology of Education*, 25, 2004. 525–544.

Khattab, Nabil, and Fenton, Steve. "What Makes Young Adults Happy? Employment and Non-work as Determinants of Life Satisfaction." *Sociology* 43, 2009. 11–26.

Kubicek, K., McDavitt, B., Carpineto J., et al. "God Made Me Gay for a Reason: Young Men Who Have Sex with Men's Resiliency in Resolving Internalized Homophobia from Religious Sources." *Journal of Adolescent Research* 24, 2009. 601–633.

Leccardi, Carmen, and Ruspini, Elisabetta (Eds.). *A New Youth? Young People, Generations and Family Life*. Aldershot, UK: Ashgate, 2006.

Massey, D. "Geographies of Responsibility." *Geografiska Annaler* 86, no. 1, 2004. 5–18.

McDowell, L. "The New Economy, Class Condescension and Caring Labour: Changing Formations of Class and Gender." *NORA—Nordic Journal of Feminist and Gender Research* 16, no. 3, 2008. 150–165.

McRobbie, A. *The Aftermath of Feminism: Gender, Culture and Social Change*. London: Sage, 2009.

Miles, S. "Understanding the Cultural 'Case': Class, Identity and the Regeneration of Newcastle Gateshead." *Sociology* 39, no. 5, 2005. 1019–1028.

Nayak, A. *Race, Place and Globalization: Youth Cultures in a Changing World*. Oxford: Berg, 2003.

Parker, S. "Working Capital: Ownership and (Some) Means of Production," in *Classed Intersections: Spaces, Selves, Knowledges*. Edited by Y. Taylor, 13–34. Aldershot: Ashgate, 2010.

Paton, K. "Making Working-Class Neighbourhoods Posh? Exploring the Effects of Gentrification Strategies on Working-Class Communities" in *Classed Intersections: Spaces, Selves, Knowledges*. Edited by Y. Taylor, 137–157. Aldershot: Ashgate, 2010.

Pini, B., R. Mayes and P. McDonald. "The Emotional Geography of a Mine Closure: A Study of the Ravensthrope Nickel Mine in Western Australia." *Social and Cultural Geography* 11, no. 6, 2010. 559–574.

Reay, D. "They Employ Cleaners to Do That: Habitus in the Primary Classroom." *British Journal of Sociology of Education* 16, no. 3, 1995. 353–371.

Reay, D., S. Hollingworth, K. Williams, G. Crozier, F. Jamieson, D. James and P. Bedell. "'A Darker Shade of Pale?' Whiteness, the Middle Classes and Multi-Ethnic Inner City Schooling." *Sociology* 41, 2007. 1041–1059.

Savage, M. "The Politics of Elective Belonging." *Housing, Theory and Society* 27, no. 2, 2010. 115–161.

Savage, M., G. Bagnall and B. Longhurst. *Globalisation and Belonging*. London: Sage, 2005.

Secomb, L. "Fractured Community." *Hypatia* 15, no. 2, 2000. 133–150.

Skeggs, B. *Formations of Class and Gender* London: Sage, 1997.

———. *Class, Self, Culture* London: Routledge, 2004.

Skelton, T., and G. Valentine (Eds.). *Cool Places: Geographies of Youth Cultures*. London: Routledge, 1997.

Strangleman, T. *Work Identity at the End of the Line? Privatisation and Culture Change in the UK Rail Industry*. Basingstoke: Palgrave, 2004.

Strathern, M. (1992). *After Nature: English Kinship in the Late Twentieth Century*. Cambridge: Cambridge University Press, 1992.

Taylor, Y. *Working-Class Lesbian Life: Classed Outsiders*. London: Palgrave Macmillan, 2007.

———. *Fitting into Place? Class and Gender Geographies and Temporalities*. London: Ashgate, 2012a.

———. "Future Subjects? Education, Activism and Parental Practices" [Special issue]. *Graduate Journal of Social Science*, 9, no. 2, 2012b. 65–85.

———. "Close Encounters of the Classed Kind: Again." *Social & Cultural Geography*, 13, 2012c. 545–549.

———. (Ed). *Classed Intersections: Spaces, Selves, Knowledge*. Farnham, UK: Ashgate Publishing, 2012d.

———. "Introduction" in Taylor, Y., *Classed Intersections: Spaces, Selves, Knowledge*, 1–10. Farnham, UK: Ashgate Publishing, 2012e.

Taylor, Y., and M. Addison. "(Re)constituting the Past, (Re)branding the Present and (Re)imagining the Future: Young Women's Spatial Negotiation of Gender and Class." *Journal of Youth Studies*, Special Issue Young People, Class and Space 12, no. 5, 2009. 563–578.

Taylor, Y., and M. Addison. "Placing Research: 'City Publics' and the 'Public Sociologist.' " *Sociological Research Online* 16, no. 4, 2011.

Taylor, Y., and K. Allen. "Sinking or Swimming? Academic Strokes, Anxious Provokes." Accessed 13 December 2013. 2011. http://sociologyandthecuts.wordpress.com/2011/11/22/sinking-or-swimming-academic-strokes-anxious-provokes-by-yvette-taylor-and-kimberly-allen/.

Taylor, Y., S. Hines and M. Casey (Eds.). *Theorizing Intersectionality and Sexuality*. London: Palgrave Macmillan, 2010.

Therborn, Goran. "End of a Paradigm: The Current Crisis and the Idea of Stateless Cities. *Environment and Planning A*, 43, no. 2, 2011. 272–285.

Thrift, N. "Intensities of Feeling: Towards a Spatial Politics of Affect." *Geografiska Annaler* 86, no. 1, 2004. 57–78.

Tolia-Kelly, D.P. *Landscape, Race, Memory. Material Ecologies of Citizenship*. Farnham: Ashgate, 2010.

Tolman, Deborah. *Dilemmas of Desire: Teenage Girls Talk about Sexuality*. Cambridge, MA: Harvard UP, 2002.

Turner, Bryan. *The Body and Social Theory*. Thousand Oaks, CA: Sage, 1984.

Tyler, K. (2004). "Reflexivity, Tradition and Racism in a Former Mining Town." *Ethnic and Racial Studies* 27, 2004. 290–309.

Valentine, G., Skelton, T., and Butler, R. (2003). "Coming Out and Outcomes: Negotiating Lesbian and Gay Identities with, and in, the Family. *Environment and Planning D*: Society and Space, 21, 2003. 479–499.

Vitellone, N. *Object Matters: Condoms, Adolescence and Time*. Manchester: Manchester University Press, 2008.

Walkerdine, V. "Steel, Identity, Community: Regenerating Identities in a South Wales Town." Edited by Margaret Wetherell in *Identity in the 21st Century: New Trends in Changing Times*. 59–75. Basingstoke: Palgrave Macmillan, 2009.

Watson, S. *City Publics: The (Dis)enchantments of Urban Encounters*. Oxon: Routledge, 2006.

Yip, A.K.T., Keenan, M., and Page, S. *Religion, Youth and Sexuality: Selected Key Findings from a Multi-faith Exploration*. Nottingham: University of Nottingham, 2011.

Young, Iris Marion. *On Female Bodily Experience*. Oxford: Oxford University Press, 2005.

———. *Throwing like a Girl and Other Essays in Feminist Philosophy and Social Theory*. Bloomington, IN: Indiana University Press, 1990.

11 The Phenomenology of Authenticity Work

Merleau-Ponty and the 'Dissonant Sound' of The Clash

Aaron Klassen

INTRODUCTION

> Punk should either send a message or simply kick some ass, it shouldn't just be a slightly more dumber and faster generic version of heavy rock.
>
> —FAN youtube.com (2011)

How can the above statement be interpreted? Originally posted on the social media site, YouTube, the blogger indicts the punk band, The Clash, for a lackluster performance at the Us Festival in Los Angeles, which was sponsored by the then-fledgling computer company, Apple (Gilbert, 2004). Whereas The Clash (along with the Sex Pistols) is widely known as a progenitor of punk (Hebdige, 1979; Laing, 1985; Marcus, 1993), the Us Festival performance in May 1983 came late in the band's career and far from its 'subcultural' point of origin in 1976 London. What makes this statement all the more curious, however, is that it was posted in 2011. Does this mean then, that punk remains an instance and even a metaphor for authentic youthful rebellion today?

Perhaps. I begin with the above quote because I think it invites us to rethink how sound, embodied perception and 'authenticity work' conspired together to produce The Clash and punk. I write this knowing a great deal of work has already been produced to account for the significance, impact and limits of punk and The Clash in relation to youth culture and political change (Frith, 1981; Hebdige, 1979; Laing, 1985; Marcus, 1989, 1993). Nonetheless I want to revisit The Clash and their connection to the emergence of punk in the late 1970s and early 1980s, because this moment is revealing of how cultural forms emerge not just as a consequence of institutions and discourses. Such developments are also the result of particular kinds of embodied perceptions and 'authenticity work' that coalesced around and, in a sense, produced The Clash and early punk. In part, I draw on R. A. Peterson's (2005) theory of "authenticity work" in developing my analysis. I also draw on Merleau-Ponty's (2012) *Phenomenology of Perception* to make sense of the experience of punk sound itself, and in particular the way punk music both signifies *and* impresses itself upon the body, a process that in turn reconstitutes punk. Ontologically, I argue that punk demarcates a sum of mutually exclusive, aggregate parts, with its music being as much a substantive feature as its institutions and discourses. For this reason, when I refer to 'punk' throughout this chapter, it is to its constitutive whole; punk is as much a music genre as it is a youth culture.[1]

I develop my position through a short review of key moments in the analysis of punk music as developed in early subcultural studies. I note those shortfalls and 'absences' that McRobbie (1980) and others have tracked in this research, and then suggest how Merleau-Ponty's phenomenology can add to youth and sound studies in several ways. Most importantly, phenomenology offers an epistemological and methodological critique that questions how the social world is known through the mediated body. Whereas Cartesian systems distinguish consciousness from the external world, Merleau-Ponty asks how it is that the body affects that knowing. I take up this question and ask how the subject-body of audiences and the object to which they attend (here The Clash themselves) come together through the sensing of sounds, spatiality and temporality (context) in a particular historical moment, thereby forging the authenticity work that would become symptomatic of the conjunction between The Clash and punk. In combining experience, which in this case would later be called punk, with historical sociology, I avoid essentializing punk while still exploring the 'structures of feeling' that characterize the cultural practice (Williams, 1977). In my analysis, I continue to draw on the three levels of analysis (the historical, the structural and the everyday life) privileged in the work of Birmingham School researchers (Jefferson and Hall, [1976] 2006). My analysis additionally attempts to account for ambiguity between subjects and objects, as phenomenology allows me to address the *emergent* quality of cultural forms, such as punk, its bands and fans. This ambiguity includes the contextually mediated body whose presence is constitutive of and by intentionality, temporality and spatiality—elements that I take to be largely overlooked in the literature. Here, I emphasize the tension that exists in the way an experience comes to be known, because of the irreducible link between experience, and political, economic and cultural structures.

YOUTH SUBCULTURE AND AFTER

The academic study of youth subcultures largely began during the interwar period in the United States with the work of Robert Park and his colleagues at the University of Chicago (Bradford, 2012). In contrast with the then dominant psychological interpretation of deviance, the 'Chicago School' took a broader approach, arguing that deviance is a normal response to normative pressures in a stratified social context (Merton, 1938). Park's colleague, Robert Merton (1957), argued that dominant groups in society define 'goals' (i.e., the pursuit of happiness) and the 'means' to achieve them. Those lacking access to legitimate means (i.e., language or education) will in turn resort to illegitimate networks and actions, including participation in teenage gangs, in order to achieve socially valued goals. Ultimately, this research would lead to influential theories such as *labeling*, wherein deviant behaviour is understood as "behaviour that people so label" (Becker, 1963).

According to Bradford (2012), Albert Cohen's (1955) work on teenage gangs influenced similar research in the UK in the post-war period. Cohen argued that 'subcultural' gangs provided a compensatory source of identity for undereducated working-class youth. His work raised key issues that have become focal points in recent work on youth cultures and subcultures in the UK: First, that subculture is expressed in values that counter or subvert 'mainstream' or authoritarian culture; second, that subculture is a source of social bonding or solidarity; and third, that subcultures emerge in relation to leisure practices and experiences (Bradford, 2012). By the 1960s, youth were thus generally conceived as socially constructed, their behaviour attributed not simply to psychology, age and biology, but to the institutions and practices of leisure and marginalization in modern societies.

It was in the shadow of these concerns that work on youth, subcultures and notions of resistance would get under way in 1964, at the Centre for Contemporary Cultural Studies (CCCS) at the University of Birmingham (Bennett and Kahn-Harris, 2004; Jefferson and Hall, [1976] 2006; Grossberg 2010).[2] According to Bradford (2012), although distinct youth cultures existed in the UK prior to the Second World War, these were typically understood according to a cohesive nationalist framework, which progressed unabated from the play of childhood to the civic responsibility of family. Scholars at the CCCS (e.g., Williams, 1961) argued instead that mainstream conceptualizations of society and youth followed a conservative line, failing to recognize the legitimacy of working-class cultures, their potential agency in history, and a broader set of changing social dynamics that followed World War II. This included diversified and diffused gainful employment among otherwise marginalized groups, including youth, women and racial minorities, challenging traditional values associated with nationalism, the church and family. The Centre incorporated a cultural-Marxist framework into their analysis, in part by way of the Frankfurt school (Adorno and Horkheimer, 2002; Marcuse, 1964), whose members argued that society was influenced—for the worse in the case of Nazi Germany—by industrial-capitalist state control, and thus standardization, of the expressive means of culture (arts and music). This led to the development of the culture industries, and the ongoing massification of society. Whereas the Frankfurt school approach was pessimistic, denying much of any sort of revolutionary impetus beyond the acts of the cultural avant-garde, the CCCS drew on Althusser's (2001) structural-Marxism and Gramsci's (1971) concept of "hegemony" to address how a dominant class exercises power over subordinate classes through ideological or cultural means, and the degree to which subordinate classes contest or negotiate such efforts. This allowed the Centre to conceive of Britain's ruling elite as influential upon the working classes, but not in a manner that was absolute. In this way, the working classes were not understood as passive consumers. They were seen rather as being capable of producing a culture and ideology of their own, one that in certain instances might resist dominant power.

Developing from this work, subculture would emerge as a key concept to describe those spaces and associations where youth engage in creative agency, including the appropriation of style, to contest, challenge and disrupt the social order. Hebdige (1979) argued that without necessarily vocalizing it, style signifies meaning by virtue of an object's cultural specificity, including the ways in which it is produced, commodified and used, or mythologized. Punks, for instance, were seen to resist perceived hegemonic pressures spectacularly, by appropriating objects and their representative meanings for their own uses. Where this work revealed interesting and new forms of youth agency, it was not without criticism.

The concept of subculture in the work of the CCCS has been the subject of substantial debate since the 1970s, both from within and beyond cultural studies. Bradford (2012) links these criticisms to three key issues: (1) the conflation of youth subculture and leisure culture; (2) the absence of attention to difference (especially in relation to gender) in early subculture work; and (3) the representativeness of those youth identified in early studies. McRobbie (1980) attributed the CCCS's focus to an aversion to the then empirical-positivist approach taken by sociologists of the family, instead choosing to problematize what came to be seen as male-dominated public activities and working-class cultural politics. Since the 1970s, critical theories and research around youth subculture have highlighted the heterogeneity of youth consumptive practices, by drawing attention to social-structural aspects of "taste cultures" (Gans 1999), including the "distinction" (Bourdieu, 1984) or obscuring (Peterson and Kern, 1996) of associations between consumption and class-background. Straw's (1991) concept of "scenes" has gained intellectual currency by virtue of its combining critical class-related analysis with anthropological theories of collectivity. Hesmondhalgh (2005) argues that 'genre' transcends the dichotomy between subculture and mainstream, and accounts for the influence of the political-economy of the cultural industries upon consumptive practice. My contribution here is to suggest that Merleau-Ponty's (2012) phenomenology, combined with Peterson's (2005) theory of "authenticity work", explains both the emergence of cultural forms and their maintenance, by framing a space and time in which they can materialize, and the conjuncture of multiple actors and their efforts (i.e., performer, audience and cultural gatekeepers) in the construction of cultural forms such as punk.

PUNK, PHENOMENOLOGY AND AUTHENTICITY WORK

Regardless of its shortfalls, the study of popular culture and music, including punk, has only proliferated since the CCCS's early work on subcultures (Clayton et al., 2012; Frith and Goodwin, 1990). I wish to contribute to this effort by tracing an ontology of punk, a task accomplished using Merleau-Ponty's phenomenology, beginning with the question: What is punk? In response, I note that punk is both an attitude and an experience, which is to say, it is both political and musical. Although punk has arguably received much academic attention since the Centre's analysis (Fox, 1987; Frith, 1981; Hebdige, 1979; Laing, 1985; Widdicombe and Wooffitt, 1990), it is true that punk continues to develop, and now is a global phenomenon (cf. numerous histories of rock: Marcus, 1989, 1993; Palmer, 1995; and subcultural anthologies: Bennett and Kahn-Harris, 2004; Kahn-Harris, 2007; Smith, 2011). Moreover, it has outlived its contemporaries (e.g., disco, hair metal), having 'passed the torch' of cultural critique, including youth resistance, on to other global scenes such as grunge and indie that, despite their own historically specific qualities, embody similar form and content (Gilbert, 2004; Hibbett, 2005). With this in mind, in the next section, I use R. A. Peterson's (2005) theory of "authenticity work" and Merleau-Ponty's (2012) phenomenology to add to our understanding of how punk emerged as a music and culture (sub- or otherwise) in a particular historical moment, and why it continues to claim 'authenticity' as an identifying marker, in spite of the contradictions and uncertainties that haunt this category.

As Stuart Hall (2006) acknowledges in the second edition of *Resistance through Rituals*, criticisms of the CCCS approach to youth subcultures commonly focus on questions of the subjective everyday life of subcultural participants (Hall cites, for instance, Hodkinson, 2002; Moore, 1994; Muggleton, 2000). However, although they have added to youth analysis (e.g., combining cohesive 'subcultural' entities on one hand, with diffuse postmodern 'hybrids' on the other hand), Hall is quick to point out that these critics go on to repeat the same 'mistake' of objectifying youth experience without explaining the ways in which experience is perceived. In contrast to this kind of move, Merleau-Ponty's (2012) *Phenomenology of Perception* helps to explain why it is so difficult to arrive at an understanding of consensually defined and bounded youth.

Merleau-Ponty's epistemology takes into account the body as it structures the perception of the object-filled world. In this way, he questions Descartes's philosophical system, which suggests that all that is knowable is consciousness itself. In contrast, Merleau-Ponty's focus on the body reminds the reader of the sine qua non of all cultural forms and non-forms including punk: that punk is not just a rational conscious construct, but a contextually mediated form shaped by the perception of sound and objects. These sounds and objects are not efficiently translated into rational discourse without losing something of their spatial-temporal quality; in other words, they are perceived in such a way as to affect emotions as much as intellect. Merleau-Ponty argues alongside other phenomenologists that to reflect upon reality is to 'bracket off' that reality, highlighting particular aspects above others as it relates to the knowing self. Throughout *Phenomenology of Perception*, Merleau-Ponty maintains a perspective that incorporates the body's perception into consciousness without reversing the trend and imposing objective consciousness onto the body. Although entirely possible—one has only to think of the disciplining of the body that happens in the acquisition of vocational skill—Merleau-Ponty wants to account for the tension that exists between perception as it affects consciousness and vice versa. He makes the important distinction that it is the entirety of sense perception that renders a particular mode of existence, not just a sum of parts. Consequently, things in the material world are not known through their objective dimensions alone, such as the measurements that are employed to define space and time; rather, things are accessed through the body's sensing of spatiality and temporality. Merleau-Ponty traces the imposition of standards upon the world to two sources: first, the 'intellectualism' of philosophy, and second, the reductionism of science. Most significantly, in identifying perception as a constitutive aspect of the knowing self, he expands the horizon of knowing the world beyond the conscious action of recognition. It is in this sense that knowing for Merleau-Ponty is always a kind of 'joining' between self and world. It is not self knowing world, so much as self and world coming together through perception.

The expansion of sense perception beyond conscious reflection is helpful in understanding the emergence of new youth cultures and music, including punk. The opening comment to this paper may be analyzed as an example of the process in which punk is perceived. In saying "kick some ass," the fan articulates a quality of his or her perception. But what does the fan mean; what is the fan referring to, exactly? The fan brings attention to an aspect of perception that remains elusive to their vernacular, leaving his or her description wanting; however, this is not because of a lack of cognitive awareness nor a lack of philosophical reflection. The fan clearly attempts to communicate what for him or her is an emotive, embodied experience. Given this, I propose that the articulation in this fan's statement suggests the expanse of senses that extend beyond conscious reflection. Read this way, we might say the fan's expression includes the sentiment that experience is reduced through description, not the inverse.

Before punk was objectified as music and culture, its practice inhered an indeterminate quality stemming from the body's perception of an atmosphere. This atmosphere crystallizes into objects and symbols through bodily action and performance. Conversely, if not for the embodied presence of objects and symbols, the objective meaning of punk would remain elusive to the subject. Punk literally did not exist before people performed it and, in a way, built on its concrete performance. One might say that the emergence of punk was 'in the air.' Historian Greil Marcus (1989, 37) captures this point, for instance, in his account of an early punk show with The Clash and Sex Pistols:

> "Now it's time for audience participation," Joe Strummer of The Clash said from the stage in late 1976. "I want you all to tell me exactly what you're doing here." As they waited for the Sex Pistols to take the stage at Winterland, probably a lot of people wondered what they were doing there—wondered why their expectations were so confused, and so fierce. In all the stories coded in that moment, at least one was simply musical. . . . It was the sound . . . of people discovering their own power.

In this passage, Marcus draws attention to the emergence of a new genre, specifically one in which the audience was afforded agency to 'make sense' of the situation. In blurring the division between objectivity and subjectivity, empirical and intellectual reflection, Merleau-Ponty highlights the originary value of our embodied experience of the world. In this way, experience is revealed as a 'facticity,' an inextricable mode of being-in-the-world that is determined by the body's schema and which gives rise to our reflection upon that world. This quality of being implies a universalism among subjects—however, one that is not qualified by means of scientific or philosophical judgment, as though its determination depends on empirical tools or careful reduction. Rather, prior to reduction there manifests in our senses a quality that is apperceived, sensed as a manifestation of the world yet characterized by the synthesis of the body schema: the apprehension of a certain *hyle,* or matter. The quality of perception is not static, but characterized or affected by constant synthesis of the body and the world. Merleau-Ponty calls this *operative intentionality*. For example, Marcus (1993, 21) recounts his first experience of the Sex Pistols, which happened to be their last performance, in San Francisco, January 14, 1978:

> The first thing that struck me, not a minute into the show, was how much stronger they sounded onstage than on their records. The music was all bite: you could reach out and touch every jagged note.

According to his description of the Sex Pistols's performance, Marcus did not just hear punk, rather, he sensed his experience as something that he could touch. Moreover, the historical description and mimesis of sounds performed from 1976 on, that is, what has come to be known as 'punk,' continues to resonate as a particular kind of 'felt' experience today, expressed in the sentiment of blogging punk fans as noted above.

The phenomenological interpretation of the phrase "kick some ass" constitutes a way of assessing a certain organization of affective experience that is later called 'authentic.' It marks a claim as to what the experience of punk music should be about, and significantly for sociologies of youth and music, a claim of 'originality' that holds currency in various fields, including the arts.[3] Indirectly then, the fan claims that punk should have a visceral, tactile effect on people, and a violent one, meaning it should startle people, shake them out of their passivity and complacency. This claim, however, articulates not just the sense of punk, but the meaning of punk as it has been claimed and legitimated over the past thirty-eight years (Gilbert, 2004); a discursive claim that works to objectivize and thus establish the particular perceptions categorically as punk (Peterson, 1997, 2005).

Punk and The Clash are not originarily authentic, but the ways in which their experience is discursively debated among fans on websites such as YouTube, and by cultural gatekeepers including historians and biographers (Gilbert, 2004; Marcus, 1993), continues to suggest that it is. Cultural sociologist R.A. Peterson (2005, 1086) argues that rather than inhering in an object or subject, authenticity is socially constructed, yet subject to continual change: "Authenticity is a claim that is made by or for someone, thing, or performance and either accepted or rejected by relevant others." Indeed, he suggests that authenticity work—as it implies a reflexive relationship—is required in order for artists and genres to stay relevant to the communities with which they interact. Kahn-Harris (2004, 2007) has made similar arguments in his work on global extreme metal scenes. Here, musicians and fans maintain an everyday life routine characterized by mundanity in order to amplify the liminal-transgressive experience of metal, with which members associate transgression. However, whereas Hebdige's (1979) theory of subcultural 'style' focuses on the external 'signifiance' of spectacular representation (cf. Kahn-Harris's (2004) critique), Peterson's theory of authenticity work follows Goffman (1959) and incorporates the internal-external work of presentation or consistency in character of a musician and his or her fan. Peterson's theory works with phenomenology in that he explains how experience becomes linked to cultural forms and their meanings, such as punk, without essentializing experience as authentic.

Peterson defines authenticity work according to five typologies, none of which are mutually exclusive: (1) authenticity to constructed self; (2) via ties to lineage; (3) claims to membership in a collective; (4) status; and (5) experience. In the case of The Clash and their fans, each of Peterson's types are reflexively performed: (1) in the presentation of the musicians and fans themselves; (2) in the occasion where the band was endorsed by 'authentic' acts such as Bo Diddley and Patti Smith (cf. Gilbert, 2004); (3) in extrinsic punk style and intrinsic punk *ethos;* (4) in The Clash's 'originality' compared to British punk trailblazers the Sex Pistols, and within the canon of Rock history; and (5) in the distinct experience of The Clash in concert. A direct correlation exists between the band's ability to claim authenticity and their critics' and fans' legitimation of the band, altogether constructing notions of 'real punk.' Arguably, without their fans' endorsement, The Clash would remain culturally insignificant. Peterson's 'authenticity work' adds to youth culture theories by drawing attention to the reflexive work that bands, gatekeepers and audiences do to claim membership, and thus produce culture, and yet without drawing deterministic assumptions about class background, age, gender or race. Situated relative to mainstream culture and the larger genre of popular music, the authenticity work behind punk's emergence becomes inextricably linked to the actors involved, including claims made in meaningfully interpreting their experiences.

In this section, I argued that it is important to note that punk authenticity work is socially and relationally constituted and not always in a rational or categorical fashion due to the phenomenology of perception. Epistemologically, by virtue of a phenomenological approach, this process is attributed in part to the horizon of perception that extends beyond its intellectual and scientific reduction, and the perceptions of experience that are lost in translation *by the practitioners themselves,* not just the theory and research of the CCCS or post-subculturalists. In the next section, I turn to the narratives of these practitioners.

PHENOMENOLOGY OF THE CLASH'S AUTHENTICITY WORK

I will now return to an historical analysis of narratives around punk in order to note the ways in which 'authenticity work' has played out since 1976 and how phenomenology can help to understand the punk experience as it is authenticated, and how its authentication is challenged by changing experiences. The key producers of authenticity work are: (1) the performers—in this case, The Clash; (2) cultural gatekeepers; and (3) fans. Sites whereby claims-making occurs includes concert performances and musicians' narrative accounts as documented in film (Temple, 2007) and biographies (Gilbert, 2004), journalist and historian renderings (Marcus, 1989, 1993), and online sites such as YouTube where fans continue to define punk through debate.

In order to illustrate authenticity work at its most elaborate, I start with a contradictory experience a few years into The Clash's career. With commercial and popular success, The Clash's band members encountered a contradiction with their anti-commercial ideals and claim to punk authenticity. For instance, in the film documentary, *The Future Is Unwritten* (2007), lead singer Joe Strummer refers back to his 'originary' experience of punk as a point of reference:

> Standing there singing those songs while it got bigger and bigger towards the end, for some reason, I began to feel worse and worse. It's something to do with what those songs are saying. When we were part of the audience, we were part of a movement. Once it became thousands of miles removed from that, I began to freak out.
>
> (Temple, 2007, 75: 25)

Joe confesses that his band's commercial success compromised punk values, which were forged in a kind of 'originary' experience. His sense of temporality allows him to sense variations in the immediacy of performance, and in the historicity of performances, allowing for comparison throughout his career. Strummer laments the changes in performance atmosphere including his relation as performer to his fans, from intimate, spontaneous, gritty and obnoxious, considered 'real punk,' to distant and overly structured, considered 'un-punk.' For instance, on the stadium stage, and for pragmatic reasons, the band and their instruments were elevated in order to remain visible from afar; however, audience members who were in close proximity were prevented from engaging the band and each other in casual violence as punk had become known for.

In punk's nascence, compared to their popular rock contemporaries that performed in stadiums and arenas, The Clash's pub shows are described as volatile to say the least. Biographer Gilbert gives an account of an early show as described by a member of the band's entourage, Jon Savage (Gilbert, 2004, 163):

> The kids were going mental like they do in Manchester and ripping this theatre up. It was just wild and I was in the press pit dodging all these chairs. It was fantastic. . . . [Clash guitarist] Mick Jones caught my eye and went, "What's going on? This is madness. Have we done this?"

Here, several conjectures are made. First, Savage's perception of fans' violence is interpreted as empowered and spontaneous, inspired by The Clash's performance, including singer Joe's embodied antagonism perceived from the stage. The violence to which Savage refers is located both in the bodies of fans and band members that were hurled into each other, an early form of moshing called pogo, and also, in the objects in the theatre. His narrative highlights the intellectual and reductive 'incoherence' of experience. In the 'chaos' of the event, Savage and Jones aimed to understand the meaning of the actions they participated in stimulating through their performance. The search for interpretation reveals a world that is first perceived prior to their conscious reflection, and that is reduced to narrative. Further, the intentionality of the concert experience is perceived in the presence of other objects whose meaning follows perception, such as 'theatre' and 'bodies.' Savage's memory of the event relies on his conscious engagement with embodied experience, including his interpretation of the operative intentionality by which it was characterized.

The body by its orientation towards the world is ambiguously free from yet servile to that world. Although capable of turning away from the world in a sense, it is only to encounter another world that continues to propel things towards the body—quite literally in Savage's account. As noted above, Merleau-Ponty calls the affecting quality of perception operative intentionality. And yet, in the experience of violence at a Clash concert, the subject is affected through his or her bodily encounter with objects and bodies. According to Merleau-Ponty (2012, 88), "To be emotional is to find oneself engaged in a situation that one is unable to cope with and yet from which one does not want to escape." Savage and Jones perceive violence through the orientation of their bodies to other objects and bodies that may or may not threaten their well-being, yet also through their inability to escape this experience. Alternatively, it is not that the subject is conflicted in his or her engagement; it is that by virtue of the structuring character of his or her embodied perception of the world, the subject experiences emotions. The ambiguity of the experience then is attributed to an operative intentionality that affects the subject.

The above reflections lead to the key question: What of the significance of the music? How is it that punk music continues to hold currency for the listening fan, whether an aging fan of the 'original' scene or a new fan? According to cultural theorists Shepherd and Wicke (1997), 'music' is as much a construct as is 'punk.' Rather, as the perception of organized sound, 'music' constitutes a significant experience in that it evokes a particular state of awareness, characterized by the body's spatiality and temporality. It would suggest that this schema, conceptually, "the sonic saddle" (ibid., 159–168), has the effect of structuring an affective state whereby memory is both evoked and challenged in order to make sense of experience. Similar to Merleau-Ponty's operative intentionality, the sonic saddle distinguishes the experience of the musical performance in real time from its conscious reflection. Contrary to Hebdige's (1979) conception of "signifiance," which overlooks the phenomenology of perception in its haste to presume that music signifies, Shepherd and Wicke argue that music becomes meaningful only after its evaluation as a medium in sound. 'Sound' is primarily significant at the level of perception, whereas 'music' is a culturally specific, arbitrary construct of a secondary order. Arguably, to claim that music signifies creates a power imbalance where the producer's musical intentions are coded, and the listener's reception is passive. Importantly, Shepherd and Wicke's theory accounts for the agency of the audience in the emergence of new cultural forms, aptly described here by Marcus (1989, 39):

> This was music that refused its own name, which meant it also refused its history—from this moment, no one knew what rock 'n' roll was, and so almost anything became possible, or impossible, as rock 'n' roll: random noise was rock 'n' roll, and the Beatles were not. . . . Punk immediately discredited the music that preceded it; punk denied the legitimacy of anyone who'd ever had a hit, or played as if he knew how to play. Destroying one tradition, punk revealed a new one.

According to Merleau-Ponty (2012, 20–23), the moment of experience is opaque to the degree that meaning is not inherent but latent in content as it awaits the subject's perceptive orientation, and eventually, conscious interpretation. On the one hand, operative intentionality characterizes the way in which objects are given to the subject, whereas on the other hand, the value of the object for the subject awaits perception before interpretation can occur. In the opacity of this evaluation, it is easy to assume that memory is projected onto experience in order to make sense of it; however conversely, memory is provoked by the physiognomy of the givens in order to complete the perception. In other words, memory is constantly challenged or entrenched by the imposition of new perceptions, given by the body's limited freedom to disengage from the world. The recollections discussed above have about them an ambiguity that suggests a refraction of experience itself. Whether described immediately after the event or, as is done here, decades later, narrative would have conveyed an ambiguity due to the problem of reduction that occurs through evaluation or translation. Shepherd and Wicke's (1997) theory, parallel with Merleau-Ponty's phenomenology of perception, suggests that reduction is inevitable when the sense of sound is translated into spoken language, and produces a limited description of the referent. In retracing experience, however, a phenomenological epistemology accounts for the 'authenticity work' that is carried out here, in the relations between producers and consumers in the emergence, establishment and maintenance of punk. And yet, the loss of valuable information in translation can be frustrating for a scene's youth and bands alike, particularly as they become used to an 'authentic' punk sentiment such as anti-commerciality.

As The Clash's fans grew in number so did the demand for larger performance venues (Gilbert, 2004). However, increasing venue size risked altering the atmosphere that was unique to pubs, and which had already become essentialized by the early 1980s, threatening to compromise the connection between the band and their fans. On The Clash's 1981–1982 tours, their manager Bernie Rhodes would attempt to preserve this connection by refusing to book larger than medium-sized venues. According to Gilbert (2004, 295):

> Bond's International Casino had been picked to host eight performances by The Clash from 28 May to 3 June [1981]. It was a cavernous sometime disco on the neon sleaze-fringe of Times Square [New York City]. With a capacity of around 4,000, it seemed a perfect Clash venue: comparatively intimate but with character. Local promoters, however, didn't understand why The Clash didn't just play a couple of nights at Madison Square Garden like everyone else.

Gilbert's account reveals a site where the authenticating work of punk was played out. The Clash used Bond's Casino as it worked to maintain an already objectivized punk, including the feel of intimacy with character that would otherwise be challenged had the band performed in an arena or stadium, where the perceived distance between band and fan is amplified.

The medium-sized venue enabled greater emotional connection than fans might otherwise experience in the expansiveness of an arena like Madison Square Garden,[4] and increased the chances of spontaneity. The gritty neighbourhood in which Bond's was located extends punk beyond the walls of the concert venue, and suggests that experience is stylized so as to claim 'street cred' and promote an 'authentic' punk experience. The subject body's orientation toward the concert allowed for the perception of space, or spatiality, and thus depending on his or her presence, differentiation in the experience of that space. Merleau-Ponty (2012, 264) states:

> Each level in which we live in turn appears when we drop anchor in some 'milieu' that is offered to us. This milieu is itself only defined spatially for a previously given level. Thus, each of our experiences in sequence, back to and including the first, passes forward an already acquired spatiality. Our first perception in turn could only have been spatial by referring itself to an orientation that preceded it.

I take this to mean here that the experience of The Clash in concert operates as a site in which the world of perception is not easily generalizable, particularly intersubjectively between embodied beings. In fact, the biographical accounts discussed above suggest that punk fans, in collaboration with The Clash, actively constructed the 'authentic' concert experience. Distinctively, The Clash's style of band–crowd participatory performances operated to level hierarchal differences between band and fan, attracting the popular and critical legitimization of punk. According to Merleau-Ponty, intersubjective signification occurs because of the body's orientation to others and the human world. Indeed, the subject's orientation toward the social world is not only to perceive objects as imbued with content, but also to perceive others as inhabited objects among uninhabited objects. On the one hand, the subject brings to existence his or her idealized history of experiences, ambiguously composed of moments which are reflected upon long after the subject has experienced them, and yet which are projected into a rationalized future. On the other hand, the subject's sense of history is made precarious because of an incessant presentation of new experiences. Thus, the presentation of new experiences works to challenge the subject's stasis, creating a habitus[5] whereby being-in-the-world becomes meaningful.

Of course, inhabited objects are perceived differently from those that are uninhabited. According to Merleau-Ponty (ibid., 364), the first cultural object, and the one whereby all other objects exist, is the embodied other. The subject's possession of a body distinctively allows for the external signification of expression and the recognition of such expression in others. And yet, it is not simply that subjects inherently constitute the world (consciousness), because that would allow for the conscious knowing of a knowing self, others and the natural world. Rather, it is the opacity of being, or not being able to know the self-knowing, that allows for communication between subjects. According to Merleau-Ponty (ibid., 374), in visual, aural and/or tactile communication with others, objectivity is suddenly broken, and the subject becomes thrown into a newly constituting relation with the other. Interestingly, Shepherd and Wicke's (1997) cultural theory similarly posits that 'music' is semantic only at the level of secondary signification, after its objectification as such, and is not inconsistent with Merleau-Ponty's phenomenology. In the intersubjectivity of communicative free-space, fans amplify their experience of 'punk' through action that is later interpreted as casual violence, DIY and anarchy.

Punk, in its event-centered combination of sounds, movement and colour, evokes awareness in the fan who is simultaneously oriented by his or her body to perceive an expression. In other words, the possession of a body allows a spontaneous response in the audience. For instance, a subject's sense of colours is not dependent on their categorization; rather, categories result from the subject's ability to sense differentiation according to the ways in which they are given to the subject prior to conscious judgment. Similarly, words have a sense that precede their articulation, and which fulfill the word's meaning, as in the intention behind a word. Despite the subject's possession of a vernacular, it is unfulfilled without the attitude, or meaning, behind the words that condition them, and which allow expression. According to Merleau-Ponty (2012, 188),

> The operation of expression, when successful . . . makes the signification exist as a thing at the very heart of the text, it brings it to life in an organism of words, it installs this signification in the writer or the reader like a new sense organ, and it opens a new field or a new dimension to our experience.

Because Merleau-Ponty refuses to separate signification and expression (linked to perception), he allows for innovative play with object-subjects prior to their becoming meaningful signifiers and in ways that produce new subjectivities. In this final narrative analysis, uncertainty was afforded space in The Clash's naming themselves:

> The band were finally named by Paul after he'd noticed the world 'clash' cropping up several times in an edition of the *Evening Standard*. It seemed to suit who they were and what they were creating: a clash of personalities, a clash against reactionary values, a clashing, dissonant sound.
>
> (Gilbert, 2004, 95)

Thus, cultural innovation can occur 'accidentally' prior to its conscious articulation or objectivization. It is telling that The Clash were named after they were formed, after they *expressed* in sound, and also, that they incorporated the ambiguity of 'dissonant sound' into their identity.

THE HAUPTPUNKT

Punk is characterized by the liminal 'chaos' of experience. In experience, the unknown—rather the irrational aspects of perception—allows undetermined responses in performers and fans, and thus holds the promise of pleasant—and not so pleasant—accidents, innovation and creativity (Negus and Pickering, 2004). A study of music and youth culture must consider the link between sound and affect, and the context of experience and 'meaning,' but with the understanding that it is narratively constructed after the fact. Moreover, a study of music and youth culture must consider object-subjects as related intersubjectively; as collaborators in the constitution, that is, emergence, establishment and maintenance, of cultural forms such as punk, and their subcultures, scenes and genres. In chronicling the history of punk as narrated by its musicians, gatekeepers and audiences, and using Merleau-Ponty's phenomenology and R.A. Peterson's theory of "authenticity work," I have noted the ways in which 'punk' has been essentialized through the combination of claims of 'originality' of experience and the authenticity work that ensues. Phenomenology allows for a space and time of ambiguity between subject agents which in turn explains the emergence of cultural forms such as punk, and accounts for the difficulty in maintaining its 'authenticity.' Really, phenomenology problematizes the notion of authenticity as involving aspects of perception that exist in tension with rational consciousness.

In the case of early punk as it was performed by The Clash and their fans, subversion was prioritized but historically specific and relative to a more or less homogeneous mainstream 1970s Britain. Arguably, today's punk retains much of the same sentiment. This does not mean that cultural modes have reached a sort of equilibrium, but the stakes may have changed. Further research into today's cultural production may find that like early punk, bands perform concerts in which arrangements of sound and light, stage and audience, style and fashion, self and conduct, are manipulated in order to claim originality and attract the support of fans and critics, and political, economic and cultural capital. New technologies such as the Internet has likely affected cultural production and consumption as well. Nevertheless, as long as performers continue to reflexively produce aural, visual and tactile phenomena, and listeners continue to project significance upon such experiences, 'authenticity work' will remain a vestige of youth identity politics.

NOTES

1 The definition of culture is highly contested (cf. Tony Bennett, 2008). Throughout this chapter, I use culture in relation to punk so as to expand my frame of analysis to include shared values such as 'anti-commerciality,' which are often overlooked in strictly musicological studies. The concept 'subculture' and its development will be discussed below.

2 2014 is something of a monumental year for the CCCS, being the fiftieth anniversary of its establishment. Sadly, it also marks the passing of one of its seminal researchers and one time director, Stuart Hall.

3 In terms of exchange value within fields of cultural production (Bourdieu, 1984), or art worlds (Becker, 1982), originality increases the legitimacy of an art object, such as a recording or performance, by its differentiation from the mainstream, yet within the rules of the legitimated field of production, or in this case, genre.

4 Madison Square Garden is an arena located in New York City that has the capacity to host up to 20,000 concert fans. It is the regular home venue of the National Hockey League team, The Rangers, and National Basketball Association team, The Knicks.

5 Although Merleau-Ponty uses the term 'habitus' somewhat ambiguously as the conjuncture of consciousness and significations of the cultural world via the body (2012, 139), it is more commonly identified with the work of Pierre Bourdieu (1977) as the site in which agents come to objectivize the world through practice, a socially structured and structuring capacity. Although Bourdieu's concept of habitus helps to avoid essentialist conceptions of experience, it tends to overly determine experience through the knowledge brought to experience based on class-based education. Simply, Bourdieu's habitus would rather see 'innovation' as 'adaptation.'

BIBLIOGRAPHY

Adorno, Theodor W., and Max Horkheimer. "The Culture Industry: Enlightenment as Mass Deception," in *Dialectic of Enlightenment: Philosophical Fragments*. Edited by Gunzelin Schmid Noerr, 94–136. Stanford: Stanford University Press, 2002.

Althusser, Louis. "Ideology and Ideological State Apparatus (Notes towards an Investigation)," in *Lenin and Philosophy, and Other Essays*. Edited by Louis Althusser, 85–126. New York: Monthly Review Press, 2001.

Becker, Howard. *Outsiders: Studies in the Sociology of Deviance*. New York: The Free Press, 1963.

———. *Art Worlds*. Berkeley: University of California Press, 1982.

Bennett, Andy, and Keith Kahn-Harris (Eds.). *After Subculture: Critical Studies in Contemporary Youth Culture*. New York: Palgrave MacMillan, 2004.

Bennett, Tony. "Sociology and Culture," in *The Sage Handbook of Cultural Analysis*. Edited by Tony Bennett and John Frow, 86–107. Los Angeles: Sage, 2008.

Bourdieu, Pierre. *Outline of a Theory of Practice*. Cambridge: Cambridge University Press, 1977.

———. *Distinction: A Social Critique of the Judgment of Taste*. London: Routledge, 1984.

Bradford, Simon. *Sociology, Youth and Youth Work Practice*. New York: Palgrave MacMillan, 2012.

Clayton, Martin, Trevor Herbert and Richard Middleton (Eds.). *The Cultural Study of Music: A Critical Introduction*. 2nd ed. New York: Routledge, 2012.

Cohen, Albert K. *Delinquent Boys: The Culture of the Gang*. Glencoe: The Free Press, 1955.

FAN. *The Clash—Us Festival 1983-Rock the Casbah*. Youtube.Com, 2011. Accessed June 13, 2011. http://youtube.com/all_comments?v=i94vKnCKgX4.

Fox, Kathryn Joan. "Real Punks and Pretenders: The Social Organization of a Counterculture." *Journal of Contemporary Ethnography* 16, no. 3, 1987. 344–370.

Frith, Simon. *Sound Effects: Youth, Leisure, and the Politics of Rock 'n' Roll.* New York: Pantheon, 1981.

Frith, Simon, and Andrew Goodwin (Eds.). *On Record: Rock, Pop, and the Written Word.* New York: Routledge, 1990.

Gans, Herbert. *Popular Culture & High Culture: An Analysis and Evaluation of Taste.* 2nd ed. New York: Basic Books, 1999.

Gilbert, Pat. *Passion Is Fashion: The Real Story of the Clash.* London: Aurum Press, 2004.

Goffman, Erving. *The Presentation of Self in Everyday Life.* Garden City: Anchor Books, 1959.

Gramsci, Antonio. *Selections from the Prison Notebooks.* London: Lawrence and Wishart, 1971.

Grossberg, Lawrence. *Cultural Studies in the Future Tense.* Durham: Duke University Press, 2010.

Hebdige, Dick. *Subculture: The Meaning of Style.* London: Methuen, 1979.

Hesmondhalgh, David. "Subcultures, Scenes or Tribes? None of the Above." *Journal of Youth Studies* 8, no. 1, 2005. 21–40.

Hibbett, Ryan. "What Is Indie Rock?" *Popular Music and Society* 28, 2005. 55–77.

Hodkinson, Paul. *Goth: Identity, Style and Subculture.* New York: Berg, 2002.

Jefferson, Tony, and Stuart Hall (Eds.) *Resistance through Rituals: Youth Subcultures in Post-War Britain.* 2nd ed. London: Routledge, (1976) 2006.

Kahn-Harris, Keith. "Unspectacular Subculture? Transgression and Mundanity in the Global Extreme Metal Scene," in *After Subculture: Critical Studies in Contemporary Youth Culture.* Edited by Andy Bennett and Keith Kahn-Harris, 107–118. New York: Palgrave Macmillan, 2004.

———. *Extreme Metal: Music and Culture on the Edge.* New York: Berg, 2007.

Laing, Dave. *One Chord Wonders: Power and Meaning in Punk Rock.* Philadelphia: Open University Press, 1985.

Marcus, Greil. *Lipstick Traces: A Secret History of the Twentieth Century.* Cambridge: Harvard University Press, 1989.

———. *Ranters & Crowd Pleasers: Punk in Pop Music 1977–92.* Toronto: Doubleday, 1993.

Marcuse, Herbert. *One Dimensional Man.* Boston: Beacon Press, 1964.

McRobbie, Angela. "Settling Accounts with Subcultures: A Feminist Critique." *Screen Education* 34, 1980. 37–49.

Merleau-Ponty, Maurice. *Phenomenology of Perception.* Translated by Donald A. Landes. New York: Routledge, 2012.

Merton, Robert K. "Social Structure and Anomie." *American Sociological Review* 3, no. 5, 1938. 672–682.

———. *On Social Structure and Science.* Chicago: University of Chicago Press, 1957.

Moore, David. *The Lads in Action: Social Process in an Urban Youth Subculture.* Farnham: Ashgate, 1994.

Muggleton, David. *Inside Subculture: The Postmodern Meaning of Style.* New York: Berg, 2000.

Negus, Keith, and Michael Pickering. *Creativity, Communication and Cultural Value.* Thousand Oaks: Sage, 2004.

Palmer, Robert. *Rock and Roll: An Unruly History.* New York: Random House, 1995.

Peterson, Richard A. *Creating Country Music: Fabricating Authenticity.* Chicago: University of Chicago Press, 1997.

———. "In Search of Authenticity." *Journal of Management Studies* 42, 2005. 1083–1098.

Peterson, Richard A., and Roger M. Kern. "Changing High Brow Taste: From Snob to Omnivore." *American Sociological Review* 61, no. 5, 1996. 900–907.

Shepherd, John, and Peter Wicke. *Music and Cultural Theory*. Malden: Polity Press, 1997.

Smith, Paul (Ed.). *The Renewal of Cultural Studies*. Philadelphia: Temple University Press, 2011.

Straw, Will. "Systems of Articulation, Logics of Change: Scenes and Communities." *Cultural Studies* 5, no. 3, 1991. 361–375.

Temple, Julien (Director). *Joe Strummer: The Future is Unwritten*. Documentary Film. Parallel Film Productions, 2007.

Widdicombe, Sue, and Rob Wooffitt. " 'Being' Versus 'Doing' Punk: On Achieving Authenticity as a Member." *Journal of Language and Social Psychology* 9, no. 4, 1990. 257–277.

Williams, Raymond. *The Long Revolution*. Harmondsworth: Penguin, 1961.

———. "Structures of Feeling," in *Marxism and Literature*. Edited by Raymond Williams, 128–135. Oxford: Oxford University Press, 1977.

12 Against All Odds

Making Underground Music in Iran

Daniel Ahadi

> The vision and idea that people in Europe and America have about Iran is not very realistic in relation to what is Iran and such vision does not allow them to think of a possibility that there is "trip-hop" culture in Iran. Knowing such things shocks them.
>
> —Lily, a female Iranian underground musician

There is a saying in Persian that sums up the following encounter I had with a group of young Iranians at a house party during a visit to Iran in 2004. The saying goes, *"Gar khahi nashavi rosva, hamrang-e jama-at sho"* ("If you don't want to get exposed, become one with the crowd"). A group of fifteen young students, about twenty years old, were sitting around a coffee table in a middle-class home in one of Tehran's suburbs. Discussion topics were diverse but primarily pertained to three topics (with some overlap): the arts, psychology and Italian culture and language.[1] I recall a lively debate on the merits of Jungian and Freudian psychoanalytical approaches over Russian vodka, Turkish beer and an eclectic French-inspired dinner menu. Adding flare to a rather surreal experience was the selection of *Buddha Bar* CDs that were playing in the background. Perhaps 'Bohemian' would best describe not only the interior decoration of the house, but also the mood of the evening. As I was sitting in a corner, feeling quite out of touch with the crowd and their conversations, I kept thinking to myself: "We are in The Islamic Republic of Iran, and yet there is nothing 'Islamic,' nor 'Iranian' about this experience." Perhaps as a nostalgia-stricken expat, who was visiting his country after many years, I was looking for a more authentic 'Iranian' experience. Towards the end of the night one of the girls walked over to the CD player, asked for everyone's attention, turned to the hosts and in an extremely apologetic manner asked whether she could change the music. She had brought a CD with Iranian dance music produced in Los Angeles. Her way of asking was quite interesting; it was as if there was something shameful about asking to play an Iranian pop song (as I will explain in this chapter, Iranian pop music produced in Los Angeles is regarded by many young people, including artists and musicians in Iran, as lowbrow music with substandard production value). Whereas the hosts graciously agreed to the change of music, the rest of the group did not respond favourably to the girl's request. Nevertheless, the CD was changed, the dance music played and, to my astonishment, one by one people started to move to the tune. On our way back, my cousin and I shared a ride with the girl who had asked to change the CD. I asked her why she was so ashamed to change the music? She smiled and responded: *"Gar khahi nashavi rosva, hamrang-e jama-at sho."* She went on explaining that most of the people at the party enjoy Iranian music, food and culture. But the version of 'Iranianness' that had been forced on youth in Iran—either by the regime, their parents, or the diasporic network (through satellite television)—was inconsistent with their needs and reality of life. She explained that what I had witnessed tonight at the party was not a complete capitulation to Western culture, and they were not being pretentious. It was a glimpse into a very typical urban youth culture that is trying to reject the identities that are imposed on them by their parents and the regime. If you want to survive and maintain your networks in this environment, she explained, you better embrace their ragout, intellectual debates about psychoanalysis, their Western music and all the other things that come with it; otherwise you will be shunned and labeled as an *ommol* (a yokel).

This experience has remained one of the singular experiences during my visit to Iran. Since then, I have retold the story numerous times in conversations I have had with friends and colleagues about Iranian culture and society. The focus of this book, and this chapter, brought back memories of my experience in Tehran and challenged me to think critically about that night's encounter—specifically around the issues of youth culture and identities, and how these condition and are conditioned by Iranian underground music. With this experience as my guiding torch, I will examine a number of questions in this chapter: What defines Iranian underground music? How significant are politics, culture, class, gender and technology in defining underground music in Iran? What are some of the challenges that the artists face? How has the underground music scene developed during the last three decades and where is it headed?

In the first section I will give a brief historical background of the political landscape in Iran and its immense impact on culture, including the music scene in the country. In the second section I lay the theoretical foundation to develop a framework for my analysis of the underground music scene in Iran. The third section—the overview of Iranian youths' engagement with underground music—draws on three semi-structured interviews (Aspers, 2009) conducted during the summer of 2010. The participants had all been involved with the so-called underground music scene in Iran for 5–10 years. Above all, I rely on a phenomenological approach to examine their situated experience as underground musicians in a country that is governed by a regime heavily invested in denying the very existence of such cultures.

BACKGROUND

Coverage of Iran and Iranians in Western media, particularly the news media, has been overwhelmingly negative since 1979. The Iranian Islamic Revolution *(Enghelab-e Eslami-e Iran),* the American hostage crisis, the war with Iraq, Iran's alleged terrorist activities and assassination of Iranian political dissidents in Europe, North America and other parts of the world, its support for Hamas in Palestine and Hezbollah in Lebanon, and its government's nuclear ambitions have contributed to a portrayal of Iran as the grand enemy to the West and its liberal democratic principles. Subsequently, media reporting on these event and trends shapes the discourse that dominates the Western imagination of Iranians. Words such as 'fundamentalists,' 'radicals' and 'jihadists' appear frequently in association with Iran and Iranians in Western media. The anti-American and anti-Israeli rhetoric of the Iranian regime have only added fuel to the fire. As a consequence, the Iranian people have come to be judged internationally by the conduct, beliefs and rhetoric of their regime. In 2009 the widely covered protests in the aftermath of the June 19 Iranian presidential election started to change the decades-old image that the West had of Iranians as backward, anti-modern and fundamentalist people. In the days that followed the allegedly rigged re-election of President Mahmoud Ahmadinejad, hundreds of thousands of Iranians took to the streets to demand a recount of the votes. After the government's refusal, the tone and focus of the protests changed to target the regime and the Supreme Leader, Ayatollah Seyed Ali Khamenei. The regime decided to ban all foreign journalists and began a brutal crackdown on the protesters and the opposition movement. Despite the banning of foreign journalists, images from street protests and conflicts were captured by ordinary people equipped with cellphones and cameras and soon went viral on the Internet and global news networks. During those days, a common reaction that I encountered from my non-Iranian friends and colleagues was their surprise over the level of dissatisfaction among Iranians towards their regime. They were also stunned by the fact that so many people had cellphones in Iran and that they were so up-to-date with technology.

What had gone missing from Western news reporting during the past three decades was the fact that Iran, despite its regime's anti-Western and anti-modern rhetoric, had invested significantly in building a communication infrastructure that had resulted in 20 million Internet subscriptions (compared to a population of 70 million), 11 million bloggers (one of the highest in the world) and 40 million cellphone users (Dutta and Mia, 2011). Since the mid-1990s, Iranians have been well connected to the rest of the world through satellite television, and despite heavy censorship, Iranians have continued to find ways to use the Internet to connect to the rest of the world. Also, the privatization of the Iranian post-secondary educational system meant that thousands of universities were built across the country, including rural areas, to cater to an ever-growing educational demand from the 'under

25-year-old' generation that by the mid-1990s came to constitute more than 65% of the population (one of the youngest populations in the world).

Demands for the liberalization of society grew as the country became increasingly technologically advanced, educated and open to the rest of the world. This culminated in the creation of the Reform Movement *(Jombesh-e Eslah Talab)* in the mid-1990s, with President Mohammad Khatami as its leader. Whereas the political domain remained relatively closed and monitored, the sector that benefited most from the moderate policies of this movement was the cultural sector. Media, especially newspaper and magazine publications, flourished (the broadcast sector remained, and still remains, state controlled), whereas the movie industry gained an international reputation with films competing at prestigious festivals such as Cannes, Berlin and Venice. But the cultural domain that probably benefited most was the music sector. Since the 1979 Cultural Revolution *(Enghelab-e Farhangi)*, all musical instruments that originated from the Western musical tradition (guitar, piano, percussion, etc.) were banned in public and private spheres. Only classical Iranian musical instruments such as *tar*, *se-tar*, and *santoor* were allowed and music stores only sold Iranian classical music albums *(musighi-e sonnati)*. Getting caught with banned instruments and music tapes or CDs could (and still can) result in severe punishments and fines. However, reforms of the 1990s radically shifted the Iranian music scene. With the lifting of the ban on instruments, pop music artists were allowed to apply for licenses to produce and distribute music, give public performances, and travel abroad for tours. The combination of a growing youth population, the aspirations of a politically and economically privileged class for economic gains, and advancement in communication and information technologies revived a sector in Iranian culture that had been suppressed and heavily censored for more than fifteen years. With the growth of the Iranian music industry, bands and individuals who were not granted license by the Ministry of Culture and Islamic Guidance (*Vezarat-e Farhang va Ershad-e Eslami;* henceforth referred to as Ministry of Culture in this chapter) to operate still had access to the technology and the instruments to produce their own underground music. By the early 2000s, Iranian underground music *(Musighi-e Zirzamini)*—mostly being produced in house basements in middle- or upper-class neighbourhoods—had become a cultural phenomenon.

MUSIC SCENES AND THE SITUATED EXPERIENCE OF EVERYDAY LIFE

Central to the discussion of underground music in Iran is the role that this cultural practice plays in society. As a cultural expression that defies the regime's codes of Islamic guidance, underground music is not only considered discursively as counter-mainstream, it is also illegal. 'Underground' as a cultural phenomenon in the West can be understood as a trend or practice that counters mainstream cultures and defies conventional and accepted cultural practices. Under the tenets of liberal democracy and freedom of expression legislations, these cultural practices are rarely regarded as illegal or morally corrupt, and often are in fact encouraged as part of the expansion and specialization of markets. In Iran, however, underground cultural practices are considered illegal and thus punishable. Given this context of strict top-down regulatory forces that governs much of Iran's cultural and political sector, it becomes tempting to read the Iranian underground music scene using the categories of subculture theory, with its emphasis on resistance. Against this, I will argue that a reliance on subculture theory limits one's ability to understand the complex nature of the Iranian underground music scene. Guided by my interviews, as well as existing literature on postmodern and phenomenological approaches to cultural practices, I argue that underground music in Iran cannot be reduced to a tool for political resistance, because it is also a cultural practice tied to everyday life.

This interplay between politics and culture is an appropriate point of departure to understand the underground music scene in Iran. Revisionist approaches to political and civic engagement have rejected definitions of 'the political' as something reserved for those actively engaged in politics (as voters or members of the political establishment), activism and debates. But, civic engagement and political expressions can take form in alternative spheres of life. According to Dahlgren (2006, 281),

> When we turn our attention to the public sphere, the traditional blinders about private domains—in which people's experience and various cultural practices can have relevance for their civic competence—hamper our understanding. Moreover, the at-times restrictive view of what ideally should take place in the public sphere, namely deliberative democracy, further narrows our field of vision in regard to civic agency and interaction.

According to Dahlgren, parallel to 'official' political resistance in the public realm—political rallies, student protests, and civil disobedience, etc.—alternative communicative practices need to form, and often do. These practices have the potential to disrupt political consensus and institutional authority across societies. Culture and cultural practices can then be viewed as spheres for civic literacy and engagement. This is particularly true in the case of Iran and its youth. Because of its restrictive political structure, including the banning of political parties, politically disenfranchised Iranian youth have found different outlets for expressing their discontent with the regime. The underground music scene is one of these outlets through which youth channel their frustration amidst the immense pressures of contemporary times.

Thinking of youth cultures in terms of subcultures is firmly grounded in structuralism and grand narratives about resistance to dominance and class warfare. But since the 1980s, developments in these debates have moved thinking away from such mechanistic models (Huq, 2006, 23). One of the fallacies of the subculture approach is the overwhelming sense that young people are somehow the living embodiments of the subculture they come to represent (Nayak, 2003). Their subjectivities are revealed as sociological types such as the football hooligan, the anarchic punk, or the ecstasy-fuelled raver. Nayak argues that such categorizations of youth identities become problematic when they reduce young lives to "the atomised essences of an imagined authenticity" (ibid., 18). In fact Nayak argues that youth formations are organized as much through commercial enterprise as in 'resistance' to the capitalist economy.

Similarly in Iran's case, the subcultural scene cannot be understood simply as a struggle of working class youth for a greater role in society. In fact, the Iranian underground music scene is almost exclusively a bourgeois project. Middle-class youth have the money to spend on music instruments, software and locale. This in fact is a class struggle in reverse: It is the urban middle- and upper-middle class that has declared war on the segments of the Iranian population that can be categorized (although somewhat sweepingly) as religious working class and the rural population.[2] Since the Islamic Revolution of 1979 the regime sought to promote certain aspects of national identity based on Islamic traditions. It sought support for this type of nation-building among the segments of the population who were excluded from the modernizing projects of the Shah in the 1970s. These were the religious working class who lived in less affluent parts of urban areas and the rural population.

In today's Iran, 'positive consumerism' has offered an opportunity for urban middle-class youth to break away from government-imposed religion-based identities. Despite government restrictions, the consumption of foreign goods has recently accelerated among young Iranians, who comprise nearly 65% of the country's seventy million population (Jafari, 2006). Historically, the decade after the 1979 revolution was characterized by an anti-Western public discourse which rejected 'all things Western' including Western goods, media and political interference. A popular slogan from that era was "Neither East, nor West, [only] the Islamic Republic." The election of the moderate President Mohammad Khatami in the mid-1990s resulted in a thaw in Iran's relations with the international community and the Iranian diaspora network. These developments, together with the emergence of cosmopolitan youth cultures, and of course the Internet, have all served to link Iranian youth to transnational cultural networks. Based on cosmopolitan ideals, Iranian youth have come to reject the heavy-handed Islamic nationalist ideologies of the Iranian regime (Nooshin, 2008).

It is in this sense that artists are projecting a different kind of national identity which reflects a growing secularism and cosmopolitanism among young people and which draws on very different signifiers (including references to Iran's pre-Islamic heritage) through music (ibid., 77). According to Nooshin, many musicians are deliberately forefronting stylistic diversity in order to transcend national boundaries, to engage in cultural dialogue and to force a debate about Iran's relationship with the outside world, particularly the West. In doing so they engage in an ongoing process of contestation over national identity, while broadening the social sphere associated with an emergent youth consciousness and civic infrastructure (ibid., 77).

Despite the forces of cosmopolitanism and globalization, including the global flow of cultural products such as music, videos and fashion through the Internet and satellite television, the music culture of Iran needs to be analyzed from a place-specific perspective. So far throughout this chapter I have resisted using the words 'industry' or 'community' when referring to underground music in Iran. Instead I have used the word 'scene.' The main source for the widespread use of the concept in cultural studies is Will Straw's influential article from 1991 on music communities and music scenes. In his essay, Straw (1991, 373) describes the music scene as a cultural space in which "a range of musical practices coexist, interacting with each other within a variety of processes of differentiation, and according to widely varying trajectories of change and cross-fertilisation." This definition is distinct from older notions of a musical community or genre, which presumes a population group whose composition is relatively stable. Drawing on the works of cultural geographers and Will Straw (1991), I argue that local processes are dependent on a vast complexity of interconnections.

Straw's notion of the 'scene' provides a useful conceptual tool to tackle Iranian underground music for a number of reasons. First, as Straw notes, the concept of scene "is efficient as a default label for cultural unities whose precise boundaries are invisible and elastic" (Straw, 2001, 248), very much like the Iranian underground music. Second, the term has an anti-essentializing effect with the capacity to disengage cultural phenomena from the more "fixed and theoretically troubled unities of class and sub-culture" (ibid.). Instead, scholars of music culture are encouraged to examine their subject of inquiry by focusing on the ways in which the relationship of different local spaces of activity takes the form of circuits "overlaid upon each other, through which particular styles of alternative music circulates in the form of recordings or live performances" (Straw, 1991, 378). Third, Straw's (ibid., 379) model for analyzing cultural practices suggests a focus on both the local (micro) and the global (macro) as sites for interaction and exchange:

> The ability of groups and records to circulate from one local scene to another, in a manner that requires little in the way of adaptation to local circumstances, is an index of the way in which a particularly stable set of musical languages and relationships between them has been reproduced within a variety of local circumstances.

Whereas the underground music scene in Iran can be regarded as a hyper-local cultural expression, limited usually to middle- and upper-class neighbourhoods in Tehran and other large cities of Iran, one should consider that it is also influenced by global flows of culture and disseminated to and influenced by a sizable diasporic network of more than three million Iranians.

Straw's approach is also phenomenological in ways that are helpful. Focusing on situated and contextual knowledge, and distancing from 'grand narratives' as a tool for sense-making of cultural phenomena and everyday life, are elements that characterize this phenomenological approach. But what counts as phenomenology?

The introductory chapter of this volume has outlined the details of such an approach. For the purpose of this particular study, essentially, a researcher subscribing to a phenomenological approach is interested in exploring participants' personal lived experiences and, at least initially, refrains from importing external frameworks for analysis and sense-making (Aspers, 2009; Finlay, 2009; Smith, 2004). This approach is a departure from a set analytical framework to allow for a more meaningful understanding of what Hannah Arendt calls the "space of appearances" (as quoted in Dillabough and Kennelly, 2010, 36). In Dillabough and Kennelly's work the phenomenological approach is used to untangle the symbolic meanings of hidden and often unrecognizable rituals and articulations of youth culture in urban areas. It is imperative for the phenomenological project to look beyond the direct or apparent meanings of events and practices to interpret the symbolic meanings expressed through youth culture. What these spatially situated and symbolic practices tell us is something about young people's place in the social order—such as new social class arrangements and urban rearrangement (ibid.).

Subsequently, in this research, the broader field of inquiry is a kind of "everyday communicative space" (Aksoy and Robins, 2003, 377), within which music makers are engaged in what Sanjay Asthana (2010) calls an "agonistic public space" (see also Chapter 2, this volume). Participation here implies a form of conflictual engagement, where collaboration and human interaction are driven by complex and often diverse realities rather than romantic notions of common ground and commonality of interest (ibid., 24).

In the section that follows, relying on my interviews, I will try to answer some broad questions pertaining to the underground music scene in Iran: How can we understand the role of underground music in Iranian society? What are some of the factors that have influenced the underground music scene in Iran in the past three decades? What problems are artists faced with? Whereas opinions are diverse, the conversations seem to suggest that the underground music scene in Iran provides an alternative space for youth to express themselves on social and political issues, without being overly focused on social resistance or political change. This space however is defined by class and geography as the majority of the stakeholders are middle class and urban. For this group of people this space serves as a therapeutic one in a society culturally and structurally coded to exclude youth from decision-making processes, both in the private and public domains. For the audience, as described by the interviewees, the type of music that is produced speaks to the very heart of the struggles and hardships that the people of Iran have endured economically, culturally and politically in the past three decades.

IRAN'S UNDERGROUND MUSIC SCENE—THE SOCIO-HISTORICAL CONTEXT

The concept of social exclusion has been used mostly in the European context to describe "the multiple dimensions of the lack of access to the means to produce individual welfare, education, jobs and income" (Salehi-Isfahani and Egel, 2007, 8). In the Iranian context, youth have become a major force on the social and political scenes and arguably served as a catalyst for the gathering strength of the Reform Movement of the 1990s and the landslide election victory of the reformist president Mohammad Khatami in 1997. But as Bayat (2010, 356) argues in the case of the Middle East, "Youth more often than not are treated as objects rather than as agents of development." In other words, youth in Iran and elsewhere in the Middle East are a tremendous force where numbers are concerned in election times. But historically the socio-political fabric of Iran, characterized by a patriarchal system, has excluded both youth and women from participating as active and autonomous agents in the public domain (Khosravi, 2008). In the pre-Revolution era (1960s and 1970s in particular), youth were active in political movements influenced by grand narratives such as Communism, Republicanism (as the opposite to Monarchism) and Islamism. In today's Iran, youth are more interested in individual freedom than political freedom (Khosravi, 2008, 128). From a sociological perspective, this can be attributed to a decline in associational life in Iran. During and in the years following the 1979 Revolution, there was a surge in the number of civil society associations, such as political parties, unions and cultural organizations. But less than two years after the Revolution, all political parties were banned and organizational life became severely restricted and monitored. Many union and political leaders were either imprisoned or executed. This drastic move by the regime severely wounded the spirit of organizational life in Iran and as a consequence cultivated a more individualistic culture among people (Emami, 2003).

This reference to 'individual agency' was brought up during my interviews with underground musicians. Amir,[3] a rock musician in his early twenties, says:

> Children and youth in Iran have very little to say when it comes to *anything*. From an early age we are brought up in a culture that has a tremendous respect for the authority of people older than us. Every decision is made by the parents without any consultation from the

> children in the family. This mentality or way of living is transferred to the outside world where young people are under tremendous pressure to conform to the Islamic norms of society.

Part of the problem underlying these sentiments is the cultural fixity of the patriarchal model that has prevented youth from taking part in the decision-making processes in meaningful ways. Amir argues that this lack of a "culture of democracy" *(farhang-e democracy)* has crippled the Iranian political system for decades.

> We [the people of Iran, as opposed to the political establishment] are in a way responsible for the political atmosphere in the country. We like to think that we are democratically minded individuals and that our country has been hijacked by an Islamic theocratic system. Maybe some of us are more open-minded than others. At least among the younger generation. But here is the thing: generally speaking we have very little tolerance for diversity of thought. And I'm not just talking about the regime and its strict Islamic laws. I think the people are also very narrow minded in terms of their values.

Working in the cultural sector in Iran as a singer, musician, songwriter and other related professions is extremely difficult. Whereas there is no law banning the various types of music that gets produced *privately* in Iran, the finished product has to be sent to the Ministry of Culture for final approval. Very few end up with official authorization and remain underground. The process of being accepted as a musician does not entirely depend on the official authorities. Social acceptance also plays a significant role. Amir explains the constraints put on him and other musicians both from the authorities and society in general:

> For example, on one hand we as musicians in Iran have to deal with the strict laws of the government when it comes to licensing and recording permissions. On the other hand, there is very little support or understanding of what we do as musicians from family and friends. Especially family members. There is a huge gap between what I experience as "home" and "nation" than say the rest of my family members or my neighbours. You spend your time, energy and money to put together a band, find a place to rehearse, and maybe if you are lucky, record a few songs and then what? No chance to get a permit to perform or release your songs.

He goes on to explain that the reason for alternative or underground music not being accepted in the Iranian society has to do with the restrictions put on them by government authorities. He believes that if they could perform and produce music freely then the Iranian society would be more accepting of their music. Elaborating on the music scene in Iran, Omid, another male Iranian underground musician, lists three different categories of Iranian music:

> From my point of view, we have three different types of Iranian music. One of them is the state sponsored music that is produced, recorded, and performed all in Iran. That is one big circle and if you are not inside that circle, you cannot get licensed; you cannot get any sort of permission to record or perform and your requests would get rejected. Hence your lyrics and your music have to be approved from the Ministry of Culture before you can publish. Even if you do get permission but you do not have connections inside the circles inside Iran, you would not be able to market it as well as other bands can. It won't be played on the national radio. That is one type of music. The second type is the Los Angeles music [produced by Iranian artists in Los Angeles]. They operate largely by the same rules that companies have to approve their music and lyrics, and so forth. There is just more freedom to be more sexier and cheesier. The third type is the underground music scene that is independent from both of these circles.

What is evident from Amir's and Omid's comments is that underground music producers in Iran are battling fights on two fronts: a fight against the government for more freedom of expression and a fight for social acceptance. The interplay between official and societal opposition to underground music has left artists like Amir and Omid in a space of liminality (Nooshin, 2008, 72)—a space of in-betweenness where musicians are pushed, rather reluctantly, to operate underground. In other words, labels like 'underground' or 'alternative' are for some artists involuntary labels. If they had the chance, they would rather operate 'overground.' Amir continues:

> I don't think there is anything alternative with the type of music that I produce. If I were living in Europe or the USA, this type of music would be considered mainstream. I don't even focus on politics or social issues in my music. What is left for me are two options: to remain independent as a musician and continue to operate underground, or to give up control over my music and lyrics in order to get government permission. Especially lyrics, because that's what the Cultural Ministry is mostly concerned about. I think this is the case for many bands. They are not alternative or radical or anything of that sort. But they are forced to operate under circumstances that *make* them underground. This is my opinion, and perhaps people out there will disagree with me.

The state censorship that Amir talks about in his interview can be traced back to the Pahlavi era (1925–1979). For over a century the governing authorities in Iran have relied on strict censorship laws to control the political environment of the country. Whereas these censorship laws, in a pre-Revolution Iran, were mainly focused on the political sphere, after the revolution, in an attempt to Islamicize the society, the government expanded the Pahlavi era's censorship policies to include cultural productions of various sorts. According to Article 4 of Iran's current Constitution, all civil, penal, financial, economic, administrative, cultural, military, political and other laws and regulations must be based on Islamic criteria (Rastovac, 2009). As for the role of music in society, the Iranian Supreme Leader Ayatollah Khomeini declared in 1980 that "music is like a drug, whoever acquires the habit can no longer devote himself to important activities. It changes people to the point of yielding them to vice or preoccupations pertaining to the world of music alone. We must eliminate music because it means betraying our country and our youth. We must completely eliminate it" (Youssefzadeh, 2004, 38). Whereas such rhetoric might have been popular in the early years of the Revolution as a measure to fight Westernization, its popularity diminished as the new regime failed to deliver on some of its key promises of Islamic justice and equality. Meanwhile, the emergence of new information technologies has made it increasingly difficult for the regime to control people's media consumption and cultural habits. One of the key changes in the cultural sector was brought about by satellite technology, which enabled television programs produced by Iranians abroad, mainly in Los Angeles, to broadcast to audiences in Iran.

The 'Los Angeles Effect'

By the 1990s Los Angeles had become the hub of the Iranian cultural scene outside of the country. Current estimates suggest that there are about one million Iranians living in Southern California, most of whom immigrated to the United States in the aftermath of the Islamic Revolution in 1979. A vast majority of Iranian entertainers and media personalities settled in the Los Angeles region as well. In the early years of settlement, these groups set up local television programs to cater to the growing number of Iranians in California. With the introduction of satellite technology in Iran in the mid-1990s it became possible for L.A. satellite stations to broadcast directly into Iran. As a consequence, the Iranian government acted swiftly and banned private ownership of satellite dishes. But in the age of globalization this battle proved to be impossible to win for the government. What was once a strictly controlled mediascape was now overtaken by television shows produced by anti-regime expats in the United States. The exact number of satellite ownership in Iran is not known. But according to conservative estimates, 40–50% of the population owns a satellite receiver (Sohrabi-Haghighat, 2011). On one hand these diasporic television programs functioned as a window to the outside world for Iranians. On the other hand, these television channels, mainly managed by entertainers from the Shah's era who by now were in their fifties and sixties, were reproducing an image of Iranian culture and nationhood that was unfamiliar to the generation born after the revolution. In his book *The Making of Exile Cultures,* Hamid Naficy (1993) makes reference to this as the "fetishization of television" by the expat Iranians in Los Angeles. He writes, "Fetishization in exile results when the exiles invest heavily in constructing certain cathexted images of homeland and the past while knowing deep down that those are forms of disavowal, or of partial representation, because they are fixed and frozen" (ibid., 127). The sense of nostalgia that the Iranian diasporic media projected was most profoundly displayed in the Iranian music and music videos that were produced in Los Angeles and showcased on Iranian satellite television (see ibid., 147–162 for a discussion of Iranian music in Los Angeles). The symbolic construction of a lost homeland in the Los Angeles music scene, found in lyrics, melody, composition and music videos, was something that had dominated the Iranian music scene since the revolution. But by the turn of the century and the coming of age of a new generation of Iranians, these references to nostalgia had little relevance for young Iranians who had not experienced the pre-Revolution life. References to homeland in the nostalgia-stricken satellite programs were far from the reality experienced by the youth in Iran. Amir's views on this are quite interesting:

> When you watch these satellite televisions it is as if the revolution never happened; as if there hasn't been a generational shift; as if the past 30 years has not taken place. It's as if time has stood still for Iranians in Los Angeles.

This sentiment is mirrored in Omid's comments on the influence of 'Los Angeles music' *(musighi-e los angelesi)*:[4]

> The main players in the Los Angeles music scene were these pre-historic record companies that were pioneers in their own right. These companies have not been able to adapt to the time change, with the pace that technology is changing. Hence, they are behind the so-called digital distribution of music and business models like i-Tunes, Rhapsody, and Napster. The way these companies make money is by buying the rights to the artist's album and selling CDs of the artist through their distribution channels. At the same time, the artist would make money by playing music on tours. They operate as a gang. Like a music mafia, who are trying to monopolise the scene. And these are the ones destroying and lowering the quality of music, with productions that are cheesy dance music, have low standards, have no message, no thought process behind it. Nothing but pure entertainment.
>
> The popularity of underground music is not because of its illegal status in Iran. I think it was because it was driven by grassroots support and people who were fed-up with this cheesy Los Angeles music. They wanted something with a substance and message and that is the reason they supported it.

Remarks like these signal a discontent among not only musicians but also youth in general with the path Iranian music had taken since the 1979 Revolution. Omid's concern is that many underground musicians are being transformed into mainstream musicians because of financial and political pressure. On the one hand, young underground musicians would like to remain independent. On the other hand, the desire to make a living from your work of art forces many musicians to compromise and give in not only to government pressure but also to market and audience pressure. The comment below from Omid is typical of the way underground musicians talk about bands and individuals who have left the underground music scene to become more 'overground':

> The underground music scene is really reliant on grassroots support. It is an independent movement. Now, you have bands like *127* that started as underground here in Iran but then I saw them one day playing on Voice of America's[5] Iranian program for the Persian new year. My point is, if you are being featured on a state sponsored television, and you are getting paid, I don't know if you still are underground.

Comments like these allude to a complex music scene that is constantly in the process of becoming. Any attempt to find a sense of cohesion in the Iranian underground music scene is misguided and based on a false notion of cultural homogeneity. Conflicts are common, but so are stories of cooperation and community building.

Conflicts and Cooperation

The segmentation of underground music in Iran runs along class lines. In other words, the type or genre of music people produce is linked to their socio-economic background. Amir explains that those involved in music, such as rock or heavy metal, that requires musical instruments tend to be from middle- or upper-class segments of society whereas those producing rap or hip-hop are from the working class. The reason is purely economic; the average cost of a musical instrument, Amir explains, could be up to two or three times the monthly salary of an average worker. This makes it very difficult for a young person to purchase music instruments and equipment. Amir recalls his first purchase of a music instrument, a blue electric guitar, as a real 'moment of crisis' in his family:

> My parents, like many other Iranian parents disapprove of me being involved in music. Most [Iranian] parents want their children to become doctors or engineers. So, to become an artist of any kind, especially a musician, brings dishonour to the family name. I purchased my first guitar when I was 17 or 18 with money I had borrowed from friends. You can imagine that my parents were not very happy when they found

> out. They told me that I had become a *motreb* [the word translates into 'singer,' but with a very negative connotation. The metaphorical equivalent in English would be to call someone a medieval 'fool' or 'jester,' or a street entertainer]. They forced me to re-sell my guitar. I sold it for far less than the purchasing price and this made my parents even more furious. They had to pay the difference so I could pay back the debt to my friends. I was grounded for weeks, with no allowance and my CD player was taken away. [He laughs.] The money was not important for me at that time. What was important was the fact that for the first time in my life I had purchased something that was mine and I no longer had to borrow music instruments from others.

The interesting aspect of Amir's story is the symbolic meaning that the guitar has for him and his parents. Whereas for Amir the guitar connotes 'independence' and 'artistic freedom,' for his parents it stands for 'moral corruption' and 'lack of prospects.' At the heart of this negotiation of symbolic meanings between the two generations rests a tangible problem: economic hardship. On one hand the inability to purchase music instruments by young Iranians has stifled many talented artists; at the same time, some have shown remarkable resilience and found ways to circumvent this problem by resorting to alternative forms of music production. Lily's comments below shed light on the socio-economic aspect of music production in Iran:

> Before, music was mostly amongst the upper class. I am not really a rich person and not from a rich family. The time when I started going to music school, most of my friends, beside one or two people, were rich and didn't have a worry in life. However, nowadays, music is more popular amongst other classes in society. Hence, the middle class is now more involved in the creation of music in the country. I can't talk on behalf of the lower class. We have a very large population who are amongst the middle-lower and lower class in the society and it is difficult for many to survive the basic needs of living. Hence, one cannot think of playing an instrument when he/she has to think how to survive. They resort to rap or hip-hop. I think music making is becoming more popular amongst the middle-class in our society. I actually like that because the more people playing music, the higher chance of making good music.

This division between the 'rap culture' and the 'rock culture' seems to be an area of conflict in the Iranian underground music scene. Omid and Lily both talked about hip-hop and rap music as a form of music with low production value. Whereas Omid focused on the cost and time that it takes to produce a hip-hop or rap album, Lily was predominantly concerned with the quality of this type of music:

Omid: Recently, in Iran, there has been a huge boom in rap and hip-hop. That kind of music is cheaper and easier to produce because you do not need to have real musicians in order to make music. This allowed musicians who could not afford expensive equipment like guitars, amplifiers, or drums to be attracted to this genre of music because it is more accessible and cheaper to produce. Moreover, the pioneers of this genre, like Hichkas, had political and social messages in their music. After a while, however, we saw that the message started to change inside the songs and became all about partying and who is hipper and cooler.

Lily: I don't consider rap musicians to be musicians. I believe they are mostly poets than musicians. The music that is playing behind the rapping *is* music. However, the singer merely recites a poem in a certain style. In Iran, beside a very few artists, most rap musicians do not have anything to say. Their poems do not have any substance. This being said, because the production of the music is easy, the content is very superficial, and young people can make themselves get noticed by releasing a song or two, many of the youth population in the country are gravitated towards this music. Simply, they get fame without much effort. I'm also a little frustrated about this matter because this rap music has reduced the taste of music amongst youth in Iran.

Clearly Omid and Lily in this segment of the interview frame themselves as middle class and take distance from rappers and the hip-hop artists. But alongside these instances of conflict there are stories of cooperation and community building. Lily talks about the network within which they work. She views the Iranian underground music scene as a kind of co-operative that is there to sustain the survival of the movement:

> Generally, the underground music community is very connected. Because of its small size, everybody knows everybody. There is always a mutual friend that you know. I have met many of the musicians who I have worked with through these types of connections. For instance, Sam, who I worked with on in [a band], was a friend of my friend who I met at a concert. There basically is a network and everyone is connected somehow. There have been many instances where musicians help each other in their bands. For example, if someone needs a bassist for a song, he is able to find one through friends and acquaintances. We basically are working in a co-operative community. So, everyone helps everyone.

Judging from comments made earlier by Lily and Omid on rap and hip-hop music, it seems like coalitions take shape around particular musical forms rather than the entire musical scene. This tendency, Straw (1991, 384) argues, is typical of a musical scene. He adds that these coalitions are not inevitably positive or disruptive but that they mirror particular social differences in society, notably those of gender, class and race. An interesting observation in the Iranian case study is that on the surface alliances are built around a particular musical form, such as rock or rap. But a closer look reveals that alliances are made along class divisions. Further, given that class is geographically defined and concentrated in urban areas, a division along class lines could also translate into a geographical demarcation of sites and territories. For example, in the case of Tehran, the middle class population is concentrated in the mountainous northern part of the city, whereas the majority of the working class population live in the southern and much older part of the city. The question is then can music blur or eradicate traditional social boundaries or is music reinforcing them to some degree? What seems to be the case is that the musical scene in itself is perhaps configured according to social boundaries and hierarchies; nonetheless, what breaks down these hierarchies and makes social relationships more asymmetrical are the tools used to distribute music, namely new information technologies.

Role of Technology

The 'trickle down effect' of technological revolution has in the past decade narrowed the digital divide between the global North and South. Countries in the global South that were once producers of consumer goods, including software and computers, or in Iran's case exporters of energy, are now serious contenders for consumer goods in the global arena. As mentioned earlier, Iranian youth have been particularly active in the blogosphere and with keeping up with new trends in mobile technology. For the underground music scene in Iran, new information technologies are vital on several fronts, not only for communication purposes within the community, but also for disseminating music. The most important impact of these new trends has been on the political economy of music production. Artists are no longer dependent on record companies in Los Angeles or in Iran to distribute their music. As Omid states:

> The underground music scene in Iran relies solely on the Internet and grassroots promotional tactics such as working with social media websites like Facebook and YouTube, and music distribution channels like CDBaby as a way of promoting and selling the music. In fact, with websites like these you really don't need a record label so long as you have the correct information and you are willing to spend several hours a day and promote yourself. From my experience, there is a lot of music out there. People do not want to buy them; they want to have the personal experience through them. They want to make a connection with the

> artists and his/her message. So, the whole business model of traditional labels is going to be extinct very soon.

Lily reaffirms Omid's idea about how the Internet changed the nature of underground music in Iran and adds:

> From one point onward, especially when the Internet was introduced to the country, the information channels were shifted. After the Internet, people had access to more information about different things including music. This also opened a new communications horizon for people to learn more about different genres of music.

Lily also talked about music literacy and the importance of the Internet in making the Iranian audience more musically literate:

> For instance, until 10 or 15 years ago, the idea of metal music amongst Iranian youth was limited to Metallica, Sepultra, and three or four other metal bands. However, nowadays, people have higher music literacy because they have access to a wider range of music of all times due to the access to the Internet. This has also led to a very noticeable change in the taste of music that different people have in Iran.

In her view, the Internet helped not only in music literacy, but also in shifting the music taste amongst Iranian audiences. This change in taste helped nurture a new set of musicians who play in different styles with influences from a variety of bands. In fact, Lily adds that when listening to a variety of genres from the contemporary underground music scene in Iran, one will find traces of Iranian classical music, Western rock and jazz in many of them.

A Labour of Love

Clearly technology has remedied some of the key problems faced by Iranian underground musicians in the areas of communication, production, distribution and music literacy. But it is not the answer to all the problems. Amir argues that there is a whole range of issues that technology cannot solve on its own. He points to the fact that Iranian music culture has been focusing too much on the content and less so on the infrastructure surrounding music production. Key players such as public relations persons and agents as well as important factors such as copyright laws have been ignored in the Iranian music industry. Lily gives an example of her band not being able to secure a visa to travel to the United States to participate in the South by South West (SXSW) music festival in Texas. Because the United States does not have an embassy in Iran, her band traveled to Dubai to apply for a visa at the American Embassy. After months of waiting they were denied a visitor's visa and had to withdraw from the festival. Lily says that the experience left the band demoralized and they decided to break up.

Generating income from producing music is also another area of concern for these artists. Perhaps the philosophy of an 'underground' cultural movement is incompatible with the desire for financial gains. Meanwhile, for many artists music production is a full-time occupation. In the Iranian case, much of the output is offered for free on various online fora for audiences to download and listen. The little money that bands generate is from underground performances. But even these private gatherings are raided by government officials and performances get cancelled. Amir shares his own thoughts on being a struggling underground musician in Iran:

> The kind of music that I have been attracted to and wanted to play is the music that has thought process and meaning behind it. It has a message and artistic standards and that's the kind of music that is hard to market and hard to make money out of. It's a labour of love. There is no real money, no income in it. I have always had a day job and that's how I pay the bills and the mortgage. Although I would like to make money out of it, it has never been that way. If you do not have connections, or commercial value to the people who are in charge, you are forced to just find you own small target audience, connect to them, and just be happy that you have a bunch of fans who listen to your music. But what drives us is the need to be able to express oneself freely. It is the desire of the freedom of expression through music, and art.

Underground music, more than anything, is a channel for artistic freedom. It is a strategy for youth to cope with the pressures put on them by a political and cultural system that seeks to manage both the public and the private aspects of life. This functions as a point of departure for many artists. But beyond this, it would be a misguided effort to try to find a common narrative among them. Lily explains that

> The situations people live in directly influence the type of music they produce. There are many problems in today's society in Iran. These problems range from political, to social, cultural and financial. For example, after what happened with the elections in Iran in 2009, almost 95% of underground music that was produced became political where the artists talked about the election and the movement after the election. This was amongst all genres including hip-hop and heavy metal where everyone were kind of angry. Before elections, however, to give you another example, most of the music that was produced was optimistic and hopeful. Now, if new changes take place, it will unconsciously influence the tone of music as well as the lyrics in the underground music of the country. Conceptually, everyone changes at the same time and with the same tone.

There is a saying in Persian that translates into, "Restrictions bring about innovation." This has certainly been the case for the Iranian cultural industry since the 1979 revolution. Artists from various sectors have found ways to cope and function *despite* being faced with monumental challenges such as social and political resistance and lack of access to rehearsal spaces and equipment. I would like to conclude this section with a comment from Omid that really sums up the importance of underground culture in Iran:

> We have an underground way of life in Iran. Everything is underground. We have underground literature that is published in blogs. We have underground fashion shows in Iran. We have underground arts in Iran. It is an underground culture and way of life. Also, Iranian people are very creative and they learn to adapt to their environment if they cannot change it. So, that is a way of adaptation and that is how this whole underground scene became bigger and bigger than before. The more restrictions we have on musicians, the more musicians will try to do everything independently and in their own way.

CONCLUSION

Against the backdrop of Will Straw's (1991) "scene theory," I have outlined above a number of forces that have conditioned the progression of Iranian underground music in the past thirty years. Scene thinking allows for a departure from deterministic frameworks of analysis that seek to understand cultural expressions as mainly political (subculture theory) or mainly economy driven (culture industry). Instead, using a phenomenological approach, I have relied on the situated experiences of three artists who live and work inside Iran. This approach enables us to analyze spatially situated practices, struggles and interactions of young Iranian musicians, taking into account the complexity of the lived experiences of individual participants to make sense of their scene of practice and understand how that scene comes into being. Furthermore, what make the Iranian underground music scene a true "space of appearance and performance" (Arendt, 2013, 198–199) are the socio-cultural and political conditions within which these actors operate. The social realities of a gender-segregated society and a government-controlled cultural landscape condition youth identities in interesting ways and prompts these actors to truly *perform* their multiple identities, and with that, negotiate moral codes and shift the boundaries between the public and the private, the legal and the illegal, and the obscene and the decent. For observers using a phenomenological approach to social research, the varieties of these shifting performances of everyday life become much more apparent, allowing for new and rich ways of understanding cultural practices outside totalizing binaries and grand narratives, such as East/West, centre/periphery, base/superstructure, and so forth.

My conversations with these artists highlighted a number of social and historical trends as contributing factors to the advancement of underground music in Iran. I narrowed these elements down to the following: (1) the liberalization of the Iranian cultural sector during the Reform years of the 1990s; (2) the backlash against the outdated Los Angeles-based Iranian music; and (3) advancements made in new information technologies. My interviews painted a complex picture of the Iranian underground music scene that is in the constant process of becoming and realignment. Whereas the struggle for freedom of speech is a common denominator for most artists, any attempt to find a common narrative among the different segments of this music scene proved to be challenging. Conflicts are common, but so are stories of cooperation and community building. What is evident is that these artists, while concerned about the political issues in Iran, are equally interested in individual freedoms. They see music as a channel through which they can express their thoughts, feelings and desires. At times they can be political and resistance-oriented, but most often they reflect other aspects of life such as love, happiness or despair. Above all, what makes their story fascinating is the resilience they show in negotiating political and social boundaries in a country so profoundly traditional, truly making it against all odds.

ACKNOWLEDGEMENTS

I would like to thank my research assistant Mr. Siavash Rokni.

NOTES

1 I should add that most of them were artists (mainly fine art) and taking psychology courses at the university. Some of them were learning Italian at the language school of the Italian Embassy in Tehran so that they could apply to art schools in Italy.
2 The so-called Green Movement that took form as a political opposition movement in the aftermath of the 2009 presidential election has also been dubbed an urban middle class movement that has lost touch with the sentiments of the broader Iranian population outside of large cities and affluent urban areas. The validity of such claims remains contested, as no empirical evidence exist for them.
3 Pseudonyms have been used in order to protect the identity of interview participants.
4 *Musighi-e los angelesi* is a term used to refer to the type of music produced by Iranian artists based in Los Angeles. It generally has a negative connotation in Persian slang culture, referring to a type of music that is commercial and culturally 'cheap,' with low artistic and production value. *Musighi-e los angelesi* was for over two decades dominated by Iranian artists who fled the country in 1979 after the Islamic Revolution. In recent years, however, a number of successful

artists have emerged as the 'next generation' of Los Angeles-based Iranian artists. As a group they are banned from performing inside Iran and their albums are only available in black markets.

5 Voice of America (VoA) is the official external broadcast institution of the United States federal government. It is one of five civilian US international broadcasters working under the umbrella of the Broadcasting Board of Governors (BBG). VoA provides a wide range of programming for broadcast on radio and TV and the Internet outside of the US in forty-three languages (Wikipedia).

REFERENCES

Aksoy, Asu, and Kevin Robins. "The Enlargement of Meaning: Social Demand in a Transnational Context." *Gazette* 65, nos. 4–5, 2003. 365–388.

Arendt, Hannah. *The Human Condition*. Chicago: University of Chicago Press, 2013.

Aspers, Patrik. "Empirical Phenomenology: A Qualitative Research Approach (The Cologne Seminars)." *Indo-Pacific Journal of Phenomenology* 9, no. 2, 2009. 1–12.

Asthana, Sanjay. "Young People, New Media, and Participatory Design," in *Media Literacy: New Agendas in Communication*. Edited by Kathleen Tyner, 11–27. New York: Routledge, 2010.

Bayat, Asef. "Conclusion: Knowing Muslim Youth," in *Being Young and Muslim: New Cultural Politics in the Global South and North*, 355–364. New York: Oxford University Press, 2010.

Dahlgren, Peter. "Doing Citizenship: The Cultural Origins of Civic Agency in the Public Sphere." *European Journal of Cultural Studies* 9, no. 3, 2006. 267–286.

Dillabough, Jo-Anne, and Jacqueline Kennelly. *Lost Youth in the Global City: Class, Culture, and the Urban Imaginary*. New York: Routledge, 2010.

Dutta, Soumitra, and Irene Mia. *The Global Information Technology Report 2010–2011*. Geneva: World Economic Forum, 2011.

Emami, Abbas. *Att Organisera Oenighet: En Sociologisk Studie av Iranska Riksförbundet och dess Medlemsorganisationer*. [To Organise Discord: A Sociological Study of Iranian National Association {in Sweden} and its Member Organisations]. Stockholm: Acta Universitatis Stockholmiensis, 2003.

Finlay, Linda. "Debating Phenomenological Research Methods." *Phenomenology Practice* 3, no. 1, 2009. 6–25.

Jafari, Aliakbar. "An Enquiry into Cultural Consumption among Iranian Youth and the Implications of Cultural Globalisation." Working Papers Series 2006, Number WP001/06, University of Wolverhampton, UK, 2006. Accessed June 23, 2013. www.wlv.ac.uk/PDF/ uwbs-wp001–06-jafari.pdf.

Huq, Rupa. *Beyond Subculture: Pop, Youth and Identity in a Postcolonial World*. New York: Routledge, 2006.

Khosravi, Shahram. *Young and Defiant in Tehran*. Philadelphia: University of Pennsylvania Press, 2008.

Naficy, Hamid. *The Making of Exile Cultures: Iranian Television in Los Angeles*. Minneapolis: University of Minnesota Press, 1993.

Nayak, Anoop. *Race, Place and Globalization: Youth Cultures in a Changing World*. Oxford: Berg, 2003.

Nooshin, Laudan. "The Language of Rock: Iranian Youth, Popular Music, and National Identity," in *Media, Culture and Society in Iran*. Edited by Mehdi Semati, 69–94. New York: Routledge, 2008.

Rastovac, Heather. "Contending with Censorship: The Underground Music Scene in Urban Iran." *Intersections* 10, no. 2, 2009. 59–82.
Salehi-Isfahani, Djavad, and Daniel Egel. "Youth Exclusion in Iran: The State of Education, Employment and Family Formation." *The Middle East Youth Initiative Working Paper 3*, 2007. June 23, 2013. http://papers.ssrn.com/sol3/papers.cfm?abstract_id=1080353.
Smith, Jonathan A. "Reflecting on the Development of Interpretative Phenomenological Analysis and Its Contribution to Qualitative Research in Psychology." *Qualitative Research in Psychology* 1, no. 1, 2004. 39–54.
Sohrabi-Haghighat, Mohammad. "New Media and Social-Political Change in Iran." *Cyber Orient: Online Journal of the Virtual Middle East* 5, no. 1, 2011.
Straw, Will. "Systems of Articulation, Logics of Change: Communities and Scenes in Popular Music." *Cultural Studies* 5, no. 3, 1991. 368–388.
———. "Scenes and Sensibilities." *Public* 22–23, 2001. 245–257.
Youssefzadeh, Ameneh. "Singing in a Theocracy: Female Musicians in Iran," in *Shoot the Singer.* Edited by Marie Korpe, 129–134. London: Zed Books, 2004.

Contributors

Editors

Jacqueline Kennelly is an Associate Professor in the Department of Sociology and Anthropology at Carleton University in Ottawa, Ontario, Canada. She is the author of *Citizen Youth: Culture, Activism, and Agency in a Neoliberal Era* (Palgrave MacMillan, 2011), and the co-author (with J. Dillabough) of *Lost Youth in the Global City: Class, Culture, and the Urban Imaginary* (Routledge, 2010). She has just completed a Social Sciences and Humanities Research Council of Canada (SSHRCC)-funded research project investigating the experiences of low-income youth in the Olympic host cities of Vancouver (host to the 2010 Winter Olympics) and London (host to the 2012 Summer Olympics), using phenomenological and visual methods. In fall of 2014, she will begin a new project funded through the Spencer Foundation's New Civics Initiative, using phenomenological and visual methods to explore the civic experiences of homeless youth in Ottawa. Her work has appeared in a number of national and international peer-reviewed journals, including *British Journal of Sociology of Education; British Journal of Criminology; Sociology; Ethnography; Feminist Theory; Sociological Research Online; Review of Education, Pedagogy, and Cultural Studies; Citizenship Studies; Visual Studies;* and *Gender and Education.*

Stuart R. Poyntz is an Associate Professor in the School of Communication at Simon Fraser University. His research interests include children's media cultures, phenomenology and theories of the public, and urban youth media production. He has recently completed the SSHRC-funded research project, *Youth Digital Media Ecologies in Canada*, and will begin a new research program in 2015, entitled *Producing Youth: Informal Learning, the State, and Networks of Culture.* He has an extensive background in the history of media literacy, is co-author of *Media Literacies: A Critical Introduction* (Wiley-Blackwell, 2012) and has published widely in a number of national and international peer-reviewed journals, including *Cultural Studies*, the *Journal of Youth Studies*, the *Review of Education, Pedagogy and Cultural Studies*, and the *Canadian Journal of Education*, as well as various edited collections.

CHAPTER AUTHORS

Daniel Ahadi is a doctoral candidate at the School of Communication at Simon Fraser University, Vancouver, Canada. His current research is on Iranian diasporic media in Stockholm. His publications include *Promoting Civic Engagement through Ethnic Media* (2010), *L'Affaire Hérouxville in Context: Conflicting Narratives on Islam, Muslim Women, and Identity* (2009) and *Urban Mediascapes and Multicultural Flows: Vancouver's Communication Infrastructure* (2009).

Sanjay Asthana, Professor, School of Journalism at the Middle Tennessee State University, earned his PhD in Journalism and Mass Communication in 2003 from the University of Minnesota. He also holds an MPhil degree in Philosophy and an MA in Communication from the University of Hyderabad in India. Dr. Asthana is the author of *Youth Media Imaginaries from Around the World,* published by Peter Lang in 2012, and *Innovative Practices of Youth Participation in Media,* published by UNESCO, Paris, in 2006. He has also co-authored *Media Information Literacy: Policy and Strategy Guidelines,* a report published by UNESCO in 2013. Dr. Asthana is currently completing an international research grant on Israeli-Palestinian working-class youth media practices funded by the Qatar National Research Grant awarded by the Qatar Foundation, Doha.

Clovis Bergère is a PhD Candidate in Childhood Studies at Rutgers University—Camden. His dissertation focuses on emerging digital cultures amongst urban youth in Guinea. He is particularly interested in the intersections of urban and virtual geographies, the changing contours of youth in Guinea, as well as inventive methods of social research, particularly cyber-ethnography and visual methodologies. His current research builds on his previous experience working as a teacher in Guinea, as well as over seven years as a local government manager in Children Services in London, UK, where he worked in sports development, children's play and education.

Victoria Carrington took up a Chair in Education in the School of Education and Lifelong Learning at the University of East Anglia in March 2010. Before joining UEA, she held a Research SA Chair at the University of South Australia and has held posts at the University of Plymouth, the University of Queensland and the University of Tasmania. Victoria writes extensively in the fields of sociology of literacy and education and has a particular interest in the impact of new digital media on literacy practices. She is co-editor of the international journal *Discourse: Studies in the Cultural Politics of Education* and sits on the editorial boards of a number of international journals. With Associate Professor Aaron Koh, she is the editor of a new book series *Cultural Studies and Transdisciplinarity in Education* (Springer).

Naghmeh Nouri Esfahani completed her PhD from the University of South Australia in 2012. Her work explores the application of a post-phenomenological framework to everyday contexts and objects. She holds a BA in Industrial Design from Iran University of Science and Technology and an MA in Industrial Design from the University of Tehran. She has been teaching in a range of undergraduate and graduate design theory and history courses. Besides her academic experiences, she has worked in the automotive industry in Iran.

Kathleen Gallagher is Professor and Canada Research Chair in Theatre, Youth, and Research in Urban Schools at the University of Toronto. Dr. Gallagher's books include: *Why Theatre Matters: Urban Youth, Engagement, and a Pedagogy of the real* (University of Toronto Press, 2014); *The Theatre of Urban: Youth and Schooling in Dangerous Times* (University of Toronto Press, 2007); and *Drama Education in the Lives of Girls: Imagining Possibilities* (University of Toronto Press, 2000). Her edited collections include: *Why Theatre Now: On the Virtue and Value of Canadian Theatre in the new Millennium* (forthcoming with Barry Freeman); *Drama and Theatre in Urban Contexts* (with Jonothan Neelands, Routledge 2013); *How Theatre Educates: Convergences and Counterpoints with Artists, Scholars, and Advocates* (with David Booth, University of Toronto Press, 2003); and *The Methodological Dilemma: Creative, Critical and Collaborative Approaches to Qualitative Research* (Routledge, 2008).

Aaron Klassen is a musician and PhD student in Sociology at Carleton University. For most of the first decade of this century, he performed in various independent bands out of Winnipeg, Canada, on tours that crisscrossed North America and Eastern Europe. These past and present performances, and the infrastructures that support them, form the basis of his cultural theory and research. 'Practice' is a key concept in Aaron's repertoire.

Ana Padawer has a PhD in Anthropology from the University of Buenos Aires (Argentina), where she is Adjunct Professor of Methodology and Fieldwork Techniques in the Department of Anthropology. As Adjunct Researcher of The National Council of Scientific and Technical Research (CONICET), she has been conducting fieldwork about knowledge and practice in rural and indigenous settings since 2008. She has published books in Spanish—*When Grades Talk about Inequality* (2008); *Middle School in Focus* (2008); *Interculturality in Debate* (2010, with G. Novaro)—and in English—*Ethnography and Education Policy across the Americas* (2002, with B. Levinson et al.)—and also articles in scientific journals like *Ethnography and Education, Horizontes Antropologicos, Educacao y Contemporaneidade, Ava,* and *Amazonica.*

Mary Lou Rasmussen is a scholar within sexualities educational research, within teacher education, and within school education. She is currently collaborating with colleagues in New York and Toronto, investigating teacher education candidates' capacity to address sexuality in the school context. She is co-editor of the Routledge edited collection *Interrogating the Politics of Pleasure in Sexuality Education.*

Leslie Robinson, Maria-Carolina Cambre, Andrew Jackson Obol, and Cathy Mashakalugo were brought together through a shared commitment to artivism, the fusion of art and activism in the struggle for social justice. Mashakalugo, Obol and Robinson are co-founding members of the *artivists 4 life* youth collective in Uganda, and Cambre is an ally and honorary member of the group. Mashakalugo is a youth leader, an HIV/AIDS counsellor and a second year student at Ugandan Christian University, Mukono, Uganda. With a fine arts degree from Makerere University, Uganda, and a diploma from Guru Digital Arts College in Edmonton, Andrew Obol works as a freelance illustrator focusing on comics and other sequential art. Robinson, a PhD candidate in Education, University of Alberta, studies community engagement and artistic processes as part of her ongoing collaborative research. Dr. Cambre teaches at King's University College at Western University, Ontario. Her work focuses on questions of representation, global communication and policy, with an eye to ethics and social justice.

Lauren Silver is an Assistant Professor in Childhood Studies at Rutgers University—Camden. She is a critical ethnographer whose research lies at the intersection of the sociology and anthropology of youth, feminist methodologies, and analyses of urban systems. Her scholarship is animated by questions of youth identity, processes of freedom and constraint, and movements across urban boundaries. Her book, *System Moms: Youth and the Politics of Regulation* (forthcoming from the University of North Carolina Press), is based on two years of ethnographic research with African American adolescent mothers and explores their identity work in a large urban child welfare system.

Yvette Taylor is Professor in Social and Policy Studies and Head of the Weeks Centre for Social and Policy Research, London South Bank University. She has held a Fulbright Scholarship at Rutgers University (2010–11) and a British Academy Mid-Career Fellowship (2013–14). Books include *Fitting Into Place? Class and Gender Geographies and Temporalities* (Ashgate, 2012); *Lesbian and Gay Parenting: Securing Social and Educational*

Capitals (Palgrave, 2009); and *Working-Class Lesbian Life: Classed Outsiders* (Palgrave, 2007). Edited collections include *Educational Diversity* (Palgrave, 2012); *The Entrepreneurial University* (Palgrave, 2014); *Mapping Intimacies: Relations, Exchanges, Affects* (Palgrave, 2013); and *Classed Intersections: Spaces, Selves, Knowledges* (Ashgate, 2010).

Paul Ugor is currently an Assistant Professor in the Department of English at Illinois State University, Bloomington-Normal. His research interests are in African Literatures and Cultures, Postcolonial Studies and New Media Cultures in the Global South. In 2013 Dr. Ugor edited a special issue of *Postcolonial Text* entitled, "Late-Modernity and Agency: Contemporary Youth Cultures in Africa." His recently completed book-manuscript, *Nollywood: Popular Video Films and New Narratives of Youth Struggles in Nigeria*, is due to be published by the University of Toronto Press in 2015.

Index

Figures/tables/photos/illustrations are indicated by an *italicized number*.

9780415720700

An environmentally friendly book printed and bound in England by www.printondemand-worldwide.com

PEFC Certified

This product is from sustainably managed forests and controlled sources

www.pefc.org

PEFC/16-33-415

This book is made of chain-of-custody materials; FSC materials for the cover and PEFC materials for the text pages.

#0023 - 211015 - C0 - 229/152/17 [19] - CB - 9780415720700